Pauline H. Tesler

Collaborative Law

Achieving Effective Resolution in Divorce without Litigation

Second Edition

**Defending Liberty
Pursuing Justice**

SECTION OF
FAMILY LAW

Cover Design by ABA Publishing.

The materials contained herein represent the opinions and views of the authors and/or the editors, and should not be construed to be the views or opinions of the law firms or companies with whom such persons are in partnership with, associated with, or employed by, nor of the American Bar Association or the General Practice, Solo and Small Firm Division, unless adopted pursuant to the bylaws of the Association.

Nothing contained in this book is to be considered as the rendering of legal advice, either generally or in connection with any specific issue or case; nor do these materials purport to explain or interpret any specific bond or policy, or any provisions thereof, issued by any particular franchise company, or to render franchise or other professional advice. Readers are responsible for obtaining advice from their own lawyers or other professionals. This book and any forms and agreements herein are intended for educational and informational purposes only.

Printed in the United States of America

Library of Congress Cataloging-in-Publication Data

Tesler, Pauline H., 1942–
    Collaborative law : achieving effective resolution in divorce without litigation / by Pauline H. Tesler. — 2nd ed.
        p. cm.
    ISBN 978-1-59031-974-1
    1. Divorce suits—United States. 2. Compromise (Law)—United States. 3. Dispute resolution (Law)—United States. 4. Attorney and client—United States. I. Title.

KF535.T47 2008
346.7301'66—dc22

2008015806

Contents

List of Tables . . . . *ix*

List of Sidebars . . . . *xi*

About the Author . . . . *xiii*

Foreword to the Second Edition . . . . *xv*

Foreword to the First Edition . . . . *xix*

Acknowledgments . . . . *xxiii*

Introduction to the Second Edition . . . . *xxv*

Introduction to the First Edition . . . . *xxvii*

Chapter 1
Why Collaborative Law, Why Now? **1**
Notes 6

Chapter 2
Overview of Collaborative Law. **9**
Notes 20

Chapter 3
Becoming a Collaborative Lawyer: The Retooling Process **23**
It's Not for Everyone 23
    Making the Paradigm Shift Happen 26
The Four Retooling Questions 27
The Four Dimensions of Retooling 34
    The First Dimension: Retooling Yourself 35
    The Second Dimension: Retooling with the Client 38
    The Third Dimension: Retooling with the Other Players 41
    The Fourth Dimension: Retooling Negotiations 43
Notes 48

Chapter 4

Overview: The Three Stages of a Collaborative Law Case **53**
Act One 53
Act Two 63
Act Three 68
Notes 74

Chapter 5

**The Nuts and Bolts of Effective Collaborative Family
Law Practice** **79**
Key Concepts and Tools 79
Notes 92

Chapter 6

Key Moments in a Collaborative Representation **97**
Making First Contacts with Other Participants 97
    1. First Communications with Your Client 97
    2. First Contacts with the Other Party 108
    3. First Contacts with the Other Collaborative Lawyer 110
    4. First Contacts with Other Collaborative Professionals 111
Preparing the Client for the Four-Way Meeting 116
The Pre-Meeting and Post-Meeting Conferences
    Between Counsel 117
Apparent Impasse in Negotiations 119
Notes 125

Chapter 7

**Statutes, Rules, Standards, and Protocols for Collaborative
Law Practice** **129**
Statutory Recognition of Collaborative Law 132
Congruence of Collaborative Legal Practice with Ethics Rules 132
Standards for Collaborative Legal Practice 133
Protocols for Collaborative Legal Practice 134
Collaborative Law in the Larger ADR Context 139
    Informed Consent: How Much, and About What? 140
    Malpractice Claims and Collaborative Legal Practice 142
Conclusion 145
Notes 150

Chapter 8

Documents and Useful Forms **155**
Comments on the Use of These Forms 157
Intra-Office Forms 157
     Initial Telephone Screening Form 157
     New Client Basic Information Form 157
     The Collaborative Retainer Agreement 157
     Sample Letters to Prospective Clients, Spouses of Clients,
        and Lawyers for Spouses 158
     Financial Disclosure Forms 159
Documents Establishing and Supporting a Collaborative Case...... 159
     Principles and Guidelines for the Practice of Collaborative Law... 160
     Participation Agreement, or Stipulation and Order 161
     Sample Letters Retaining Collaborative Neutral
        Experts/Consultants 163
     Sample Recitations Re: Collaborative Representation
        and Informal Discovery to Include in Marital
        Settlement Agreements 163
     Sample Provision Re: Resolving Future Disputes to Include
        in Marital Settlement Agreements 164
Documents Ending a Collaborative Representation 164
     Amendment of Participation Agreement When Clients Elect
        Mediation 165
     Final Letter at Time Divorce Is Concluded 165
     Notice of Withdrawal of Collaborative Counsel............. 166
     Notice of Termination of a Collaborative Case.............. 167
Data-Gathering Forms 168
     Internal Data-Gathering and Evaluation Form 168
     Practice Group Data-Gathering and Evaluation Forms........ 168
     IACP Survey Form 169
Notes 169

Chapter 9

Developing and Marketing Your Collaborative Practice........ **171**
Practice Groups: The Sine Qua Non for Practice Development 171
Other Practice Development Ideas 184
Conclusion 187
Notes 187

Chapter 10

Collaborative Law Beyond Family Law **191**
Notes 204

Chapter 11

Frequently Asked Questions About Collaborative Law **207**

Appendix I

Tools and Resources for Lawyers **221**

Appendix I-A

Intra-Office Forms **223**
1. Initial Telephone Screening Form 223
2. New Client Basic Information Form 224
3. The Collaborative Retainer Agreement 226
4. Sample Letters to Prospective Clients, Spouses of Clients,
   and Lawyers for Spouses 233
   (a) Initial Letter to Client Providing Information
       about Collaborative Law 233
   (b) Initial Letter to Client Providing Information
       about Collaborative Law 235
   (c) Extended Letter to Client after Initial Consultation Re:
       Collaborative Representation 236
   (d) First Letter to Nonclient Partner or Spouse 239
   (e) First Letter to Nonclient Partner or Spouse 240
   (f) First Letter to Nonclient Partner or Spouse 241
   (g) Initial Letter to Other Collaborative Lawyer 242
5. Financial Disclosure Form 243

Appendix I-B

Documents Establishing and Supporting a Collaborative Case . . **249**
1. Principles and Guidelines for the Practice of Collaborative Law/
   Collaborative Divorce 249
2. Participation Agreement or Stipulation and Order 257
3. Sample Letters Retaining Neutral Collaborative
   Experts/Consultants 263
   (a) Real Estate Appraiser 263
   (b) QDRO Specialist 265

4. Sample Recitations Re: Collaborative Representation
    and Informal Discovery to Include in Marital
    Settlement Agreements 267
5. Sample Paragraph Re: Resolving Future Disputes to Include
    in Marital Settlement Agreements......................... 269

Appendix I-C

Documents Ending a Collaborative Representation **271**
1. Amendment of Participation Agreement When Clients
    Elect Mediation 271
2. Final Letter at Time Divorce Is Concluded 273
3. Notice of Withdrawal of Collaborative Counsel............. 275
4. Notice of Termination of Collaborative Case............... 277

Appendix I-D

Data-Gathering Forms **279**
1. Internal Data-Gathering and Evaluation Form 279
    (a) Letter to Client Re: Evaluation of Collaborative Process..... 279
    (b) Evaluation of the Collaborative Process 281
2. Practice Group Data-Gathering and Evaluation Forms........ 285
    (a) Data-Gathering Report for Lawyers Only (An Example
        Focusing on Objective Facts)......................... 285
    (b) Client Evaluation Questionnaire (An Example Focusing
        on Client Satisfaction).............................. 289
3. IACP Survey Form 293

Appendix I-E

A Collaborative Divorce Case History...................... **295**

Appendix I-F

Lawyer Conference Checklist................................ **301**
First Meeting between Lawyers.............................. 301

Appendix I-G

First Four-Way Meeting Checklist.......................... **305**

Appendix I-H

Metaphors for Collaborative Practice...................... **309**
Whitewater Rafting.. 309

Mountain Climbing/Rock Climbing 310
The Journey through the Deep, Dark Woods 310
Divorce as a Trip from Here to There 311
Airplane Travel as a Divorce Metaphor 312
Divorce as a Birthing Process 312
Durable Power of Attorney. 312
A Peculiar Sort of Marathon. 313
The Sack Race. 314
Training Horses 314

Appendix I-I

IACP Ethical Standards **315**

Appendix I-J

When a Collaborative Case Is in Trouble **321**

Appendix I-K

ABA Committee on Ethics Opinion **325**

Appendix I-L

Bibliography **331**
Articles 331
Books 333
Websites and Web Pages. 335

Appendix II

Client Handout **337**

**Collaborative Divorce Handbook: Your Choices for Professional
Legal Help with Ending a Marriage or Domestic Partnership** . . . **339**

Index. *363*

List of Tables

Table 1   Retooling Yourself. 38
Table 2   Retooling with the Client 39
Table 3   Retooling with the Other Players 41
Table 4   Retooling Negotiations 45

List of Sidebars

Reconciliation and Collaborative Law 13
Professional Help in Divorce Dispute Resolution 15
The Lawyer's Relationship to the Issues: Traditional Adversarial
    Representation 16
The Lawyer's Relationship to the Issues: Collaborative
    Representation 16
Estimating the Cost of Collaborative Law Representation 18
A Medical Analogy 20
Making the Paradigm Shift Happen 36
With Whom Are Your Clients Talking? 44
Reading Yourself, Relaxing Yourself 46
Making the Paradigm Shift Happen 47
Think about the Physical Space. 48
Watch Your Language 56
The Conflict-Resolution Menu 57
What Does Flooding Have to Do with Collaborative Law? 62
Five Ways Mediators and Collaborative Lawyers Can
    Work Together 64
Collaborative Agenda Management and Conflict Management
    in the Second Act 65
Recalibrating from Conflict to Solutions. 67
Advising Clients about the Law 69
Detaching from Solving the Problem. 70
Interest-Based Bargaining: Asking for Everything You Need 71
Helping Your Client Connect with Highest Intentions
    for the Divorce 73
Helping Clients with Children to Remain on the High Road 74
Three Two-Way Communications (Old Paradigm). 81
One Six-Way Communication (New Paradigm) 81
Screening Collaborative Law Clients. 99
Expanding the Pie in Interest-Based Negotiations: The Story
    of the Orange 105
Starting on the Right Foot with Your Client. 106

Basic Communications Skills for Lawyers and Clients 107
Road Map of a Collaborative Case. 109
What about the Kids? 112
Peeling the Onion 114
Preparing Your Client for the First Four-Way 115
Strategies and Tactics for a Successful First Four-Way Meeting 117
A Step-by-Step Guide to Brainstorming 120
Negotiating Styles 120
Ghost-Reading Letters 121
Food and Collaborative Law 122
Keys to Success in Four-Way Meetings 123
Negotiating Collaboratively: Propose, Explain, Upgrade 123
Getting the Most out of the Last Four-Way 124
Confidentiality and Privilege in Collaborative Legal Practice 136
A Practice Group Membership Agreement 148
Six Ways Your Office Staff Can Support the Collaborative
    Paradigm Shift and Build Your Collaborative Practice 175
Judge's Letter to People Filing for Divorce 179
Knowledge Is Power 180
Quality Assurance in the Collaborative Community 180
Nine Rules for Magnetic and Effective Practice Groups 181
Making Practice Group Meetings Irresistible (Ideas for
    Content-Rich Meetings) 183
Publicizing Collaborative Law: Learn to Use "The Hook" 186
Seven Reasons Why Collaborative Conflict Resolution Should Be
    Appealing to Civil and Commercial Clients 192
In Conflict Resolution, as in Show Business, Timing Matters 193
10 Questions for Business Clients Wondering Whether to Choose
    Collaborative Law. 196
Your Local Judge Can Raise Awareness of Civil and Commercial
    Collaborative Legal Practice 199
EDS: A Pioneering Multinational Corporation 201
Business Roundtable Executives Want Collaborative Law—But
    Just Don't Know It Yet! 202
Further Information about Collaborative Law for Civil, Business,
    and Commercial Clients 203
Impasse: The Magic Moment 214
Collaborating with Attila the Hun 218
Divorce: Collaborative vs. Litigation 345
Some Ground Rules During the Collaborative Law Process 347

About the Author

Pauline H. Tesler practices family law in Mill Valley and San Francisco, California, where she has been a state-certified family law specialist and a fellow of the American Academy of Matrimonial Lawyers since 1984. After years of providing litigation and appellate services to clients, in the mid-1990s she became a pioneer in developing and extending the practice of collaborative law in the United States and internationally. Since 1998 she has limited her practice with clients to collaborative representation and consultation.

Ms. Tesler is a founder of the San Francisco Bay Area Collaborative Practice Group and of the International Academy of Collaborative Professionals, where she served as its first president. She was founding co-editor of *The Collaborative Review,* the first publication in the United States to focus on this powerful new dispute-resolution option, and writes its *Dear Collaborator* column. She co-authored, with psychologist Peggy Thompson, a book for general readers entitled *Collaborative Divorce: The Revolutionary New Way to Restructure Your Family, Resolve Legal Issues, and Move On with Your Life* (Harper Collins, 2006). More information about that book can be found at www.collaborativedivorcebook.com.

The first edition of this book, *Collaborative Law: Achieving Effective Resolution in Divorce without Ligation,* published in September 2001, was widely praised by lawyers and other divorce professionals as the first book-length treatise for collaborative lawyers. Soon after its publication Ms. Tesler received the first annual "Lawyer as Problem Solver" award from the American Bar Association's Dispute Resolution Section.

In addition to speaking widely and writing about collaborative law, Ms. Tesler has trained thousands of lawyers (as well as mental-health and financial professionals) in how to become more skilled at collaborative practice, in North America, Europe, Australia, and New Zealand. She also provides mentoring, coaching, and case consultation to lawyers and other professionals who are learning how to practice collaboratively or whose cases are in difficulty. More information about Ms. Tesler's work can be found on her blog, www.collaborativedivorcenews.com, or at her website, www.teslercollaboration.com.

Foreword to the Second Edition

Collaborative law (CL) is one of the most important developments in the American legal system in the past 25 years—an ironic statement when one considers that the whole point of collaborative law is to foster out-of-court settlements. CL has now become a worldwide phenomenon, and the author of this wonderful book, Pauline Tesler—one of the pioneers of the CL movement and one of its most sought-after trainers—is responsible for much of this growth.

Pauline and the founder of the CL movement, Minnesota lawyer Stuart Webb, were recognized in 2002 for their achievement in the growth of CL when they received the American Bar Association's first "Lawyer as Problem Solver" Award, an annual prize from the ABA's Section of Dispute Resolution. The ABA's decision to publish this book is itself a noteworthy recognition of the importance of CL.

Another important sign of the arrival of CL as a major component of the American legal system is the creation in 2007 of a Drafting Committee on CL by the National Conference of Commissioners on Uniform State Laws (NCCUSL), the organization responsible for drafting such uniform laws as the Uniform Commercial Code and Uniform Arbitration Act. The NCCUSL Committee has already begun drafting a model statute authorizing the use of CL.

Pauline was the co-founder and first president of the International Academy of Collaborative Professionals (IACP), the leading organization in the CL field. From its beginnings as a kitchen-table cabal in the late 1990s, IACP has grown to an international organization with more than 3,000 members. Today, IACP estimates that more than 10,000 lawyers and other professionals throughout the world have received CL training.

The Foundations of the Collaborative Law Movement

Many streams have converged to form the CL movement. First, the practice of negotiation has been transformed in the past 25 years by the growing use of interest-based, rather than positional, bargaining. This approach to negotiation was described in the path-breaking book *Getting to Yes: Negotiating Agreement Without Giving In* by Roger Fisher, Bill Ury, and Bruce Patton.[1] First published in 1981 and now translated into 25 languages, *Getting to Yes* introduced the ideas of (a) separating the people from the problem, (b) using principled benchmarks for arriving at agreement on contested issues, (c) assessing each party's BATNA (best alternative to a negotiated agreement) when considering settlement options, and (d) communicating about the parties' underlying interests to enable mutually advantageous exchanges. Prior to the publication of *Getting to Yes*, negotiation theory and practice focused primarily on competitive techniques for gaining advantage; Fisher, Patton, and Ury opened the door for a more collaborative approach.

Second, as litigation has become more costly, complex, and time-consuming, a broad range of private dispute-resolution methods has developed. One of the important sources of change in this area was the 1979 article "Bargaining in the Shadow of the Law: The Case of Divorce," by Robert Mnookin and Lewis Kornhauser.[2] The article described, and legitimized, a system of negotiation in which courts play an essential role (even though very few cases are resolved there) by providing guideposts and benchmarks that enable the parties to make informed choices about settlement terms. Mediation and other forms of alternative dispute resolution (ADR)—such as arbitration, case evaluation, and CL—have greatly expanded the range of options for the private resolution of conflict. In the United States, ADR is now taught in virtually every law school, and ADR programs exist as adjuncts to virtually every state and federal court system.

Third, the American Bar Association's publication of the book *Unbundling Legal Services* by Forrest Mosten in 2000 validated a new approach to lawyering based on the recognition that some clients might not want, or might not be able to afford, the full range of services that lawyers offer.[3] Clients who use "unbundled" legal services want to be actively involved in handling their case and seek only a limited number of the following legal services: advice, research, drafting, negotiation, review/editing of contracts or agreements, and court appearances. Another important manifestation of unbundling has appeared in the area of family law, in which a number of lawyers—many of them devoted to the full-time practice of CL—have begun limiting their practices to advice and negotiation and refer their clients to other counsel if a court appearance is needed.

Collaborative Law Today

CL, which among its other characteristics is a prime example of unbundling, has grown dramatically since 1990, when Stuart Webb first began representing clients solely for the purpose of negotiation. Although it originated as a form of family law practice, CL is now used in nonfamily cases as well.

During the CL process, the parties and counsel sign a participation agreement in which all agree that, if litigation is needed, (a) the lawyers will withdraw and new counsel will be hired, and (b) current counsel will be disqualified from further involvement in the case. The purpose of the withdrawal/disqualification provision is to align everyone's economic incentives toward settlement. These and other important features of the process are discussed fully and with brilliant practical insight in this book. However, it is worth mentioning at least one of those features here: for proponents of CL, a major part of the value of the process comes from the enhanced trust that can be created in negotiations. Because the parties do not have to fear that they will one day face the other party's lawyer in adversarial proceedings in court, they are able to achieve deeper levels of communication and resolution.

Another important contribution of CL is the development of an interdisciplinary approach to negotiation. It is common in CL cases—particularly in divorce and other family matters—for the lawyers and clients to work with a child specialist, a financial specialist, and/or "coaches," whose job is to assist the parties with their communications and the psychological/emotional aspects of the negotiation. In some forms of CL practice, such as collaborative divorce, interdisciplinary teams are used in every case.[4] It is a rare family case that does not have financial and psychological issues, and a team-based approach can provide a richer, more three-dimensional solution to the clients' problems.[5] When legal historians look back at the development of CL, and where it has taken us, this more holistic perspective on legal practice may turn out to be one of its most important legacies.

The achievement of this important book—the first text in the CL field and still the touchstone for anyone seeking to practice CL—has been to combine the focus on achieving deeper levels of peace and resolution with an abundance of practical advice on how to get there. The section on "metaphor"—the root meaning of which is "to bring about change"—is by itself worth the price of admission.

The entire CL movement owes an enormous debt of gratitude to Pauline Tesler, a pioneering practitioner, trainer, and author, for helping to forge the tools that enable us to craft creative settlement solutions, and thus bring peace and hope into the lives of our clients.

David Hoffman
Boston, Massachusetts

Notes

1. *See* R. Fisher, W. Ury & B. Patton, Getting to Yes: Negotiating Agreement Without Giving In (2d ed. 1991).

2. *See* R. H. Mnookin & L. Kornhauser, *Bargaining in the Shadow of the Law: The Case of Divorce*, 88 Yale L. J. 950 (1979).

3. *See* F. S. Mosten, Unbundling Legal Services: A Guide to Delivering Legal Services a la Carte (2000). Mosten first outlined the concept of unbundling in a 1993 keynote address to lawyers in Australia.

4. For an excellent discussion of collaborative divorce and the use of interdisciplinary teams, *see* Pauline Tesler's second book, P. Tesler & P. Thompson, Collaborative Divorce: The Revolutionary New Way to Restructure Your Family, Resolve Legal Issues, and Move On with Your Life (2006).

5. For a discussion of the legal, ethical, and practical issues associated with forming a multidisciplinary practice, *see* D. Hoffman & R. Wolman, *Multidisciplinary Practice: Three-Dimensional Client Service* Mass. Psychol. Ass'n Q., (Summer 2004) (available at www .BostonLawCollaborative.com).

Foreword to the First Edition

I

Pauline Tesler is an inspiring evangelist bringing a message of renewed hope and exciting new possibilities for divorce lawyers and their clients. I am a divorce lawyer and my story illustrates the pressing need for Pauline's excellent manual. During my 32-year legal career, I have handled hundreds of family law matters. Like most of my colleagues, I chose this specialty because I wanted to make a positive difference in the lives of clients going through stressful life transitions. I was the consummate warrior. I fought passionately for my clients and "won" many battles. However, I was often disappointed when my "victories" did little to reduce the pain of my clients and their children. Sometimes I had the disturbing thought that, despite our most noble intentions, divorce lawyers did more harm than good in many situations.

It became clear to me that the courthouse was not the optimal forum to resolve family disputes and restructure family relationships. The adversarial legal model works for automobile accidents and criminal matters but is ill-suited to address the complex dynamics of family relationships. Nevertheless, well-meaning divorce lawyers have continued to drop families into the litigation meat grinder because there was no known alternative.

Although we had hoped to reduce the divorce court body count when mediation came into vogue, it has not been the panacea that was envisioned. In some mediation models, the parties do not have lawyers during the process and unjust results occur. Other types of mediation are little more than a subpart of the litigation process: after the parties have spent a considerable amount of financial and emotional capital preparing for trial, they then mediate. The case may be settled, but avoidable damage to the spouses and their children occurs as a result of the temporary hearings, written discovery, depositions, and acrimonious meetings and correspondence that precede mediation.

Several years ago, after concluding one of the most bitter and expensive divorce cases of my career, my dissatisfaction with the family law litigation model was at an all-time high. I set out on a worldwide quest to find a more humane alternative to the way family law was taught and practiced. During my travels, I discovered the therapeutic jurisprudence movement, which seeks to optimize client well-being and humanize the legal profession.

In the summer of 1999, my quest took me to the International Conference on Law and Psychology in Dublin, Ireland, where I heard Pauline Tesler lecture on collaborative family law. I was immediately hooked! Pauline was one of the most eloquent, powerful, and passionate speakers I had ever heard. She presented a logical explanation of the reasons why divorce clients are unhappy with their lawyers and divorce lawyers are unhappy with themselves.

Pauline pointed out that our training as gladiators does little to prepare us for assisting clients through a major life passage. In most cases we are the only professional helpers available to them. She explained that most divorce lawyers, by temperament and training, are poorly suited to deal with the strong emotions that are the primary currency of family law. She also developed a fascinating new concept—the "relational estate." Divorce lawyers are accustomed to dealing with the marital property estates and the separate property estates of the spouses. However, little or no attention is paid to the nonquantifiable relationship concerns that will impact the parties and their children as well as friends and extended family for years after the divorce has been concluded.

During her most informative lecture, Pauline did much more than define the problem—she offered a solution. She outlined her use of the collaborative family law model, wherein the spouses and their attorneys contractually agree the case will be resolved outside the adversarial litigation system. In other words, the parties agree that under no circumstances will they go to court in the collaborative process and that if the matter is not settled through collaboration, the lawyers for both spouses will be required to withdraw from the case and the spouses will be forced to hire new lawyers. If experts are needed, joint neutral experts will be selected by both spouses, eliminating the costly and divisive "battle of the experts" that is one of the most vexatious aspects of the adversarial system.

As Pauline concluded her remarks to thunderous applause, the light bulbs were exploding in my head. I could only exclaim "Wow!" as I pondered the limitless possibilities of her approach. I was energized by new hope for my profession and I resolved then and there to bring Pauline to Texas as a mentor for my colleagues.

Pauline graciously accepted my invitation and has spoken to enthusiastic audiences of Texas lawyers on three occasions. She has now taught collaborative family law to hundreds of Texas divorce lawyers. She continues to receive rave reviews from the Texas Family Law Bar. Her masterful presentations have dramatically changed my life and law practice and have favorably impacted the lives and law practices of countless other lawyers.

My practice is significantly enriched by Pauline's oral presentations. I eagerly await the publication of her *Collaborative Law Manual*. It is my profound privilege and honor to introduce this manual and recommend it to family law practitioners everywhere. It is a most readable and user-friendly treatise. The concepts and practices of an outstanding collaborative lawyer are explained concisely, with forms and examples gleaned from Pauline's many successful collaborative law cases. The material has been refined and enriched by the many trainings she has presented for lawyers in the United States and Canada. I believe this manual is the best investment a family lawyer can make, and it will be a must for the libraries of all family lawyers.

If the singular contribution of Pauline's manual illustrates a more humane model of family law and revolutionizes the practice, it will be an extraordinary contribution. Incredibly, there is more. In Pauline's sections on how lawyers can retool their practices and their professional relationships, she makes another significant contribution—she is teaching the lawyer how to be a better human being.

The lawyer who becomes a successful collaborative practitioner will inevitably become a more caring, compassionate, and creative person. To do this work well is to develop human competencies, skills, and understandings that enhance and enrich all aspects of life. Bravo and well done, Pauline Tesler!

John V. McShane
Dallas, Texas

II

In 1993, I had been practicing collaborative law for a little over two years when I received an inquiry about collaborative law from Pauline Tesler, a San Francisco–area lawyer. I sent her some materials and soon learned she and others had formed a collaborative family law group. Her organized group was probably the first to demonstrate that collaborative law could be—and would be—"transplanted" geographically. They helped prove that collaborative law was, indeed, "an idea whose time has come."

A year later, I had occasion to converse directly with Pauline by telephone. At that time I was still finding it difficult to communicate with lawyers about the collaborative concept. The idea that the collaborative lawyer had to withdraw from representation if adversarial proceedings loomed was a foreign concept to the bar and one that met with a fair amount of resistance. In talking with Pauline I quickly discovered that she understood the process and all the implications that flow from that requirement. Pauline deals with these issues very cogently in her manual.

Since that time, Pauline and I have presented collaborative trainings and assisted in collaborative divorce trainings together. We have trained in many cities, including San Francisco, Dallas, Houston, Scottsdale, Vancouver, Minneapolis, Philadelphia, and Honolulu.

Let me tell you what it's like to participate with Pauline in a collaborative law training. She's like the manual—thorough, detailed, and intelligent. We have different styles and approaches to training, but these differences are enfolded in a context of profound respect for each other. You will find that working with Pauline's manual is a collaborative training in itself.

If you become a successful practitioner of collaborative law, you must and will experience the paradigm shift Pauline addresses so lovingly. It will happen—and it will change your practice and your life. Pauline is an example of this truth.

I invite you to enjoy this collaborative law manual and to find a way to practice its principles.

Stu Webb
Minneapolis, Minnesota

Acknowledgments

For their help in rethinking the material on the ethics of collaborative law that appears in the greatly expanded Chapter 7, I thank my fellow members of the Ethics Task Force of the International Academy of Collaborative Professionals: David Hoffman, Don Royall, Peter Sandmann, Nancy Cameron, Sue Hansen, Diane Diel, and Ann Gushurst. For materials and suggestions relating to civil and commercial collaborative practice that I have incorporated into the expanded Chapter 10, particular thanks to Peter Sandmann, David Hoffman, Larry Maxwell, and Brad Hunter. Thanks also to Sonia Song, a very capable and helpful volunteer researcher who appeared just when she was needed most; to Peggy Thompson, Ph.D., for her invaluable interviews with collaborative clients; to Liz Ferris for showing me the importance of effective strategic planning and public education; to the many collaborative colleagues in England, Scotland, the two Irelands, France, Switzerland, New Zealand, and Australia (including, to name only some of them: Jane Oakes, Roger Bamber, Rachel Wingert, Ruth Smallacombe, Richard Sharp, Anne Dick, Cath Carlin, Gillian Crandles, Caroline Boston, John Reavey, Muriel Walls, John MacDaid, Noel Doherty, Patricia Mallen, Charlotte Butruille, Elisabeth Bannister, Kate Woodd, Cassandra Pullos, and Lorraine Lopich), who are teaching me how to adapt North American collaborative practice to their legal cultures; and to the hundreds and hundreds of remarkable collaborative practitioners across the United States and Canada whose leadership has supported the growth of this extraordinary international movement and whose work continues to teach and inspire me.

Introduction to the Second Edition

Since the first edition of this book was published in 2001, there has been an explosion of interest in collaborative law among family lawyers. In 2001, this was the sole book-length treatise on the subject; now, in 2008, the second edition will join a sheaf of excellent books on collaborative practice, some local in focus, others broad and inclusive, some for professionals, and others for general readers.

My purpose in doing the substantial revision and expansion that is reflected in this second edition was to keep this book current and useful as a broad, comprehensive introduction to effective collaborative legal practice for lawyers entirely new to the field, and as a reference book for more experienced practitioners. So many lawyers and collaborative practice organizations have contributed both theoretical and practical advances to our work over the years since 2001 that this second edition includes not only brief updates, but also a great deal of entirely new material. The chapters on ethics, on civil and commercial collaborative law, and on marketing and public education are substantially enlarged from the first edition. Appendix I, which presents forms in use in collaborative practice, includes many new documents from a variety of sources.

It has been gratifying to me that collaborative colleagues continue to tell me that they keep this "blue book" on their shelves and refer to it often. My hope is that this second edition will continue to be useful to them for some years to come.

Introduction to the First Edition

What dispute-resolution model offers rewards, challenges, and benefits sufficient to make successful family lawyers all over the United States, Canada, Europe, Australia, and New Zealand eager to become beginners again, to discover how to practice family law in an entirely new and different way?

What dispute-resolution model encourages family lawyers to become true counselors to their clients?

What dispute-resolution model engages the unique problem-solving skills of lawyers solely in service of helping clients devise the best solutions they are capable of embracing for the post-divorce restructured family?

What dispute-resolution model aims at serving the client's enlightened self interest, seen in the long view?

What dispute-resolution model teaches lawyers to listen, and to value key noneconomic interests as highly as our clients do?

What dispute resolution model encourages a voice for the children in divorce-related decisions that will powerfully affect their lives, as required by the United Nations Convention on the Rights of the Child?

What dispute-resolution model encourages lawyers to work collegially with financial and mental health professionals to meet the entire spectrum of needs typically presented by divorcing couples and families?

Collaborative law is that model. Collaborative law has transformed my work as a lawyer. Since first hearing of it in the early 1990s,[1] I have offered it to my clients, and by the time of the second edition of this book, clients in 18 nations across North America, Europe, Australia, New Zealand, and elsewhere now have this service available to them and are choosing it in growing numbers. The power of this model to help clients through the divorce passage with integrity and satisfaction continues to astonish and delight me. The ability of collaborative law to engage the most positive and creative problem-solving abilities of lawyers often astonishes and delights clients.

In the collaborative legal process, clients are supported by their lawyers to aim for reasonable, mutually respectful agreements as the normal, expected way to resolve divorce-related disputes, and are taught to regard litigation as the "emergency room cum intensive care unit" of the legal system. As a matter of course, settlements are reached that expand the pie and customize outcomes in ways that few courts are able to achieve. In the process, fees and costs are contained, high-quality legal counsel and negotiating assistance are built in, and the ability of divorcing spouses to cooperate and co-parent after divorce is maximized.

In collaborative law, each spouse is represented by specially trained collaborative counsel throughout the negotiation of a divorce agreement and processing of the legal divorce, but the sole purpose of the limited-purpose retention is to reach an agreement meeting the legitimate needs of both spouses and any children, to the maximum degree possible. This limitation has teeth: a binding agreement disqualifies both counsel from further participation if either party threatens to or elects to go to court. Written commitments to adhere to respectful, constructive good-faith negotiations, including full and early disclosure of relevant information, adequate compensation for both lawyers, and attention to legitimate needs and interests of each party and any children, constitute the foundation for the settlement process. The process terminates and both parties must find new litigation counsel if either spouse elects to take matters to court, or if there is a violation of the fundamental commitments to integrity and good faith made at the start of the process.[2]

It was expected that this model might produce well-thought-out agreements compared to the results of other settlement modalities, because of the commitment to settlement from the beginning of the legal representation and because of the integral involvement of counsel from the start of the negotiation process, rather than at the end of or ancillary to the settlement process.

What was unexpected is the degree of creativity that often arises during collaborative negotiations. When the sole agenda is settlement, and when the sole measure of lawyer success is helping clients reach an agreement both can fully accept, and when the lawyers have been instructed by their clients not to include court-based resolution as part of the range of possible solutions for a given problem, a quantum leap in problem solving frequently occurs: both lawyers and both clients marshal their creative energies toward finding solutions for each problem that could work well for both parties. A concentration of intellectual energy is brought to bear solely on solving the problem that is unmatched in any other kind of negotiations I have experienced in my practice.

A second unexpected gift of the collaborative process is how frequently divorcing spouses and their lawyers find the process itself to be rewarding—even sometimes a source of insight. Skilled collaborative lawyers find themselves modeling positive problem-solving behaviors for their clients. "Shadow" feelings (anger, fear, grief, and the like) are expected and accepted—"normalized"—but not permitted to direct the dispute-resolution process. The client sees two other adults responding appropriately and constructively to the shadow behavior of the spouse, without being manipulated, angered, or frightened by it. Each lawyer takes responsibility for moving each client from artificial bargaining positions to the articulation of real needs and interests. Needs that appear to be in conflict, perhaps even irreconcilable, are nonetheless recognized as genuine; lateral thinking often reveals unexpected areas of congruence, and sometimes yields not just acceptable but even "win-win" solutions. The lawyers structure the pace of negotiations to encourage a foundation of successes upon which trust and a sense of competency in negotiation can grow. The client sees the spouse behaving reasonably, perhaps even generously, and can be moved to respond in kind. Out of all this, a sense grows that something positive is being achieved—that rather than officiating at a prolonged death, the lawyer is nurturing the transformation of a relationship into something different and less intimate, but no less valuable.

I first understood that something inherently more valuable in human terms than my traditional law practice was occurring when, at the end of a particularly challenging collaborative meeting, the wife of my client hugged me as she left, saying, "I know you are my husband's lawyer, and not mine, but I can't call you 'opposing counsel'—you've got to find a more accurate name for what you do here." Only in my collaborative practice do the two lawyers and two clients routinely share a champagne toast over the signing of the settlement agreement. Only in my collaborative practice have cases routinely gone on "hold" after clients discover a desire to explore the possibility of reconciliation. It is not that divorce is, or should be, a happy event, or that marriages are always better than divorces. Rather, treating divorce as a normal, predictable life passage that can be handled well rather than badly helps many divorcing couples to retain their human decency and self-respect as they move with dignity toward separate households and separate lives.

Collaborative lawyers are helping to shape a long overdue cultural shift from viewing third-party decisions in divorce as appropriate and customary, to a new expectation that divorce-related issues normally ought to be resolved by the parties themselves without court battles, in a process with integrity that values and preserves the residual core of positive connection that divorcing spouses can often retain toward one another. Such an expectation has obvious importance for couples with children who will continue to meet over a lifetime at births, graduations, marriages, and deaths. It can be equally important for childless couples whose ties to one another's extended families can be deep, or who simply do not wish to despoil through the divorce process a quantum of personal life history that had profound meaning and value in its time and who therefore wish to part with respect and dignity. Having such an expectation as a core value in our daily work with divorcing couples means that collaborative lawyers are engaging in work of the highest possible societal importance: helping people end intimate relationships in a way that allows them still to do the best possible job of raising their children, the next generation that every culture is responsible for protecting and nurturing if it is to remain viable.

Passing on to other lawyers what I have learned about how to do this kind of legal work well is the purpose of this book. Every collaborative representation teaches a lesson; the patterns that have emerged from those lessons in my work with my clients are presented here, in the hope that they will be of use.

Notes

1. Stuart Webb, a family lawyer from Minneapolis, Minnesota, originated the idea in 1990. It has spread so rapidly that by the time of this second edition, collaborative law and interdisciplinary collaborative divorce practice are recognized throughout the English-speaking legal world as important modes of resolving divorce issues constructively. Nearly every major urban center in North America, the United Kingdom, Ireland, and Australia now has well-trained collaborative lawyers offering services to divorcing couples. This is an idea whose time has come.

2. A note on terminology currently in use among collaborative lawyers. "Collaborative law" is a specifically legal mode of conflict resolution in which lawyers, bound by all applicable ethical mandates and standards of practice, provide representation for their respective clients in a structured process governed by contractual agreements that preclude the lawyers from appearing in court on behalf of these parties and that set forth consensual resolution outside the court system as the sole purpose of the legal retention. "Collaborative divorce" refers to collaborative conflict-resolution services provided in the context of domestic relations matters, and usually integrates services of professionals from the fields of finance and mental-health counseling in addition to collaborative lawyers. "Collaborative practice" is a more generic term that embraces collaborative conflict-resolution in both domestic and general civil matters, and that embraces conflict resolution services provided solely by collaborative lawyers as well as conflict-resolution services provided by interdisciplinary teams of professionals from the fields of law, finance, and mental health.

Chapter 1

Why Collaborative Law, Why Now?

"Peace cannot be kept by force. It can only be achieved by understanding."

—Albert Einstein

Roughly one out of every two marriages in the United States ends in divorce,[1] and for nonmarital relationships, the breakup rates are higher. The rates are similar for all industrialized Western countries where divorce is freely available. Divorce,[2] in other words, is a predictable life passage for couples to anticipate, not a rare catastrophe that happens only to the unlucky or undeserving few. Although other major life passages—births, deaths, graduations, marriages—involve professional guides (often in black or white garb) whose job includes helping the participants rise to the occasion and behave in socially acceptable ways, in the case of divorce, the only professional who is usually involved is the divorce lawyer. Historically, until well after the end of the second World War, divorce was widely regarded as shameful and was fault-based as a reflection of that social opprobrium. The divorce lawyer's job was to guide clients through the structured conflict of court-based proceedings. Consequently, until the advent of collaborative law and collaborative divorce, although most family law cases did (and do) eventually settle, those settlements generally have taken place on the courthouse steps (literally or figuratively), after most of the damage of litigation has occurred: inflammatory court papers have been filed on the public record, positions have polarized, clients have been encouraged to believe the black-and-white oversimplifications of reality that constitute a "theory of the case," large sums of money have been spent, and the children have been at best forgotten or at worst drawn into the center of the battle zone.

The consequences of the traditional adversarial approach to divorce—which is still unfortunately alive and well[3]—are devastating, not only for the children but for the adult participants as well. As the culture's de facto "high priests" of divorce, we family lawyers have for the most part officiated at and even caused avoidable catastrophes when we have cast the normal issues facing a restructuring family into the highly polarized positions of court-based dispute resolution. Because of the nature of traditional adversarial divorce practice, our clients' perception of the divorce lawyer's role often resembles the cartoon stereotypes of television and the tabloids. Clients turn to lawyers when they want a gladiator or hired gun to wreak vengeance on their divorcing spouses, yet at the same time, in recent decades they have been turning away from family law professionals in record numbers. Pro per litigants are clogging the courts[4] and commentators believe this is not only because they cannot afford the services of divorce lawyers, but also because they fear the damage to families often caused by conventional legal proceedings.[5]

Courts are not good places for resolving the issues that arise when families break down and restructure. Psychologists Janet Johnston and Vivienne Roseby, specialists in the damage done by high-conflict divorce, deplore the faulty reasoning that asks courts and judges to:

> take on and resolve family dilemmas that other professionals and the community at large have failed to resolve—cases that attorneys have failed to negotiate and mediators have failed to settle, for families that counselors and therapists have failed to help. Inexplicably, there is an assumption that judges have some special capacity to resolve the most difficult, the most complex of all family problems. Is it any wonder that family court assignments are so unpopular, so often avoided, and usually staffed by rotating assignments to prevent burnout?[6]

Hon. Anne Kass, a family law judge in Albuquerque, New Mexico, has explained in more detail the reasons why families who take their problems to court generally get only grief in return:

> Too few judges and lawyers have examined their personal beliefs, attitudes, and expectations about family matters in any depth, and that leaves them vulnerable to becoming emotionally entangled in divorce and custody cases, sometimes quite unconsciously. . . . What does reach their conscious awareness is that they are extremely uncomfortable, but they haven't the skills to reflect on their discomfort through introspection. In short, family law has the propensity to diminish objectivity and blur boundaries for judges and lawyers and thus cause emotional overload.[7]

The same thoughts were summarized pithily by retired California Court of Appeals justice Donald M. King: "Family law court is where they shoot the survivors."[8]

Family lawyers have led the way in developing procedural alternatives to litigation, precisely because we operate on the front lines, watching the catastrophes unfold as the litigation matrix inflames the normal differences and concerns that arise when a family dissolves and restructures itself.[9] Mediation, as a private dispute-resolution mode, originated among family lawyers dissatisfied with the courts as a place for resolving those issues and spread from there into the mainstream of civil dispute-resolution modalities.[10] But early hopes that mediation might become the normal first resort for divorcing couples faded somewhat as family lawyers began to recognize many situations in which mediation was proving ineffective or inadvisable.[11] Learning from the family law mediation experience, family lawyers have very quickly embraced the next-generation family law dispute-resolution mode: "collaborative law."[12]

Researcher Julie MacFarlane, Ph.D., observes, "The exponential growth of 'collaborative family lawyering' (CFL) is one of the most significant developments in the provision of legal services in the last 25 years."[13] According to Christopher Fairman, associate professor of law at Ohio State University, "Collaborative law is clearly the hottest area in dispute resolution."[14] Collaborative law is an extremely valuable conflict resolution option for divorcing couples and other disputants committed to a civilized, creative, contained, and cost-effective way of reaching settlement entirely outside the court system.

Collaborative law combines the explicit commitment to settlement that is at the core of mediation with the enhanced creative power of a model that builds legal advocacy and counsel into the settlement process from the start, as well as conflict management and guidance in negotiations. Unlike mediation, which uses a neutral either as the sole professional or as the dispute-resolution manager of a process that includes adversarial counsel for the parties, collaborative law, by contrast, has each party represented in negotiations by separate counsel whose role is limited to helping the clients reach agreement. If the process breaks down and the parties go to court, the collaborative lawyers are disqualified from further participation. In other words, in collaborative law as in no other dispute-resolution modality, the risks and costs of failure are distributed to the lawyers as well as the clients. The lawyers and the clients enter into written contracts governing the negotiation process,[15] in which they undertake to engage in respectful good-faith bargaining, to provide early and complete voluntary discovery, and to protect the interests of children. All expert consultants are ordinarily retained jointly within the collaborative process and, like the lawyers, they are disqualified from participating in subsequent litigation if the collaborative process breaks down.[16] No one may resort to the courts or threaten to do so during the pendency of a collaborative law representation, though the clients may terminate the process and litigate—with the help of new lawyers—at any time.

With experience, collaborative lawyers learn to behave in ways that significantly enhance their clients' ability to achieve their stated goal of amicable settlement.[17] These behaviors differ dramatically from how lawyers learn to represent clients in law school and from how they behave in conventional litigation practice.[18] Effective collaborative lawyers cultivate thought processes, attitudes, and skills entirely different from the armaments of a trial lawyer. Many collaborative lawyers report that as they embark upon learning this new craft, their understanding of the dynamics of divorce and the appropriate role of lawyers in the divorce process undergoes profound shifts.[19] These lawyers report that their clients tend to emerge from the process satisfied, relations with fellow collaborative attorneys become cordial, negotiations are characterized by creativity, "outside-the-box" thinking among all participants becomes commonplace, and the lawyers' sense of integration and satisfaction in their work grows and deepens. Clients often report that their attitudes about lawyers undergo positive transformation during collaborative representation. Much to their surprise, for some of them the divorce process becomes a learning experience with rewarding and even enjoyable moments. For many clients, the collaborative process fosters a sense of a job well done, enhanced problem-solving and communication skills, and a feeling of optimism about resolving future issues with the former spouse.[20]

Absent from these reports are the war stories commonplace when old-paradigm family lawyers gather together, about the vicious behavior of the opposing party or the outrageous demands of the opposing counsel or the angry client who refuses to pay and threatens to sue. Even when collaborative cases fail to reach complete agreement, it is rare for clients to regret having attempted to do so collaboratively.[21] Collaborative clients and lawyers promise in writing to treat one another with respect, and with few exceptions, they keep those promises.

The value for lawyers, clients, and families of a positive, client-centered, apparently effective consensual dispute-resolution model like this cannot be overstated. The literature demonstrating the pernicious effects on litigants and their children of high-conflict divorces leaves little doubt that divorcing spouses who care about their integrity and about the economic and emotional well-being of themselves and their children ought to avoid litigation and seek consensual resolution of their differences.[22]

At the time of this second edition, 18 years after the birth of the collaborative law movement, no other dispute-resolution modality presently available to divorcing families matches collaborative law in its ability to manage and resolve conflict, elicit creative out-of-the-box solutions, facilitate respectful communications and self-determined outcomes, protect children, and support parties in realizing their highest intentions for their lives after the legal process is over. While not every couple will realize all those benefits, collaborative law is structured to encourage and support clients in a divorce process that values and aims for those laudable qualities of process and resolution.

Not least of the benefits of collaborative practice is that it seems to evoke in those lawyers who embrace it a rekindled joy in the practice of law. Effective collaborative lawyers find that what matters most in one's personal value system can finally be brought to the office, and that integrating one's deeply held personal values into one's work not only is possible in this model, but actually improves one's effectiveness in collaborative law. Good collaborative lawyers recognize that they are, at last, members of a helping and healing profession.[23]

This book offers a structured, step-by-step orientation to how collaborative law works and how one can begin developing the attitudes, skills, and behaviors that enhance collaborative legal practice. Also provided here are documents, checklists, bibliographies, and other materials collaborative lawyers will find useful in their cases and suggestions for practice development and marketing, as well as a handbook about collaborative law for use with clients. Finally, this book presents in "sidebar" format a broad sampling of quotations, perspectives, checklists, and similar supporting material to enrich the reader's understanding of the more structured information presented in the chapters and to spark further reading, inquiry, and experimentation.

Each lawyer brings a personality and value system to this work, and will develop a unique personal style of collaborative lawyering. Most of the material in this book is intended to inspire and "jump-start" you in the process of discovering your own techniques and style. For example, some lawyers are uncomfortable with the stress-reduction and visualization techniques that are presented, instead preferring a "strictly business" approach to collaborative law. Others find that with some clients, there is receptivity and appreciation for incorporating spiritual dimensions into the collaborative process. There is really only one irreducible minimum condition for calling what you do "collaborative law": *You and the counsel for the other party must sign papers disqualifying you from ever appearing in court on behalf of either of these clients against the other.* Beyond that requirement, all else is artistry, and you are free to accept, reject, and adapt what is presented here to suit your personal style, within the growing body of collaborative standards and protocols. The techniques presented do work for many lawyers, and you are encouraged to experiment with them before deciding whether they do or do not work for you.

Notes

1. U.S. Bureau of the Census, U.S. Gov't Printing Office, Marriage, Divorce and Remarriage in the 1990's (Current Population Reports) 5 (1992). More recent data for 1997 suggests that half of all first marriages can be expected to end in divorce, while 60% of second marriages so end. (Divorce magazine web report at http://www.divorcemag.com/statistics/statsUS.shtml, citing as its sources data from the U.S. Census Bureau, National Center for Health Statistics, Americans for Divorce Reform, Centers for Disease Control and Prevention, Institute for Equality in Marriage, American Association for Single People, and Ameristat, Public Agenda).

2. As a convention, this book will refer throughout to divorce, but the concepts described herein apply equally to nonmarital domestic partnerships and same-sex relationships.

3. While no-fault divorce has become available nearly everywhere in North America and Europe, "no fault" relates to the grounds for awarding a divorce and the evidence that therefore will be relevant and material. "No fault" in the legal sense does not equate to "no shame, no blame" in the minds and hearts of our divorcing clients, and the advent of no-fault divorce has by no means ended high-conflict divorce proceedings. Courts lack the power in "no fault" divorces to label one spouse the guilty party and consequently, evidence of bad behavior is largely irrelevant, but family lawyers are well aware that clients with a high level of animus growing out of guilt, shame, and blame will find some justiciable issue upon which to attach the emotional stakes that matter most to them: establishing who was blameless, and who wasn't. This may be one reason (among many, admittedly) for the troubling increase in custody litigation—36% more contested custody filings over the past decade, as compared to no increase in divorce filings. *See National Center for State Courts, State Court Guide to Statistical Reporting,* 2003, at 31 (2003), *available at* http://www.ncsconline.org/D_Research/CSP/2003_Files/2003_DomRel.pdf, cited in Andrea Kupfer Schneider & Nancy Mills, *What Family Lawyers Are Really Doing When They Negotiate,* Fam. Ct. Rev. 44 (4), 612–22, n.33 (2006).

4. *See, e.g.,* Roderic Duncan, *Pro Per Do-It-Yourself Divorce,* Cal. Law., Jan. 1998, at 44. In 2001, more than 50% of custody and visitation filings were by self-represented litigants; some urban courts report pro se divorce filings in excess of 80%. In Maricopa County, Arizona, pro se litigants doubled in number between 1980 and 1985 and by 1990, 88% of all divorces involved one self-represented party, with more than half of all divorces involving two unrepresented parties. In one study, 82% of those with incomes over $75,000 per year disagreed with the statement that lawyers can "make a divorce simpler and less painful," as compared with 63% of participants making less than $35,000. Ayn H. Crawley, *Helping Pro Se Litigants to Help Themselves,* a report prepared by the Maryland Legal Assistance Network, *available at* www.courtinfo.ca.gov/programs/cfcc/pdffiles/HelpThemselves.pdf. A study in the early 1990s by the National Center on State Courts of 16 large urban trial courts' domestic relations dockets concluded that lack of money does not appear to be the reason for the prevalence of pro per filings. *Id.,* p. 2.

5. *See, e.g.,* Roderic Duncan, A Judge's Guide to Divorce: Uncommon Advice from the Bench (2007) ["Whatever you do, try to keep your case out of divorce court. . . .

The divorce-court system stinks."] Duncan, a retired family law judge, advises laypeople to avoid court because there are no winners there, only losers—especially the kids. He urges divorcing couples to reach out-of-court agreements, and recommends collaborative law.

6. JANET JOHNSTON & VIVIENNE ROSEBY, IN THE NAME OF THE CHILD 223 (1998).

7. Anne Kass, *Clinical Advice from the Bench*, 7 J. CHILD & ADOLESCENT PSYCHIATRIC CLINICS OF N. AM. 247, 251–53 (1998).

8. Justice Donald M. King, Address at *New Ways of Helping Children and Parents Through Divorce*, a conference sponsored by the Judith Wallerstein Center for the Family in Transition and the University of California, Santa Cruz, Quail Lodge, Carmel Valley, California (Nov. 21, 1998).

9. For a more extended discussion of why family lawyers are turning to collaborative law, *see* Pauline H. Tesler, *Collaborative Law: What It Is and Why Family Law Attorneys Need to Know About It*, 13 AM. J. FAM. L. 215–25 (1999).

10. Joan B. Kelly, *A Decade of Divorce Mediation Research*, 34 FAM. & CONCILIATION CT. REV. 373–85 (1996).

11. Imbalances in power, sophistication, emotional attitude, and stability of the parties, as well as dishonesty, foot-dragging, and other less-than-good-faith orientations to the mediation, can render effective mediation by a single neutral professional difficult or can compromise the evenhandedness and stability of the mediated outcome. Also, the role that must be played by the consulting attorneys is structurally challenging and despite good intentions all around, can impair the effectiveness of mediation. Since the lawyers often give their advice from the sidelines, outside the mediation process, and since their primary job is seen as ensuring informed consent and careful deliberation rather than moving the parties toward consensual resolution, the work of the mediator can be undone by the equally conscientious work of the lawyer participating from the sidelines. Where conventional lawyers participate directly in the mediation sessions, there is nothing to prevent them from behaving as positional advocates, more or less as they would in an evaluative judicial settlement conference. In such situations it takes considerable skill and force of personality on the part of the mediator to facilitate a client-centered resolution.

Bernard Mayer, in his brilliant and thought-provoking BEYOND NEUTRALITY (2004), addresses these and other challenges facing the conflict-resolution movement as he looks at why mediation (apart from court-annexed mandatory mediation) has failed to achieve the widespread popularity among clients that was originally hoped for. He notes, "In many arenas, if mediators had to rely on people voluntarily asking for their services, they would have almost no business. Instead, people must be persuaded, cajoled, or mandated to use mediation and related services." *Id.*, Chapter One (*available at* http://www.mediate.com/articles/mayerB1.cfm). Mayer urges putting aside the emphasis on neutrality that has characterized the mediation movement and focusing instead on what he identifies as the six characteristics of effective conflict resolution—all of which I believe can be found in "best practice" collaborative law. See note 17, *infra*.

For these and other reasons, many family law practitioners as well as some academic commentators take the view that divorce mediation, especially without the presence of private attorneys, can be recommended as working effectively only for a relatively small group of "high-functioning, low-conflict" spouses. For more challenged couples, their view is that a mediator alone cannot eliminate the inevitable power imbalance between the parties, while collaborative law, with its built-in advocacy and legal counsel in service of consensual resolution, can be appropriate for a much broader spectrum of divorcing couples. *See, e.g.,* Charles M. Goldstein & Dori Smith, *Collaborative Law: Getting Clients Out of the War Zone of Litigation into Peaceful Problem Solving*, THE HENNEPIN COUNTY LAWYER (official publication of the Hennepin County Bar Association), February 20, 2007, citing John Lande, *Possibilities for Collaborative Law: Ethics and Practice of Lawyer Disqualification and Process Control in a New Model of Lawyering*, 64 OHIO ST. L.J. 1315, 1325 (2003); John Lande & Gregg Herman, *Fitting the Forum to the Family Fuss: Choosing Mediation, Collaborative Law, or Cooperative Law for Negotiating Divorce Cases*, FAM. CT. REV. 42 (2), 280, 282–83 (2004).

12. For a short history of the collaborative law movement, *see* Pauline H. Tesler, *Collaborative Law: Where Did It Come From, Where Is It Now, Where Is It Going?* 1 THE COLLABORATIVE QUARTERLY 1 (1999). (This journal was renamed THE COLLABORATIVE REVIEW in 2001.)

13. Julie MacFarlane, *The Emerging Phenomenon of Collaborative Family Law (CFL): A Qualitative Study of CFL Cases,* p. 19 (Department of Justice, Canada, 2005).

14. Jill Schachner Chanen, *Collaborative Counselors: Newest ADR Option Wins Converts, While Suffering Some Growing Pains,* 92 A.B.A. J. 52, 53 (June 2006).

15. There has been some attention from commentators to the question of whether lawyers should sign the contracts that the two clients enter into regarding the collaborative process commitments (often referred to as "participation agreements"), or whether only the clients should sign them, or whether it matters, and why. See Chapter 7 for further discussion of this and other questions of legal ethics.

16. Collaborative trainers and experienced practitioners generally agree that while clients should not be barred from seeking second opinions and other independent advice outside the collaborative process during its course, it is a "best practice" that the fact of the outside consultation be disclosed, to avoid the appearance of bad faith. It is also generally agreed that maintaining a relationship with "shadow counsel," who waits in the wings preparing papers for the eventuality of litigation, is in bad faith and not consistent with the collaborative commitments.

17. Bernard Mayer identifies six qualities of effective conflict resolution professionals: a focus on the integrative potential of conflict, a needs-based approach, a focus on communication, a commitment to empowering disputants, process focused, and system focused. *Supra* note 11. These qualities are characteristic of good collaborative legal practice and practitioners, and would be emphasized in most good introductory collaborative law trainings that meet the standards of the International Academy of Collaborative Professionals.

18. *See, e.g.,* Julie MacFarlane, *supra* note 13, at 19; ANTHONY T. KRONMAN, THE LOST LAWYER: FAILING IDEALS OF THE LEGAL PROFESSION (1993); SUSAN SWAIM DAICOFF, LAWYER, KNOW THYSELF: A PSYCHOLOGICAL ANALYSIS OF PERSONALITY STRENGTHS AND WEAKNESSES (2004).

19. For a discussion of how and why this conflict resolution work of collaborative lawyers changes over time, *see* Pauline H. Tesler, *Collaborative Family Law, the New Lawyer, and Deep Resolution of Divorce-Related Conflict,* 2008 J. DISP. RESOL. ____.

20. There is as yet no empirical research that compares client outcomes and perceptions in collaborative cases with those in other dispute-resolution modalities. The observations in this chapter are derived from the author's own nearly 15 years of work with clients (as of mid-2007) and her conversations with many hundreds of collaborative practitioners and trainers in the course of more than a decade of teaching, writing, and speaking.

21. Clients from time to time observe that even when a case terminates short of full resolution, the collaborative process—while it lasts—encourages important child-related issues to be discussed honestly and productively, and that the information-sharing and voluntary discovery done during the process advance negotiations in a cost-effective way. When comparing their experience in collaborative law with what happens later in litigation, clients whose cases terminate short of resolution may in hindsight be even more able to see the benefits of collaborative conflict resolution than they were during the process. Another common observation of such clients is that they are glad they made the best effort that they were capable of to resolve matters out of court, even if the effort did not fully succeed.

22. *See, e.g.,* Ron Neff & Kat Cooper, *Parental Conflict Resolution. Six-, Twelve-, and Fifteen-Month Follow-Ups of a High-Conflict Program,* FAM. CT. REV. 42:1, 99–114 (2004); Marsha Kline Pruett, Glendessa M. Insabella, & Katherine Gustafson, *The Collaborative Divorce Project: A Court-Based Intervention for Separating Parents with Young Children,* FAM. CT. REV. 43 (1), 38–51 (2005).

23. *See,* generally, JULIE MACFARLANE, THE NEW LAWYER (2007), which examines profound changes in how collaborative and other "new lawyers" conceive of their role and undertake their advocacy on behalf of clients, and David Hall, *In Search of the Sacred,* 7 THE COLLABORATIVE REVIEW 27–29 (Winter 2005).

Chapter 2

Overview of Collaborative Law

"Often, the best way to win is to forget to keep score."
—Marianne Espinosa Murphy

At its simplest, the collaborative law process consists of two lawyers and their respective clients who sign binding agreements defining the scope and sole purpose of the lawyers' representation: to help the parties engage in creative problem solving aimed at reaching a negotiated agreement that meets the legitimate needs of both parties.[1]

In the collaborative law process, the parties agree that no one will threaten or engage in litigation to coerce compromises. The parties retain their right of access to the courts, but if either party does resort to the courts for dispute resolution, both lawyers are automatically disqualified from further representation of either of the parties against the other. Expert consultants are retained jointly within the collaborative law model and are similarly disqualified if the process breaks down. During the process, although the lawyers remain advocates for their respective clients, bound by all applicable professional standards and ethical mandates, they share a commitment to keep the process honest, respectful, and productive on both sides—a commitment confirmed with the lawyer's agreement with the client, and in the participation agreement signed by both lawyers and both clients at the start of a collaborative case.

Collaborative law is a close cousin to other modes of reaching agreement without litigation, but with important differences that make it a particularly powerful process for resolving family law issues.

Collaborative law combines the constructive problem-solving focus of mediation with the built-in legal advocacy and counsel of traditional settlement-oriented representation. In collaborative law representation, however, important and unique characteristics give rise to potentialities not generally found in other dispute-resolution models. In collaborative law representation, the lawyers and their clients commit to work honestly and respectfully toward a negotiated settlement as the sole purpose of the retention. The hallmarks of the process are:

- Full, voluntary, early, and ongoing discovery disclosures.
- Acceptance by the parties of the highest fiduciary duties toward one another, whether imposed by state law or not.
- Voluntary acceptance a priori of settlement as the goal and respectful, fully participatory process as the means.
- Transparency of process.
- Joint retention of experts.
- Commitment to meeting the reasonable goals of both parties if possible.
- Avoidance of even the threat of litigation.
- Disqualification of all lawyers and experts from participation in any legal proceedings between the parties outside the collaborative law process.
- Four-way settlement meetings as the principal means by which negotiations and communications take place; no bargaining through agents.

Like mediation, collaborative law utilizes skilled dispute-resolution professionals who are committed to helping parties reach customized solutions to divorce-related disputes. Like mediation, collaborative law offers more control, more privacy,[2] individualized results, the likelihood of greater compliance, and (at best) a more civilized process than can be found in the divorce courts. Unlike mediators, however, collaborative lawyers function as active legal advisors and negotiators alongside their clients at the center of the dispute-resolution process rather than on the sidelines, as is generally the case in family law mediations.[3]

That single element of difference between mediation and collaborative law can make a very big difference in process and outcome. For example, one structural challenge built into family law mediations where the parties work directly with a single neutral and without the direct involvement of their legal counsel is that problems often arise if significant imbalances exist between the parties in such areas as their emotional reaction to divorce, their respective stages of recovery from the grief associated with ending a marriage, their skill in negotiating, their knowledge of family finances, or their tendencies to buy peace at any price. This is because the mediator's neutrality can be compromised by the need in such situations for professional help in leveling the playing field on which such parties meet in mediation. A second structural challenge built into mediation occurs when consulting lawyers for each party review the resulting mediated agreements outside the process, as is often the case. The agreement arrived at by the parties and the mediator can be swept aside by the impact of essential legal advice that has come too late to be constructive.[4]

In collaborative law, on the other hand, these structural weaknesses have been addressed by building legal representation and advocacy into the core of the process. Two skilled legal advocates work with individual clients in a way that a neutral mediator cannot, to ensure that the playing field is leveled, at the same time that two skilled legal minds are engaged to help both parties arrive at fully informed "win-win" (or "good enough") solutions wherever possible.

Thus:

- In the collaborative model, both parties are represented by experienced family lawyers, neither of whom is expected to be neutral. The lawyers have the same ethical obligations to their clients as any lawyer, plus the additional responsibilities imposed by the collaborative law participation agreements (some contractual, others simply aspirational) that are signed by lawyers and clients.
- In the four-way settlement meetings that constitute the principal means of advancing collaborative negotiations, the parties and their counsel together ask questions, share information, brainstorm, evaluate alternatives, and offer proposals.

The negotiations that are at the heart of a collaborative process take place at "four-way" meetings, in the presence of and with the active involvement of all four participants, bringing rich benefits.

- Dynamic legal advice is built into each session.
- Seasoned negotiators bring their respective experience and skill in the craft of dispute resolution to bear upon the process.
- Four minds engage together in "real-time" creative problem solving.
- The lawyers do not own the case and do not control the flow of information or negotiations. Their work becomes more open and transparent to one another and to both parties than in conventional legal negotiations, causing all participants to take more personal responsibility for the content and forward movement of negotiations.

- The playing field becomes more level in cases where a broad range of possible imbalances between parties might render mediation difficult or impossible.[5] Essential advice and counsel about the law is built into the process constructively, in support of informed decision making by the clients.

- A difficult party can be assisted by his or her own counsel to make compromises, to modulate unreasonable expectations, to assert legitimate needs, or to manage anger or other negative emotions without fatally upsetting the balance necessary for successful negotiations.

- Unlike any other kind of family law representation, the risk of failure is distributed to the lawyers as well as to the clients in collaborative law. In conventional representation and in mediation consultation, the lawyer's work generally continues until there is a judgment, no matter how adversarial or cooperative the process employed. However, in the collaborative law process, the lawyers have no further role if a suitable settlement acceptable to both clients cannot be fashioned within the collaborative process.[6]

These unique characteristics of the collaborative law process can help clients to participate in face-to-face negotiations, especially clients who lack sufficient self-confidence in the presence of the other party to succeed at mediation; the support of collaborative counsel can enhance the ability of many such clients to achieve their goal of successful out-of-court dispute resolution. Each person in a collaborative law representation has the benefit of experienced family law counsel participating at every step of the process. The lawyers advise, advocate, negotiate, and maintain a level playing field, side by side with the two clients. The single six-way conversation that is the norm in collaborative four-way negotiation sessions maximizes the possibilities for creative lateral thinking and imaginative proposals for settlement, and minimizes the risk of miscommunication, inadvertent errors, misunderstandings, and lack of accountability. Hardball tactics, threats, tactical delays, hidden agendas, and "hide-the-ball" are barred from the process via good-faith aspirational undertakings memorialized in a formal agreement signed by both parties and their lawyers that sets as the only goal the achievement of mutually acceptable solutions on all significant issues.[7] If anyone acts in bad faith, uses threats, or resorts to the courts, the process must terminate, each party must retain new counsel, and never again can either collaborative lawyer represent either party in opposition to the other.

The best family lawyers have always offered settlement-oriented representation when appropriate, wherein discovery is voluntarily given and received, procedural efficiencies are stipulated to, and agreements are sought and achieved in place of trials. Indeed, it is commonly estimated that well over 90 percent of divorce cases end short of trial with negotiated terms of judgment, whatever dispute resolution modality is employed.[8] That being so, lawyers often ask how collaborative law differs from that pragmatic orientation toward settling cases. Lawyers with no direct experience of collaborative representation sometimes assert that there is nothing particularly new about it—that they already do it in their usual family law practices.

This is not a perception shared by lawyers who actively practice collaborative law. Lawyers often come to collaborative law from the ranks of the most seasoned family lawyers—people who have facilitated settlement agreements over decades of practice—and are in the best position to compare it to the traditional "friendly negotiations" approach to settlement. Collaborative law is described by those who do it well as a dramatically different way of

RECONCILIATION AND COLLABORATIVE LAW

Just because you are a divorce lawyer, don't assume that the client needs a divorce. Sometimes clients make appointments in the wrong office and really need a psychologist, or a financial counselor, or a clergyperson. Sometimes clients need only information and time to chew on it. Sometimes they need a postnuptial agreement that restructures financial understandings and debt responsibilities.

Sometimes, the experience of being in a respectful, productive collaborative process can reduce the static generated by situational difficulties sufficiently to allow clients to remember what originally brought them together. When that happens, clients sometimes consider reconciliation. Collaborative lawyers need to keep that possibility open and to listen for its emergence. They do well to avoid precipitous movement toward divorce. They serve clients by remaining aware that clients who arrived at the first meeting eager to be divorced may be too embarrassed to discuss reconciliation with their lawyers later on. Clients may worry that the lawyers may disapprove, or feel their time has been wasted, if there is a turn toward reconciliation.

Remember also that those hasty and argumentative court filings that irrevocably polarize a couple have no place in collaborative divorces. Practitioners find that one incidental benefit of the orderly progress of a collaborative case—from information sharing through communicating interests and considering options before reaching solutions—is that clients develop confidence and sometimes a renewed sense of possibilities as they are guided through a contained, constructive, and civilized discussion of problems that may have been the source of frustrating conflict toward the end of the marriage.

Consider including a discussion of these possibilities in your initial meetings with the client, making it clear that the door is open to consider alternatives other than divorce for solving the problems facing the couple.

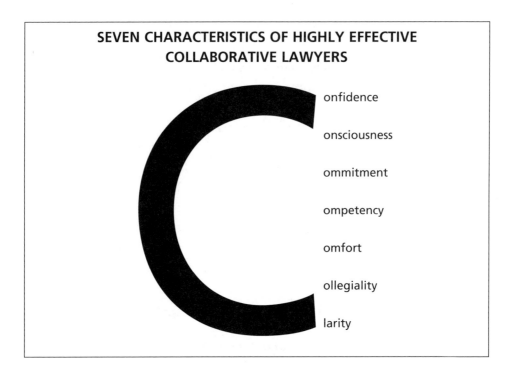

SEVEN CHARACTERISTICS OF HIGHLY EFFECTIVE
COLLABORATIVE LAWYERS

onfidence

onsciousness

ommitment

ompetency

omfort

ollegiality

larity

representing clients, and a potentially far more powerful dispute-resolution tool, than what is typically available in conventional representation.

The differences lie in the profound effects that the formal written commitments made at the start of the process have upon the state of mind of the parties and of their lawyers. First, both clients entering a collaborative law process commit to selecting counsel who understand and accept explicit prearranged ground rules. Ideally, the clients choose lawyers who have a history of working cooperatively and effectively on opposite sides of divorce cases.[9] Second, everyone signs a statement of understanding about how the process will be conducted, which remains in effect as long as all participants conduct themselves in good faith. Third, a core element of the written agreement is that the process continues only as long as no one threatens or pursues litigation as a means of conducting negotiations. Fourth, if the process breaks down, either because of bad faith or because one party or the other feels obliged to turn to the courts for relief, the lawyers must withdraw and thereafter cannot represent either party against the other. While departing collaborative law counsel must assist in an orderly transition to litigation counsel, the financial and emotional costs of starting over with new representation will often be significant.

These stipulated commitments become powerful "carrots" and "sticks" encouraging immediate engagement in good-faith problem solving on all

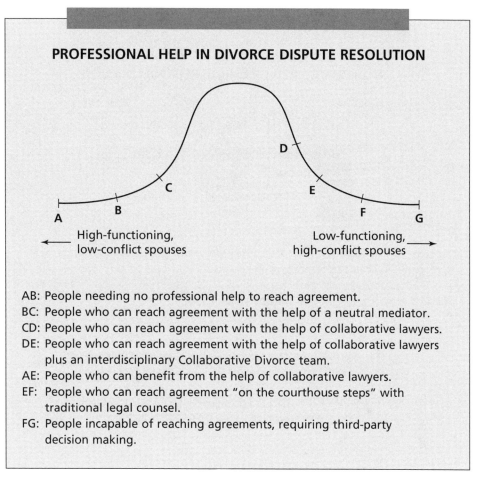

PROFESSIONAL HELP IN DIVORCE DISPUTE RESOLUTION

D

C

E

A B F G

High-functioning, ←
low-conflict spouses

Low-functioning, →
high-conflict spouses

AB: People needing no professional help to reach agreement.
BC: People who can reach agreement with the help of a neutral mediator.
CD: People who can reach agreement with the help of collaborative lawyers.
DE: People who can reach agreement with the help of collaborative lawyers plus an interdisciplinary Collaborative Divorce team.
AE: People who can benefit from the help of collaborative lawyers.
EF: People who can reach agreement "on the courthouse steps" with traditional legal counsel.
FG: People incapable of reaching agreements, requiring third-party decision making.

sides and discouraging the parties from lightly electing to litigate. The process itself places pressure on all participants to remain within the format. The suspicion and paranoia that can be present in the early stages of separation and divorce decline dramatically in collaborative cases as compared to conventionally negotiated divorces because far more of the process takes place in the presence of both parties, the lawyers are expected to manage conflict and guide negotiations, and the explicit commitment on both sides is that collaborative law counsel will withdraw if they have any reason to doubt the good faith of their own clients. Because everyone agrees in advance that win-win—or at least "good enough"—solutions are the preferred goal and a measure of lawyer success, the process encourages imaginative lateral thinking at a high level among all participants from the start. None of these effects is impossible to achieve in a traditional settlement negotiation, but nothing about the traditional lawyer-client relationship fosters these effects in a manner similar to collaborative law.

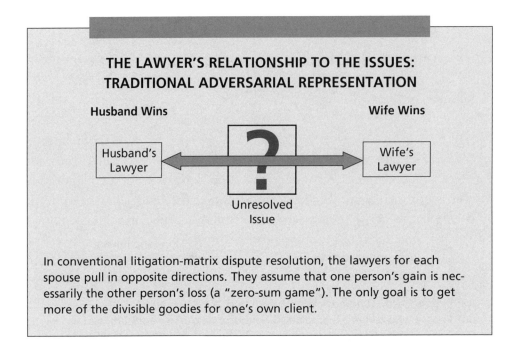

THE LAWYER'S RELATIONSHIP TO THE ISSUES: TRADITIONAL ADVERSARIAL REPRESENTATION

Husband Wins   Wife Wins

Husband's Lawyer ← **?** → Wife's Lawyer

Unresolved Issue

In conventional litigation-matrix dispute resolution, the lawyers for each spouse pull in opposite directions. They assume that one person's gain is necessarily the other person's loss (a "zero-sum game"). The only goal is to get more of the divisible goodies for one's own client.

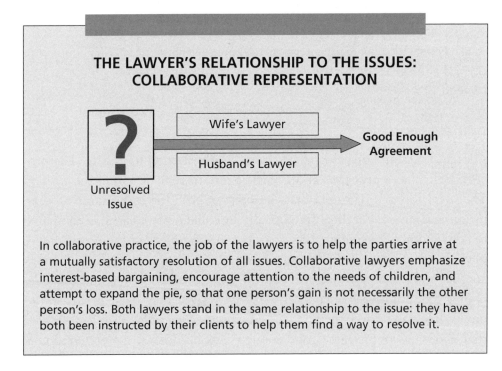

THE LAWYER'S RELATIONSHIP TO THE ISSUES: COLLABORATIVE REPRESENTATION

? → Wife's Lawyer / Husband's Lawyer → **Good Enough Agreement**

Unresolved Issue

In collaborative practice, the job of the lawyers is to help the parties arrive at a mutually satisfactory resolution of all issues. Collaborative lawyers emphasize interest-based bargaining, encourage attention to the needs of children, and attempt to expand the pie, so that one person's gain is not necessarily the other person's loss. Both lawyers stand in the same relationship to the issue: they have both been instructed by their clients to help them find a way to resolve it.

The clear commitment by everyone that decisions will not ordinarily be made by any third party dramatically alters how each participant engages in negotiations: each participant, whether lawyer or client, bears personal responsibility from the start for generating creative alternatives that might meet the legitimate needs of both parties. That is the sole agenda. When unilateral resort to third-party decision making remains an acceptable issue-resolving mechanism, as in traditional family law practice, one's responsibility for keeping the focus on settlement is diminished—sometimes subtly, sometimes dramatically.

Collaborative lawyers report that because resort to the courts means the termination of the collaborative process, their very thinking about dispute resolution changes in important ways compared to how they think when not involved in a collaborative law representation. Litigation for a collaborative lawyer is not merely another item on a menu of dispute-resolution options, as it necessarily must be for even the most collegial of traditional family lawyers. In the collaborative law process, litigation represents a failure of intention and imagination because it represents a failure to meet the objective for which the client hired the lawyer.

When lawyers think differently, they behave differently and counsel their clients differently. Of course, collaborative lawyers advise their clients about the law, about prioritizing goals, and about how to achieve the best outcome, as all lawyers do, but they do so in a context in which the clients have identified reaching a reasonable, acceptable settlement as the highest priority. The parties retain the right to go to court in a collaborative divorce, but the collaborative model makes it clear that doing so constitutes the end of a creative process, not the continuation of it. Because there is no way for the collaborative lawyers to do the job they were hired for other than devising pathways to a solution that might work, solutions can—to the amazement of the participants—sometimes be crafted out of the most unwieldy elements. The doorway leading from impasse to solution is the disqualification stipulation, the indispensable component of the collaborative law model. When apparent impasse arises, the model works because of it.[10] Once in a while, parties come up against a truly either-or ("zero-sum" or distributive) issue where they cannot compromise—perhaps, who will keep the family residence, or, whether the residence of the children may or may not be changed by a primary parent. Rather than requiring the collaborative law process to terminate in such cases, in some communities of collaborative practitioners it is possible to include in the participation agreement for collaborative law representation one or more procedural options for addressing such narrowly delimited issues, by mutual agreement only. These include by inviting a "meta-mediator" into the four-way meetings, or by submitting the issue to a designated arbitrator or private judge,[11] within the collaborative law process. These procedural options give parties who in good faith reach impasse a means to open the logjam without thereby opening the floodgates

of litigation, or allowing threats of litigation to become a legitimate negotiating technique within the collaborative container. Because of the privacy
and control that come with staying outside the formal court system, the
collaborative law process is well-suited to public figures and people of substantial means who often prefer to keep their financial and personal affairs

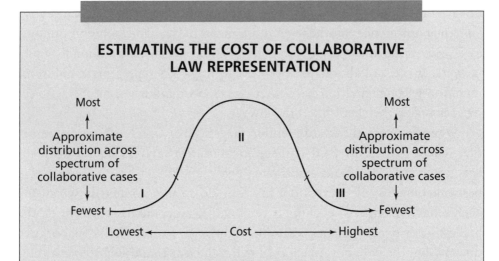

ESTIMATING THE COST OF COLLABORATIVE LAW REPRESENTATION

I: No complex issues; high-functioning clients
   a. Two or three four-way meetings equal 10 to 20 hours of lawyer time
      for each party* multiplied by the hourly rate for each lawyer.
   b. Court costs—filing fees.
   c. Expert fees—appraisals?
II: More issues or more complex issues; adequately functioning clients
   a. Three to seven four-way meetings equal 14 to 30 hours of lawyer time
      for each party* multiplied by the hourly rate for each lawyer.
   b. Court costs—filing fees.
   c. Expert fees—appraisals, accountancy fees, child consultant, inter-
      disciplinary collaborative divorce team, etc.
III: Complex and/or numerous issues and/or dysfunctional clients
   a. Seven or more four-way meetings equal a minimum of 30 and
      probably significantly more hours of lawyer time for each party*
      multiplied by the hourly rate for each lawyer.
   b. Courts costs—filing fees plus arbitrator or private judge.
   c. Expert fees—collaborative divorce team, custody consultant, CPA,
      appraisers, etc.
*Meetings, preparations, telephone time, research, correspondence, draft-
  ing, etc.

out of the public record. At the same time, the efficiency, cost-control, and high level of post-agreement durability satisfaction associated with success-ful collaborative law negotiations make it an attractive option for families with limited means as well.

For family lawyers, too, the rewards of this mode of practice can be great. While contentment with one's role as a family lawyer can be in short supply in divorce court because the legal process so often facilitates entirely avoidable family tragedies, contentment—even pleasure—in the practice of collaborative law is common. This is true largely because in electing to work out their differences in this way, collaborative clients have by definition placed as much or more value on the intangible benefits of treating the other party with consideration and good faith, and of ending an intimate relation-ship with dignity and integrity, than they place on such typical family law litigation goals as achieving the highest possible marginal dollar gain in out-come or the greatest absolute number of custodial hours.[12]

Helping a client to achieve a satisfactory, self-generated settlement that the client, fully informed and fully advised, believes is in his or her long-term best interests is satisfying work for a lawyer. Similarly satisfying is the recognition that in helping clients to reach settlements in this way, col-laborative lawyers are helping to strengthen the positive residual ties that survive the divorce, whether in co-parenting the children of the marriage, or in maintaining long-standing relationships with the extended family of the other party. It is not overstating the matter to say that working with other lawyers in such a model allows one to feel a rekindled sense of pride in the practice of law itself.

A successful collaborative representation not only resolves the legal issues associated with divorce, it can also help the clients aspire to and achieve tran-sition through an extremely difficult life passage with dignity and a sense of recovered competency and wholeness.[13] The best collaborative lawyers bring to their work a perspective, communicated directly and indirectly to both parties throughout the representation, that divorce is normal, that stress, grief, fear, vengefulness, anger, and the whole panoply of strong feelings attendant upon divorce are predictable, normal, and manageable, and that those feelings will pass and the clients will heal. For that reason, collabora-tive law is being recognized among academicians as belonging not only under the rubric of alternate dispute resolution, but also in the realm of two rela-tively new academic disciplines, "therapeutic jurisprudence" and "preventive law."[14] From that perspective, collaborative law allows us as family lawyers to embrace a view of ourselves as members of a healing profession.[15]

A MEDICAL ANALOGY

The legal profession is experiencing dramatic changes resembling the transformation of the health-care profession from a doctor-controlled to a patient-centered model that has taken place in the past 20 years or so. We can learn a lot about where we are going, and where we need to go, by analogy to the medical profession.

- Family lawyers would do well to adopt the first principle of the Hippocratic oath: "First, do no harm."
- In a medical emergency we must have high-quality emergency rooms and intensive care units available to deal with crises. But they are bad places to go for primary health care. In a legal emergency, we must have high-quality courts and litigating lawyers available to deal with the crisis. But courts are terrible places of first resort for resolution of divorce-related issues.

- We family lawyers might well consider adopting by analogy the medical principle of conservative treatment: start with offering the least invasive, least intrusive professional services that could handle the problem.

- We family lawyers need to hold ourselves to rigorous standards of informed consent when we advise clients about the risks associated with the dispute-resolution options available to them—including litigation—just as we expect physicians to explain fully the medical options and associated risks and to allow their patients to make fully informed choices for treatment.

Notes

1. See Chapter 7 for a discussion of ethical aspects of signing collaborative participation agreements.

2. From the perspective of some clients, control and privacy can be the most important advantages of alternate dispute-resolution modes such as collaborative law. In the court system, procedures and time lines are governed by intricate statutes, statewide rules of court, local rules, and practices of the individual judges who are the absolute authority figures within their courtrooms. Decisions are made by the judge, who rarely has the time, information, or authority to craft solutions tailored to the unique needs of the particular family. *See* Anne Kass, *Clinical Advice from the Bench,* [No. 2] 7 J. OF CHILD & ADOLESCENT PSYCHIATRIC CLINICS OF N. AM. 247, 251–53 (1998). In the collaborative law process, on the other hand, the parties and their lawyers control every step of both process and outcome. Similarly, it is common in many U.S. jurisdictions (California among them) for all aspects of litigated divorce proceedings, from motions and declarations through financial disclosures, hearings, trials, and all rulings, to be matters of public record, often causing embarrassment to adults and children alike, and at times putting the adults at risk for identity theft. In the collaborative process, the parties can readily insulate private information and agree on what will become public record. Mediation shares these attributes of privacy and control, but without the important advantage of advice and advocacy at the core of the process itself.

3. Joan Kelly, Ph.D., notes that the term mediation embraces a wide spectrum of different models, rendering generalizations about "mediation" of limited utility. Kelly, *A Decade of Divorce Mediation Research,* 34 FAM. & CONCILIATION CT. REV. at 373–75 (1996). In

northern California, the locus of the author's practice, family law mediations, whether conducted by lawyers or by mental health professionals, generally do not include direct participation by counsel for the parties. If independent counsel are retained, they advise and consult privately, outside the mediation process. Even in locales where family lawyers do participate directly in mediation sessions, their role is quite different from that of the mediator with respect to the goals of the mediation. Their responsibility is to provide independent advice and advocacy for the benefit of the individual client, whether or not the mediation results in an agreement. The risk of failure in mediation, in other words, is shared by the parties and the mediator, but not by the lawyers, who simply proceed to court with their clients if the mediation breaks down.

4. *See, e.g.,* Charles M. Goldstein & Dori Smith, *Collaborative Law: Getting Clients Out of the War Zone of Litigation into Peaceful Problem Solving,* THE HENNEPIN COUNTY LAWYER (official publication of the Hennepin County Bar Association), February 20, 2007, citing John Lande, *Possibilities for Collaborative Law: Ethics and Practice of Lawyer Disqualification and Process Control in a New Model of Lawyering,* 64 OHIO ST. L.J. 1315, 1325 (2003); John Lande & Gregg Herman, *Fitting the Forum to the Family Fuss: Choosing Mediation, Collaborative Law, or Cooperative Law for Negotiating Divorce Cases,* FAM. CT. REV. 42 (2), 280, 282–83 (2004).

5. Of course, not every client is well-served by the collaborative law model, any more than every lawyer is temperamentally suited to work well as a collaborative lawyer. Not every collaborative representation results in a comprehensive agreement. As long as the lawyers have worked together to provide the best possible opportunity for the couple to achieve an acceptable settlement, the fact that the couple did not fully succeed does not necessarily mean that they shouldn't have tried, nor that the lawyers necessarily failed to do their job.

6. For a discussion of the inherent tensions between lawyer and client in collaborative representation, *see* Pauline H. Tesler, *Collaborative Law: A New Paradigm for Family Law Attorneys,* 5 PSYCHOL., PUB. POL'Y L. 967, 976, n.24 (December 1999). *See also* ROBERT H. MNOOKIN, SCOTT R. PEPPET, & ANDREW S. TULUMELLO, BEYOND WINNING: HOW LAWYERS HELP CLIENTS CREATE VALUE IN NEGOTIATION (2000), Chapter Three. Of course, precisely the same tensions exist between the interests of lawyer and client in conventional representation, and indeed between any professional and his or her client, though this is rarely noted by critics of collaborative law. Highlighting this concern with respect to collaborative law alone seems without foundation. It would be of interest for commentators who are particularly concerned about this with respect to collaborative law to engage in an evenhanded assessment of the relative potential for conflict of interest in conventional representation as well. See Chapter 7, *infra,* for further discussion of ethical concerns.

7. Some elements of the written agreements are contractual and enforceable—for instance, the provision disqualifying both lawyers from ever appearing as counsel of record or as witness in adversarial proceedings between the parties—while others are aspirational and set the standard by which good faith and conduct consistent with the collaborative process can be measured. It is good practice for retainer agreements between lawyer and client, as well as participation agreements signed by both parties and both lawyers, to contain clear recitations that neither lawyer is in privity of contract with or owes a direct duty to the other lawyer's client.

8. *See, e.g.,* David Hoffman, *Colliding Worlds of Dispute Resolution: Towards a Unified Field Theory of ADR,* 2008 J. DISP. RESOL. ____.

9. *See* Ronald J. Gilson & Robert H. Mnookin, *Disputing Through Agents: Cooperation and Conflict Between Lawyers in Litigation,* 94 COLUMBIA L. REV. 509 (March 1994); and Rachel T.A. Croson and Robert H. Mnookin, *Does Disputing Through Agents Enhance Cooperation? Experimental Evidence,* 26 JOURNAL OF LEGAL STUDIES 331–45 (1997).

10. Settlements can of course be reached out of court without a disqualification stipulation, but the power of this particular model lies in keeping parties—and their lawyers—at the settlement table, and in a constructive frame of mind, far longer than other models. This seems to arise from the commitment of the lawyers to do the job they were hired to do,

their skill in maintaining the collaborative "container" around the clients, the serious written aspirational commitments to the collaborative model made by the participants, and the substantial incentives and disincentives built into the model itself.

11. The option of including a designated limited-purpose private judge or arbitrator in collaborative participation agreements had some popularity throughout the 1990s but was rarely invoked even when included as a process option. The reasoning was that clients would feel more comfortable knowing they had an intermediate option short of terminating the collaborative process if negotiations stalled. More recently practitioners seem to have concluded that where the collaborative professionals are skilled in interest-based negotiations, there is little need for such a process option. Provided it is resorted to rarely, and only in exceptional circumstances, however, it remains a possibility where both parties and both lawyers wish to elect it—as does any mutually agreeable process option other than resort to the court system. But the consensus among experienced collaborative practitioners is that any resort to third-party decision making will be less satisfactory to divorcing parties in the long run than even the very same decision made by the parties themselves.

12. Traditional, court-based family law practice can be compared in this respect to the kind of narrow, specialty-based medical care that the patient rights and alternative health-care movements have transformed so profoundly over the past quarter-century. Physicians who specialize in a particular procedure or body part while ignoring the impact of their care on the entire person resemble lawyers who refuse to look beyond a narrow range of truly legal issues they consider their bailiwick, to see the long-term impact of their work on the actual lives of their clients once the divorce is over. Just as surgeons joke that "the operation was successful but the patient died," retired California Court of Appeals Justice Donald M. King acerbically concludes, "Family law court is where they shoot the survivors." King, Address at *New Ways of Helping Children and Parents Through Divorce,* conference sponsored by the Judith Wallerstein Center for the Family in Transition and the University of California, Santa Cruz, Quail Lodge, Carmel Valley, California (Nov. 21, 1998).

13. It is commonly accepted in the mental health professions that divorce ranks as one of the most stressful experiences one can endure as an adult, second only to the death of a child, and that people going through divorce may experience transient diminished capacity to deal with the ordinary demands and stresses of life to a greater or lesser degree. Our work as conventional lawyers allows us little scope to recognize or respond effectively to that reality about our clients' experience of divorce. Collaborative law invites and is enhanced by such a perspective and clients are helped to deal constructively with that reality when they are educated to understand and expect it rather than being treated as if it were not happening.

14. Therapeutic jurisprudence studies the intended as well as unintended therapeutic and antitherapeutic consequences of people's involvement with law and the courts. Preventive law looks at the responsibility of lawyers to anticipate and assist their clients to plan for legal difficulties likely to arise in the future. *See* Dennis P. Stolle, David B. Wexler, & Bruce J. Winick, Practicing Therapeutic Jurisprudence: Law as a Helping Profession (2000). Collaborative lawyers do this work not only when they normalize the immediate divorce process and the emotional impact of the grief and recovery process, but also when they take the long view of clients' interests and needs, and advocate for long-term solutions that will serve the relational as well as the immediate financial interests of the clients, and when they build into negotiated collaborative agreements recitations about predictable future areas of disagreements and procedures for reaching negotiated agreements when such issues arise.

15. Such a perspective may strike hardball litigators as having little to do with the real work of lawyers. But therapeutic jurisprudence scholars point out that whether we like it or not, every encounter that our clients have with us and with the courts operates in service of healing or against it; little or nothing that we do with clients enduring so stressful a life passage can be seen as therapeutically neutral. We can choose to ignore the scarring impact of our work as litigating family lawyers, but that does not make the damage we do less real; it merely makes us willfully ignorant. *See* The Affective Assistance of Counsel: Practicing Law as a Healing Profession (Marjorie Silver ed., 2007).

Chapter 3

Becoming a Collaborative Lawyer: The Retooling Process

"Discourage litigation. Persuade neighbors to compromise when-ever you can. Point out to them how the nominal winner is often the real loser in fees, expenses, and waste of time. As a peacemaker the lawyer has a superior opportunity of becoming a good [person]."
—*Abraham Lincoln*

It's Not for Everyone

Deciding to practice collaborative law is easy. Doing it well is not.[1] The adversarial default setting exerts so much power, and its workings are so invisible to most of us—especially those of us who have been successful litigators for most of our careers—that without a substantial commitment of time, energy, and introspective reflection, chances are high that aspiring collaborative lawyers will offer their clients something they are unprepared to deliver. In terms of malpractice prevention, professional responsibility, consumer protection, and truth in advertising, it is the premise of this book that no one should engage in collaborative representation without under-standing that doing this work well requires examining a professional life-time of conscious and unconscious habits, and requires rebuilding from the bottom up an entirely new set of attitudes, behaviors, and habits that have been measured by their effectiveness in collaborative cases. To do this work well, we must become beginners and unlearn a bundle of old automatic behaviors before we can acquire the new, more conscious attitudes, behav-iors, and habits of a good collaborative lawyer. Without this effort, the pull toward conducting conventional settlement negotiations will be strong, and the risk of unsuccessful collaboration will be relatively high. As the old saying reminds us, "If you keep on doing what you've been doing, you'll keep on getting what you've been getting."

That being so, it is useful before going any further to pose the question, "Why should a successful lawyer at the peak of his or her professional career want to become a beginner again?" The answer is simple: because doing so is challenging, rewarding, prudent, and socially useful.

1. **Challenging:** By the time most of us reach our prime professional years, we have mastered our craft. We know the substantive and procedural law. We know how to interview a client, shape an argument, and try a case. The experienced litigator's calendar is full and the days are demanding: we constantly meet new people and try new issues, but we are rarely called upon to master an unknown skill. Learning the craft of collaborative lawyering involves mastering knowledge and skills that were not taught to us in law school and that few of us learn in the course of our litigation practices. Lawyers like challenges; learning to do this work is a particularly engaging challenge.

2. **Rewarding:** At the end of an adversarial representation, few family law clients express genuine appreciation for the work we have done for them—even if we won a remarkable victory in court.[2] As Washington Supreme Court Justice Bobbie Bridge has remarked, roughly 90 percent of the ostensible winners in family law matters emerge unhappy with both the process and outcome of the proceedings, and it is safe to assume that 100 percent of the ostensible losers feel the same way.[3] We work very hard when we do trial work. If we get recognition for a job well done, it is more likely to come from the judge or a colleague than from the client for whom we toiled. In collaborative practice, however, it is common for clients who reach agreements to express profound gratitude for the work done by both lawyers. Wanting to be appreciated for what we do is a basic human desire that tough old litigators simply learn to suppress because the need is so rarely met.[4] Collaborative lawyers learn to enjoy the appreciation of the clients they serve as a regular feature of their work.

3. **Prudent:** Many family lawyers, observing the striking increase in numbers of self-represented litigants over recent years,[5] conclude that the market share of family law clients who want to hire a lawyer to manage their entire divorce within a litigation matrix from start to finish is diminishing. Increasingly, even clients who can afford such representation do not want it. These trends obviously

are linked to the fear of lawyers endemic in our culture:[6] fear of escalating costs and conflict, fear of loss of control and privacy, and fear of turning over important life issues to the decision of a disinterested judge. Many clients ask for mediation and for unbundled legal services, preferring to act as their own general contractors for legal services rather than to turn the case over to the all-powerful lawyer of record. Where collaborative law is available, clients want it.[7] Certainly litigation counsel will always be needed for clients who cannot or will not resolve their issues by agreement, but available evidence suggests that clients want, and are well-served by, alternate dispute resolution.[8] From a strategic planning perspective, lawyers who want to serve the needs of the market by offering a full menu of dispute-resolution options will need to be familiar with collaborative law.

4. **Socially Useful:** If Justice Donald M. King is correct in asserting that "family law court is where they shoot the survivors,"[9] and if commentators on the catastrophic impact upon children and families of highly conflicted divorce proceedings are to be believed,[10] then it is apparent that we serve not only our clients but our larger society by offering collaborative law and by learning to do it well. In this regard, collaborative law is in the forefront of an upwelling of change in the legal profession, and in the ways that lawyers relate to their clients, that legal scholars and ethicists have been exhorting for nearly two decades.[11]

As important and valuable as collaborative law is, it isn't for every client and it isn't for every lawyer. Clients who may be poor candidates for the collaborative model include people with clinically significant psychiatric problems (such as major depression, unmedicated bipolar disorder, psychosis, and certain character disorders), drug or alcohol abusers, families with active domestic violence/abuse problems, fundamentally dishonest or unscrupulous people, people unwilling to take responsibility for making choices and decisions in their own lives and living with them, and people unwilling or unable to follow through on commitments, both substantive and procedural, made during the collaborative process.[12]

Lawyers, too, vary widely in their openness to collaborative law and in their ability to learn the new skills and habits of collaborative lawyering. Collaborative law's success in a community depends on the emergence of a sufficient critical mass of interested and competent collaborative lawyers in the locale who put out a consistent core message—individually and collectively—about collaborative law, so that clients and referral sources become familiar with the availability and respectability of the model. One of the first tasks in introducing collaborative practice to a community is having a means for identifying to opinion makers, clients, lawyers, and referral sources those lawyers who are making the commitment to learn how to practice collaborative law effectively. Identifying like-minded colleagues, drawing them into practice groups,[13] bringing in capable trainers,[14] meeting regularly for case conferencing, preparing and distributing public information and marketing materials collectively, educating referral sources, mounting individual and group websites and blogs that emphasize collaborative practice, and similar methods, can assure that there is a sufficient cohort of good collaborative lawyers known to clients and referral sources in a locale, so that couples are aware of adequate professional resources from which to select their respective collaborative lawyers.

Making the Paradigm Shift Happen

The phrase that many have adopted to describe the process of unlearning adversarial behaviors and learning collaborative behaviors is "making the paradigm shift." The shift comes more easily to some lawyers than to others, and in the process of learning collaborative behaviors, lawyers develop individualized styles of practicing collaboratively. No two lawyers will end up practicing collaborative law in exactly the same way, any more than two lawyers will try the same case in exactly the same way. Nonetheless, the process that one engages in to make the paradigm shift occur has a clear four-part conceptual structure to it and mastering, in one's own way, each of the four dimensions is the foundation for competent collaborative lawyering. One develops the skills in all four dimensions of the paradigm shift more or less simultaneously, but for purposes of this chapter, we will look at them in sequence. Remember, though, that all four dimensions play out simultaneously whenever we take on a new collaborative case and the "beginner's mind" of the collaborative lawyer must be directed to all four dimensions, not just one.

Each of the four dimensions of the paradigm shift includes both inner and outer transformations; in other words, transformations of the lawyer's inner perception of who he or she is and what he or she is doing, and transformations of objective, visible behaviors toward the clients and other professionals involved in the collaborative case. As you read and think about the rest of this chapter, bear in mind that understanding the meaning of the words you are reading is not the same thing as mastering the skill. Reading this chapter (or this book) will not suffice to transform you from an adversarial to a collaborative lawyer. However, you will perhaps have taken the essential first steps: recognizing that you want to practice collaborative law and recognizing that there is considerable work ahead of you to master this new craft.

The Four Retooling Questions

As you enter the realm of the paradigm shift and begin the task of becoming a competent collaborative lawyer, four overarching questions will help you to stay in the beginner's mind, the inner state in which the work takes place of deconstructing your combative habits and replacing them with a range of choices embodying collaborative behaviors and beliefs. Make it a practice to reflect on these questions each time you move to a new task during your day—opening the mail, answering the telephone, writing a letter, meeting with a client or lawyer.[15]

1. Who Am I?
2. Who Is the Client?
3. What Is the Task?
4. How Do I Do This Task?

Let us consider each of these questions for a moment.

1. **Who Am I?** No question is more powerful than this one in helping us to see and free ourselves from the automatic, unthinking adversarial behaviors of the gladiatorial litigator.[16] Reflecting on this question means developing a much richer range of choices about how we will respond when faced with needless, excessively argumentative or overreaching behavior on the part of other lawyers and with unreasonable, unattainable, or self-defeating demands from our clients—the demands that arise out of fear, anger, vengefulness, grief, shame, and other powerful emotions poorly correlated with identification and achievement of a client's long-term enlightened self-interest. Embracing this question "Who am I?" can take many forms and lead in a number of valuable directions, including the following.

A. Am I behaving like a gladiator at this moment? What is a gladiator? What is a gladiator's job description? What does a gladiator believe about his or her role and responsibilities? How does a gladiator behave when faced with the complexities of human feelings and relationships? Do I want to behave in that fashion? Why? How does it help me to advise and advocate for my client's enlightened self-interest to employ the behaviors and beliefs of a gladiator at this moment?

B. When I am doing my very best work for my clients, the work that most helps them to make a considered and constructive transition from married to single, what skills and understandings am I employing? Would those skills and understandings be useful at this moment? Can I improve those skills and understandings? Are there related skills and understandings that I would like to draw upon at moments like this? How can I learn them?

C. In moments of stress that require quick responses, what is my usual default setting? How do I usually respond to a crisis (real or imagined) when I don't have time to think and plan ahead? How effective has that style been in the past? How useful is it likely to be in this immediate situation? In this case, with these people, what style of response to stressful situations might be most useful if I am to help clarify and advance my client's genuine long-term interests? What do I need to learn to make that new style automatic? Are there any visceral cues that could alert me when I have fallen into an unwanted habitual style of response? Are there any conscious habits or cues that I could build into my daily practice that could help me at stressful moments to access the new styles of response that I am developing?

D. Considering all that, what metaphors for my new role as a collaborative lawyer can I incorporate into my own consciousness that can replace the litigating gladiator as a template for measuring and changing my own attitudes and behaviors?[17]

2. Who Is the Client? A conventional family lawyer would rarely think to ask this question. The client, in conventional practice, is simply the person who arrives for legal consultation with a checkbook and with a story that can be efficiently analyzed and reduced to key justiciable issues. The client, in the dominant paradigm, is little more than the owner of those key issues. Soon enough, we learn that the client also has a longer life story, past and unfolding, most of which a conventional lawyer will determine to be irrelevant to the professional task. The client also has feelings, which also are irrelevant to conventional legal work and can interfere with it. If those feelings are strong and unmanageable enough, we will be forced to deal with them in the dominant paradigm, generally by referring the client to a mental health professional for individual psychotherapy or counseling—or by being fired or resigning from representation.

This question "Who is the client?" has a very different and more dynamic meaning in collaborative legal practice. Indeed, constant awareness of this question is a vital tool for the collaborative lawyer's management of conflict and guidance of negotiations. Being attentive to this question is also the foundation for the collaborative lawyer's ability to help normalize for clients the stormy nature of the divorce process and to help them expect and achieve the good divorce.

We know from firsthand professional experience, buttressed by solid research, that divorce and family breakup are second only to the death of a child in traumatic impact upon the survivors. Our clients frequently consult us in transient states of more or less diminished capacity, as a consequence of waves of strong, even unmanageable negative emotion washing over them—grief, rage, fear, and vengefulness prominent among them. In that sense, our clients often are in a "shadow" state when they consult us and when we devise with them the goals and strategies for our representation of them. In other words, in the dominant litigation paradigm, we take our professional marching orders from clients who often are flooded by feelings so intense and destabilizing that their ability to cope and even to think clearly about cause and effect, much less to make well-considered plans for the future, may be compromised.[18] Yet, these same clients will also experience transient but gradually lengthening periods of fully restored rational coping capacity, until eventually, they are more or less reliably back to the functional level that preceded the divorce. By that time, however, our work for them may be long since finished. To put it another way, we are dealing with people facing some of the most complex challenges and decisions of their lives, at a time when their thinking and coping abilities often are at an all-time low.

In the dominant paradigm, our clients come to us expecting gladiators and they call us to schedule appointments when they want a gladiator's intervention. We devise our game plan during those meetings, when the client's least competent shadow state is in control and fear, rage, or grief is calling the shots. An emotion-driven opening salvo by one client can be expected to produce an equal or greater salvo in return. The clients do not call us a week or two later to report that things are looking better, that they are communicating and cooperating better with their spouses, that the take-no-prisoners litigation plan we worked out needs to be reconsidered. Such conversations can be embarrassing, and in addition, the lawyer's time is expensive. No wonder, then, that family law cases so often careen toward the courthouse, despite genuine desire on both sides for a negotiated resolution.

What if, instead of accepting at face value the shadow client that so often presents himself or herself to us, we were to ask ourselves questions like the following whenever we meet or speak with our clients.

A. Am I speaking at this moment to my client's highest-functioning self? Or to a client gripped to a greater or lesser degree by overwhelming shadow-state emotions?[19] Is my client at this moment in the same state of competent functioning that he or she was in when I was first retained as a collaborative lawyer in this matter? If my client is in a highly competent state at this moment, is he or she likely to experience other, more overwhelming emotional shadow states before this divorce is completed? Does he or she know that? Have we fully discussed that probability in planning how this divorce process will be handled? Have I asked this client whether he or she wants major decisions about the divorce and the future life of the post-divorce family to be made when he or she is gripped by a shadow-state emotion, with biochemically diminished ability to weigh options? What instructions have we put in place during this client's highest-functioning meetings with me about how to handle those shadow periods? How will I recognize when this client is in a shadow state, and how will I most effectively remind him or her of the process agreements we have made for waiting it out? How clearly have I explained to this client that dramatic ups and downs on both sides are par for the course in divorce and need to be planned for? Have I used this shadow template to help my client understand and respond effectively to negative behaviors from his or her partner? If not, why not? How clearly have I linked these concepts to the proposition that achieving the good divorce depends in part on how effectively we anticipate and deal with the inevitable shadow states?

B. In setting goals and priorities for this case at this moment with this client, have I been engaged with my client at his or her highest-functioning self? Is my client able at this moment to take a long view, and to recognize and plan for maximizing enlightened self-interest, his or her own and that of the people he or she loves? Has this client made an informed decision that I am expected to plan for conduct of the divorce only with the highest-intentioned persona of my client, not the shadow self that is here today? How will I go about reframing the task today in light of the fact that I am meeting with the "shadow" client, rather than the higher-functioning client who retained me and set the goals and expectations for the representation?

3. What Is the Task? All lawyers "know" that we have a "duty of zealous representation" of our clients, just as we "know" that satisfying that duty means that we must always use our most diligent efforts to get maximum advantage for our client, whatever the cost, by all lawful means.[20] Put most simply, we believe that we satisfy our duty of zealous representation of family law clients when we aim for nothing more than to get the largest possible share of the quantifiable widgets for our own client.

This deeply ingrained belief and the way that we construe its meanings have helped create the dominant paradigm, but in reality, our duties to our collaborative family law clients are—and should be—considerably more complex than merely obtaining the greatest piece of the pie regardless of collateral damage, just as families themselves are considerably more complex entities than a damaged automobile fender. Just as effective collaborative lawyers constantly ask themselves, "Who is this client that I am representing at this moment, and who is the client that retained me?," we also ask, "What is the task that this client retained me to achieve? What are the interests that this client retained me to advance or protect during this representation, and are we working toward those goals or in unintentional opposition to those goals at this moment?"

A conventional litigation lawyer might well assume that achieving the greatest quantifiable outcome for each of the legally cognizable issues is the obvious and sole task of representation, and might therefore (as trained to do in law school) probe efficiently from the first interview to spot the issues, weed out irrelevancies, and shape the messy facts into a theory of the case for trial. In contrast, the collaborative lawyer does something different: he or she begins the representation by listening carefully, asking searchingly, and encouraging the long view, enlightened self-interest, and appropriate attention to relational as well as economic issues, attention to people and personal values as well as dollars. He or she assumes nothing about the goals to be achieved.

Experienced divorce lawyers know that it is extremely common in a first interview for the client to say something like, "I only want what's fair." We tend to discount such statements, because "fair" is an inherently self-referential concept that can interfere with setting goals and reaching solutions. (If the client defines his or her favored outcome as "fair," anything short of that is likely to be viewed as "unfair.") But our clients do mean something important when they say that, and when collaborative lawyers learn to conduct a different kind of initial interview, we can help our clients reframe that thought so that they have a better chance of achieving the reframed goal. Often, what is meant is something like this: "I want a contained and reasonably civilized divorce process, one that keeps the kids safely out of the firing line, and while I want a good financial outcome, I don't want to be perceived as greedy or over-reaching." In other words, when they say "I only want what's fair," our clients are saying in effect that they want a "good divorce." The skilled collaborative lawyer begins from the first conversation with the client to place responsibility on the client's shoulders for the choices that will make such goals achievable—or impossible. At the same time, the lawyer educates the client about what really happens when spouses take their differences to court: the limits of judges' jurisdiction, time, skills, knowledge, and patience; the focus on allocating consequences resulting from the past rather than on planning for the future; the oversimplification at the heart of trial practice; the political and accidental origins of legislation and the ambiguities contained within statutes; the difference between what the law allows courts to do and what the individual family may need and want; the economic and relational costs of litigation and likely impacts upon the family members' capacity to make a healthy transition through the divorce process; the usual range of outcomes in litigation; the fact that most cases settle (even if on the courthouse steps); and the many other practical truths about divorce litigation that are well-known to lawyers and entirely unknown to most clients, whose view of family law may have been shaped chiefly by television shows. The purpose of all this listening, questioning, and educating is simple: to disabuse clients of their unrealistic expectations that they will find justice and vindication in domestic relations court, to focus their attention on the true and hidden costs of conflicted divorces, to place responsibility for choices that lead to good or bad divorces with the clients, and to educate about the importance of realistic expectations, mutual good faith, a well-managed process, and attention to the needs of the children, in achieving the "good divorce."

In light of these truths, as good collaborative lawyers we ask ourselves over and over again during the course of representation, "What is the task?" Here are some ways to think about the meaning of that question.

A. What has my client (at his or her most competent and clear-thinking) identified as his or her most important priorities in this divorce? Does that list give attention to the needs of the children and other significant family members, now and over the foreseeable future? In setting goals and priorities, have I ensured that my client weighed the importance to himself or herself of maintaining valued connections with extended family members on both sides? With the former spouse? Will trying to achieve any of the identified goals thwart any important needs of the post-divorce restructured family? Does my client understand the connection between appropriate attention to these matters and achieving a good divorce?

B. Is my client paying attention to issues of personal integrity and self-respect in prioritizing goals and setting strategies for this divorce? Have we discussed the implications of those aspects of divorce sufficiently for my client to make well-considered choices and decisions in this regard?

C. In setting goals, have my client and I spent sufficient time distinguishing between positions and true interests? Does my client understand the difference between the two, and the importance of interest-based bar-gaining for expanding the settlement pie, building consensus about solutions, and achieving a good divorce?

D. Is my client in this moment taking a broad perspective? Or a narrow one? Is my client thinking clearly about building a satisfactory future after the divorce, or is he or she reacting in the grip of overpowering but transitory emotions? Am I helping my client see the possible long-term costs of marginal short-term gains? Is this conversation/goal/tactic likely to advance my client's highest stated intentions for this divorce, or is it more likely to thwart those highest intentions?

4. How Do I Do This Task? In a conventional, litigation-driven family law practice, the question "How do I do this task?" is typically asked only by the newest practitioners. Once we have been at it for any length of time, we master our craft, and while there is challenge involved in figuring out how to structure and present an issue for a victory, few of us feel any need to re-examine how we go about our work in any fundamental sense. We already know how to interview our clients and witnesses efficiently, how to find, retain, and prepare our experts and prevent them from going astray; how to get the best edge for our clients in court-appointed custody evaluations; how to deal with a difficult opposing party in a deposition or trial; how to advocate effectively for the best outcome in a judicial settlement conference; and how to shape and simplify complex facts for effective presentation at trial. We operate out of habits and learned behaviors and practices that are second nature, and that are well-suited to a litigation-driven practice in which preparation for trial is the matrix for gathering information, organizing facts, obtaining orders, and navigating settlement conferences.

Lawyers who commence a collaborative representation without asking at every juncture, "How do I do this task?" are likely to impose unthinkingly that same litigation matrix onto the collaborative process. Doing so imposes process elements (speed, efficiency, narrow standards of relevancy, limited jurisdiction, lawyer control) that rarely suit the needs of collaborative clients and that in fact impede offering the best opportunity for these clients to achieve their optimal terms of resolution—the one overarching promise a collaborative lawyer must make and keep with clients and colleagues.

Seeing and deconstructing what we already know about how to do our job opens spaces for learning how to do a new job, that of the collaborative lawyer. Questions like the following, asked every day, help us do this deconstruction job.

A. What do I need to do before sitting down with this client today that will help me do this task with beginner's mind? What do I need to attend to during our conversation that will invite my client to tell me the entire story I need to know?

B. In this moment, as I am interviewing my client, what do I want to achieve? What do I want to communicate to this client about myself and my role? What do I need to find out about my client right now before I can perform my tasks well?

C. What meta-messages about our professional relationship and our respective responsibilities are communicated by my physical environment?

D. What am I doing now, and what will I do, to educate my client about conflict, conflict management, dispute resolution, negotiations, the courts, the power and effect of emotions in divorce, child development, the dynamics of grief and recovery, and the good divorce?

E. In what I say to and about the other participants in the divorce process today, am I modeling collaborative behavior and intention for my client?

F. What preconceptions about outcome do I bring to this situation today? Where do they come from? Are these preconceptions useful in working collaboratively toward a mutually acceptable agreement? If not, what will I do about them?

G. How will I recognize self-defeating adversarial behavior on my own part today? How will I respond to similar behavior in others? How can I invite constructive problem-solving behavior and discourage counterproductive behaviors in myself and others? What can I do today toward those ends?

H. What tools do I need to use today to provide the best possible conditions in which my client and the other party can achieve their highest intentions for this divorce in terms of process and outcome?

The Four Dimensions of Retooling

The four questions we have looked at above are like spotlights, questions to focus your attention inward at specific moments on challenges that will help you leave behind automatic habits of mind so that you can enter the more open space of the beginner's mind. Once there, you begin to develop the attitudes, skills, and behaviors of a collaborative lawyer. In this section, we will broaden to a floodlight focus aimed outward at observable behaviors. We will scan the entire range of retooled behaviors, attitudes, and skills that a capable collaborative lawyer will want to develop. These new capacities grow over time, not all at once, nor in any particular order. In the remainder of this chapter, we are mapping out in a four-dimensional model the universe of new learned behaviors that all of us enter as we begin doing collaborative work.

The First Dimension: Retooling Yourself

My first collaborative practice group of 18 pioneering family law specialists came into being in 1993 in San Francisco. One of the perplexing issues that emerged early on in that group was a phenomenon that I have seen repeated in community after community in my work as a trainer since then. Although all of us were well-known and respected family lawyers with flourishing practices, and all expressed interest in learning this new way of practice, some of us quickly began taking in many new collaborative cases, while others encountered few if any clients willing to try this new model. How could this be? We all had similar caseloads and represented similar kinds of clients; we all settled most of our cases; we believed that we shared a consistent, well-defined understanding of collaborative law; we all had committed considerable time and energy to developing and refining the model and meeting together monthly to get our practice group off the ground. What did some of us apparently have that was attracting collaborative law clients that others of us apparently lacked?

After a while, the answer became clear to me: the lawyers whose collaborative practices were flourishing were those whose enthusiasm and conviction about collaborative practice were so genuine and intense that they simply could not contain their excitement when they spoke about how the collaborative process works. These lawyers reacted to the inevitable uncertainties associated with introducing a new and (at that time) untried model by assuming that solutions to any problems that might arise in collaborative cases would emerge naturally from the work itself. This sense of assurance was transmitted from the very first words that these lawyers exchanged with a potential new client. Their belief in the superiority of collaborative law as a conflict-resolution model caused them to provide honest yet wholly confident responses to questions from potential collaborative clients. I came to understand that the depth and breadth of the lawyer's belief in the collaborative model, or lack thereof, was being communicated in words and nonverbal cues to clients so forcefully that clients were accurately receiving the messages sent. For the successful collaborative lawyers, the message was: "Collaborative law is something I really believe in, and even though it is still new and there isn't yet research to prove I'm right, I have confidence that I can offer superior professional services to you in that model." For those with languishing collaborative practices, the message was more like: "This is something interesting, new, and untried; maybe it will work and maybe it won't, but I'm willing to try it if you are." Clients who heard the former tended to select collaborative representation, while clients who heard the latter tended to reject it.

From this understanding flows the first dimension in the outer-world work of becoming a collaborative lawyer: retooling *yourself* so that from the very first communications with any client to the last, you are sending honest, consistent messages about your conviction that collaborative law is a powerful, safe, creative conflict-resolution process that can greatly benefit the clients who choose it and commit fully to it.

MAKING THE PARADIGM SHIFT HAPPEN

THE FOUR DIMENSIONS OF TRANSFORMING YOURSELF INTO A COLLABORATIVE LAWYER

Remember as you explore these four dimensions of the paradigm shift that you are not just learning a new set of behaviors. More important, you are examining and reshaping your beliefs about your profession, your role, your relationships, and what it means to do your job well.

FIRST DIMENSION: RETOOLING YOURSELF

Thinking, Feeling, Speaking, and Acting Like a Collaborative Lawyer:

- Doing the inner work: seeing and resetting your automatic gladiatorial reactions

- Retooling how you think about law, your role, your responsibilities

- Retooling how you use language

- Understanding your role as de facto "priest" of divorce

- Learning to apply new concepts and skills from many disciplines

SECOND DIMENSION: RETOOLING WITH THE CLIENT

Being a Collaborative Lawyer from the First Contact:

- Placing and eliciting responsibility: retooling alter-ego behavior

- Active, deep listening

- Presentation of dispute-resolution continuum and client self-selection

- Retooling pace: make haste slowly

- Orienting client in time and space and process

- Encouraging focus on highest goals for the future, including attention to the relational estate, vs. strategizing for maximum quantifiable outcome (the lawyer comfort zone)

- Normalizing shadow behavior

- Normalizing the good divorce
- Evoking, contracting with, and validating working from the higher self
- Setting and maintaining a safe, constructive, respectful container: metaphors and agreements

THIRD DIMENSION: RETOOLING WITH THE OTHER PLAYERS

Embodying New Thoughts and New Behaviors:
- Retooling how you think and talk about the other party
- Retooling the relationship with the other lawyer
- Retooling the relationships with other professionals
- Deconstructing and transcending turf issues
- "Win big" vs. "win-win" (or "good enough")
- Building shared understandings about good faith, trust, honesty, civility, and termination of process
- Building shared understandings about negotiating style: interest-based vs. positional styles

FOURTH DIMENSION: RETOOLING NEGOTIATIONS

Managing Conflict, Guiding Negotiations:
- Agenda management and control: planning for success, highlighting success
- Pre-meetings and debriefing meetings
- Caucusing agreements
- Normalizing the shadow, managing shadow behavior
- Managing and educating about pace
- Holding to a clearly defined process: buy-in or commitment; information-gathering and analysis; expansion and evaluation of options; negotiations and resolution; closure
- Modeling effective communication and conflict resolution skills
- Learning to use a new toolbox: metaphors, upgrades, shadow writing, brainstorming, reframing, "more law not less," "right language,"[21] and a host of other techniques
- Becoming adept at constructive criticism/self-criticism/transparency/apology
- Learning to recognize and make effective use of transference and countertransference
- Attending to and enhancing ceremonial aspects of the divorce process
- Working collaboratively with mediators and mentors
- Working with a team
- Ensuring progress and closure
- Troubleshooting and solving process problems

TABLE 1. Retooling Yourself[22]

Adversarial Lawyers:	Collaborative Lawyers:
See winning as the goal and losing as the alternative	See completing the divorce transition with integrity and mutual satisfaction as the goal
Consider "win big" the best outcome	See "win-win," or "good enough," as the best outcomes
Focus on bottom-line outcome with little openness to creative problem-solving	Remain detached from focus on outcome, and focus instead on creative problem solving techniques
Measure professional success by magnitude of immediately quantifiable, measurable outcomes	Measure professional success by how well the client's larger life goals are served by the collaborative process
Believe one must be aggressive to win	Understand the difference between aggression and assertion
Consider emotions and feelings to be distractions from the real work	View emotions and feelings as important elements of the collaborative process that need to be acknowledged and appropriately managed
Hide real self and personal values behind armored professional persona	Reveal self and integrate personal values and ethics into work
Operate within a metaphor of "lawyer as gladiator" or "lawyer as hired gun"	See themselves as wise counselors with special skill in managing conflict and guiding negotiations
Believe life experiences happen to us	Believe life experiences often reflect who we are
See apology as risky and forgiveness as weak	See apology and forgiveness as strengths
Define the scope of the work in terms of jurisdiction of court and predictions about behavior of judges	Define the scope of the work as all matters the clients wish to address, regardless of whether courts can issue orders about them
See pacing as a by-product of court's procedural rules and requirements	See pacing as a valuable and flexible tool
Regard the litigation process as a proper template for resolving disputes	Regard litigation as a last resort for resolving disputes

The Second Dimension: Retooling with the Client

Attending to the second dimension of the paradigm shift means becoming aware of habitual behaviors and beliefs that come into play when we are working with a client, and retooling those behaviors and beliefs so that they will serve, not thwart, collaborative conflict resolution.

Habitual attitudes about what is the client's responsibility and what is the lawyer's, what is relevant and irrelevant to the representation, what is possible and what is not, and what the proper relationship between lawyer and client should be are the focus of this retooling dimension. Reflect on this list and add your own retooling perceptions to it.

TABLE 2. Retooling with the Client

Adversarial Lawyers:	Collaborative Lawyers:
Sit behind a desk	Sit face to face with client
Regard encounter with client as an exclusively intellectual process	See encounter with client as synergistic, involving thoughts, emotions, sensory perceptions
Ignore client's physical and emotional comfort	Attend to client's physical and emotional comfort
Remain unaware of meta-messages communicated by physical space and placement	Make conscious, constructive use of physical space and placement to support intentions of representation
Consider efficiency to be paramount	Consider integrity and authenticity to be paramount
Spend limited time with client; emphasis is on getting the work done efficiently	Spend as much time as needed with client; time with client is central to the process
Focus on legal analysis: issues, facts, law	Focus on what client requires to make healthy transition from married to unmarried
Apply legal relevancy screen from the start in gathering information and analyzing justiciable issues	Apply no predetermined screen in helping client identify and achieve long-term enlightened interests
Use focused and leading questions for efficient retrieval of essential elements of case	Use active listening for comprehension of entire situation: history, context, goals, priorities, fears
Ask close-ended questions to fit facts into legal framework	Ask open-ended questions to elicit full understanding of complex situation
Categorize clients by issues presented	Receive each client as presenting a fresh story with an unknown potential outcome
Rely on prepared or standard questions in early interviews with client	Allow information-gathering communications to follow a natural course guided by client concerns
Support client in beliefs about others, including negative beliefs	Encourage respect for all participants

(continued)

Adversarial Lawyers:	**Collaborative Lawyers:**
Align with client's view of facts in role as alter-ego advocate	Understand client's inevitable coloring of facts in role as wise counselor
Support client's self-concept as victim	Question client's assumptions that undermine personal responsibility
Take directions that may arise from client's anger, fear, guilt, or grief	Help clients differentiate true, long-term interests from emotion-based impulses and reactions
May adopt without change client's initial view of genesis of, and solutions to, problems	Support client in developing balanced view of genesis of problems and range of potential solutions
May foster, or may disregard, client's unrealistic or illusory perceptions	Counsel and challenge client to transform understanding of what is real and what is not
May support client's desire for revenge and advantage	Encourage compassion and enlightened self-interest
May support client's shifting of responsibility for actions and consequences to others	Educate client to accept personal responsibility for consequences that naturally follow actions taken
See client's low self-esteem as a given when addressing problems connected to it	See client's low self-esteem as possible cause of conflict, and susceptible to change
Believe clients come to lawyers to shift responsibility for resolving conflicts	Believe clients come to lawyers for skilled guidance in resolving issues arising from making a major life transition
Take on client's problem as gladiator/ hired gun/alter ego	Explain and maintain role of counselor, advisor, negotiator, conflict manager— client's problem remains client's problem
May foster unrealistic goals	Work with client toward mutual understanding of what is possible and what is useful
Support unequal, power-based relationship	Support partnership and shared decision making
Share client's belief that lawyer is responsible if case goes badly	Are truthful with client about mutual challenges arising from case going badly
Tell client the game plan and control all case preparation and negotiations	Help client clarify goals and priorities, support client involvement in evaluating options and arriving at resolution, expect active client participation in all stages of work
Prefer that clients leave the law to the lawyers	Invite client to understand the limitations and strengths of law as a guide in consensual conflict resolution
Believe other side must change for agreement to be reached	Accept possibility that change may have to come first from client

The Third Dimension: Retooling with the Other Players

The third dimension of retooling to achieve the paradigm shift focuses on the collaborative lawyer's relationship with the other professionals involved in the case: the other lawyer, the collaborative divorce team (if any),[23] and the neutral experts and other consultants and professional helpers who may be called upon to assist in the matter. Those whose habits of control and suspicion and whose attachment to size of outcome as the measure of professional success die hard will find this the most challenging aspect of becoming a collaborative lawyer. On the other hand, collaborative lawyers who measure their professional success by the degree to which they deliver on their promise to provide clients with the best possible opportunity to arrive at a high-quality, lasting consensual resolution soon recognize the value of incorporating other professionals into the collaborative process as a team to provide integrated, consistent professional services. While some of the tasks performed by these other professionals will resemble the work done in litigation by opposing forensic experts (e.g., business valuations), other functions will be unique to the collaborative process (e.g., communications skills coaching). Whatever the role and function of the other professionals, the collaborative lawyer will need to develop new ways of working with these colleagues. Consider the following table in constructing your own list of points for this dimension of retooling.

TABLE 3. Retooling with the Other Players

Adversarial Lawyers	Collaborative Lawyers
Insist on control over all contacts with client related to case	Value a team approach to providing services for clients, including mental health coaches and financial consultants
Regard the case as the lawyer's turf	See themselves as providing only one of a range of professional services that most divorcing couples and families will benefit from
Regard the other lawyer solely as an adversary	Regard the other lawyer as a fellow problem solver
See conflict with the other lawyer as normal	See conflict with the other lawyer as counterproductive
Prefer lawyers to conduct negotiations without clients present	Prefer clients to participate actively in all phases of negotiations
See other professionals as intrusive unless retained by the lawyer and acting under the lawyer's direction	See themselves as a members of a client-centered professional team

(continued)

Adversarial Lawyers	Collaborative Lawyers
Fear that other professionals will compromise the lawyer's ability to "win big"	See the task as working collaboratively with all retained professionals to help the clients achieve their optimum consensual resolution
Regard the client's forthcoming work with an accountant, mental health professional, or other professional as occasion for exerting maximum control, advance strategizing, and risk-avoidance planning	Work collegially with the other professionals and client as a team to further the highest goals identified by the client
Rehearse and stage-manage client's communications with other professionals, and instruct client to play cards "close to the chest" with other professionals	Understand that the quality of professional services to the client depends on the quality of the client's engagement with that professional, and help the client reframe potentially difficult issues for positive work with other professionals
Try to influence advice and conclusions of other professionals involved with the client, and resist accepting information from other professionals that does not fit the lawyer's theory of the case	Value sound input from other disciplines as an aid to providing highest-quality services to the client, and respect potential contribution of other disciplines in problem solving
Resist information that calls into question client's worldview or perceptions	Appreciate the dynamic nature of family systems; help the client see the bigger picture; foster high-quality humanistic problem solving grounded in reality-based understanding of client and client's relationships with others
Question other professionals largely to find weaknesses in the positions presented by them	Confer with other professionals collegially in order to strengthen the quality of the legal and other services provided to the client
Consider the work of other disciplines ancillary to the main task, legal work	View the legal issues in a divorce as a subset of a larger, longer, and more complex human transition

Lawyers who learn to use the resources of the professional team (ad hoc or planned) that is assisting the client through divorce typically find their own professional performance enhanced, their levels of stress reduced, and their clients' functionality and ability to participate effectively in negotiations enhanced. By sharing responsibility for the case appropriately and effectively, the lawyer is freed to concentrate on guiding negotiations and managing conflict, while the mental health professionals (coaches and child specialists) can attend to the clients' shadow emotional states and to educating the clients about child development and training them in effective communication skills. The financial consultant can facilitate cost-effective marshaling of documents, preparation of budgets, and disclosure of asset and income information and documentation, as well as educating the less-knowledgeable spouse in basic money-management skills. When clients are assisted by a smooth-functioning team of client-centered collaborative professionals who send consistent messages about aspiring toward civilized, respectful interest-based conflict resolution and who are committed themselves to transcending turf-based competition for the client's scarce resources, one "iatrogenic" source of conflict in divorce (dueling professionals working at cross-purposes to one another) is removed. In that situation, each professional helper is freed to do high-quality work from the perspective of his or her specific discipline. Clients are quick to recognize the value of this interdisciplinary collaboration and are generally grateful for it.

The Fourth Dimension: Retooling Negotiations

The fourth dimension of retooling to achieve the collaborative paradigm shift involves transforming how the lawyers approach the heart of the representation—the negotiations that lead toward settlement. In conventional litigation-driven settlement negotiations, bargaining takes place figuratively, if not literally, on the courthouse steps, in the sense that stages of legal work are defined and pacing is driven by the inexorable progress toward trial, and relevancy and materiality are determined by the court's specific jurisdiction to make orders. Moreover, in conventional negotiations, positional bargaining is a nearly inescapable given, dictated by the basic facts of adversarial litigation: judges' time and attention are limited, complexity is almost always trumped in trial by simplicity, and litigants generally ask for much more than they want because they will never get 100 percent of their requests. Positional bargaining by its very nature does violence to the complex reality of relationships unraveling and reforming themselves, and by its very nature it fosters and flourishes in a context of black-and-white oversimplification of complicated family dynamics into cartoons of villains and victims. It is perilously seductive for clients to believe the oversimplifications that their lawyers construct to persuade busy judges, and thus perilously hard for even the best-intentioned lawyers to guide litigation-driven settlement negotiations into the civilized interest-based mode that collaborative lawyers know is the wellspring of creative problem solving.

Retooling negotiations means detaching fully from the litigation matrix and starting fresh, with a beginner's mind, to examine what we do, why we

WITH WHOM ARE YOUR CLIENTS TALKING?

Litigators often instruct clients to stop talking with their spouses, so that the lawyer's control over the case remains intact and the ability to shape positions and facts for trial isn't undermined. In collaborative law, as we detach from outcome as the measure of our success, we often take a dramatically different view. So long as they are able to do so productively and cordially, we may advise clients to work with their spouses freely between four-way meetings on specific tasks if they are comfortable doing so, as a way of streamlining the process and keeping costs down. We advise them to avoid negotiating resolution outside the meetings, so that brainstorming and legal advice can be factored in before solutions are reached, and we provide legal counsel about applicable law and ranges of outcomes transparently, as needed. In so doing, we are recognizing the reality that in a civilized divorce process, conversation between spouses should be encouraged, because successful information sharing and problem solving without direct professional assistance are skills that many of our clients will need to use together long after our work with them is done.

Conversations with well-meaning friends and relatives are another matter. These conversations can undermine clients' confidence in the collaborative process, without good reason. Few friends or relatives will have direct prior experience with or knowledge of collaborative law. Their database of divorce information may be drawn from the high-conflict horror stories that friends gossip about. The accuracy of their reports about how much support the judge awarded to Mary, or how much custodial time John was able to win at trial over Sally's objections, tends to be low, and their awareness of the specific facts that lead to unusual outcomes in litigation tends to be nil. Furthermore, friends' and relatives' understanding of the costs and procedural complications of litigation can be quite confused, and misguided loyalty can lead them to demonize the other spouse in ways that undermine collaboration. For these reasons, collaborative lawyers often advise clients from the start to use great caution in discussing the details of their divorce process with friends and family, and to invite their support in other, more constructive ways.

do it, and what might work better, as we structure and plan for and debrief from the events that move the collaborative process to closure: the four-way meetings. It means developing a wholly new toolbox of behaviors and attitudes that will become second nature to us as collaborative lawyers, just as introducing documents into evidence, making objections, and posing hypothetical questions to expert witnesses become second nature to litigators. Among these many new tools are: planning and managing agendas to enhance clients' competency at negotiations and to build the expectation of success; use of pre- and postmeetings with the client, the other collaborative lawyer, and the other professionals to manage conflict and guide negotiations; use of pacing, ritual and ceremonial elements, language, and metaphor to build and maintain a safe container for the process; teaching and modeling new conflict resolution skills for clients; and teaching and modeling transparency of process.

Consider the following table as you begin your work of learning how to retool negotiations, and add to it as you work with collaborative clients and colleagues.

TABLE 4. Retooling Negotiations

Adversarial Lawyers	Collaborative Lawyers
Operate within litigation paradigm from first meeting with client	Explain the full spectrum of conflict resolution modalities, and expect the client to choose the appropriate one
Prepare for court battle from the very beginning of representation	Consider court as a last resort; collaboration is first
Devise and communicate credible threats about process and outcome as primary approach to pretrial settlement discussions	Implement and refine methods of working transparently and collegially with clients and professional colleagues to facilitate mutually beneficial resolution for clients
Assume negotiations mean positional bargaining in the context of third-party decision making	Assume negotiations mean client-centered, interest-based conflict resolution
Focus on obstacles in the way of agreement or success at trial	Challenge reality of obstacles in the way of agreement
Play "hide the ball" and blame the other side for all difficulties in process	Work transparently and assume that all difficulties represent mutual challenges
Control process to achieve efficient, task-oriented meetings	Appreciate need for: —allowing everyone to be heard and acknowledged —creating an environment of honesty and good faith —helping each party to develop comfort with the other party's lawyer —forging process commitments that will be honored —incorporating ceremonial elements at start and finish of collaborative process
See impasse as trigger for hearing or trial	See apparent impasse as gateway to enhanced creative process
Resort to compromise late, as escape from ongoing strains of legal action or solution for exhaustion of client funds	Aim always for agreement as first and best mode of resolution

READING YOURSELF, RELAXING YOURSELF

We lawyers love challenge and control. We prefer *doing* to *being*. The fight-or-flight adrenal state is familiar and comfortable for us. Many lawyers report that when working they are so concentrated intellectually that their awareness extends only from the neck up.

What's wrong with that? Nothing, if you are going into battle. Plenty, if you want to be receptive as well as active, if you want to be aware of the subtext as well as the text, if you want to read the emotional cues and body language of those you are working with. These are rich sources of information that we miss when we are in fight-or-flight mode.

Also plenty, if you understand the impact of your own physical and emotional state upon others. If you are tense, aggressive, or hyper-alert, your physical bearing and voice may well cause discomfort or distrust in others, reducing your effectiveness as a collaborative problem solver without your even knowing it.

Experiment and see if you agree. To do so you need to become aware of when you are in the charged, tense fight-or-flight mode, and when you are more relaxed and receptive. Physical cues will tell you. Many people observe the following about themselves when they are in fight-or-flight battle mode:

- Their breathing is shallow, high in the chest rather than low in the belly.

- Breathing may be irregular rather than smooth.

- The jaw may be tight or clenched.

- The muscles around the diaphragm and belly as well as in the jaw may be tense.

- The shoulders may be tight and lifted rather than drawn down and relaxed.

- There may be a pounding sensation in the temples.

Learn to recognize the physical cues that alert you to being in fight-or-flight mode. Observe the demeanor of those you are working with when you are in that state. Observe how effectively people are communicating with one another and you, and whether they seem at ease or uncomfortable with you. Ask yourself how much "broadband" information you have been taking in about the people around you—that is, how much have you learned from sources other than the actual content of the words they have been speaking, such as their physical posture and bearing, their tone, where their eyes are looking, what their hands are doing.

Then, experiment with simple relaxation techniques. Each time you shift from one task to another (answering the telephone, starting a letter, sitting down at a conference, and so forth), take an inventory of the physical cues that tell you whether you are in fight-or-flight mode or not. If you are, take a moment to consciously relax your body before continuing:

- Take several slow breaths that extend deep into the abdomen, and exhale slowly and fully.

- Wherever you notice tensed muscles (jaw, shoulders, diaphragm, abdomen), do this with each tensed area one at a time: first deliberately tighten the muscle more—as much as possible—while inhaling. Then, on the exhale, relax the muscle fully.

- Finally, focus your awareness for a moment at a point deep in the abdomen about two inches below your navel, and imagine that your breath enters and exits from that point rather than from your throat. This is an easy technique to use for quick relaxation whenever you notice a return of tension.

Once you are in a more relaxed physical state, observe the demeanor of those you are working with, and as before, notice how much "broadband" information you are taking in from those around you.

These simple techniques are powerful ways to retool some unconscious gladiatorial habits that we tend to be quite unaware of. These habits can have big effects on how others behave with us, and how effectively we communicate with others, and changing them can have dramatic positive impact on your work.

MAKING THE PARADIGM SHIFT HAPPEN

IMPORTANT KNOWLEDGE AND SKILLS FOR COLLABORATIVE LAWYERS

- A sophisticated understanding of the psychodynamics of divorce for adults.

- A working understanding of child development and of the impact of divorce on the development of children.

- A working understanding of the dynamics of transference and counter-transference in the lawyer-client relationship and in marital relationships.

- Mastery of interest-based bargaining techniques, including use of the "BATNA" and "WATNA."*

- Understanding of the difference between immediate and long-term goals and interests of the client, and ability to bring the client to an appreciation of the difference.

- Familiarity with the spectrum of conventional and alternate dispute-resolution methods.

- Understanding of the types of clients who are well-served and less well-served by each dispute-resolution method, and of how and when to present this information to clients.

- Skill in the management of clients' anger, grief, anxiety, and fear during the negotiation process.

- Ability to use and teach clients how to use effective communications and problem-solving techniques.

- Mastery of how to structure and manage a collaborative representation to enhance success, including agenda planning and goal setting, agenda management, conflict management, use of story and metaphor, orderly stages of work, and other practical techniques.

- Mastery of techniques for working collaboratively with other professionals, including the other lawyer, within the duty of zealous representation of the client and the lawyer-client privilege.

* Terms popularized by Roger Fisher and William Ury in *Getting to Yes* (1981).

THINK ABOUT THE PHYSICAL SPACE

- Where will you sit in relation to your client? In relation to the other spouse and lawyer? Who will sit next to whom? Does this arrangement place anyone in a superior or inferior position? Does it encourage relaxed listening and talking?

- What lies in the line of vision of each participant? Clutter? Case files? Something beautiful? Something that expresses a positive value such as cooperation or communication? A window?

- Are the chairs comfortable? Is the room adequately ventilated, heated, cooled?

Notes

1. One colleague, a successful family law litigator, describes the move from litigation to collaboration as a shift from "checkers to 3-D chess." Because he is fascinated with the expanded potential for helping clients that the collaborative model offers, he looks for the moments when a collaboration can move into creative hyperspace and, conversely, the moments when it is at risk of sinking into contentious adversarial "business as usual." He sees his job as maximizing the possibilities for the former and minimizing the emergence of the latter. Less attentive lawyers can unintentionally precipitate controversy and stifle creative problem solving. If they see collaborative law as merely what they already do, but without the trial at the end, they can sink a collaborative case by their unexamined habitual adversarial behavior without ever recognizing their failure to provide competent collaborative representation.

2. The reasons for their dissatisfaction are familiar to most family lawyers. First, litigation costs far more money than most family law clients can spare. Second, the results of litigation can be crude solutions ill-tailored to the specific needs of the family, imposed from above by an overworked judge who has been presented on both sides with oversimplified facts designed to persuade more than to inform. Third, clients' expectations from litigation

can be quite unrealistic. Family law clients often enter litigation seeking justice (or revenge, or vindication), but at best they come out of it with only certainty. And because they generally expect to win, and family law litigation rarely produces a winner, they are unhappy. Often, looking for someone to blame for all this disappointment, the client focuses on his or her own lawyer, and efforts to collect the fees we work so hard to earn can too often trigger a malpractice suit. Malpractice insurance carriers warn of the direct relationship between client unhappiness and malpractice litigation. Divorce lawyers learn to fear their clients for that reason. Illustrating this point, in a 2005 survey of divorce lawyers done by an organization of financial planners, "more than a few lawyers related their greatest fear in any client relationship: the dissatisfied client." http://www.fpanet.org/journal/BetweenTheIssues/YourPractice/030105.cfm.

3. Justice Bridge made this observation on February 10, 2006, during her introductory remarks beginning a two-day collaborative law training given by the author in Seattle, Washington.

4. The consequences for lawyers of this prolonged lack of appreciation are serious. Many studies trace rising levels of dissatisfaction with the practice of law, and practitioners generally regard family law as one of the most stressful specialty areas. Typical is this 2006 law school blog posting: "Family law practice is a high burn-out field and our students should be repeatedly cautioned to take care of themselves and get help before they become overwhelmed, lest they find themselves harming clients and out of the profession entirely." http://lawprofessors .typepad.com/family_law/attorneys/index.html. To understand the impact of this job-related distress on lawyers, *see, e.g.,* ABA Commission on Lawyer Assistance Programs, Law School Outreach Subcommittee Literature Review Committee Report: Limited Annotated Bibliography, which cites several studies with conclusions similar to this: "Depression is not the only awful affliction that impacts the legal profession. Alcohol and drug abuse also plays a prominent role, and endures past law school graduation. In fact, the findings of this cross-sectional study of lawyers across practice years suggest alcohol problems are progressive in nature and profoundly affect the profession. In this large, stratified random sample of lawyers that used well-validated, reliable measures, 70% of the lawyers in active practice had a lifetime prevalence of clinically significant negative consequences related to alcohol abuse. Another set of surprising findings showed that for female lawyers, positive relations within a primary relationship served as stress protector. But the percentage of divorced female lawyers proved to be twice that of physicians and three times that of teachers. Female lawyers are the least likely to remarry of these occupational groups. When compared with the findings of a normal population, female lawyers remain significantly more angry in their primary relationships while male lawyers remain significantly more stressed." Connie Beck, Bruce Sales & G. Andrew H. Benjamin, *Lawyer Distress: Alcohol-Related Problems and Other Psychological Concerns Among a Sample of Practicing Lawyers,* 10 J.L. & HEALTH 1, 1–60 (1995–1996). The problem is acute enough that Villanova University's Law School Advising Program warns entering students, "The fact that staggering numbers of lawyers are unhappy in their jobs is one sad reality of modern practice" and continues, "In addition to being disenchanted, lawyers report[ed] that they are 'in remarkably poor health.' Researchers found that lawyers 'are at a much greater risk than the general population for depression, heart disease, alcoholism and illegal drug use.'" http://www.villanova.edu/artsci/college/advising/development/law/succeed.htm. Given the very high stress levels associated with family law practice, it is reasonable to assume that family lawyers experience these problems at least as much as, and probably more than, lawyers in other areas of practice.

5. In Florida, approximately 65 percent of all divorces and 80 percent of all family law cases have at least one self-represented party. Kari Deming, *Changing the Face of Legal Practice,* http://www.michbar.org/journal/article.cfm?articleID=159&volumeID=14. Even *Time* magazine has noted the phenomenon. In *Who Needs Lawyers?* (June 12, 2000) the magazine links the escalating number of self-help filings in courts everywhere across the United States with frustration, havoc, and delay in courtroom proceedings. *See also* Chapter 1, *supra,* note 4.

6. To say that clients generally don't like lawyers would seriously understate reality. Even sober scholarly articles conclude that our clients dislike us, and find good cause for that dislike; *see, e.g.,* Roger E. Schechter, *Changing Law Schools to Make Less Nasty Lawyers,* 10 Geo. J. Legal Ethics 367 (1999). *See also* Marsha Kline Pruett & Tamara Jackson, *The Lawyer's Role During the Divorce Process: Perceptions of Parents, Their Young Children, and Their Attorneys,* 33 Fam. L.Q. 283 (Summer 1999). Popular humor websites often have a special category for jokes about lawyers. *See, e.g.,* http://www.lawyer-jokes.us; http://scroom .com/SCROOMtimes/Humor/Lawyer.shtml; http://www.ahajokes.com/lawyer_jokes.html. These are only the tip of the lawyer-joke iceberg, and no other profession is singled out for this quantity and quality of attention. Lawyers even put the same scornful lawyer jokes on their own websites. *See, e.g.,* http://www.duhaime.org/LegalResources/LawFun. The jokes have numbingly repetitive themes: Lawyers are greedy, unethical, crooked; they will do anything to keep litigation going and build up higher fees; they cheat their clients and anyone else they deal with. They are routinely compared to rodents, snakes, and other vermin and found to be less admirable. Many of the jokes involve killing lawyers, with the punch lines suggesting that nobody could possibly grieve for them and that a service to society has been done thereby. This is chilling material when read alongside the disturbingly frequent news reports of lawyers being shot and killed by clients and adverse parties. In California, the two courtrooms that routinely have metal detectors at the entrance are the criminal and the domestic relations departments.

7. See interview with collaborative lawyer John McCall, by Pauline H. Tesler, *The Good, the Bad, and the Ugly: Collaborating with Anyone Who Shows Up,* 2 The Collaborative Q. 1 (May 2000) (now, The Collaborative Review).

8. *See* Joan Kelly, *A Decade of Divorce Mediation Research,* 34 Fam. & Conciliation Ct. Rev. at 373–75.

9. Donald M. King, Address at *New Ways of Helping Children and Parents Through Divorce,* a conference sponsored by the Judith Wallerstein Center for the Family in Transition and the University of California, Santa Cruz, Quail Lodge, Carmel Valley, California (Nov. 21, 1998).

10. *See, e.g.,* Janet Weinstein, *And Never the Twain Shall Meet: The Best Interests of Children and the Adversary System,* 52 Univ. Miami L. Rev. 79 (1997); Judith S. Wallerstein & Joan Berliner Kelly, Surviving the Breakup: How Children and Parents Cope with Divorce (1980); Janet R. Johnston & Vivienne Roseby, In the Name of the Child (1998).

11. For example, Anthony T. Kronman, former dean of Yale Law School, wrote of a "spiritual crisis" in which the legal profession is in danger of "losing its soul." The Lost Lawyer: Failing Ideals of the Legal Profession (1993). Sol M. Linowitz, who was both a respected lawyer and an ambassador in both Republican and Democratic presidential administrations, linked the widespread unhappiness of lawyers with a loss of the sense that the legal profession involves service to society at large. In The Betrayed Profession: Lawyering at the End of the Twentieth Century (1994), he urged lawyers to return to a more traditional understanding that the lawyer's role is as a wise counselor who advises not only whether certain conduct is legally permissible, but whether it is wise and just, and to decline to represent clients who are uninterested in that advice. More recently, David Hall, former dean of Northeastern University Law School, wrote, "the [legal] profession's strong adherence to the adversarial model has provided many benefits, but it has also cost us our soul." Hailing collaborative law as a movement promising the "revitalization and transformation of the legal profession," he concluded, "Collaborative law is not just law with a twist; this is law as it was meant to be." Hall, *In Search of the Sacred,* 7 The Collaborative Rev. 27–29 (Winter 2005). These views of the proper role of a lawyer are consistent with comments to Rule 2.1 of the A.B.A. Model Rules of Professional Conduct: "It is proper for a lawyer to refer to relevant moral and ethical considerations in giving advice. Although a lawyer is not a moral advisor as such, moral and ethical considerations impinge upon most legal questions and may decisively influence how the law will be applied" and "A lawyer

ordinarily has no duty to initiate investigation of a client's affairs or to give advice that the client has indicated is unwanted, but a lawyer may initiate advice to a client when doing so appears to be in the client's interest." For an insightful analysis of the sea change taking place in how lawyers work with their clients, *see* JULIE MACFARLANE, THE NEW LAWYER (2007).

12. Of course, many of these clients may be equally ill-suited for all dispute-resolution models; in litigation, they often become the high-conflict recidivists, the hot-potato cases that even judges shudder to handle. Lawyers in the early stages of establishing collaborative practices in their locales may be wise to confine themselves to representing clients who are likely to do well with the model, so that the lawyers can develop their skills more readily and so that word-of-mouth reports about collaborative law will more likely be positive. Once the model is well-known in a locale, lawyers may be open to giving even poorly suited clients the option of collaborative representation if they understand the process fully and insist they want it, though it will be especially important for appropriate warnings and disclaimers to be made and for there to be fully informed consent before the model is elected. Such clients will have much greater prospects for success in the collaborative law process if they choose interdisciplinary collaborative divorce team-based services including mental health coaches, child development specialists, and financial consultants. (*See* www.collaborativepractice.com for more information about that team-based model. COLLABORATIVE DIVORCE: THE REVO-LUTIONARY NEW WAY TO RESTRUCTURE YOUR FAMILY, RESOLVE LEGAL ISSUES, AND MOVE ON WITH YOUR LIFE, by Pauline Tesler and psychologist Peggy Thompson, explains in detail for clients and other general readers how collaborative lawyers can work with the two other professions in a team approach to optimize a couple's ability to make the divorce transition well. *See* www.collaborativedivorcebook.com.

13. See Chapter 9 for a description of what a collaborative practice group is and how to form one.

14. Information about the author's speaking and training schedule can be found at www.teslercollaboration.com and www.collaborativedivorcenews.com.

15. Initially, posting the questions next to your telephone and computer screen, or at the front of your calendar, may be helpful.

16. The point is not that all litigators behave unthinkingly all the time. On the contrary, a seasoned litigator has an impressive array of conscious skills to draw upon. At the same time, temperament, training, experience, and cultural zeitgeist join to produce an equally powerful array of unconscious habits and knee-jerk "default settings," which may be useful in litigation but that can defeat effective collaborative work. The goal is not to abandon the useful skills acquired in litigation, but rather to expand and see clearly the full range of behaviors available to us as collaborative lawyers, and to select in each moment the behaviors best-suited to the client and the task.

17. See Appendix I for some useful metaphors that serve this purpose.

18. It is well established that strong emotions trigger the primitive fight-or-flight response, which from a physiological perspective means that the endocrine system is flooded with cortisol. Cortisol flooding causes us to revert to immediate, habitual responses to threat, increasing heart rate and blood pressure and switching our mental processes from the higher frontal lobes, where considered evaluation of a range of choices and new responses is possible, to the more primitive parts of the brain that make a quick choice among three reactive options: fight, flight, or "play dead." The focus is on assessing immediate danger for purposes of immediate survival; hypervigilance and a tendency to see elevated threat levels are usual. The capacity to envision long-term consequences of choices and the capacity to consider new options for behavior are temporarily unavailable during an episode of cortisol flooding. Such episodes typically last for about 20 to 30 minutes after the triggering stimulus is no longer present, but in the face of prolonged stress, the fight or flight "emergency response" mode can become chronically entrenched. In other words, when we are working with an extremely fearful, angry, or grief-stricken client, we are working with a person who—at least for the moment, and sometimes longer—quite literally cannot think straight. (Simplified

descriptions of the physical, mental, and emotional aspects of the fight or-flight response suitable for use with clients can readily be found on the Internet. *See, e.g.,* http://www.mayoclinic.com/health/stress/SR00001; http://en.wikipedia.org/wiki/Flight_or_fight_response.)

19. In asking ourselves questions like these, we are not engaging in diagnosis or therapy, and we require only the knowledge of a skilled collaborative lawyer, not the knowledge of a mental health clinician. Nor are we substituting our own views for those of our client. Awareness of the psychological and counseling dimensions of family law practice is a basic tool of even the traditional domestic relations specialist. (For example, in California, a state bar-certified family law specialist is required to take six continuing education units in psychology and counseling during each five-year recertification cycle to maintain specialist certification.) A collaborative lawyer benefits from going further into this same terrain, and from applying that knowledge in a significantly more pervasive way than an adversarial lawyer is likely to consider during the course of the representation, but still as a lawyer, and in no way as a therapist.

20. While the phrase "zealous advocacy" or "zealous representation" still remains in some state ethical canons, its importance as a touchstone for ethical conduct has been in steady decline for nearly half a century, and can no longer be seen as a convenient rationale for a role-defined morality in which the lawyer pursues every advantage for the client that is not prohibited by law. The current version of Rule 1.3 of the ABA Model Rules of Professional Conduct states: "A lawyer shall act with reasonable diligence and promptness in representing a client." References to zealous advocacy appear only in the commentary and the preamble to the rule. Comment 1 to Rule 1.3 states that "a lawyer must also act with commitment and dedication to the interests of the client and with zeal in advocacy upon the client's behalf," but Comment 1 emphasizes that the rules do not require a lawyer to: (1) "press for every advantage that might be realized for a client"; or (2) "use offensive tactics or preclude the treating of all persons involved in the legal process with courtesy and respect." The preamble similarly circumscribes attorneys' role as advocates by stressing their duties as officers of the court: "A lawyer is a representative of clients, an officer of the legal system and a public citizen having special responsibility for the equality of justice. . . ." See Chapter 7, *infra,* for further discussion of the ethics of collaborative legal practice.

21. Attention to the assumptions buried in our language is essential in the retooling process: for instance, the other lawyer no longer can be called "opposing" counsel unless opposition is what you want and expect.

22. This comparison table and the three that follow in this chapter are adapted with permission from a similar comparison of adversarial and holistic lawyering by William Van Zyverden, founder of the International Alliance of Holistic Lawyers. These four tables contrast certain characteristic extremes of thought and behavior, and should not be read as a literal description of all adversarial or all collaborative lawyers.

23. *See* http://www.collaborativepractice.com/ for a concise explanation of interdisciplinary team collaborative divorce practice, and Collaborative Divorce: The Revolutionary New Way to Restructure Your Family, Resolve Legal Issues, and Move on with Your Life, by Pauline Tesler and psychologist Peggy Thompson, a book-length explanation of interdisciplinary team collaborative divorce suitable for general readers.

Chapter 4

Overview: The Three Stages of a Collaborative Law Case

"Litigation is to collaborative law as bowling is to curling."
—*Chip Rose*

Before exploring specific techniques for becoming an excellent collaborative lawyer, looking at the big picture will help you create a mental armature onto which you can build your more detailed understanding of this new mode of practice. A well-managed collaborative representation unfolds in three sequential phases, which we can liken to a well-constructed three-act play.[1]

Act One

The curtain opens in a collaborative representation with your first contact with your potential collaborative client. This first act will continue through completion of the first "four-way" settlement meeting. Just as in a play the characters, themes, and potential challenges are introduced during Act One, similarly in this first act of a collaborative case all participants will get to know one another and get a beginning sense of what the collaborative work will need to address. In this first act, just as in a traditional divorce representation, each lawyer must get to know the client and the basic facts about the relationship and separation. In addition, there are many tasks specific to collaborative practice that must be accomplished during Act One—and in order to accomplish them successfully, it will be necessary *not* to do some of the things that conventional divorce lawyers would routinely undertake during the early stages of a new case, because they are not consistent with starting out on the right foot collaboratively.

During Act One, each lawyer must lay a foundation for a successful collaborative representation by communicating a great deal of information to the client. The client needs information about the many choices available for professional conflict-resolution services during a divorce, the philosophy and practice of collaborative conflict resolution, negotiation theory, the place of the law in conventional and collaborative negotiation, psychological factors associated with family restructuring during divorce that affect the conflict-resolution process, and much more. In this stage, the lawyer and client forge basic understandings and agreements about how they will work together. The lawyer provides the information needed for the exercise of informed consent, and asks the client to make informed process choices. At this stage the lawyer also puts in place with the client some basic tools (or "process anchors") that the lawyer will rely upon throughout the representation for guiding negotiations and working constructively with potential conflict. At the same time, the lawyer begins helping the client to identify and clarify substantive goals and priorities. Together, they begin the work that will lead eventually to collaborative negotiations during Act Two.

During Act One, the two collaborative lawyers also do important foundational work with one another that will shape the course of the entire representation. During this phase, the lawyers take steps to build or to reinforce a trusting and productive professional relationship with one another.[2] Further, they make or confirm basic agreements with one another about procedures for the collaborative representation and they communicate essential information that will assist both of them to work as effective collaborative advocates on behalf of their respective clients in the case. Also, they do the detailed planning that will precede the first of a series of carefully orchestrated four-way meetings.

Finally, during Act One, the clients and lawyers together form a working team and establish a working relationship with agreed-upon rules, commitments, and understandings.[3] This core team can expand or contract from the start, or later on during the representation,[4] but the fundamental first-act task is for the lawyers and clients to exchange enough information and establish the groundwork for a sufficiently constructive working relationship so that the documentation confirming that this will be a collaborative case can be signed. The signing of these documents is the defining event of Act One. Once it has occurred, everyone knows that this is a collaborative case, and until it does occur, the curtain does not go down on Act One. Both the clients and the lawyers must know with certainty whether this is or is not a collaborative case before any substantive work in the divorce begins.[5]

Critical points during the first act include the following.

1. **First contacts with your client.** In the first conversations with a potential collaborative client, every word, gesture, tone, and expression of the collaborative lawyer is fraught with heightened significance, communicating both intended and unintended, conscious and unconscious messages to the client about the lawyer's expectations and beliefs concerning the legal process, divorce, family transition, conflict resolution, and the law itself.[6] Collaborative law works powerfully when the collaborative lawyers hold out consistent, congruent, clearly expressed expectations that their clients can and should resolve divorce-related differences in a civilized manner—the expectation that with help, the clients can achieve the good divorce.

   Holding out such expectations calls for a particular kind of conscious and focused attentiveness from the lawyer, beginning with the very first words exchanged with the client.[7] The task is to ensure that in word, deed, and gesture, consistent messages—and only consistent messages—are flowing from the lawyer to the client,[8] messages that evoke and support the client's highest intentions for the divorce process and help the client become aware of how to achieve the good divorce.

2. **Making a fully informed choice of the appropriate conflict-resolution mode.** The day is past when a competent lawyer can simply bring to bear on a client's problem the conflict-resolution mode that the lawyer happens to prefer without offering the client a meaningful opportunity to make an informed choice from the growing menu of dispute-resolution options now available.[9] Taking as much time as is necessary to explore the range of choices available, the advantages and risks associated with each choice, the kinds of people and problems that can generally be addressed effectively utilizing each of the options, and the customary acceptability and durability of the outcomes associated with each, is time well spent, and it does the client a serious disservice to truncate this advice. After an in-depth

WATCH YOUR LANGUAGE

Our words both reveal and shape how we think about a situation. Instead of inadvertently allowing the high-conflict language of the argument culture to cast your collaborative work in a conflict-based mold, work at matching your language to your goals and intentions. This careful attention to words will speak directly to the old reptilian brain—yours and those of the other participants. The surprising use of a collaborative word where an adversarial one is more customary grabs attention and underscores intention.

Instead of:	Try using:
opposing party	other person, spouse
opposing counsel	other lawyer, collaborative counsel, collaborative colleague
dispute	issue, subject, challenge
counterproposal	upgrade
adversary	colleague
arguments	ideas, thoughts
position	concept, suggestion
my client	John, or Mary

conversation of this kind, the client has the necessary tools to make the process choice that will shape everything that follows.

The choice always should be the client's, and no matter how much a lawyer may want to expand a collaborative practice, it is unwise to persuade or direct a client to choose any of the conflict-resolution modalities, collaborative law included. For the client to make the initial process choice places responsibility for the decision, and accountability for its subsequent ramifications, where they belong—with the client. Experienced collaborative lawyers present information about collaborative law in the context of information about the spectrum of conflict-resolution options, during the first extended conversation with the client. They develop ways of communicating the reasons for their own enthusiasm for collaborative practice without selling collaborative law to this particular client. Since part of the collaborative lawyer's toolbox for guiding negotiations and managing conflict involves keeping the client personally responsible for the progress of negotiations, it is important that the client make a knowledgeable choice of the process in the first instance, so that such accountability is a reasonable expectation.

3. **Opening communications with the other party and/or other lawyer.**
    Sometimes, your client will be the primary mover in restructuring or
    ending the intimate relationship and will not yet have informed the
    intimate partner of the situation, in which case your job will include
    either advising your own client about how to enlist the spouse or
    partner in a collaborative process, or making a direct first over-
    ture yourself to the other party. Sometimes, the other party initi-
    ates the separation or divorce and may have already taken steps
    toward selecting legal representation. Inevitably, there will be times
    when the other party will already be represented by a lawyer new to
    or entirely unacquainted with collaborative law.[10] In each of these
    instances the skilled collaborative lawyer uses conscious care in
    communications, to enhance the likelihood that the other party will
    choose collaborative representation, and to enhance the possibility
    that both the other party and the other lawyer will participate effec-
    tively in the collaborative process.

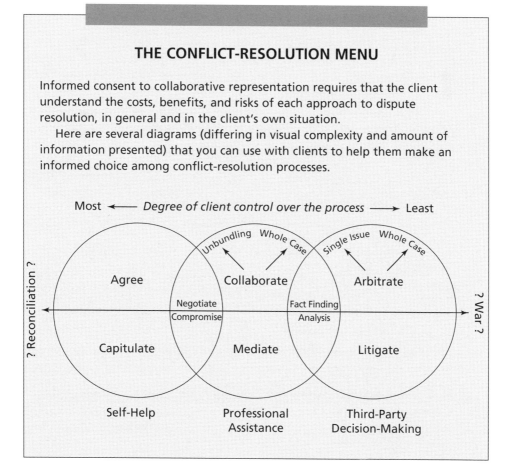

THE CONFLICT-RESOLUTION MENU

Informed consent to collaborative representation requires that the client
understand the costs, benefits, and risks of each approach to dispute
resolution, in general and in the client's own situation.

Here are several diagrams (differing in visual complexity and amount of
information presented) that you can use with clients to help them make an
informed choice among conflict-resolution processes.

Most ← *Degree of client control over the process* → Least

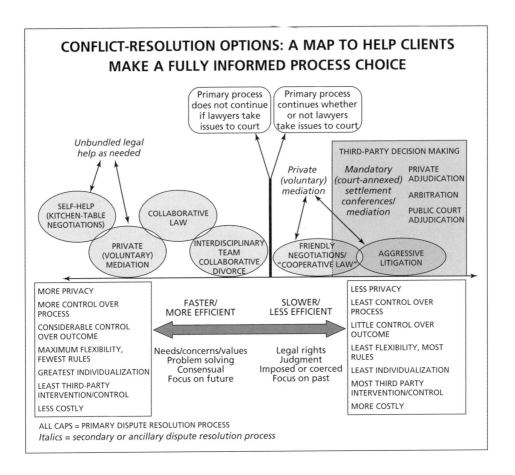

CONFLICT-RESOLUTION OPTIONS: A MAP TO HELP CLIENTS MAKE A FULLY INFORMED PROCESS CHOICE

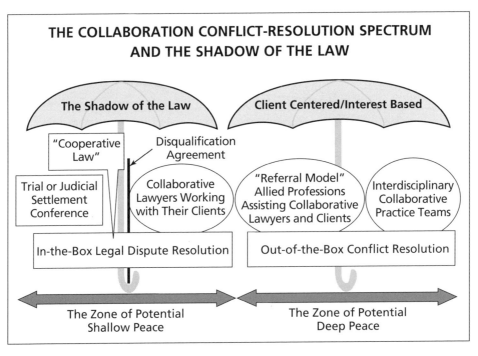

THE COLLABORATION CONFLICT-RESOLUTION SPECTRUM AND THE SHADOW OF THE LAW

4. **Setting the Agenda and Preparing for the First Four-Way Meeting.** The first four-way meeting is the first event when the clients will experience that the collaborative conflict-resolution process is indeed under way. By the end of that meeting, a great deal of process management groundwork must be in place if the case is to move forward effectively toward resolution. Consequently, the first four-way meeting requires careful preparation by the lawyers if it is to achieve the "container-setting"[11] objectives that launch a collaborative representation in a constructive manner toward resolution. The preparation normally includes at least two pre-meetings: one with your client,[12] and one with the other collaborative lawyer.

You will listen to the client's concerns about the substantive issues, but you will not address them as a priority yet, because initially it is more important to discuss the procedure and the philosophy underlying collaborative representation and other conflict-resolution modes and facilitate an informed process choice. If collaborative representation appears to be the preferred choice, you and your client will review the formal documentation that will be signed at the first four-way, setting forth the binding commitments that constitute the collaborative process.[13] Also, you will discuss with the client any short-term or urgent needs that must be addressed early in the process, and will review with the client the stages of the collaborative process and the very limited agenda that can be undertaken at the first four-way meeting. Exploring whether there are urgent matters that need to be stabilized will provide important information about how soon after the first four-way meeting the second one should take place.

The two most important elements of the pre-meeting with collaborative counsel for the other party (both for the first and for subsequent four-way meetings) are tasks that are unique to collaborative representation: (a) exchanging information about potential "hot buttons" (e.g., client's emotional state, information-processing styles, recent stressful events, and the like) and (b) planning in detail the agenda for the forthcoming meeting, including not only what will be addressed, but also what must be postponed. The skill of the lawyers is mobilized at the agenda-planning stage to ensure that the process-management container will be firmly in place by the end of the first four-way; to ensure that sufficient time is devoted at the first four-way to discussion of how the work will be done; and to ensure that the agenda for the first four-way includes only matters that have a likelihood of resulting in immediate success. The usual container-setting goals for the first four-way that the lawyers should confirm during their pre-meeting involve reaffirming transparently and publicly, in one another's presence, the good-faith bargaining agreements that will guide the process, and building the clients' sense of competency and optimism by ensuring that in the first meeting, they are able to succeed in the agenda that was planned and confirmed in advance. The agenda typically will include: inviting clients to express their highest goals for the process; reviewing the participation documents and collaborative commitments; signing the documents; discussing involvement of an interdisciplinary collaborative divorce team; explaining how to obtain a legal divorce in the state; explaining interest-based negotiations; describing the road map of the collaborative process; explaining collaborative minutes and e-mail protocols; discussing the agenda for the next meeting; giving homework assignments; and setting a schedule of several future four-way meeting dates. Best practice is to exclude from the agenda for the first meeting negotiations over any substantive issues.[14]

5. **Conducting the First Four-Way Meeting.** If the lawyers have prepared their clients and themselves well, the first four-way meeting usually proceeds in an orderly, planned, almost choreographed manner. Unlike all subsequent four-way meetings, in which the clients will be at the forefront and their active engagement with the subject matter is key, the lawyers are at center stage in this defining first four-way meeting. The most important purpose of this meeting is to confirm face-to-face the formal ground rules and informal understandings for the process. The clients' execution in one another's presence of the binding agreements confirming those understandings takes on a solemn, almost ceremonial quality when done well. The signatures on the documents are not the point of the exercise; rather, they memorialize the fact that a direct confirmation of mutual intention and commitment has taken place. The function of this almost ceremonial review and execution of participation documents is one that impatient, goal-oriented, rational problem solvers (i.e., most family lawyers and many of their clients) might be tempted to overlook or minimize. That would be a serious mistake. Experience has shown that confirming together the process that will guide all participants as they do the work together amounts to a commitment that most people will wish to honor later in the process when impasse, anger, or other obstacles to settlement can be

expected to emerge. The time spent in this first meeting on setting the container gives the lawyers indispensable tools for managing potentially destabilizing behaviors down the road.

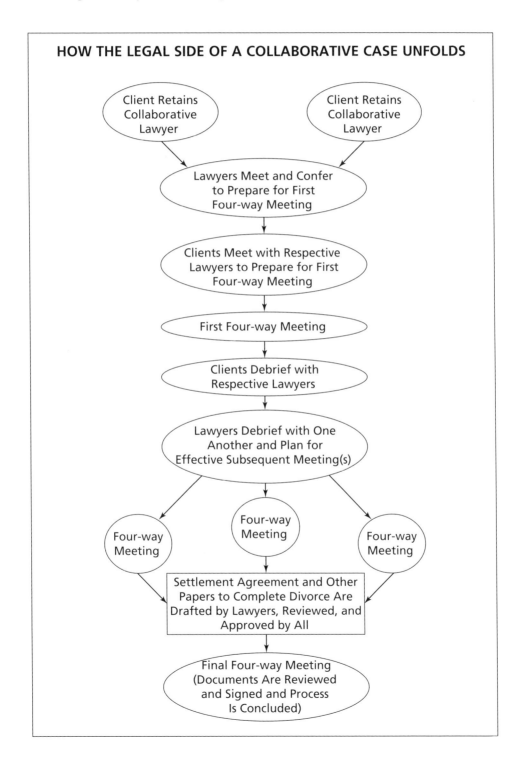

HOW THE LEGAL SIDE OF A COLLABORATIVE CASE UNFOLDS

Client Retains Collaborative Lawyer

Client Retains Collaborative Lawyer

Lawyers Meet and Confer to Prepare for First Four-way Meeting

Clients Meet with Respective Lawyers to Prepare for First Four-way Meeting

First Four-way Meeting

Clients Debrief with Respective Lawyers

Lawyers Debrief with One Another and Plan for Effective Subsequent Meeting(s)

Four-way Meeting

Four-way Meeting

Four-way Meeting

Settlement Agreement and Other Papers to Complete Divorce Are Drafted by Lawyers, Reviewed, and Approved by All

Final Four-way Meeting (Documents Are Reviewed and Signed and Process Is Concluded)

WHAT DOES FLOODING HAVE TO DO WITH COLLABORATIVE LAW?

No, we are not talking about riparian rights when we talk about flooding. The term describes a physiological phenomenon of the endocrine system that occurs in all of us when we are overcome by sudden, intense emotion. Although fear, sorrow, shame, and other emotions will arise, anger is the one we will most commonly encounter in our work as collaborative lawyers—our own, that of clients, and that of the other lawyer. The physiological accompaniments of flooding at times of sudden flare-ups of anger are familiar to us all: a surge of heat ("he was hot under the collar"), a narrowing of our field of vision ("I was blinded by anger"), a speeding of the heart rate ("my heart was pounding"), a sense that our blood pressure has somehow run amok ("my blood was boiling; I saw red"). These sensations are the immediate reactions of our body to a sudden inflow of cortisol into the bloodstream, and there is nothing fanciful about our descriptions: our bodies are experiencing literally what our words portray.

Psychologists studying the phenomenon tell us some facts about the flooded state that are important for collaborative practice. First, our capacity for rational thought—no matter who we are or how smart we are—plummets during the surge of flooding. When we are in the grip of anger, we literally cannot think straight. This is true for clients, and equally true for lawyers. Second, there is a predictable interval required physiologically before the endocrine surge that caused the flooding has receded sufficiently for our bodies (including our brains) to resume normal functioning. Generally, that interval is about 15 to 20 minutes for women, and 20 to 30 minutes for men.

Be alert to flooding in yourself and others. Explain the phenomenon beforehand to your clients. Use caucusing and time-out breaks freely when flooding occurs. Don't make the mistake of thinking an act of will can overcome this physical reality. No good work can be done when a participant at the collaborative table is flooded.

An effective first four-way meeting reassures most clients. Meeting the other spouse in a controlled environment with a predictable agenda that is honored relaxes fearful clients. Worries about whether the other spouse's lawyer will be difficult or intimidating generally evaporate in a well-structured first meeting; each lawyer makes efforts to establish rapport with the other party and each lawyer offers to be held accountable by the other participants. Basic education about the interest-based negotiation process and the work that will be done in each of the three "acts" of the collaborative process takes place collegially, with both lawyers sharing the tasks smoothly. The lawyers help the clients understand the emotional stages of the divorce process. They lay a foundation for managing strong emotions and conflict by normalizing their occurrence, predicting their emergence, and eliciting agreement about how such events will be handled. The agenda for the next meeting is agreed to by all; "homework" assignments are made and a schedule of future meetings is confirmed. In most instances, the first meeting proceeds smoothly and predictably and the clients emerge relatively relaxed and with enhanced confidence about the collaborative process.

6. **Conducting the Debriefing.** Immediately after the close of the first four-way meeting comes the last task in Act One of a collaborative representation, the "debriefing." This consists of a conference or "post-meeting" with the client and one with the other lawyer to review what took place in the first four-way meeting.[15] These conferences can be very brief indeed, perhaps little more than a private word or two as the participants leave the first four-way. More often, the lawyer and client will confer (either in person or via telephone) a day or two after the first four-way to allow time for reflection. Next, the two lawyers will share perceptions (their own and their clients') about what worked well and what could be improved. If either lawyer has inadvertently offended the other party, this is the time to share that information and agree about how both lawyers will repair the situation. If unanticipated conflict emerged, or anyone violated the agenda agreements, the lawyers at this stage discuss what went wrong and what should be done. If a lawyer or client behaved with commendable grace or restraint, that might be acknowledged.

By the end of the debriefing process, if the tasks of Act One have been done well, the lawyers and clients can move forward with a clear understanding of the process agreements that all will adhere to. Equally important, the parties and lawyers will have developed sufficient confidence in one another's good-faith intentions and in the collaborative process to move into Act Two, where the real work gets done.

Act Two

The curtain rises on Act Two as both lawyers prepare their clients for the second four-way meeting. In this phase of the collaborative process, all participants roll up their sleeves and begin to share information, clarify and communicate goals and priorities, brainstorm possible resolutions, devise and evaluate proposals, and—finally—reach agreements. The work is done systematically in that order, because leaping to a quick-fix deal before the

FIVE WAYS MEDIATORS AND COLLABORATIVE LAWYERS CAN WORK TOGETHER

1. **Collaborative lawyers make great consulting lawyers in cases where mediation is the clients' choice of primary conflict-resolution mode.** The collaborative participation agreement is modified to reflect this role change, and the collaborative lawyers remain barred from participating in litigation. An extra layer of protection for the clients' choice of settlement is in place as compared to utilizing consulting lawyers who will litigate if the mediation breaks down and whose advice and advocacy may be positional and not supportive of consensual resolution.

2. **Collaborative lawyers can strengthen and enrich the mediation process itself.** In mediations where the clients' consulting lawyers are in the room participating, mediators who develop good working relationships with collaborative lawyers can enjoy the advantages of having two other professionals in the room who know about interest-based conflict resolution, whose legal advice will be built into the negotiation process, and who are skilled at out-of-the-box problem solving.

3. **If a collaborative case runs into problems, a "meta-mediator" can help everyone get through the challenging phase.** Sometimes a "perfect storm" of challenging clients and challenging issues can stall a collaborative negotiation. If a mediator who understands the collaborative process is brought in to hold responsibility for managing the negotiating session, the lawyers can be freed to work more intensively with their respective clients. And, a third conflict-resolution professional in the room can sometimes help undo logjams in creative problem solving.

4. **Where new mates or extended family are undermining the collaborative process behind the scenes, a mediator can help return the process to integrity and transparency.** A mediator can work with the outside family members and help them or the client bring any legitimate interests involving them to the collaborative table for constructive discussion.

5. **If the collaborative lawyers run into difficulties with one another, a mediator can help.** A mediator who understands the collaborative process can be an effective facilitator or mentor who can help the two professionals communicate about what is going wrong, and help them get back into a more helpful mode with the clients.

parties have had time to evaluate all the facts, goals, priorities, and possibly superior options for resolution will not be the best pathway to the optimal outcome that might be possible for these parties.

In this phase of the work, agenda setting and early warning about potential "hot spots" continue to be key responsibilities of the lawyers as specialists in conflict management and guided negotiations. They will use pre- and post-meetings consistently to achieve those ends. Although the clients can be expected to push for advancing particularly vexing issues earlier on the four-way agenda, the lawyers will marshal their skills to counsel and elicit patience so that the meetings remain organized to build a series of successes. Ideally, no issue is put on a four-way agenda until both lawyers are reasonably confident that the clients are ready to resolve it, or until all readily resolvable issues have already been discussed and only the difficult issues remain.[16]

The number of four-way meetings required to reach the end of Act Two (a complete, agreed framework for settlement) varies with the number of issues to be resolved and their complexity, and with the temperament and flexibility of the clients and their emotional stance toward the divorce. The skill of the collaborative lawyers to manage conflict and guide negotiations also has a powerful effect on the efficiency and forward movement of the process. At the short end, some cases can be resolved fully during Act Two in as few as two to four four-way meetings.[17] At the more complex and challenging end of the spectrum, in a small percentage of cases it could take as many as seven or more four-way meetings to resolve all issues.[18]

Elapsed time in Act Two from the first four-way meeting to the last will vary. Even the most positive, cheerful, creative, and high-minded four-way meetings involve stress for the participants, from which recovery time is needed. Time to mull, to let ideas percolate, and to gather additional information is important, too. Neutral appraisers or consultants may need to complete reports before the big picture becomes clear. A house or other asset may need to be sold. Collaborative coaching to develop a suitable parenting plan may need some additional input from a child-development specialist. A dependent spouse may need career counseling. Leaving sufficient breathing room between meetings allows this productive work to take place in the spaces between, while pushing for too compressed a schedule compounds stress and reduces the quality of information-gathering, thinking, and negotiating. Experienced collaborative lawyers become sensitive to the

---

COLLABORATIVE AGENDA MANAGEMENT AND CONFLICT MANAGEMENT IN THE SECOND ACT

Collaborative lawyers manage four-way meetings for several purposes:

1. To avert needless anxiety and address conflict constructively if it arises.
2. To build client competency and confidence in negotiations.

3. To build a congruent understanding of all information important for resolving each issue—including goals, priorities, values, and information about the law—before resolution is addressed.

The clients control the substance of the agreements reached, but the lawyers are responsible for the procedure, including: pacing, tone, sequence, planning, and follow-through.

Some simple guidelines will help you manage your four-way agendas:

- Always plan the specific content of the four-way agenda in advance and be sure the lawyers are in agreement about the agenda.

- Always review the agenda for the forthcoming four-way in advance, with the other lawyer and also at your pre-meeting with your client.

- Never bring into a four-way meeting an issue that is not on the agenda. Even an emergency can be discussed privately, before the meeting, with your collaborative colleague and collegial process management about when and how to address the issue can take place.

- Never be the bearer of bad tidings to the other party. Never force your collaborative colleague to bear bad tidings to your client. Use pre-meetings for this purpose so that bad news or criticism is brought to the client by his or her own lawyer—ideally before the four-way.

- Highlight all acts of grace and generosity. Praise civility. Use "stop-motion" to invite the participants to take time to acknowledge important moments of collaborative cooperation.

- Plan agendas to build on success. Include in an agenda only what the lawyers are confident the clients are ready to address. Start with easy issues to build momentum and confidence. Save hard issues for later.

- Sometimes the only thing that can be agreed upon is the date for the next meeting. Sometimes that is a big accomplishment.

- Invite the other party to call you to account if you revert to adversarial or contentious mannerisms. Apologize quickly, sincerely, and frequently for your errors. Take more than half of the responsibility for collective missteps.

- Always discuss the agenda for the next four-way before concluding a four-way meeting.

- Always have several future four-ways on the calendar before adjourning a four-way.

- Always have one of the lawyers prepare and distribute a post-meeting memorandum summarizing what was accomplished, what was agreed upon, what was promised, who has what homework assignments, and what comes next.

RECALIBRATING FROM CONFLICT TO SOLUTIONS

A simple, powerful technique to apply when clients get embedded in positions that bog the process down is to recalibrate whoever is stuck (it may be more than one person) back to the original process agreements made at the start of the collaborative representation. This technique would ordinarily be used privately with your client. With practice, with a trusted colleague, and with careful preparation, this technique can sometimes be used to great effect at a four-way meeting.

"Do you recall that when we began this collaborative process, we all confirmed the shared goal of reaching an agreement that both of you could find acceptable? And do you recall that we all agreed to adhere to the Principles and Guidelines for Collaborative Law in our work toward arriving at agreement?"

"Let's review together how we get from here to the agreement that is your goal, and also your partner's goal. It seems that at this moment, you are expressing a strong view that. . . ."

"Would you agree that Mary does not seem to share your perspective on this point? In fact, would it be fair to say that her viewpoint right now about this specific point appears to differ in significant, fundamental ways from your viewpoint?"

"That being so, let's look at what choices you have to try to get from here to a resolution. You could hold onto your position and argue with Mary about it, but has that approach ever produced good results for you? You could give up and go to court and let someone else tell you both what you are going to do about this, but are you ready to give up all control over what happens here? Can you see anything else that we could do that might be more productive than arguing, and that might lead us to a solution? Would you consider brainstorming all your ideas for how this problem could be resolved, from sensible all the way to crazy, without saying whether you'd actually accept the idea or not, and asking Mary to do the same thing? And seeing what emerges from that exercise in creative problem solving?"

"If not, what other ways can you envision for doing the job we agreed to do here?"

pace and rhythm of the specific case and plan the schedule of forthcoming meetings accordingly. Once in a while circumstances require closely spaced meetings (for instance, if one party must travel long distances to attend) but rarely is such a situation optimal.

Litigation-mode negotiations will frequently include insistence by a party or lawyer that no piecemeal agreements will be considered—that the case must settle in its entirety all at once, or not at all. Such a stance has little compatibility with collaborative practice since by its very nature it is an arbitrary strategic position unrelated to any inherent needs arising from the lives of the parties. Insistence on global settlement or nothing causes ill will, frustrates progress, and should be avoided. The work of Act Two in cases involving more than a few issues will usually proceed via a series of interim agreements or tentative understandings, issue by issue. Whether the parties elect to be bound by interim agreements or merely to agree tentatively, subject to final comprehensive agreement, is up to them, with advice of counsel, but what is to be avoided is an insistence on a sequence of global comprehensive proposals and counterproposals as the bargaining mode.

Act Three

As in a well-wrought play, all ends are tied up in Act Three of a collaborative case, both in the literal sense (all issues are resolved, so that the parties know where they stand now and for the near future, both financially and as parents) and in a more symbolic or ceremonial sense (a major and emotionally challenging life transition, the divorce, is about to be completed). The last terms of agreement will have been reached at the end of Act Two, and during the third act the lawyers will undertake drafting an acceptable agreement, preparing the court papers necessary to obtain a divorce judgment, and completing related technical paperwork tasks such as Qualified Domestic Relations Orders (QDROs) and title transfers.

In a conventional settlement situation, completing those paper tasks ends the work. In a collaborative matter, however, there is a significant human dimension to be acknowledged and supported. The formal papers marking the end of the legal divorce (the agreement and the judgment) may have little emotional significance to our clients, while the reverberations of the fact that the marriage or relationship and the negotiating process itself are ending may be immense, yet may be quite invisible to the lawyers. This truth is the source of the phenomenon familiar to adversarial family lawyers: whether after a settlement conference or after a trial, the terms of judgment are finally agreed, the judge has signed the papers, the judgment is entered, a file-marked copy is sent to the client, and then the client telephones the lawyer to ask, "Is it over yet?"

In collaborative law practice, the lawyers recognize the human need of many clients to reach emotional closure at the end of the process. For that reason, elements can be built into the final events of the representation that help clients achieve a kind of homeostasis or resting place with respect to the life passage that divorce represents for them. Accordingly, goals in the third act of a collaborative representation include these:

ADVISING CLIENTS ABOUT THE LAW

As lawyers (and unlike mediators), part of our responsibility is to ensure that our clients understand their legal rights as they negotiate collaborative agreements. But collaborative lawyers put much thought into when and how that legal advice will be provided, so that the clients understand what might happen if the matter were litigated in the local courts, without the legal context being accorded dispositive power over the negotiations or outcomes. For traditional, rights-bounded lawyers, the only concerns worth discussing with a client are those about which motions can be filed and court orders can be issued. Good collaborative lawyers take a more expansive view of the task. As interest-based bargainers, we know that our clients care greatly about many matters that lie outside the jurisdiction of the family court. When we negotiate collaborative agreements, we can include resolution of issues for which no legal remedies would be available in court. That being so, our clients may make trade-offs in collaborative negotiations that yield outcomes on the legally cognizable issues markedly different from what might usually happen in court. In return, they may gain outcomes that no judge could ever order.

Traditional lawyers may look at the resulting agreements with horror, because the client did not insist on getting every dollar or every asset that a judge might have awarded, while ignoring the nonquantifiable or nonjusticiable goals valued greatly by the client that have been met in the collaborative process. When advising clients about the role of the law in collaborative matters, collaborative lawyers generally include contextual information such as this, that lawyers are well aware of and clients are not:

> The family courts don't dispense justice, and trials are not about winning or losing. What the courts dispense is certainty. If you and your spouse— with the help of the collaborative lawyers and other collaborative professionals—are unable to craft an individualized, custom-made solution about the issues affecting your family after the divorce, the courts are available to give you certainty and closure. But the judge can never know as much as you know about the needs of the family and will never have as much time or interest as you do in crafting solutions that will work. Any couple with the desire to do so can do better than any judge in designing solutions that will work and that will last. If you make your own decisions about the post-divorce family, you keep control over your finances and your parenting where it was when you lived together—with yourselves. Furthermore, the judge is required to work with a straitjacket and blinders on, called the Family Code. This is a collection of laws made by elected officials who may know little or nothing about family dynamics and who may have been lobbied by vocal special interests. We need to know about those laws, and we can apply them here if they seem to produce the results you both prefer. As a last resort, the court can do it for you. Think of it as the emergency room. If you value privacy and control over your own destiny, keep decision-making power here; don't give it away and don't put on the straitjacket here that the judge is required to wear in court.

- To help clients reflect back upon the successes and acts of grace that occurred in the collaborative process and to acknowledge acts of generosity and ethical, civilized behaviors.
- To mirror for clients their proven competency at resolving disputes and disagreements with their partner or spouse.
- To normalize for clients the expectation that future disagreements or conflicts are predictable and can also be handled with grace, civility, and integrity.
- To build into the agreements and into the clients' expectations adequate tools and procedures for resolving future disagreements.
- To provide for clients who wish it a ceremonial marker for the end of their legal relationship. This might include an opportunity for apologies and forgiveness, or something as simple as a champagne toast or a hug. At a bare minimum it generally will include face-to-face signing of the agreement and the divorce papers by the clients and their collaborative lawyers.

The vehicle for achieving these third-act goals is a final four-way meeting with the pragmatic agenda of reviewing and signing the settlement agreement and other documents required to process the divorce. Of course, those papers could be signed separately in the lawyers' offices or mailed around for signatures, but to do so would be to leave the clients without a clear, meaningful ending to a highly significant experience.

DETACHING FROM SOLVING THE PROBLEM

Lawyers love solving problems. We are impatient when we cannot move quickly to the solution. We *know* what the result ought to be, and we can become frustrated when our clients stubbornly hold onto problems and focus on small quibbles rather than seeing the big picture. It is not uncommon for conventional litigation-matrix lawyers to push and prod reluctant clients into accepting a settlement the lawyers conclude is the best achievable outcome. It is also not unusual for the clients to resent such negotiations and to be dissatisfied with the results and the lawyers who facilitated them.

In collaborative law, we lawyers are guardians of the process. Good collaborative lawyers know that responsibility for solving the problem needs to be kept firmly on the shoulders of the clients. There is no surer way to maintain progress in moving from issues to comprehensive agreement than to insist that clients assume responsibility for considering, weighing, and deciding among the available options.

When the lawyer tries to solve the problem, the client often responds with criticism of the solution. Experiment with detaching entirely from the solution and focusing the client on the process of identifying, evaluating, and selecting the best of the available options. The lawyer's job is to ensure that all feasible options have been developed accurately and considered carefully and reasonably. One option always is terminating the collaborative law process and going to court. There generally are other, perhaps better choices. If so, then with help, the client will be able to see that reality as clearly as you can. If the client does not see an acceptable solution that is achievable within the collaborative process, never try to persuade him or her otherwise. You will regret it if you do.

Tell your client:

I support whatever choice you believe will bring you closest to the best possible outcome for yourself and those you care about and I am available to help you implement your choice.

Ask your client:

- What do you see as your choices at this point?

- What are the consequences, for better and for worse, of selecting each choice? How do you expect that choosing this option will bring you closer to the goals you have identified as important? How could it take you further from those goals? What are the costs of choosing this option, financial and emotional, for you and your children? Do you have enough information to make this assessment? If not, how can you get the necessary information? Would my experience in this area be helpful?

- Given that analysis for each option, what would you prefer to do here and now?

INTEREST-BASED BARGAINING: ASKING FOR EVERYTHING YOU NEED

Try counseling your client at the first meeting about this important concept in collaborative, interest-based bargaining: ask for everything you need, no more and no less.

This means avoiding artificially inflated demands motivated by fear. It also means avoiding guilt-ridden offers that are much too generous and requests that would yield far less than is needed. Such stances can be motivated by feelings of guilt or shame about how one left the marriage. Experienced family lawyers know that guilt and shame tend to have short half-lives. In hindsight a year or two down the road a client can regret making such an agreement. Clients are in charge of the substance of the final agreement, and generosity is to be admired, but collaborative lawyers need to be alert when generosity or self-abnegation appears self-defeating, and/or seems motivated by transient negative emotions rather than considered thought. In best collaborative practice, the focus is on helping clients devise solutions that will look as good 10 years downstream as they look today.

A typical sequence of events at the final four-way might unfold like this: first, the lawyers would conduct a review of the settlement agreement with the clients before it is signed. The lawyers might alternate summarizing the meaning of the sections of the agreement, beginning to end, giving more attention to complex or especially significant sections, and merely highlighting the effect of the "boilerplate" sections.

As the review proceeds, the conversation can naturally include recognition of important concessions or acts of generosity during the collaborative process that resulted in particular points of agreement in the final document. Or, if a provision represents a hard-won achievement after apparent impasse, or an act of creative imagination, these successes too should be acknowledged. Also, as the review proceeds, the lawyers can weave into the conversation a discussion of areas where predictable future life changes may require revisiting the present provisions. For example, children get older, income rises or falls, divorced spouses remarry or move, and special medical or educational needs arise.

The lawyers will serve the clients well by including in the agreement (and reviewing in the final four-way meeting) the steps that the clients will take to resolve future issues as they arise. Building in the expectation of change, and normalizing for the clients the need for flexibility and future renegotiation of terms using the collaborative process are valuable steps in the third-act process.

After the documents are reviewed and signed, many clients will be in an emotionally charged state, recognizing the importance of what has just occurred, and not knowing an appropriate way to express their feelings or to conclude the event. It is at this stage that the collaborative lawyers provide a great service by offering the opportunity for an appropriate closing ceremony for the process. This ceremonial quality is inherent in the occasion, and tends to emerge quite naturally if time is allowed for it. A conversation reviewing and evaluating the collaborative process itself is a good way to bring clients into a reflective state (as well as an excellent source of feedback for the lawyers about what did and did not work well in the representation). That conversation often will lead clients to feel comfortable enough to express directly to one another something of their relief, appreciation, sadness, acceptance, forgiveness, or other feelings toward the partner about the divorce itself. Rarely do clients go through this final four-way process in a well-managed collaborative case without expressing appreciation toward one another and toward the lawyers who assisted them. Often, the meeting closes with hugs, smiles, and tears. All this marks the event for the clients as important, successful, and complete. Collaborative clients whose divorces end this way do not ask, "Is it over yet?"

HELPING YOUR CLIENT CONNECT
WITH HIGHEST INTENTIONS FOR THE DIVORCE

The essence of the collaborative process for clients is that it evokes, supports, and works to achieve both spouses' highest intentions for the divorce and for the post-divorce restructured family. But our clients will sometimes be so preoccupied with the tensions and fears associated with the early stages of divorce that they become temporarily overwhelmed with immediate, short-term concerns. Here is a technique for recalibrating your client's perspective from the immediate grievances and irritations of the separation period to a broader focus on highest intentions for the future. Remember that you can be completely transparent about this. Tell your client what you are doing and why you are doing it.

Ask your client's permission to do a simple exercise with you* that will give the client a vivid sense of what it means for you to represent the client's highest-intentioned self rather than the client's shadow self, as follows:

- Ask your client to make himself or herself physically comfortable and to close his or her eyes and take a few deep breaths.

- Ask the client to spend a few minutes remembering some of the positive aspects of the marriage. Perhaps it might be the honeymoon, the birth of a child, or a time when the spouse was particularly supportive.

- Then ask the client to look a bit further back, to the time that the couple decided to marry, remembering the proposal and the acceptance, and the hopes that both had for their marriage and life together. Ask the client to recall his or her own positive feelings toward the other spouse, and the commitments and positive intentions that the client had for how he or she would behave during the marriage toward the other.

- While holding the memory, ask the client to imagine that some trusted counselor or friend back then had said, "Though you consider the possibility unthinkable at this moment, I want you to know that divorces do happen and that divorce could possibly happen to you and your spouse sometime down the road. Loving and respecting your spouse as you do at this moment, what promises and commitments can you make about how you will behave if you should have to divorce someday in the future?"

- After your client has spent a few moments imagining what you have suggested, invite your client to open his or her eyes. Tell him or her that keeping that image in current awareness will help the client act with dignity and civility during the divorce process—that remaining aware of that perspective will help the client move through the divorce process with integrity and help preserve a memory of that which was valuable in the relationship that is ending. Ask the client whether he or she would like to be reminded of this perspective when—inevitably—strong emotions arise during the divorce process.

*I am indebted to my colleague Larry Wilson for this visualization, which he and I often use at the start of the first four-way meeting in cases we work on together.

HELPING CLIENTS WITH CHILDREN TO REMAIN
ON THE HIGH ROAD

Here is a technique (sometimes called a "process anchor") that you can use to help clients get back into constructive, highest-intentioned problem solving when they slip into emotion-driven focus on old grievances.

Early in your work with the client, discuss whether the client would value holding in mind during divorce negotiations questions like these: "What would my children think of my conduct during this divorce if they had been watching this conversation/meeting? How would I like my children to believe I conducted myself during this time? How would I behave right now if I knew my child could someday watch a videotape of this meeting?"* Clients often are quite moved by this conversation, and many welcome an understanding that their lawyer will remind them of it later, during difficult periods in the collaborative negotiations.

In your first pre-meeting with your collaborative counterpart, propose presenting this concept as a process anchor at the first four-way meeting. Then, during Act Two discussions and negotiations, either lawyer can remind the parties of the conversation at the first four-way meeting during which they agreed that they would like to behave during the collaborative process in a manner that would model for their children a respectful, caring way to resolve differences.

---

*Clients represented by litigation counsel who file inflammatory divorce-related motions are often entirely unaware that in California and most other U.S. jurisdictions, divorce files are public records that older children can freely view should they ever care to.

Notes

1. In the first edition of this book, this chapter was organized using an extended chess metaphor. Some readers pointed out that chess is a war game and thus that the chess metaphor was inherently conflict-based rather than collaborative, for which reason this edition has shifted to a theatrical metaphor. This is yet another illustration of the degree to which conflict pervades our language and therefore our thought and discourse, in ways that are difficult even to see, much less to avoid.

2. Whether the representation is collaborative or traditional, the ability of the two lawyers to trust one another and to negotiate together constructively is a key predictor of how efficiently—or dysfunctionally—the divorce process will unfold. *See* Robert H. Mnookin & R. Gilson, *Disputing Through Agents: Cooperation Between Lawyers in Litigation,* 94 COLUMBIA L. REV. 509 (1994).

In collaborative practice, where facilitating consensual resolution is the sole purpose for which the clients retain their lawyers, this aspect of the professional relationship is central to the lawyers' ability to do the job they were hired for.

3. While each lawyer can represent one and only one client, and takes on no contractual duty to the other party, the overarching goal of each party in a collaborative case is the same:

find workable solutions that both parties can accept as the resolution of all divorce-related issues. This goal implies and requires a kind of teamwork that emerges quite naturally when the collaborative lawyers know their craft, without compromising the lawyer's primary ethical duty to his or her own client. In this author's very first collaborative case, after the first four-way meeting, my client's wife embraced me and chided, "You've got to find another name to replace 'opposing counsel.' I know you represent my husband and you don't represent me, but there's nothing 'opposing' about what you're doing."

In an excellent pioneering study, *The Emerging Phenomenon of Collaborative Family Law (CFL): A Qualitative Study of CFL Cases* (2005), at http://canada.justice.gc.ca/en/ps/pad/reports/2005-FCY-1/2005-FCY-1.pdf., law professor Julie MacFarlane cites a few troubling comments in this regard from practitioners to the effect that their loyalty is to "the family as a unit," or the "whole family." *Id.* at 46. It is important to put the remarks in context. Professor MacFarlane's research design from which the comments emerged did not select for, or aim to investigate, practitioners' level of experience or training. A number of the lawyers who participated in the study were beginners at collaborative practice who had handled few if any cases prior to the ones MacFarlane included in her research protocol. While one does not expect best practices to be the rule in this kind of study, it does provide important early warning of some questionable practices emerging in some collaborative communities and therefore is proving helpful in setting standards and training for best practices.

4. It will ordinarily be decided very early in Act One whether to work with an interdisciplinary collaborative divorce team of coaches, child specialist, and financial consultant who will come on board right away during Act One, or instead to bring in neutral advisors and consultants on an "as-needed" basis during Act Two.

5. This is a principle of "best practice" with important ramifications for professional ethics and professional responsibility. See Chapter 7 for discussion of the importance of fully informed consent in collaborative representation. That there be no uncertainty whatsoever as to whether the lawyers are or are not barred from subsequent adversarial representation before substantive work on divorce issues begins is of fundamental importance, and no client should be permitted to embark on discussing settlement objectives and priorities or to begin making factual disclosures in a collaborative divorce until the participation documents have been discussed and signed.

6. Family law clients often come to their lawyers in the early stages of grieving for the unexpected loss of a primary relationship. They may be far more confused and fearful, as well as far less capable of absorbing and organizing new, complex information, than they appear. That being so, it is safest to assume that your new client will benefit from a slow pace and careful reiteration of important points. It is also wise to assume that your client may misinterpret or misremember the explicit content of the first few meetings, and may take as much meaning from the unintended subtext of your early meetings as from the content of what you intentionally present. Chapter 3 includes a series of four tables comparing adversarial and collaborative lawyering, with illustrations of some of the habitual, unconscious behaviors and attitudes that collaborative lawyers need to become aware of and to reshape for consistency with the explicit mutual undertakings of the collaborative process.

At a more nuanced and sophisticated level, becoming more aware of the potential ramifications for the client of being in a dependent relationship, at a time of particular vulnerability and stress, with a powerful, wise professional advocate is a journey of exploration that all domestic relations lawyers would benefit from and that is essential for becoming highly effective at collaborative representation. Insights from clinical psychology about transference and countertransference are a good starting point, as well as study of the dynamics of grief and recovery in divorce. Beyond that, there is an expanding universe of understanding in the behavioral sciences—particularly in the realm of cognitive neuroscience—about how human beings think, communicate, influence one another, and make decisions, that is fascinating, pertinent, and well beyond the scope of this book. A layperson's look at the tip of the iceberg can be found in Malcolm Gladwell, Blink: The Power of Thinking Without

THINKING (2005); *see also*, e.g., JOSEPH LEDOUX, SYNAPTIC SELF: HOW OUR BRAINS BECOME WHO WE ARE (2002); TIMOTHY D. WILSON, STRANGERS TO OURSELVES: DISCOVERING THE ADAPTIVE UNCONSCIOUS (2002); RAN R. HASSIN, JAMES S. ULEMAN & JOHN A. BARGH, THE NEW UNCONSCIOUS (Oxford Series in Social Cognition and Social Neuroscience) (2005).

7. See Chapter 9 for ideas about how your office staff and office procedures can support the messages you will want to reinforce with your collaborative clients.

8. One easily overlooked aspect of consistent message is what you pay attention to. If you spend time during the first meeting discussing utility bills and other monthly budget line items, for instance, you are instructing your client to regard the utility bill as the most important matter to think about when embarking on a divorce. While it must be paid, there are far more important concerns to address at the start of Act One.

9. *See* ABA MODEL RULES OF PROFESSIONAL CONDUCT, Rule 1.4, Comment [5]: "... when a matter is likely to involve litigation, it may be necessary under Rule 1.4 to inform the client of forms of dispute resolution that might constitute reasonable alternatives to litigation." Some jurisdictions mandate that lawyers offer "alternate dispute resolution" options to their clients at the start of a representation. *See, e.g.,* TEX. CIV. PRAC. & REM. CODE § 154.001–073; Clarke v. England, 715 So. 2d 365, 366 (Florida); Howard v. Drapkin, 222 Cal. App. 3d 843, 858 (California). Professional standards for mediators require them to explain to potential clients the range of dispute-resolution options available before agreeing to provide mediation services to them. *See, e.g., Model Standards of Practice for Family and Divorce Mediation, Standard III,* 39 FAM. CT. REV. 121 (2001), at 128. A growing body of opinion supports the idea that whether expressly mandated or not, lawyers too fail to provide adequate services if we fail to advise our clients that there are more ways available to them for resolving their disputes than simply going to court. *See, e.g.,* Robert F. Cochran, Jr., *Professional Rules and ADR: Control of Alternative Dispute Resolution Under the ABA Ethics 2000 Commission Proposal and Other Professional Responsibility Standards,* 28 FORDHAM URB. L. J. 895–914 (2001) ["I have suggested elsewhere that lawyers should present the option of pursuing alternative means of dispute resolution (ADR) to clients as a matter of good practice, and that lawyers might be subject to malpractice liability if they fail to do so. My argument here is that the rules of the legal profession should require lawyers to present such options to clients."]; Marshall J. Breger, *Should an Attorney Be Required to Advise a Client of ADR Options?,* 13 GEORGETOWN J. LEGAL ETHICS 427 (2000); Carrie Menkel-Meadow, *Ethics in ADR: The Many "Cs" of Professional Responsibility and Dispute Resolution,* 28 FORDHAM URBAN L. J., (April 2001) ["Every lawyer ought to have an ethical obligation to counsel clients about the multiple ways of resolving problems and planning transactions. A few states have included this obligation in precatory language, although very few have done so in required language. I think that this ethical obligation should be mandatory, and I have suggested this in my idealized Ten Commandments of Appropriate Dispute Resolution."]; Carrie Menkel-Meadow, *Ethics and Professionalism in Non-Adversarial Lawyering.* 27 FLA. ST. U. L. REV. 153, 167–68 (1999). [All internal citations and notes omitted from quotations.]

10. Whether or not to sign a collaborative participation agreement when the other party is represented by counsel you do not know, or worse, by counsel you know to be ineffective at or ill-suited to collaborative representation, is the subject of an interview by the author with John McCall; see Chapter 3, *supra* note 7. At minimum, most collaborative lawyers would require that the other lawyer have been trained in collaborative law and be a member of a collaborative practice group before advising their own client that it is prudent to sign the collaborative participation agreement. All effective collaborative representation requires communication and process management with the other lawyer between meetings, but a much higher degree of communication will be necessary to do a minimally competent job with an ineffective or unskilled lawyer as collaborative counterpart. Many practice groups recommend designating a more experienced group member as mentor from the beginning in such situations, to be available on request when either lawyer feels the other is failing to

facilitate constructive collaborative negotiations. Practice group protocols for case management also help greatly.

11. When collaborative lawyers work skillfully together and with their respective clients to clarify, restate, reinforce, and apply the specific process agreements (agreements about good-faith bargaining, conflict management, and sequencing of events) that characterize an effective collaborative representation, they often refer to this accomplishment as setting or maintaining a collaborative "container" around the parties and the issues.

12. Better practice is to plan on two or more preliminary meetings with the client before the initial four-way meeting. The order of conversation is not as important as ensuring that there is enough time to confer without pressure or haste, and enough time for the lawyer to really listen to the client The client needs to learn about the lawyer, the divorce process, the collaborative process, interest-based negotiations, the legal divorce process in the jurisdiction, and also needs to be prepared specifically for what will and will not take place at the first four-way meeting. And of course, the lawyer needs to learn about the client, get a preliminary sense of the facts and potential issues, and decide whether to represent collaboratively—or at all.

13. In the author's locale (California), these documents typically are: the collaborative retainer or fee agreement with the individual lawyer, and two documents signed by all participants: Principles and Guidelines for Collaborative Divorce, and Stipulation and Order for Collaborative Case. See Appendix I for sample forms of these documents.

14. A second meeting can be scheduled immediately after the first if genuinely urgent issues must be addressed in order to stabilize the situation of the parties, but true urgency arises far less frequently than conventional litigating family lawyers might assume.

15. A post-meeting, or debriefing, takes place after each four-way meeting. It can be as brief as a few words, or a short telephone call. The debriefing that takes place after the first four-way can be particularly important in completing the "setting of the container." Later in the case, if matters are proceeding smoothly, the debriefing conversation can sometimes be accomplished at the same time as the pre-meeting to prepare for the next four-way.

16. This emphasis on addressing issues only when they are ripe for resolution illustrates a major distinction between the role of the collaborative lawyer and that of the adversarial lawyer. Since the process will have failed to achieve the clients' identified goal if all issues cannot be resolved to both clients' satisfaction, it follows that the collaborative lawyers serve their clients' interests best by acting as guardians of the collaborative dispute-resolution process as part of the work of helping their own clients reach solutions that they find acceptable. Counseling and educating clients about how one "gets to yes" becomes a vital part of the effective collaborative lawyer's job. Litigating lawyers may be able to get by for an entire career simply acting as their clients' alter egos, but a collaborative lawyer is unlikely to get the job done at all with such an attitude.

17. These estimates are in addition to the first "container-setting" four-way, which as a matter of best practice is limited solely to establishing the procedural parameters and good-faith commitments.

18. These estimates address the number of meetings required to bring the immediate sheaf of divorce-related issues to agreement in the great majority of collaborative cases. Many cases will require subsequent post-judgment renegotiation of support and custody issues, because many couples, particularly those who have minor children or who are ending a long relationship, will find the period of 18 to 24 months following entry of judgment to be more challenging even than the period between separation and entry of judgment in terms of the enormous changes that typically take place place during that time, as divorced partners consolidate new lives and households. These estimates do not include future collaborative proceedings to address such changes. These estimates also do not apply to the small number of collaborative cases involving serious addiction or other psychopathology in one or both clients. Such cases will be complicated and difficult for any professional to handle in any context, whatever the conflict-resolution mode. Best practice for collaborative lawyers working

without other professional team resources is to decline collaborative representation in such cases, not because any other conflict-resolution choice is better, but because of the unacceptably high likelihood that the collaborative process will fail to reach the identified goals. With sufficient support from experienced mental-health professionals (ideally via a collaborative divorce team) collaborative law can remain an option provided a careful informed-consent protocol is followed. Even with the necessary interdisciplinary professional team resources, collaborative lawyers who decide to handle such cases should expect and advise their clients to expect significant process challenges and long-term professional involvement.

Chapter 5

The Nuts and Bolts of Effective Collaborative Family Law Practice

"My joy was boundless. I had learnt the true practice of law. I had learnt to find out the better side of human nature and to enter men's hearts. I realized that the true function of a lawyer was to unite parties riven asunder. The lesson was so indelibly burnt into me that a large part of my time during the twenty years of my practice as a lawyer was occupied in bringing about private compromises of hundreds of cases. I lost nothing thereby—not even money, certainly not my soul."
—*M. K. Gandhi*

This chapter presents a variety of practical concepts, techniques, and approaches to keep handy in your collaborative law "toolbox." These tools work. They have evolved from the experiences of many lawyers working with many clients.[1] Try them out; experiment; add your own techniques and refinements as you develop your own style of collaborative lawyering.

Key Concepts and Tools

We begin with concepts and tools that you will use again and again in collaborative practice. Become familiar with these terms and how you will explain their meaning to new clients and to lawyers unfamiliar with collaborative practice. Apply them often. Remind clients when you are using a tool that you defined for them early in the process.

Paradigm Shift: The paradigm shift refers to the alteration in consciousness whereby lawyers retool themselves from adversarial to collaborative lawyers. The paradigm shift first requires the lawyer to become aware of unconscious adversarial habits of speech, as well as automatic adversarial thought-forms, reactions, and behaviors. The second step in the paradigm shift is to adopt the beginner's mind, learning new ways of thinking, speaking, and behaving as a collaborative lawyer.[2]

Container: In collaborative practice, the "container" is the invisible structure (foundation, walls, and roof) that holds the clients and the lawyers together in a working collaborative team during the ups and downs of the divorce process. It consists of a shared philosophy, shared goals, and shared procedural agreements, some of them formal and written, and some of them informal and unwritten, but all of them explicit. At its most basic, the container consists of the written stipulation or participation agreement that disqualifies the lawyers from appearing in court on behalf of these clients and that recites the limited-purpose retention of counsel. It also includes all the additional understandings and commitments about good faith, transparency, negotiation style, and conflict management that the four participants share and apply as the case proceeds.

Transparency: Transparency is hard to define, but easy to recognize in collaborative practice. It includes the following: honesty and candor about what one is doing and why one is doing it (both lawyers and clients); conduct of information exchange and negotiations in four-way meetings attended by both clients and both lawyers so that all important conversations are six-way communications experienced directly by each participant; candor about goals, priorities, and reasoning; and accountability and acceptance of responsibility. When transparency is present, there are no hidden agendas or hidden balls; there is no secret tactical maneuvering; there are no triangulated attempts to blame absent persons for faults never disclosed to them; there is no taking advantage of misunderstandings or errors. Complaints are aired promptly and apologies are made quickly and publicly; ideas are presented and improvements are suggested with the direct participation of all players. The lawyers vouch for the completeness of the information presented. Accountability is immediate, direct, and apparent to all participants.

The Invisible (or Relational) Estate: In conventional family law representation, the lawyers' work focuses on identifying and allocating economic interests in two estates, the marital and the separate, owned by the parties. Legal rights constitute the universe within which thinking and advocacy take place, focusing primarily on size of quantifiable outcome. In collaborative representation, the lawyers attend to the separate and marital estates, but in addition they commit to preserve and value a third estate owned by

THREE TWO-WAY COMMUNICATIONS
(OLD PARADIGM)

Lawyers control communications in conventional litigation-template representation. With rare exceptions, every communication is a two-way communication between the lawyer and one other person, a lawyer or a client. This communication mode maximizes control and minimizes transparency and accountability. It looks like this:

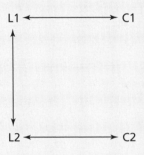

ONE SIX-WAY COMMUNICATION
(NEW PARADIGM)

In collaborative law practice, the negotiating work is done almost entirely in four-way meetings attended by both lawyers and both clients. This communication mode maximizes creativity, transparency, and accountability. It looks like this:

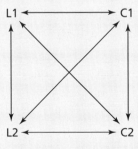

the parties and their family: the invisible or relational estate. This estate consists of a range of interests vitally important to clients but generally ignored and often unthinkingly destroyed during conventional family law representation.

The invisible estate attended to by clients and their collaborative lawyers includes: relationships with members of the spouse's extended family (the clients' in-laws, who are the grandparents, aunts, uncles, and cousins of both parties' children); the web of friendships shared by both spouses; the ability of the spouses to co-parent effectively after the divorce; the ability of the clients to meet comfortably in the future at major life passages such as births, christenings, graduations, bar mitzvahs, marriages, and deaths; the ability of each client to look back on his or her own conduct during the divorce with comfort, self-respect, and a sense of dignity; the preservation for each spouse of the integrity that comes from valuing what was positive in the marriage—an important chapter in one's own life history; the ability of each client to feel that he or she behaved consistently with deeply held religious and ethical values in moving through the divorce passage.

Process Anchors: The term "process anchor" refers to stories, metaphors, and techniques that collaborative lawyers introduce to clients during Act One of the collaborative case as part of educating them about collaborative conflict resolution. Experience has shown best practice to be a transparent explanation of how the process anchor might be used in the future to manage conflict or guide negotiations. These process anchors later can be used at times of confusion or emotional distress to help the client return to a clearer state of thinking. They are also used as tools to manage uncivil or other dysfunctional client behavior during the collaborative process. Their particular virtue in the collaborative toolbox is their simplicity and clarity. When a client is in the grip of cortisol flooding and is not thinking clearly, tossing out a process anchor may be the most useful response in the moment to stop a dysfunctional process and help the parties return to constructive problem solving.

Some process anchors are quite tangible, such as placing objects in the four-way meeting room that encourage parties (and lawyers) to focus on identified highest goals and constructive behavior at times of stress. For example, some collaborative lawyers whose clients have identified protecting their children as a high priority like to invite them to bring photographs of the children to four-way meetings, and to place the photos at the center of the table. Artwork in the collaborative conference room with images of parents and children (human or animal) can remind parties of the same priority. One practitioner has had little metal "coins" the size of silver dollars made that are engraved on both sides with the word "win." Anything that potentially carries meaning that supports the specific goals of the parties or the good-faith process commitments of collaborative law, and that might become the subject of small talk between breaks, becomes a process anchor when attention is directed to it.

Other process anchors are verbal in nature. Teaching stories and meta-phors fall into this category, as does the use of an unexpected, thought-provoking word ("upgrade" in place of "counterproposal," for example). And some can even be physiological—a reminder to take a deep breath, or a suggestion that everyone stand up and stretch for a moment to change the energy in the room.

The Shadow Client and the Highest-Functioning Client: The term "shadow client" refers metaphorically to the client whose thought processes may be impaired by the temporary upwelling of intense and primitive emotions such as fear, rage, grief, or shame. It being well-established that a divorce is second only to the death of a child in the intensity of resulting emotional distress, it follows that our divorcing clients come to us in varying stages of recovery from intense trauma. A client experiencing a burst of strong emotion is never in a state of mind well-suited to long-term planning for the best interests of children and the post-divorce restructured family, or even for the client's own long-term best interests. The shadow client is the one most often being rep-resented by conventional divorce lawyers in the slide toward the courthouse. In a collaborative representation, on the other hand, the work is done by the client in his or her highest-functioning state, when there is the capacity to plan for his or her enlightened long-term self-interest and the interests of children and other loved ones. In best collaborative practice, the client is brought to the four-way table to do the work only when the client is in a functional cog-nitive state, able to give appropriate attention to those highest intentions for the divorce that he or she has identified earlier in the collaborative process.[3]

Collaborative lawyers first educate, and then make agreements with their clients, about how the indisputable biological facts of cortisol flooding and temporarily impaired cognition should be handled during negotiations in light of the higher goals, interests, and intentions that the client has identified as pri-orities. A simple metaphor for this nuanced conversation is that the collabora-tive lawyer will listen to and counsel the shadow client when he or she appears, but will not take direction from clients who find themselves during a four-way meeting experiencing a temporary shadow state because that would have the effect of thwarting goals and interests the client has identified as significant.[4]

The ADR Continuum, Client Self-Selection, and Client Accountability: Conventional family lawyers often find themselves vulnerable to the appeal of clients who see them as gladiators and want them to jump on a white horse and attack the other party, who is seen as embodying all evil just as the client embodies all good. In that mode of black-and-white adversarial practice, attention is rarely given to advising clients fully about the predict-able emotional, relational, and financial costs involved in legal battle, nor is much time typically spent advising clients about the growing spectrum of low-conflict dispute-resolution choices available to them. Good collaborative lawyers begin building client accountability and empowerment from the start by educating their new clients about the entire spectrum of dispute-resolution options, the profile of clients who typically do well in each mode, and the obvious and hidden costs and benefits of each approach. Good collaborative lawyers also avoid pushing or selling any one option.[5] Instead, clients are given as much information as possible with emphasis on the importance of choosing for themselves. These techniques are the first steps in keeping the client responsible for the decisions that lead toward or away from the good divorce. To the extent that the lawyer takes over responsibility for deciding how the case will be handled, and whether it will be collaborative law, or mediation, or litigation, the client is justified in holding the lawyer responsible if the process is a poor fit. Consequently, it is important for collaborative practitioners to develop easily presented, easily understood descriptions of the range of dispute-resolution options available in the jurisdiction, and a readily explained summary of which people and which cases do well in each mode. It is also important to explain carefully and to have your client sign a fee or retainer agreement tailored for collaborative practice that sets out specifically the unique characteristics of collaborative representation, for purposes of informed consent and malpractice prevention.

Flooding: Research confirms that at times of high emotional stress, the body's "fight-or-flight" mechanism comes into play, flooding the physical body in a hormonal soup that alters cognitive functioning. Mental-health professionals who work with divorcing clients summarize the practical consequence of flooding as a temporary and dramatic eradication of the ability to engage in effective rational thought. Whenever lawyers are working with divorcing clients, and particularly when both spouses are working together in the same room (as is the norm in collaborative practice), flooding is a possibility. The shadow client almost by definition lives in a state of perpetual flooding. Mental-health colleagues advise that there is a predictable interval before the capacity for reasoning returns to normal. For women, the interval is said to be about 15–20 minutes; for men, about 20–30 minutes. The importance to collaborative lawyers of understanding and working with this phenomenon should be obvious: a flooded client is not able to participate effectively (or even respectfully) at the collaborative four-way table. Caucusing, time-outs, and possible adjournment of scheduled meetings become important tools for managing flooding. Preparing clients for its occurrence permits normalizing it and reducing its destabilizing impact. Effective collaborative process management must involve planning for flooding and making collective agreements in advance for managing it rather than ignoring it and allowing it to become the "500-pound gorilla in the middle of the table" that will subvert or destroy the collaborative process.

Guiding Metaphors: One of the most valuable tools for managing conflict and maintaining the integrity of the collaborative container is the "guiding metaphor." Collaborative lawyers draw upon a growing sheaf of metaphors for these purposes, and each successful collaborative practitioner will make use of favorites and will devise his or her own new ones. Collaborative lawyers systematically incorporate metaphors into every stage of the collaborative process, from the first meeting onward. Gradually, their use becomes second nature. By guiding the client to think in these metaphorical terms, the collaborative lawyer develops a bundle of shorthand terms (process anchors) with which to communicate effectively even when the client is flooded in a shadow state (itself a metaphor). These metaphors are used in the first meetings with the client, again in the first four-way, then as needed in the mid-game stage, and again in summing up the accomplishments of the parties at the final four-way meeting. You will find a collection of commonly used metaphors for collaborative practice in Appendix I.

Interest-Based Negotiations: Interest-based (or needs-based) negotiation is the preferred mode of bargaining employed in collaborative practice. Unlike the bargaining styles commonly used in adversarial legal negotiations,[6] interest-based bargaining requires considerable groundwork between collaborative lawyer and client before any issue is brought to the four-way table for discussion. In this mode of bargaining, lawyer and client examine every one of the client's identified goals and priorities under a microscope, "peeling the onion" down from what the client initially states as goals and priorities, to examine why the client wants each goal, what benefits achieving the goal would bring to the client, whether there might be other ways of achieving the same benefits that are as good as or better than the means the client has identified, and whether the goal can be described at the four-way table in terms that any reasonable person of good faith would recognize as legitimate. Since no collaborative agreement will result unless both parties can agree, it follows that presenting goals in the most reasonable manner possible and finding modes of reaching the identified goals that are compatible with the other party's legitimate interests will provide the best chance for optimal settlement—the overriding goal in service of which all collaborative lawyers are retained. Peeling the onion is a kind of work that conventional civil litigators, steeped in the dance of Mediterranean-marketplace bargaining, rarely engage in. It is the gateway to lateral thinking, and the key to identifying solutions acceptable to both parties that expand the settlement pie beyond what is available in court.[7]

Attention to Language: Most of us are aware in a general sense of the powerful impact carried by words and their associations. Linguistics scholar Deborah Tannen has contributed greatly to our understanding of how men and women use language differently[8] and how crude adversarial battle metaphors that suffuse our colloquial speech dominate and limit our ability to think or communicate outside our culture's adversarial straitjacket.[9] To avoid falling into the tenacious habits of adversarial thought and speech is difficult and requires determination. Thoughtless use of a litigator's habitual fighting words and metaphors can instantly destroy months of work spent building the atmosphere of safety and trust that must be present for collaboration to work well. Conversely, creative, conscious use of language can be a potent tool to reframe how the participants think about what they are doing. For instance, consider the dramatically different climate created at the four-way table by meeting a comprehensive settlement proposal from the wife not with the husband's "counterproposal," but rather, with his "upgrade."

Managing Agendas for Success: Clients whose marriages are unraveling generally come to their lawyers at a nadir of effective problem solving as a couple. Indeed, the distance and separation that couples need to achieve as they end their marriages often occur by rejecting the intimacy-based habits and unstated agreements about mutual problem solving that developed during the marital relationship.[10] Your client may come to you bewildered about why every effort to have a civilized discussion about differences results in bitter argument and feeling incompetent to discuss anything at all effectively with the spouse. It is common for a client to hold a deep desire to use the collaborative law process and an equally deep doubt that it could possibly work in this client's particular case. The collaborative lawyer's confidence that this ambivalence is normal and explainable may help a client to overcome doubt and give collaborative law a try.

This phenomenon (the demise of effective problem-solving skills within the couple and the need to rebuild competency and confidence in ways not premised on intimacy) is a key reason why careful agenda management in the early stages of a collaborative representation is so very important.[11] A related phenomenon is the tendency of fearful, anxious clients to fasten on specific issues and to insist upon their immediate resolution, in the mistaken belief that if only this issue can be resolved, fear and anxiety will go away. An issue that is negotiated prematurely will rarely be resolved successfully, and the impact on the collaborative process itself of allowing clients to force inappropriate early agendas is nearly always damaging. If the lawyers confer and shape the early four-way meeting agendas so that each early meeting ends with success and hot-button issues are deferred, most clients relax, begin to feel confidence, and feel renewed competence to tackle and solve increasingly challenging problems with the spouse. Conversely, if the clients' anxieties are allowed to control agendas, so that difficult issues are tackled before adequate competency and confidence have been built, it is likely that each client's worst fears will be realized, and the process will terminate without an agreement. Metaphors—particularly, "the forest and trees" and "the three-legged race"—are helpful in explaining the importance of agenda-management to clients.[12]

Reinforcing and Mirroring Success and Competency: A corollary to agenda management for success is the technique of highlighting collaborative successes as they occur. Our clients may be so anxious during early four-way meetings, preoccupied with worries and fears, focused on a private internal agenda, or so attached to negative expectations for how the spouse will behave, that important moments of grace or generosity may pass unnoticed and unremarked. Good collaborative lawyers are alert to those moments and use a variety of "stop-action" techniques to ensure that all four participants acknowledge and appreciate them when they occur. Think of yourself as operating a theatrical spotlight that you can shine on a participant for a moment. Or, think of the four-way as a videotape with freeze-frame capability. The goal is to highlight each success, each example of an individual or the collaborative team achieving something more than might have been expected. At the end of each four-way, leave time in the agenda for brief reflection on the successes of the meeting and for expressions of appreciation.[13]

Modeling Effective Problem Solving: The fact that each client has a committed, skilled collaborative lawyer at his or her side during all four-way meetings brings an ancillary feature that the lawyers can make good use of, in that each client will witness one and possibly two other adults communicating and reasoning effectively with the spouse and with one another. As a component of rebuilding the clients' competency to resolve issues directly with one another in a new way that does not require intimacy, this modeling function that the collaborative lawyers bring to the table is a valuable benefit of the dispute-resolution process that can add significant value to the invisible estate.

Using the Expanded Professional Team: Once lawyers develop comfort with collaborative law practice, retooling themselves into collaborative rather than adversarial advocates, the next step tends to be recognition of the value of working in new collaborative modes with the other professionals who may counsel clients during a divorce: therapists, child-custody evaluators, forensic accountants, and financial planners. Instead of the possessive turf battles of the adversarial lawyer (who generally sees other professionals as threatening the lawyer's control over the case) or the conflicting signals given to the clients by isolated advisors offering incongruent advice from the perspective of each separate professional discipline, the expanded professional team approach to collaborative practice offers clients a coordinated, consistent, and efficient group of professionals who know how to work together effectively to serve the interests of the restructured post-divorce family in the conflict-resolution process the clients have chosen. The most carefully thought-out and well-structured approach to interdisciplinary professional collaboration is the collaborative divorce team model,[14] which allows clients economical access to communications skills coaches, child-development specialists, and financial professionals trained in collaborative teamwork with the lawyers who provide the collaborative law representation. When this kind of resource is available, collaborative law becomes a feasible dispute-resolution option for a much broader spectrum of clients than is possible without it.[15]

Attention to Physical Space and Logistics: Attention to seemingly small details can have a large effect on a collaborative representation. With the beginner's mind, look at every aspect of where people sit, what they see, what they experience at a physical level during four-way meetings, and what meta-messages you are conveying, intentionally or otherwise. For example, at your first meeting with a new collaborative client, where do you sit? Behind a desk cluttered with files and papers? Or at a clean round conference table? Or on comfortable chairs around a coffee table? Are you in a room filled with evidence of your work on other cases? Or in a conference space designed for comfort and relaxed concentration?[16] What does the client see on the wall: your certificates of admission to various courts? A soothing landscape? A gently humorous cartoon? Are there flowers and plants or only fax machines and computers? It should be obvious that there will be as many answers as there are lawyers. The point is not to manage these matters in only one way, but rather to make decisions about these matters with conscious awareness rather than by default, since each element carries meaning.

Similarly, consider who will sit where during the four-way meetings, and why. Consider what provisions you can make for a comfortable, attractive private caucus space. Consider what will be on the table when people arrive, and why. For example, many collaborative lawyers agree that it is helpful to provide plentiful wholesome food and drink during four-way meetings, arrayed at the center of the four-way table.[17] Discuss in advance whether the clients do better with morning or afternoon meetings[18] and whether it is important to alternate locations for four-way meetings or not.[19]

Attention to the Body/Mind Continuum: Although intellectual work is the stock in trade of the legal four-way meeting process, the best intellectual work is facilitated by paying attention to the physical needs and foibles of the participants as a regular part of your work as a collaborative lawyer. First, at the most basic level, people who are physically uncomfortable are unlikely to relax and be effective at problem solving. It is worth the investment to create a comfortable, relaxed conference space.

Second, people absorb and process information differently. For some, reading information is the most effective channel, while others do better listening. If the information is important, present it via multiple channels (e.g., distribute copies and read aloud as clients follow along; or, accompany a brainstorming session with use of a flip chart to note important points). Some lawyers have large poster boards, or PowerPoint projection capability, that can reinforce oral communications.

Third, even with ample food on the table, clients and lawyers alike may become cranky and inefficient at the tail end of long meetings; agree in advance how long a meeting will last (usually not more than an hour and a half) and stick to the agreement. Trying to add one more item to the day's agenda when all are tired is a recipe for conflict and frustration rather than comfort and success.

Fourth, the body is a source of useful information about the negotiating process: a person who is confident, creative, and enthusiastic sits forward, makes eye contact, and is visibly animated, while a person who is angry or resistant will appear rigid, sit with arms and legs crossed, and otherwise send physical signals. These signals can be subtle as well as obvious; use body language as a monitoring device for how things are going.

Self-monitoring also provides invaluable information to the collaborative lawyer. For example, many lawyers report that when they fall into old-paradigm behaviors, they tense physically and their awareness shrinks to the area above the collar. It is possible with practice to use body awareness to reverse that process, relax oneself, and become more conscious again by taking deep breaths, and directing breath and awareness to the belly and the extremities. Also, it is possible to become aware of physical cues that help one recognize anger or frustration before it grows out of hand and to use breath and body awareness to relax and recover composure.

Finally, the body-mind connection can be used affirmatively to improve what happens during the four-way. For example, clients can be coached to use breathing or other relaxing methods when the lawyer notices signs of tension or distress. Or, the lawyer's careful use of touch—something as simple as a tap on the hand—can help remind clients of agreements or bring awareness of unintended behaviors.

Ceremonial Aspects of Four-Way Meetings: There is reassurance that comes from preparing the client for what will happen, then noting that it is happening, and then summarizing what did happen. Doing these steps consciously can be seen as having a ceremonial function, in the sense that an orderly progression of events is planned, occurs, and is seen to occur. For example, clients are prepared to expect that certain specific procedural steps will take place at the first four-way meeting. At the meeting, they are again told what will occur and each step is identified and highlighted as it takes place. At the end of the meeting, clients are reminded of the importance of what was accomplished.

Post-Meeting Memoranda: It can be difficult to recall late in a collaborative representation exactly what has and has not been agreed to earlier in the process. It can be frustrating to make commitments about information exchange or other between-meetings tasks and have follow-through not occur. A wise habit that becomes a protocol in most collaborative practice groups is to follow each four-way meeting with a memorandum of what took place, what each participant agreed to do next, and what the agenda for the next meeting will be. The responsibility for distributing the memorandum can alternate between the two lawyers. It can be reviewed and corrected by the clients so that an accurate record of the collaborative work is created as a matter of course. Misunderstandings are much easier to straighten out when this technique is used.[20]

Keeping It Moving Forward: One of the potential hazards of collaborative law practice arises from the reality that there is no externally imposed structure or momentum. While the best pacing and schedule will vary from case to case depending on the issues and the stage of grieving and recovery that each client has achieved, it is usually true that at least one of the clients wants speedy movement toward completion. Without court clerks, discovery deadlines, and trial calendars to keep matters moving forward, collaborative lawyers must depend on themselves and their self-imposed rules, protocols, and habits of best practice to protect against cases falling into limbo. One excellent rule of practice is to ensure that at all times, at least three or four forthcoming four-way meetings are on the calendar, even if they may later prove unnecessary and be canceled. Each time a four-way meeting convenes, the agenda should include scheduling additional sessions before the participants adjourn. Something as simple as being sure to bring one's calendar to four-way meetings can make the difference between a smooth and a rocky collaborative process.

The Apparent Impasse and the Magic Moment: In conventional settlement negotiations, whether extended over time or taking place in a single settlement conference, it often occurs that one or more issues reach what appears to be an impasse. At that point, once efforts to resolve the problem have been exhausted (and sometimes much earlier, as part of the strategizing for settlement negotiations), the conventional adversarial lawyer considers resort to judicial decision making—a hearing or a trial. For collaborative lawyers, the disqualification stipulation means that unilateral resort to judicial resolution is the end of the collaborative lawyer's role in the case. For that reason, the collaborative lawyer is far less likely than the conventional lawyer to leap to thoughts of judicial intervention in the face of apparent impasse. The conventional lawyer bears none of the risk of failure when settlement negotiations break down, while the collaborative lawyer shares the risk of failure with the clients. The impact of this fact upon how impasse is handled in collaborative law as distinct from conventional settlement practice is immense and cannot be overstated. In collaborative practice, apparent impasse is simply when the sleeves get rolled up. If all four participants have not understood this fact earlier, this is the time when they face the reality that if a satisfactory solution to the problem is not found, they will never meet again as a problem-solving team because the lawyers will have to withdraw. If, at this moment of apparent impasse, the lawyers are skillful enough, they will simply be quiet and let silence do its work. Far more often than not, as the silence continues, that awareness of having reached the end of the collaboration percolates, and eventually one party or the other is likely to say, "Well, I suppose that. . . ." When that happens, there is an experience of being catapulted into a kind of creative hyperspace where the hard work in Act One of forging the container and building commitment to the process bears fruit, and ideas flow, and solutions emerge. That is why collaborative lawyers often refer to "apparent impasse" and to the "magic moment" that it triggers. It is after experiencing such moments again and again in collaborative practice that lawyers understand the profound creative power of the collaborative model. Without the possibility of disqualification, neither lawyers nor clients would have remained for long in the silence that eventually unblocks the impasse, because their thought processes would long since have moved to planning for motions, hearings, and trials. Without transparency and the commitment to work solely in direct four-way negotiations, the enhanced creative power of simultaneous six-way communications would not be brought to bear on the apparent impasse. With the possibility of disqualification plus transparency, collaborative law again and again triggers the magic moment.[21]

Buyer's Remorse, Seller's Remorse, Advocate's Remorse: Experienced litigators know well the phenomena of buyer's and seller's remorse, the clients' morning-after discomfort about terms of settlement agreed to in courthouse-steps settlement conferences, where the threat of trial is imminent and the pressure to settle can be intense. In effective collaborative law practice, these phenomena are rare, because of the attention paid to appropriate pacing, careful and measured examination of interests and needs, and good-faith transparent bargaining. Hasty settlements do not occur in good collaborative legal practice; careful consideration of all important elements of settlement is a hallmark of good collaborative negotiations. Instead, collaborative lawyers should be alert to the risk of advocate's remorse, a phenomenon specific to collaborative practice that lawyers have begun to notice. It occurs toward the end of the case, when most or all issues have been tentatively resolved, but drafting the agreement remains to be done. At that point, some lawyers become anxious about whether they have advocated vigorously enough on behalf of their client's bottom line, and instead of remaining an advocate for a win-win[22] agreement that both clients find reasonable, they begin to push for a greater piece of the distributive pie on their own client's side of the table.

The key to recognizing this phenomenon for what it is lies in noting whether the drive for a bigger share arises from becoming aware that in some way the interests of the client have not been addressed appropriately, or from the lawyer's fear that he or she has failed as a "real lawyer," one who always gets for one's own client the biggest share of whatever is being distributed. Rarely does the latter orientation produce two clients equally content with the outcome, since obviously both cannot get the biggest piece of each pie. Process is the best remedy in this situation. Instead of yielding to the temptation to jockey for advantage with the other lawyer, confer with your own client in terms of the client's own goals, priorities, and satisfaction with the proposed resolution. If there is a problem, resume collaborative negotiations, and if there is not, get out of the way. A lasting resolution that clients are satisfied with must be a resolution they themselves reach. If you allow yourself to revert to habitual adversarial habits in the third act of the case, you won't be helping your client achieve the good divorce, and your efforts will almost certainly reduce the mutual trust between the two lawyers in future collaborative cases.

Notes

1. My thanks to the thousands of lawyers and mental-health and financial professionals I've trained and practiced with, and particularly to Stu Webb, Larry Wilson, George Richardson, Peggy Thompson, Nancy Ross, John McCall, and Chip Rose, whose perspectives have enriched mine. The collaborative community is generous in sharing ideas. Every time

someone is inspired to solve a new problem in a case and shares the results, whether in a training, or at an IACP Forum, or at a local practice group meeting, or in an article in the COLLABORATIVE REVIEW, the toolbox grows.

2. See Chapter 3 for a deeper discussion of the four paradigm shift questions, and for extended discussion of the four facets of retooling.

3. A client who has no higher intentions for the divorce process, either for himself or for anyone else in the family system, is a poor candidate for success in a collaborative representation because without this perspective as a motivator and process anchor, the collaborative lawyers will lack a vital tool to help clients remember that at times of cortisol flooding, reactive habits replace and can derail careful rational thinking and weighing of priorities and goals. Good collaborative lawyers do not instruct their clients that relational values should matter, or that they should trump more material concerns. Rather, the collaborative process itself invites clients to pay attention to the indisputable fact that the relational estate is often ravaged as collateral damage in family law litigation, without the lawyer ever warning the client about this or asking whether it is an acceptable outcome. We invite clients at the very start of the representation to think about whether destruction of those relational interests is acceptable. We invite them to think about the kind of relationship they want with the ex-partner after the divorce, and how much of a priority that is for them. We educate them about what can happen to children, extended families, and friendship networks if attention is not paid to protecting them during divorce, and we ask whether avoiding thoughtless damage to these interests is of importance. This is part of the clarification of goals and priorities during Act One of a well-managed collaborative case. If the client's answers are that these interests do not matter, or that they pale in comparison to improving the economic bottom line, then collaborative law may not be the best process choice for that client. The lawyer should respectfully but firmly point out the reasons why this is so. If these interests do matter to the client, then the lawyer has a responsibility to advocate, not just with the other party but also with the client, to ensure that the client remembers the value he or she placed on these interests during emotional rough passages in the divorce process. *See* ABA MODEL RULES OF PROFESSIONAL CONDUCT, Rule 2.1, which delineates the lawyer's role as counselor and advisor: "In representing a client, a lawyer shall exercise independent professional judgment and render candid advice. In rendering advice, a lawyer may refer not only to law but to other considerations such as moral, economic, social and political factors, that may be relevant to the client's situation."

4. It is important to remember that divorcing clients often think of lawyers as gladiators or sharks, stereotypes deeply embedded in our culture. They call upon their divorce lawyers not when they are feeling most competent and confident, but rather when they feel most frightened or angry and in need of a hired gun. That is when adversarial lawyers and their clients plan strategies and goals for a divorce representation, and devise the lawyers' marching orders. The client rarely calls back to report that things are going well with the spouse and things look more positive, less gloomy. Clients recovering from the trauma of divorce spend increasingly less time in the shadow states of powerful negative emotion, and increasingly greater time in their more high-functioning pre-divorce state of competency and capacity, as they move forward toward full recovery from the divorce process and a more reliably even state of mind. However, since both clients tend to call upon their respective adversarial lawyers while experiencing transient shadow states of strong emotion, and plan goals and strategies in that fearful and reactive state, it should not be surprising that divorce cases so often slide inexorably toward high-conflict litigation despite the honest assertions of each spouse that he or she wants only a reasonable outcome. When lawyers present this perspective on divorce to potential collaborative clients, using the "shadow client" metaphor and implicitly or explicitly posing the question, "Would you rather make the most important and difficult decisions of your life when you biochemically cannot think straight, or when you can?," clients simply do not say, "Thanks anyway, but I prefer to make major decisions and plan goals and strategies for myself and my children when I am so upset that I cannot think." No client, however distressed or righteously indignant, consciously chooses to make decisions with such long-term and high-stakes consequences from a shadow state when presented with the alternative

of being helped by the lawyer with reminders and cues that could help the client step back, regain a more composed state of mind, and engage in more competent and better-informed divorce decision making. The choice is always the client's, not the lawyer's. There is an old saying that criminal lawyers see bad people at their best, while family lawyers see good people at their worst. The question is whether the lawyer will serve as a wise counselor, reminding the client who identified the "good divorce" as the goal that some choices and behaviors are likely to lead to better outcomes than others—or whether the lawyer will act as an alter-ego warrior for good people at their worst, oblivious to predictable collateral damage and failing to counsel temporarily grieving and angry clients that "this too shall pass."

5. Some collaborative practitioners use a contrarian approach at the start of the case, describing collaborative law as a process requiring the highest ethical intentions and good-faith conduct on both sides, and emphasizing that it certainly is not for every client or every divorce. Most clients, hearing this, will prefer to see themselves as a person who wants and can do collaborative law. In other words, they will reach for highest intentions rather than focusing on fear and anger. Their hesitancies, if any, will usually concern whether their spouse is or is not capable of these high-level process undertakings.

From that perspective, holding out high expectations for how one must behave in order to be likely to succeed in collaborative law and to achieve the "good divorce" encourages distressed clients to understand that they are in fact (whether the lawyer points it out or not) making process choices at the start of a divorce that have immense implications for better or worse outcomes for themselves and their children. Inviting clients to decide consciously and carefully whether they prefer to proceed from best hopes or from worst fears, in a situation where both possibilities exist as driving forces for the divorce, and where the consequences of operating from fear rather than hope can have a significant negative impact on the client's ability to move through the divorce and into a healthy restructured life, surely is important and responsible legal advice and counsel. Surely a lawyer who fails to provide this kind of advice at the start of the representation about the predictable consequences of conflict-resolution process choices is failing to give divorcing clients vital information that the lawyer has, and the client lacks.

Collaborative lawyers should not be mindless Pollyannas about the choice of collaborative law. Some clients and some couples don't have a sufficient commitment to the good-faith, interest-based approach of collaborative practice for the chances of success to be good. Collaborative lawyers ought to be confident they can help the client make the collaborative journey to "the good divorce," before agreeing to provide collaborative representation. But inviting clients to reach for the best rather than fearing the worst is not inconsistent with such realistic assessment by the lawyer.

6. Clients can be educated about negotiating styles in a manner that helps them think more clearly about the most effective way to present their goals in the collaborative process. They can, for instance, be given workbooks that help them transform positions into interests, such as ROGER FISHER & DANNY ERTEL, GETTING READY TO NEGOTIATE: THE GETTING TO YES WORKBOOK (1995). Excellent training courses to help lawyers develop interest-based bargaining skills are readily available, and completing at least 30 hours of such training is part of the minimum standards for collaborative lawyers adopted by the International Academy of Collaborative Professionals.

7. An outstanding book on interest-based bargaining is ROBERT H. MNOOKIN, SCOTT R. PEPPET, & ANDREW S. TULUMELLO, BEYOND WINNING: HOW LAWYERS HELP CLIENTS CREATE VALUE IN NEGOTIATIONS (2000). See the bibliography at Appendix I for further resources from the substantial literature on this subject that are of particular value in collaborative practice.

8. TANNEN, YOU JUST DON'T UNDERSTAND (1990).

9. TANNEN, THE ARGUMENT CULTURE: MOVING FROM DEBATE TO DIALOGUE (1998).

10. I am indebted to my colleague Larry Wilson for sharing his ideas about the connection between ending intimacy-based behavior as part of the emotional divorce process, and rejecting the problem-solving habits that existed during the marriage.

11. This is because clients usually are anxious and uncomfortable in the first meeting with the other spouse and lawyer, and in a poor state of mind to address problematic mat-

ters. Their recent history as a couple may well have been characterized by failure to agree and consequent bickering or even rage, a history that gives rise to pessimism or fear about their competency as a couple to resolve their own issues without judicial intervention. That recent history and resulting anxiety can be allayed by experiencing one or two successful collaborative four-way meetings before difficult tasks are tackled. Meeting the other lawyer, coming together as a working team, reiterating the process agreements that all agree to be bound by, explaining negotiating theory and the dispute-resolution continuum, assigning homework, and planning a schedule of meetings and a specific agenda for the next meeting all take time—usually at least an hour and a half to two hours to do well. Tackling actual negotiations at that point (or even worse, before any process agreements have been confirmed) rarely results in success and can damage the prospects for a successful collaborative representation, sometimes irreparably. Waiting until the clients have experienced a successful first meeting, and have relaxed into the process, is in the long run a safer as well as more efficient approach. If each meeting is structured to maximize the prospects for comfort and success, then by the time the harder issues appear on the agenda, the clients are likely to be more comfortable with the process and more capable of engaging in the kind of interest-based bargaining that leads to agreements. One does not ensure a speedy, efficient process by rushing into difficult negotiations prematurely. In the words of my high school Latin teacher, "Festina lente"—"Make haste slowly." Or, as Midwestern farmers say, "You've got to plow, plant, water, and weed before you can harvest."

12. See Appendix I, *infra*.

13. With some especially contentious couples, the main successes in the early stages of collaboration may be little more than avoiding active argument, honoring the planned agenda, and scheduling the next meeting. Don't make the mistake of minimizing those achievements; for this couple at this moment, those achievements may have taken enormous focus and self-control. It may have taken a great deal of work with their lawyers to agree not to leap prematurely into conflict over substantive issues. Acknowledging the fruits of the clients' efforts at self-control and cooperation is positive reinforcement that may make it easier for them to accomplish more next time.

14. Information about the model can be found at the IACP website, www.collaborative practice.com and in TESLER & THOMPSON, COLLABORATIVE DIVORCE: THE REVOLUTIONARY NEW WAY TO RESTRUCTURE YOUR FAMILY, RESOLVE LEGAL ISSUES, AND MOVE ON WITH YOUR LIFE (2006). The IACP website also maintains a calendar of trainings for professionals, including interdisciplinary team training.

15. It is not unusual for clients to be drawn to the idea of a good divorce and yet lack the emotional balance or the communications skills to be able to work effectively at the collaborative four-way table. Skilled collaborative lawyers can redress some of these imbalances, but the more challenging the clients, the less sufficient the skills of lawyers alone will be in facilitating effective collaborative negotiations. Trained communications skills coaches and child-development specialists can provide the expanded and reinforced container that might allow clients to function in the collaborative process when they would fail at it without that resource. Or, it may be that one or both parties to the divorce has an emotional or cognitive disorder that requires extra assistance in order for the lawyers to be able to provide good-faith collaborative representation. Again, mental-health professionals trained in the coaching function of collaborative divorce practice can sometimes make it possible for the clients to achieve the good divorce. The work of collaborative divorce coaches is entirely different from conventional therapy, just as collaborative law is entirely different from litigation. A therapist who has not been trained in collaborative divorce practice will not have the specific skills required to work effectively in a team model. IACP has promulgated standards for each of the professions, financial and mental-health, who participate in a full collaborative divorce team. Standards for practitioners and trainings can be found at www.collaborativepractice .com; navigate to the "Standards" section of the website.

16. In some communities—for instance, Minneapolis, Minn., and Santa Rosa and San Diego, Calif.—collaborative lawyers and other professionals have located their offices under

the same roof to facilitate clients' access to interdisciplinary collaborative services. In some instances the various collaborative professionals share conference facilities.

17. First, food ensures that the anxious client who could not eat before the meeting will have sufficient energy for the event. Second, chewing on nuts or chips helps many people discharge tension. Third, and perhaps most important, breaking bread together seems demonstrably to elevate standards of civility—perhaps triggering childhood memories of parents admonishing that we do not squabble at the dinner table.

18. Many clients, when asked, reveal difficulty sleeping at night during the divorce process and may be far more effective participants at meetings if their preferences are considered regarding time of day for meetings.

19. Some clients attach ideas of fairness or balance to the notion of alternating the meeting location at each lawyer's office. Others place higher value on meeting at the most convenient location for most participants. Some like the comfort of one office over the other. The lawyers should not automatically assume that clients prefer to alternate offices.

20. In the author's practice group, one meeting was dedicated to looking at post-meeting memoranda prepared by a number of members of the group. The differences were considerable. Some lawyers included mention of every subject discussed at the four-way, while others noted only major topics. Some recited the differences that preceded agreement, while others recorded only the agreements that were reached. Some aimed for very brief minutes, while others aimed for as complete a record of the conversation as possible. One lawyer used as a header for all his minutes the "mission statements" or "statements of highest purpose" that the clients had identified very early in the collaborative representation. One lawyer used a bold font to highlight all action items. Some lawyers distributed the minutes to lawyers and clients via e-mail, requesting errata to be sent via "reply all," while others expected minutes to be reviewed and edited by the lawyers until both were satisfied, before e-mail distribution to the parties. Having such a discussion with your colleagues in the practice group will improve the quality of memoranda and avoid misunderstandings.

21. Some commentators have worried that because collaborative lawyers cannot take matters to court, they will become so determined to reach settlement that they will coerce their clients into agreements the clients don't really want. This concern is not taken as a serious issue by lawyers experienced in collaborative practice because of the emphasis good practitioners place on client responsibility for decision making, and the corollary emphasis on lawyers detaching from outcome as a measure of their success in collaborative practice. Their view is supported by the absence of any malpractice filings against collaborative lawyers in the 18 years from the inception of the model through the date of this second edition. In any case, an imagined tension between the interest of a collaborative lawyer in encouraging a client to continue to work toward collaborative resolution, and the possible interest of a client in terminating the process because of a hope that litigation might yield a better outcome, is no different than the tensions that exist in any professional relationship between the interests of the professional and the interests of the client. For instance,

> "... it is frequently the case that (a) litigation counsel have a vested interest in avoiding settlement if they are paid on an hourly basis, and (b) counsel retained on a regular basis by the same insurer could be perceived as having a vested interest in satisfying the insurer when the lawyer's sole duty must be to the insured. These and many other examples point to the fact that our legal system requires us to place enormous trust in the fiduciary responsibility of workaday lawyers whose financial interests are often in tension with those of their clients." IACP Ethics Task Force [D. Hoffman, P. Sandmann, D. Diehl, P. Tesler, D. Royall, N. Cameron, S. Hansen], *The Ethics of the Collaborative Participation Agreement: A Critique of Colorado's Maverick Ethics Opinion* (2007), p. 5, http://www.collaborativepractice .com/documents/IACPEthicsTaskForcearticle.pdf.

22. "Win/win is an attitude, not an outcome." Don Boyd

Chapter 6

Key Moments in a Collaborative Representation

"It is not what a lawyer tells me I may do; but what humanity, reason and justice tell me I ought to do." —Edmund Burke

Making First Contacts with Other Participants

Now that you have some understanding of the stages of a collaborative representation, the transformations required to become an effective collaborative advocate, and some of the new tools and concepts you will be applying in your collaborative work, let us examine in more depth some considerations to bear in mind when making first contact with your own client, the other party, the other lawyer, and the other collaborative professionals who may become involved in the case.

1. First Communications with Your Client

A collaborative case begins with the first inquiry from the potential client. At least three different tasks go on simultaneously as the lawyer handles these initial communications. First, what you say and how you say it in these early communications will determine whether the client seriously considers selecting the collaborative process or not. Second, and perhaps even more important, viewing each communication as an opportunity to lay pieces of the foundation for a successful collaborative process helps create the paradigm shift, in both lawyers and clients, that makes the collaborative process work. And third, the lawyer is eliciting screening information that forms the basis for deciding whether you can conscientiously recommend collaborative law for the client and, if so, whether you yourself want to be the lawyer who goes on the collaborative journey in this particular case.

Because every communication with the client matters, think through and set up a system for how initial client inquiries will be handled and who in your office will have what responsibilities, to ensure that you and your staff are giving out informative, consistent, and confident responses about collaborative law.

In our office, the support staff asks all potential family law clients whether they are aware of collaborative law and our office's commitment to it, and whether they would like to receive our information packet about it. If possible, we send out this packet so that it can be read and considered before the client's first conversation with a lawyer. We also give potential clients the link to our firm's website and blog, where they can find more information about our collaborative practice, and other links about collaborative divorce that they can suggest to their spouses or partners. Support staff fill out a brief questionnaire (see Appendix I for a sample form) to elicit basic screening information before the lawyer's first conversation with the client, which can be by telephone or at a scheduled consultation. This form includes information about whether the spouse is represented and by whom, whether any court papers have been filed, how the client heard about our firm, and whether there are any issues requiring urgent attention.[1] The form also asks how the client learned about collaborative law. These questions will give you useful information about referral sources, how widely the model has been disseminated in your community, and about your client's potential misconceptions about divorce and collaborative representation.[2]

Once the client has received and reviewed the collaborative law information packet, the first consultation between lawyer and client sets the stage for both to decide whether the case is appropriate for collaborative representation. The dialogue in the first meeting educates the client about the divorce process, conflict-resolution options generally, and collaborative law specifically, so that the client can make an intelligent decision about whether the collaborative law process is likely to serve him well. The dialogue also yields information directly and indirectly that helps the lawyer decide whether or not to recommend that the client go forward with collaborative law. Many clients will want to discuss how to engage the other party.

Persuading a client to try collaborative law in the face of resistance or hesitancy is always a mistake. The key to success in collaborative representation is the degree of commitment of both parties at the start and the ultimate ability of all participants to say "yes" to an outcome that inevitably will be less than 100 percent of everything the client might have wished for at the start of the divorce. Persistent hesitancies at the start signal less-than-wholehearted commitment to the process.

SCREENING COLLABORATIVE LAW CLIENTS

Is there a way to tell at the start which clients will benefit from collaborative representation, and which clients would be better off not trying it? Is there a profile of the ideal collaborative client, and of the clients who are sure to terminate the process without reaching agreement? We have no reliable predictive screen, but there are common-sense guidelines.

- Couples who come to collaborative lawyers with a commitment to avoid litigation, and who express genuine respect for and trust in one another, usually do well in collaborative law. They tend to do well however they decide to handle their divorce.

- People who express strong commitment to positive co-parenting of children after the divorce can do well in collaborative law.

- People who need to blame others for all the problems they are facing without a willingness to accept personal responsibility for their part in the situation tend to do poorly in collaborative law, just as they do poorly in other dispute-resolution models, though with skilled collaborative mental-health coaching or counseling they may be able to make effective use of the process.

- People who are in the very early stages of the grief/recovery process may present problems in any modality, including collaborative law, because of their need to proceed slowly. Experienced collaborative lawyers working together with collaborative divorce coaches can make collaborative law a feasible option in such cases, though it will be particularly important that the lawyers work well together and that the other spouse be a good candidate for collaborative work.

- People who have great difficulty managing their emotions will have difficulty handling the stresses of collaborative four-way negotiating sessions. Skilled collaborative lawyers and collaborative divorce coaches may be able to help them make the process work. Sometimes face-to-face collaborative meetings may prove too challenging for these clients, in which situation "friendly negotiations" by traditional lawyers may provide necessary distancing and may be a more feasible option. Candid in-depth discussion of this factor can help clients make an appropriate process choice.

- Active domestic violence presents very serious problems for collaborative lawyers—as for all professional helpers. Collaborative lawyers working on their own should exercise great caution in taking on such matters. Domestic violence advocates point out that coercive judicial orders are not self-effectuating and may in fact provoke violence, for which reason many believe that with a full interdisciplinary collaborative team on board, collaborative divorce may be the best available option for the victim, inasmuch as it provides containment, congruent professional services, and the opportunity for consensual interventions to address the violence. The client who is at risk of harm must be carefully counseled about risks and benefits of each choice and lawyers should insist the client make the ultimate process choice. The choice is two-part: If the client wants a collaborative divorce, you must then decide if you have the skills to be the collaborative lawyer for this client. If not, make an appropriate referral.

- People with serious psychiatric diagnoses (e.g., major depression, bipolar disorder) that are unresponsive to medication tend to do poorly in the collaborative process.

- People with character disorders (e.g., borderline or histrionic personality disorder) and/or substance abuse problems tend to have difficulty keeping the commitments central to the collaborative process. Such clients are challenging for any professional to work with. Unless the client is willing to include a full collaborative divorce team, think carefully about taking on such a case collaboratively, because of the higher risk that it will terminate short of full agreement. Even a full team can be challenged greatly by such clients.

- Take easy cases at first, while you build your skills. After a while, you may be comfortable providing collaborative divorce services even with unlikely clients. Few of them will be better off in court. Some of them will surprise you with their ability to rise to the occasion, particularly with the support of an interdisciplinary collaborative divorce team.

What works better than persuasion is sound information presented with enthusiasm and confidence. In our firm, family law clients always learn in their first consultation about the entire spectrum of process choices people have for resolving the divorce-related issues facing them.[3] Rather than urging the prospective client to choose mediation, collaborative law, "unbundling," or traditional representation, the emphasis in the first meeting is on self-selection founded upon full information.[4] Clients frequently are confused about the differences and cannot make informed choices until they understand each model clearly enough to self-select intelligently. The client learns what each conflict-resolution mode consists of, what kinds of people typically do well with each mode, the benefits, challenges, and risk factors (including emotional and relational costs) associated with each approach, and the typical range of expense and duration of process experienced by others who have selected each mode.

Particular attention is paid to distinguishing collaborative law from mediation, and from traditional settlements. Some points usually covered in the first interview and again just prior to the first four-way meeting include these:

- Litigation invariably polarizes the parties and by its nature casts issues in oversimplified black-and-white terms. It is almost always bad for children. Rarely is either litigant happy with the outcome, and rare is the family that can afford litigation economically. Dissatisfaction with results and financial ruin are commonplace consequences of litigation, which dispenses certainty and crude equity, but not "justice."

- Mediation[5] involves a single professional who must maintain neutrality both as a matter of professional ethics and as a practical necessity in order to remain effective. Independent legal advice and advocacy enter the process in many jurisdictions only from outside the mediation room. In collaborative law, the two legal advocates are intimately involved in the negotiations, solely for the purpose of helping to forge a satisfactory settlement, and the protocols for collaborative practice in the community will generally be well known to practitioners because of membership in practice groups.

- Mediation typically works best where the clients feel some degree of comfort negotiating face-to-face, have similar levels of information about family finances, have basic respect for one another, and are similarly comfortable about—or at least accepting of—the need for a divorce, because of the absence of an ally/advisor participating at the client's side in most forms of divorce mediation.

- Divorce mediation is often associated with speed and economy, and many mediators aim expressly to help the parties arrive at an agreement both parties are willing to sign, as soon as possible.

- In collaborative divorces, the direct involvement of legal advocates at every stage, and the widespread availability of trained interdisciplinary collaborative divorce teams working together with collaborative lawyers in a clearly defined structure, can level the playing field in ways that a mediator might find difficult to achieve: for example, where there are strong imbalances in emotional reaction to the breakup, stages of adjustment to it, or sophistication about money matters. In other words, collaborative law expands the universe of clients for whom the good divorce may be a realistic goal, in a way that mediation, from a structural perspective, does not.[6]

- Because there are two skilled advocate/problem solvers present who will fail to achieve the clients' goals if they do not facilitate effectively the clients' efforts to arrive at acceptable solutions, the potential for creative outcomes is enhanced in the collaborative process. Because each lawyer interacts in the negotiation process with his or her own client, the other lawyer, and the other party, a rich gathering

of intellectual and creative resources is brought to bear on solving
the problem. Structurally, collaborative law always builds in two
problem solvers as compared to one in mediation, and when the
interdisciplinary team is added to the mix, the coordinated and specialized professional problem-solving resources available to collaborative clients simply cannot be matched by other conflict-resolution
modalities.

- Traditional settlements (and even mediations in some locales) often
take place at or close to the time of trial, by which time considerable friction and expense will already have been generated. Collaborative legal representation is a "front-end" pre-litigation modality
with a sole agenda of finding the way to a settlement that satisfies
all, entirely outside the court system. Commitments of good faith,
full disclosure, and attention to the legitimate needs of both parties
help avert runaway conflicts before they begin. When collaborative
divorce coaching is part of the process, conflict-management techniques can become very sophisticated and can help a very broad
range of clients reach the "good divorce."

- Traditional legal counsel tend to weigh each issue in light of the
probable outcome if it were litigated. The scope of thinking and
discussion is bounded by the jurisdictional limits of the family law
court, and the timing and content of work on the client's case—
whether it ultimately settles or not—are governed to a greater or
lesser degree by the procedural rules of litigation in the jurisdiction.
These factors narrow the scope of creative lateral thinking, so that
the results may typically be less imaginative and less individually
tailored than the results of a collaborative negotiation.

- Collaborative representation works best when there is trust in the
fundamental honesty of the other party. Parties may be angry or
disappointed but will still usually have a fairly reliable sense of
whether they can trust the other to tell the truth about money,
assets, and other material facts concerning the legal divorce. Without that baseline trust in the other's honesty, the collaborative process cannot work well. As the old saying goes, "Praise Allah and
tether your camel." Collaborative practitioners gather the same
financial documents that a traditional lawyer would assemble for
informed settlement negotiations. As a best practice, collaborative lawyers (and the collaborative financial consultant or neutral
CPA, if any) insist that all questions of either spouse must be fully

answered before negotiations for resolution will begin.[7] It is common for suspicion to evaporate during this collaborative disclosure process, and if it does not, responsible collaborative lawyers will consider whether bad-faith concealment is happening and will recommend termination if it is.

- For the collaborative process to work most effectively, each client must have some goals in the divorce that are more profound than merely maximizing his or her share of immediately quantifiable "goodies." Such goals might include: remaining friendly with the other party after resolution of divorce issues, being able to co-parent children with mutual trust and respect, being able to retain positive connections with in-laws and extended family, completing the divorce process with a sense of personal integrity and self-respect, wishing to ensure that the other spouse is adequately provided for, being able to meet the former spouse at marriages, births, graduations, and other life passages without tension or anger, raising children to the maximum degree possible in a conflict-free zone after the divorce, and many more. Best practice in many collaborative communities is for the lawyers to encourage their clients to articulate these higher intentions at the first or second four-way meeting, as part of the "Act One" process of commitment to collaborative divorce. These statements then become part of the minutes that are the ongoing record of the work accomplished, and will often be referred back to as part of evaluating and choosing among options for resolution.

- If either party lacks a substantial reason for choosing collaborative law, there may be problems ahead during the inevitable rough spots in negotiations. Problems can include bad-faith participation, delay, lack of follow-through, and other difficulties. The collaborative lawyers and other collaborative professionals may or may not be able to work effectively with such a person.

Described in these concrete terms, the various options for divorce dispute resolution become comprehensible to the client in a way that makes intelligent choices possible. The lawyer can express conviction and optimism about the advantages of collaborative law in an appropriate situation, with people who are well-suited to it, without trying to sell it to the particular client sitting in the room. A realistic picture of the advantages and disadvantages of each choice is presented, and in effect, the lawyer holds before the client a picture of the kind of person who is likely to flourish with collaborative representation, with the client responsible for deciding how closely he or she resembles that picture. If the client has reservations about selecting collaborative law, he or she may be saying, "I don't see myself in the picture you are drawing for me." In that case, it is wiser for the lawyer to agree that the client's situation might not be well-fitted to the collaborative model than to persuade the client to put aside the concern. Indeed, it often happens that a somewhat contrarian approach (for instance, "It may be that your goals are more focused toward money at this point than toward the kinds of unquantifiable relationship benefits that need to be considered important for collaborative law to work well") elicits from the client more interest in collaborative law than persuasion ever could.

Once the client expresses informed interest in the collaborative law process, the lawyer must ensure that the client understands the seriousness of the specific commitments involved. The client needs to know, for instance, that he or she loses his or her own lawyer and must retain new litigation counsel if the collaborative process fails to reach satisfactory agreements. If money is in short supply, spending resources on a collaborative process that terminates badly may leave the client without sufficient funds to pay the retainer of litigation counsel.[8] It is also essential to stress the degree of good faith that will be expected on both sides: full voluntary disclosure of all relevant facts, good-faith attention to meeting the legitimate needs of both parties to the extent feasible to do so, maintaining the highest fiduciary duties to the other spouse throughout the negotiating process, correcting any errors or mistakes rather than taking advantage of them, and so forth. This means going line by line through your retainer or engagement letter and through the "Principles and Guidelines for Collaborative Law" with the client, ensuring that the client understands and accepts fully the undertakings he or she would be making.[9]

Perhaps most important of all as a foundation for successful collaborative representation, the lawyer must emphasize from the start—and repeat as the representation proceeds—the differences between "position-based" and "interest-based" bargaining. The client must understand and accept that the lawyer's work will be unlike traditional alter-ego gladiatorial advocacy. A good collaborative lawyer will always begin by sorting out priorities and goals with the client and then peeling back the onion concerning positions the client initially expresses to expose the interests—the real needs—that the client believes would be served if the stated position prevailed. The lawyer and client work together to refine goals that seem potentially achievable from the practical perspective. They work to refine goals that will meet the

EXPANDING THE PIE IN INTEREST-BASED NEGOTIATIONS: THE STORY OF THE ORANGE*

The story of the orange helps clients understand the creative potential of interest-based conflict resolution and helps them see why leaping to obvious solutions without first exploring facts and interests fully can lead to less satisfactory outcomes.

Imagine that the entire marital estate in the divorce of John and Mary consists of one large, ripe, juicy orange. Their two conventional divorce lawyers "know" that in their jurisdiction, the judge is going to just cut that orange in half. Or maybe if John were really unlucky and Mary were really lucky, she might get 51 percent, but the high litigation fees and costs involved in a trial would eat up the value of her possible larger share. So each lawyer urges each client to save themselves a lot of time and money by signing an agreement for an equal split of the orange—after all, that's what's going to happen in court anyhow, so let's just get it done, they urge. John and Mary reluctantly sign, and both lawyers feel proud of their efficiency and commitment to quick pretrial settlement. But back at their respective law offices, John's lawyer can see that John is very unhappy with the settlement, and Mary's lawyer sees that Mary is, too.

"What's wrong?" the lawyers ask. "I got you just what the judge would have ordered, and I saved you thousands of dollars in fees and months of stress and waiting."

"Well," Mary tells her lawyer, "I like to make potpourri. What am I going to do with all that wet pulp?" John, meanwhile, tells his lawyer, "I really like orange juice. What am I going to do with all that peel?"

A process that began with listening to John and Mary, rather than telling them what the legal-template solution was likely to be, would have given John and Mary each 100% of what they wanted.

---

*Adaptation of a teaching story about interest-based bargaining, which appears in ROGER FISHER, WILLIAM URY & BRUCE PATTON, GETTING TO YES: NEGOTIATING AGREEMENT WITHOUT GIVING IN (1991).

client's needs in a creative, efficient manner, and that can perhaps be seen as appropriate by the other side. The lawyer, in other words, will not act as a hired gun. No goal or priority will be addressed in negotiations with the other spouse until the lawyer and client, together, sort out how the client's real, long-term human needs will be served by an agreement that includes the identified item and can explain that need in a way that any reasonable person can be expected to understand. The client must accept from the start that the negotiations in collaborative law are not horse trading, not poker playing, not threat-based, and not the Mediterranean-style bazaar bargaining. Negotiations in a collaborative representation begin and end with goals and priorities that have internal integrity. The client is encouraged to ask for everything he or she really needs—no less, and no more.[10]

To do this, the client will need to appreciate the differences between short-term and long-term benefits, between quantifiable and nonquantifiable goals, and between narrowly defined immediate self-interest and longer-term, more enlightened self-interest.[11] Few divorcing clients arrive at the lawyer's office with an evolved understanding of these matters. But many can be educated to see the overriding importance these understandings can have for the quality of their lives after the divorce is long over. The lawyer's understanding of the avoidable tragedies that occur when divorces are hotly litigated is important knowledge from the trenches that only we can bring to help our clients make intelligent choices about what kind of divorce they want to have.

Covering all this ground in the initial meetings with the client will take time—perhaps a good deal more time than family lawyers are used to devoting to preliminary matters in conventional divorce representation. In cases where a judge will decide pendente lite support and custody matters via an early motion filed on behalf of your client, it is not terribly important or

STARTING ON THE RIGHT FOOT WITH YOUR CLIENT

Goals and strategies for the first meeting with your client:

- Establish rapport
- Establish clear roles for the lawyer and client in the collaborative process
- Place responsibility on the client for achieving the "good divorce"—with your help
- Provide full information about the menu of conflict-resolution process options so that the client can self-select a mode intelligently
- Ask open-ended questions to help you assess the client's appropriateness for the collaborative process
- Discuss how to engage the other spouse in the collaborative process
- Listen for interests rather than spotting issues
- Help the client peel the onion from positions to interests
- Engage the client in understanding the function and value of the interdisciplinary collaborative divorce team
- Express new-paradigm values in what you say and how you say it

BASIC COMMUNICATIONS SKILLS
FOR LAWYERS AND CLIENTS

SPEAKING SKILLS:

- Make "I" statements, not "you" statements.

- State what you observe with your senses. (For example, "I noticed that twice this month times that were scheduled for the children to be with you simply did not happen.")

- State how you feel about what you observe. (For example, "I feel worried and unhappy about this.")

- State what you think about what you observe. (For example, "I think it is bad for the children to have scheduled time with you that does not happen.")

- State what you would like to do about what you observe. (For example, "I want you to propose a schedule that could be put into place for visits that would not result in the children being disappointed in that way.")

- Avoid using the terms "fair" and "unfair." Words like "acceptable," "workable," "agreeable," and their converses, "unacceptable," "unworkable," "not agreeable" are preferable in that they allow room for reasonable people to differ.

LISTENING SKILLS:

- Listen fully while the other person speaks; avoid thinking about your reply until the speaker has finished.

- Ask for more information on any points that aren't completely clear to you.

- Check out how accurately you understand what the speaker said by restating your understanding in different words.

- Ask for more information.

- Keep doing these steps until the speaker agrees that you have fully understood what was said and what was meant.

- Remember, you can say "I understand" without meaning "I agree."

useful to be surgically precise about the difference between your client's wants and needs or positions and interests. In the collaborative process, attention to these distinctions from the beginning of the representation is a foundation for mutual trust and an effective working relationship between lawyer and client and is essential if the parties are to arrive at mutually acceptable agreements.

2. First Contacts with the Other Party

In many instances, your client will be the first to explore collaborative law and will ask you how to involve the other party in a collaborative representation. Sometimes your client will already have discussed collaboration with the partner and will know that both intend to select collaborative law. In that instance, your task is easy. You may advise your client to suggest that the other party select collaborative counsel—ideally from your own practice group—and have the other lawyer contact you to begin the process. Or, circumstances may dictate filing a divorce petition for your client (in propria persona, of course) and mailing it to the other party with a friendly cover letter including information about collaborative law and a suggestion that he or she consider choosing collaborative counsel.[12] Your client may take an information packet, or one of the *Collaborative Divorce* books you have in bulk supply in your conference room, to the spouse, or may ask a trusted friend to pass it on. Or your client may simply ask that an information packet or book, with an explanatory cover letter, be sent to the other party. Any of these steps can result in the other party contacting your office to ask for information, referrals, or the like.

Occasionally, clients ask for a joint informational meeting with one lawyer where collaborative law and other dispute-resolution options are explained. So long as the parties are clear that joint representation is not possible and that you can represent only one of them, this may be an acceptable approach, provided they execute the necessary releases. Indeed, sometimes clients have been known to toss a coin after such meetings to decide which party will be represented by that lawyer and which will select some other collaborative lawyer. Be careful to conform to ethical mandates of your state in responding to requests for a joint meeting with you.

When communicating with a party that you will not be representing before that person has legal counsel, pay special attention to avoid the habits of "lawyer speak" and curtness that can grow out of years of attention to our professional obligation not to take advantage of unrepresented parties and not to communicate directly with parties represented by counsel. It is easy for brusque words, impatience, or inadvertent adversarial language to creep into communications with the other party, poisoning the well before the collaborative process ever begins. If this should happen in any of your cases, immediate and sincere apologies and an explanation of how unconscious adversarial behaviors are the "clay feet" of lawyers learning to practice collaboratively may rescue the case from falling out of the collaborative model.

ROAD MAP OF A COLLABORATIVE CASE

- First meeting(s) with the client and retention of the lawyer.
- First contact with the other party and/or other lawyer.
- First four-way and associated pre-meetings and debriefings: setting the container.
- Mid-game four-ways and associated pre-meetings and debriefings: "walk around the estate," gather and exchange information, involve neutrals, brainstorm, evaluate options, float and negotiate proposals, get to "yes."
- Draft and revise documents.
- Final four-way: review, sign, appreciate, anticipate, evaluate, celebrate.
- Final file-stamped paperwork distributed to participants and asset transfers completed.
- Lawyers and other professionals remain available to assist during period of rapid change following entry of judgment.
- Lawyer's file is closed.

Sometimes a client will ask you to recommend specific collaborative lawyers to the other party. Since selecting two lawyers with a good track record of working well together is one of the best predictors of a successful collaborative process, lawyers may want to offer an annotated practice group membership list, indicating those with whom one works most effectively. Bear in mind, this can backfire. The other spouse may use that list to eliminate any lawyer that is perceived as too closely aligned with you, the initiating spouse's counsel. Also, of course, it is important to provide a long enough list that there is no appearance of having selected the other party's counsel for him or her.

Sooner or later you are likely to encounter a situation in which your client tells you that the other party simply will not retain any counsel at all (this often happens if the other party is a lawyer himself or herself). Remember: It is not possible to provide collaborative law representation unless both parties are represented by collaborative counsel pursuant to a disqualification stipulation and it is important to make this fact clear to clients. You may be able to provide capable, civilized dispute-resolution assistance in other ways, but you will not be providing collaborative law services unless there are collaborative lawyers on both sides of the matter who work with their own clients to facilitate constructive conflict resolution, pursuant to an agreement that the lawyers can never go to court in that case.

Also fairly common is the client's fear that the other spouse will be unwilling to select collaborative law, or incapable of participating effectively in a collaborative process. Since neither you nor your client has any control over whether these fears materialize or not, it is generally sufficient to counsel your client that surprises are common in divorce. One surprise might be the spouse's willingness to try collaboration, once provided with the necessary information. If your client paints a picture of a fundamentally dishonest spouse, or one with a character disorder or serious emotional or behavioral disturbance, use caution in advising going forward collaboratively even if the other spouse selects collaboration, since you may later need to withdraw or terminate the process and your client will lose you as counsel.[13]

3. First Contacts with the Other Collaborative Lawyer

Whether you are the first or second lawyer retained in the case; whether the first overtures are made by you or the other collaborative lawyer; whether you know the other lawyer well or not at all; whether you have a good, mediocre, or poor working relationship with the other lawyer; all these factors require conscious attention as you and the other lawyer take first steps toward forging the working relationship that will sustain you and the clients through the collaborative representation. Some considerations to bear in mind during these first communications with the other lawyer include:

- If you haven't worked together before, or if prior encounters have been less than satisfactory, would it be wise to begin with a meeting over lunch or coffee to forge a smoother professional connection? Do you need to process or apologize for anything that occurred in a prior encounter? Do you need to propose a mentoring agreement in case difficulties arise in this case?[14]

- What documentation, protocols, and ground rules will be in place during this representation? Who will prepare initial paperwork? Will there be alternating responsibility for post-meeting memoranda? How and when will these memoranda be distributed, and how will errors be addressed? Will agendas be considered inviolable except by agreement? Is there an agreement to confer before each four-way meeting?

- Whose client is further along in the divorce-recovery process? Whose client has greater financial and other resources? Does either client have emotional issues or other hot-button concerns that the other lawyer needs to be aware of? These and similar potential imbalances and destabilizing forces need to be discussed transparently between counsel from the very first communications.

- Will the other lawyer cooperate with you in agenda management and conflict management understandings? Do you have agreement about the procedural agenda for the first four-way meeting? How will you handle urgent temporary support and parenting matters to stabilize circumstances while avoiding premature negotiation of difficult issues?
- If the other lawyer is relatively new to collaborative practice, do you have a plan for how to work effectively in collaboration with that lawyer and the clients without patronizing him or her?
- Have you considered proposing a side agreement that anticipates and provides a means for resolving potential future difficulties between counsel, such as a designated mediator or mentor, retained at the lawyers' expense to recalibrate counsel to effective communications?
- Have you and the other lawyer worked out understandings about how to deal with typical problems that might arise during the representation?
- How will client delays or bad faith be handled by counsel? Does the other lawyer share your explicit commitment to withdraw and/or terminate the process if one's own client is in persistent bad faith?
- Do you feel sufficient confidence in your ability to collaborate with this lawyer to go forward with a formal collaborative representation?

4. First Contacts with Other Collaborative Professionals

During Act One (opening moves) of a collaborative case, the clients will be encouraged to consider working with a full interdisciplinary collaborative divorce team. Many practice group protocols now include the expectation that clients will have at least one preliminary interview with collaborative divorce coaches during Act One, so that this decision will be fully informed.[15] During Act Two, the work of the interdisciplinary team will proceed on its own time line, with the legal and other professionals communicating regularly and adjusting the pace of their respective work appropriately. In addition, during Act Two you and the other participants may decide to make use of the services of a business or real estate appraiser, a forensic accountant, a vocational consultant, a neutral financial consultant, or a stock options specialist, to name a few. Even if there is no complete collaborative divorce team, the clients might still choose at this stage to work with collaborative coaches or a child development specialist on a parenting plan. Attention needs to be paid to how such professional helpers are selected, who first contacts them, and how they are brought formally into the collaborative process. The basic ground rule is that all experts are retained jointly as neutrals under the collaborative umbrella, and if the process should terminate prior to settlement, the neutrals are disqualified from testifying in court just as the lawyers are disqualified from representation or other participation in court proceedings. The consultants and experts need to understand these terms of retention and sign documentation binding them to these understandings.

Ordinarily, the collaborative lawyers will either agree on the person who should be retained, or will recommend several from whom the person will be selected. Usually both counsel generate a list of professionals, and

WHAT ABOUT THE KIDS?

Children are the forgotten parties in most divorces. Research shows that most children receive less than 10 minutes' worth of information from their parents about why the divorce is taking place and what will happen to the children in its wake. At a time when children need more and better attention than ever from their parents, divorcing spouses have less time and energy than ever before for parenting their children.

Parents may have fought bitterly over how to parent the children during the course of their marriage. These differences do not disappear simply because the marriage ends. But parents, who may be exhausted from the stresses accompanying divorce, or wracked with guilt because of leaving the marriage, may lack the energy to have essential conversations about how the children are doing and how they might be helped to do better. Or the divorcing couple may feel hopeless about ever agreeing on parenting matters and simply give up on any coordinated efforts to provide consistent rearing of their children, settling instead for unilateral control while the children are in each home. These parents may simply "cut a deal" that ends the disputes, without regard to what the children need in order to flourish. Many lawyers and mediators believe that any agreement the parents are willing to accept regarding parenting the children during and after the divorce is ipso facto good enough for the children. Few collaborative mental health professionals would agree.

A collaborative divorce team that includes mental-health coaches and a child specialist will help parents to have essential conversations about how to do the best parenting job possible after the divorce. The conversations about how to accomplish high-quality joint parenting will be based on accurate input from the children, transmitted safely by the child specialist. This team remains available to help adjust parenting plans as needed during the period of rapid change that usually occurs in the year or two following entry of judgment.

Parents who make use of these team resources often report that they are doing a better job of shared parenting after the divorce than they were able to do while married. Many return for assistance from the collaborative divorce coaches when their children reach adolescence—a time of challenge for parents even in intact families and a time when children's welfare and even safety may depend on the quality of communications and cooperation between the divorced parents. This is an area where interdisciplinary collaborative divorce teams can facilitate solutions far superior to what even the best collaborative lawyers can accomplish working on their own.

the parties themselves interview and choose. It is probably wise for both lawyers to make the initial contact with the chosen consultant or expert, to ensure that the consultant understands how the collaborative law process works and what is expected of the person as a professional participant in a collaborative matter. If a neutral expert such as a real estate appraiser is going to generate a formal report to be used in negotiations, it is wise for collaborative counsel to agree together in advance about procedures to be followed if methodological or other errors are seen in the expert's work product.

Counsel need to assess the likelihood that the expert consultant could effectively participate in a collaborative "five-way" meeting in making the selection of experts for collaborative purposes. Not every forensic expert has the necessary evenhandedness, patience, empathy, or other "people skills" required for collaborative work. Financial consultants and mental health professionals who have been trained in the interdisciplinary collaborative divorce team model should have no difficulty participating in a collaborative matter pursuant to a role definition other than that of the collaborative divorce team.

Occasionally there is good reason for a collaborative lawyer to propose that a client work with other than a jointly retained collaborative consultant. Provided this is done openly and the lawyer maintains clear boundaries for the consultant's involvement this can sometimes be useful, though it should be done carefully and collegially. If this is handled well, such a consultant can sometimes work constructively and evenhandedly at the four-way table even though not retained jointly.[16]

Because the collaborative consultants and experts will never need to be cross-examined in court or testify at a deposition, their reports can be relatively informal—perhaps even delivered orally at a four-way, with a later written report only if needed and requested subsequently. For these reasons, experts usually like working in collaborative cases, and will often agree to lower fees for their work than in conventional litigation practice.

PEELING THE ONION

Collaborative negotiations proceed via interest-based rather than positional bargaining. Your client's identified goals may initially take the form of positions. Your job as collaborative counsel is to refine positions with your client until they can be expressed as interests. Only interests, not positions, are brought to the collaborative bargaining table. A position can be defined as an arbitrary demand that exists on its own terms without reference to objective justification. A position generally is one-dimensional (e.g., "The family residence must be sold now"): only one solution satisfies a positional demand. An interest can be defined as a need or concern or goal that can be explained in a way that a disinterested person of good will would recognize as worthy of respect. To recognize an interest as legitimate means only that it makes sense, not that it can necessarily be achieved in the collaborative process. Interests generally can be met with more than one possible solution (e.g., "I would like to acquire housing of my own that is more or less equivalent to yours"). Moving from positions to interests with the client can be visualized as "peeling the onion." It consists of politely and persistently probing with the client, asking questions like these:

- Why does the client want the goal stated in the position—why is it important to the client?

- What underlying human need will be met if the client obtains the goal stated in the position?

- How would achieving the identified goal improve the client's lot over the long haul?

- Would anyone else's interests be compromised by the client achieving the identified goal?

- What alternative ways exist that might also meet the need underlying the identified goal of the position?

- Can the need underlying the identified goal be explained to a third person as reasonable under all the circumstances currently known?

PREPARING YOUR CLIENT FOR THE FIRST FOUR-WAY

Many clients approach the first four-way meeting with trepidation. Meet with your client about a week before the event for two purposes: first, put the nervous energy to work, and second, allay fears by providing clear information about what will and will not happen at that meeting. Once the first four-way has been navigated successfully, most clients approach subsequent four-ways with greater confidence.

Some helpful approaches in preparing your client for the first four-way:

• Review the principles and guidelines for collaborative law. Reassure your client that the others at the four-way will be adhering to those principles and guidelines.

• Review the agenda for the first four-way. Reassure your client that nothing except what is on the agreed agenda will be addressed at that meeting— that "no surprises" is one of the commitments the lawyers adhere to.

• Ask your client to tell you her greatest fears or worries about the first four-way. Work out understandings with your client about how you and she will handle each situation if it should arise. Remind your client that breaks and caucuses can be called at any time by any participant.

• Ask your client to tell you how you will be able to recognize if the other party is upset or unhappy in the four-way. Ask your client what physical cues might give early warning if the spouse is getting angry or frustrated and urge your client to pay particular attention to those cues during the four-way.

• Teach your client simple stress-reduction techniques to use at the four-way: deep breathing, muscle relaxation, simple visualizations (surrounding himself with a protective shield of light, or seeing an angry wife as a two-year-old having a tantrum).

• Ask your client to prepare two lists for you: (1) his highest goals and intentions for himself, his spouse, and his children during and after the collaborative process; and, (2) the specific outcomes, if any, that are his highest priorities in the divorce. Remind him that the second list is a work in progress and that as the negotiations unfold it may change.

• Explain to your client that you will need to form a positive working relationship with the other spouse and other lawyer at the meeting and that establishing rapport with them is important to create a favorable climate for constructive negotiations.

• Ask your client to write for you a "crib sheet" or road map of how to evoke the spouse's highest, most comfortable, most generous self at the four-way table. The crib sheet should address these points: How does the spouse prefer to think of herself or himself; how does the spouse want others to see him or her; what are the spouse's hot buttons—what makes him or her angry or frustrated? Does the husband prefer to see himself as someone who always takes care of the family's needs? Or does he want everyone to pull their own weight as soon as possible? Is it vitally important to the

> wife to be seen as a competent primary parent? Or does she feel she has
> sacrificed her career goals for too long and want a full parenting partner?
> Your client will know this kind of information and it can be very helpful
> to you in establishing rapport, in framing discussions constructively, and in
> presenting possible solutions.

Preparing the Client for the Four-Way Meeting

Most clients benefit from meeting with their own collaborative lawyer several days before the first four-way meeting, and again a half hour or so before the first four-way, in order to review the meeting agenda, discuss concerns and anxieties, and prepare the client for the procedural objectives the lawyer is working toward during the first four-way. Some repetition may occur during these preparatory meetings, but many clients will benefit from the repetition to overcome the negative effects of anxiety on retention of detail. During these meetings, consider accomplishing the following:

- Review the agenda for the meeting and make sure the client understands what will and will not be addressed at the meeting.
- Inquire what events of significance may have occurred since the last meeting with the client that you need to be aware of during the forthcoming four-way meeting. (Sometimes a child will exhibit sudden emotional problems, a house will sell, there will have been a violent argument between spouses, someone will have lost or found a job, a trial separation will have transmuted into a divorce or vice versa, a client's parent or new partner may be pressing unsolicited advice, the client may just have stepped off a flight that lasted 14 hours, or the client may be coming down with the flu.)
- Confirm whether previous financial arrangements are continuing or have been interrupted and what new needs may exist in this regard.
- Give the client homework, due prior to the first four-way, to begin constructing priority lists and gathering information and documents that will help you. (For instance, you might ask the client to keep a calendar of actual time-sharing with the children, to write a "mission statement" for the collaborative process, to prepare a budget, or to gather tax returns and deeds and other essential documents.)
- Educate the client about the importance of forming effective working relationships at the first four-way, and invite your client to educate you about what you can do to elicit the highest-minded and most confident participation and trust from the other spouse, as well as what you should avoid doing so as not to cause anxiety, fear, or paranoia.[17]

STRATEGIES AND TACTICS FOR A SUCCESSFUL FIRST FOUR-WAY MEETING

- Use pre-meeting with the other collaborative lawyer to confirm process protocols and achieve agenda-management and conflict-management agreements.

- Arrange physical space to foster comfort, cooperation, and trust.

- Decide which lawyer will prepare and distribute the post–four-way memorandum.

- Use metaphors to help achieve "buy-in" to formal collaborative law divorce process.

- Present, discuss, and sign formal collaborative divorce documents.

- Establish schedule for future four-way meetings.

- Assign homework for next four-way meeting, for clients and lawyers.

- Discuss agenda for next meeting.

The Pre-Meeting and Post-Meeting Conferences Between Counsel

Experienced collaborative lawyers make it a point to confer with counsel for the other party regularly, before and after four-way meetings, not for the purpose of conducting substantive negotiations, but rather to keep the collaborative process moving forward smoothly, transparently, and effectively. These conferences can be brief—as little as a few sentences on the telephone or during the break in a bar association meeting. When necessary the conferences can be longer face-to-face meetings, perhaps to look over complicated fringe-benefit documents that the lawyers need to understand but the clients don't wish to master, perhaps to plan how to present information about the law collegially at a four-way meeting, perhaps to brainstorm options for conflict management if one client or the other is having repeated difficulty handling the stresses of four-way meetings—indeed, for any purpose that strengthens the ability of the lawyers and clients to work effectively in four-way meetings. The greater the mutual trust and candor of the lawyers with one another, the greater the potential utility of the pre-meetings. In tone, these meetings bear little or no resemblance to adversarial alter-ego communications between counsel. The most effective collaborative lawyers are candid about the difficulties their clients may be having with the process, such as shadow-client behaviors that may be emerging at four-ways, tensions between lawyer and client and how to deal with them best, or the reception various settlement approaches are likely to receive from the client and how to prepare the ground for a more positive response to suggestions worth considering. A broad range of discussion that amounts to a review of how things are going, substantively, emotionally, and in the working relationships of the players with one another, and a conversation about how to make the process work better for all concerned, are the hallmarks of effective collaboration.

Pre-meeting conferences often include heads-up warnings between counsel about events that may have occurred since the previous four-way that could affect the attitudes of the parties going forward, as well as suggestions based upon what went well and what went poorly at the most recent meetings. These conferences are so fundamental to the collaborative process that it is a good idea to include a routine call to the other lawyer a day or two before a four-way meeting as part of the regular preparation protocol. Such a call can prompt the other lawyer to confer with his or her client if that has not occurred and can prevent false starts and miscommunications that can frustrate and thwart collaborative results.

Post-meeting conferences serve precisely the same purposes as pre-meeting conferences, but instead of a prospective focus, the lawyers look backward to critique and review what occurred at the four-way meetings. Ideally, the post-meeting conferences between counsel take place after there has been at least a day or two for the client to mull over the events of the four-way meeting and after each lawyer has had an opportunity to confer privately with the client about what took place. Often, the post-meeting conversation will be brief and positive: "That was a great meeting—I really appreciated how you approached the house sale issue, and so did my client." Or, "Your client really showed admirable restraint when Mary lost her temper at the end of the four-way. Please thank him for me, and for Mary as well, though I'm pretty sure she'll do it herself at the next four-way." Sometimes the post-meeting conferences will be more complicated—perhaps a valuable piece of jewelry has disappeared during the packing of the departing spouse's belongings and each party is accusing the other of some malfeasance; the lawyers need to plan carefully together to prevent the issue from eclipsing the real progress being made collaboratively on other important matters while helping the parties reach some closure about the lost jewelry.

When collaborative lawyers pay attention to these key stages in the forward movement of the collaborative process, they are doing the necessary maintenance work to enhance the likelihood that the four-way meetings will move forward cordially, productively, and efficiently.

Apparent Impasse in Negotiations

During Act Two of a collaborative case, best practice is to defer negotiations until the time is ripe, the foundation is solid, and the parties are fully prepared to engage in constructive problem solving. This kind of careful process management and groundwork by the collaborative lawyers is the best way to prevent apparent impasses from derailing the orderly progress of a collaborative representation. While anxiety often causes clients to leap prematurely to solutions in the vain hope that the pain will end if the process ends, good collaborative lawyers insist that sticking to the road map is the best way to get to the destination.

While the clients will be encouraged to identify their most positive hopes for the collaborative process during the first or second four-way meeting, good collaborative lawyers discourage a focus on more concrete goals and priorities until the fact-finding and disclosure process is moving toward completion. With a shared fund of congruent information, constructive problem solving is far more likely than if clients are allowed to hijack the orderly process and leap to solutions while information is still spotty and incomplete and factual questions remain unanswered. Even after all financial disclosures are complete, the income, expenses, assets, and debts are fully understood, the legal context has been explained, and the personal goals, interests, and priorities of the clients have been explored, there remains another important step before discussing resolution: brainstorming, or expanding the spectrum of options.

Best practice is to insist as process managers that devoting time to expanding the range of options is time well spent. Naturally, there are some issues as to which the obvious and best solution simply rises to the surface and is recognized by all. But where there are more complex issues, or issues as to which clients have expressed potential differing or even opposing interests, brainstorming[18] as many potential solutions as possible and then evaluating them carefully in light of which are most congruent with the big picture hopes and the specific goals and interests of each client can yield surprisingly constructive results.[19]

If an apparent impasse does arise once it is time to reach resolution of issues, good collaborative lawyers, in Stu Webb's words, "roll up their sleeves." Because the collaborative participation agreement creates substantial incentives to keep working, as well as disincentives that discourage bolting to court too quickly, there is time for such techniques as reframing, mutualizing, exploring differences in timing and risk preferences, further brainstorming, taking a break to allow other perspectives to emerge, and for one of the most powerful techniques of all: silence.[20] Impasse is rarely identified as a cause for termination of a collaborative case, because when the clients take time to reflect on their priorities and options, they generally recognize that if they submit the matter for resolution by the court, the decision will be based on less information,[21] and will take less account of personal goals and priorities,[22] than is available at the collaborative table. Now and then a client will prefer to have the judge make a decision, but this is much less common than practitioners new to collaborative practice might imagine.

A STEP-BY-STEP GUIDE TO BRAINSTORMING

- Define the issue that is being brainstormed as precisely as possible.

- Keep the session focused on the problem.

- Use a flip chart or poster board so all ideas can be noted and seen.

- Don't permit criticism or commentary about ideas; just write them all down. A good brainstorming session is fast-moving and creative.

- Encourage the clients to enjoy the exercise by emphasizing that naming a possibility has nothing to do with whether one would ever agree to it.

- Loosen inhibitions and preconceived notions by instructing everyone to offer at least two ideas that are privately considered unthinkable and even ridiculous, without identifying which they are.

- Both lawyers and clients can participate. Don't label the source of ideas; just write them down.

- Save evaluation for later. Consider using the "four-square" method at that point for evaluating possible solutions to difficult issues.

NEGOTIATING STYLES

Interest-based bargaining

- Preferred in collaborative law

- Addresses needs and concerns, not arbitrary positions

- Presents needs and interests in context of reasons

- Aims at win-win or mutually acceptable solutions
- Aims at expanding the pie
- Expands range of possible solutions before evaluating options and working on resolution
- Requires careful listening and understanding of viewpoints
- Looks for congruence, not victory
- Uses differences as sources of potential solutions rather than sources of conflict
- Handles distributive ("zero-sum") issues with reference to external measures or other evenhanded techniques, not with power plays or arbitrary posturing

Positional bargaining

- Discourages creative development of a range of options for resolution
- Proceeds via successive arbitrary demands for unitary solution
- Allows no room for reasoned exploration of viewpoints
- Places no value on understanding the concerns of the other party
- Treats differences as a basis for conflict
- Uses a "Mediterranean-marketplace" style: dance of successive arbitrary, extreme positions toward an arbitrary meeting place that often can be predicted from opening bids
- Uses a "Soviet–Cold War" style: extreme ultimatums and threats based on power
- Uses a "Scandinavian" style: apparently reasonable position presented as "fair," leaving no opportunity for discussion or consideration of alternatives

GHOST-READING LETTERS

We have all experienced the shock of writing a letter that we thought innocuous in tone and content, and then learning from the other spouse's lawyer that it caused a firestorm of angry reaction. Sometimes we even write letters thoughtlessly that we never should have mailed. As e-mail communications displace paper, the risk of hastily written communications harming consensual problem-solving efforts increases. The other party in a collaborative case can be particularly upset by such errors on your part and can lose trust in your commitment to collaborative work. Keeping written communications to a minimum and doing the work in person or via telephone is always wise. Confining emails to scheduling and other routine case management matters is a best practice. If you do need to write a letter, consider this technique:

- Ask yourself why this letter is necessary. Maybe it isn't.

- If it is necessary, prepare the letter as a draft and mark it clearly, "Draft—not for distribution."

- Call your collaborative counterpart in the case, explain why you need to send a letter, and ask if she would be kind enough to pre-read the letter and edit it for tone, as you want to be sure you don't inadvertently offend her client. Make it clear that you need to send a letter about the content but you would welcome improvements to the tone.

- If you are the receiving lawyer, edit the draft as if your client were reading over your shoulder. Don't try to change what is being said, but do your best to render the tone inoffensive. Send it back to your colleague.

- Now, the letter can be prepared in its final version, signed, and sent. Now it can be given to the other party.

Another tip: If, on reading your draft letter, your collaborative colleague calls and says, "Is there any way you could postpone sending this letter to me? I think for the following reasons that it would be unwise for my client to see this right now . . ."—*listen*, and consider doing as asked.

FOOD AND COLLABORATIVE LAW

Many collaborative lawyers make a practice of offering plentiful, wholesome food (breads, cheese, nuts, and fruit) at the collaborative four-way table. Here are some good reasons for you to consider doing the same:

- Most of us were raised with the rule that it's rude to argue or bring strongly negative attitudes to the dining table. Seeing platters of food on the four-way table seems to trigger this atavistic childhood rule of good manners.

- People get tense at collaborative four-way meetings. Crunchy and chewy foods give people something to do with their mouths and hands, and the chewing seems to discharge tension.

- Occupational therapists tell us that the physical act of chewing is associated in many people with enhanced clarity of thinking.

- Clients sometimes are too anxious to eat before a four-way meeting and can become irritable as a result of hunger, especially toward the end of a long meeting. Lawyers who overschedule their days may have omitted breakfast or lunch, with the same result.

- Food can sometimes make the difference between a good meeting and a frustrating one. It never does any harm to provide it.

KEYS TO SUCCESS IN FOUR-WAY MEETINGS

- Use *pre-meetings* to agree with other lawyer about agenda control and conflict management.

- Consider *five-way or larger meetings* if issues or the process would benefit from the presence of a neutral consultant, expert, or collaborative divorce team member.

- *Prepare the client* in advance for the agenda.

- Prepare the client for how *conflict* and *shadow behaviors* will be handled at the four-way.

- Arrange *physical space* to foster comfort, cooperation, and trust.

- Start the meeting by *confirming the agenda*.

- Refer to *guiding metaphors, statements of highest hopes/intentions,* and *signed documents* as conflict-management tools (process anchors).

- Use *caucusing, reframing, mutualizing, and similar* conflict-management techniques.

- *Confirm agreements* about homework, agenda, and timing for the next meeting.

- Use *ceremonial elements* to close meetings: confirm positive achievements; confirm understandings of what is to happen next.

- Conduct *post-meeting debriefings* to evaluate and improve the process.

NEGOTIATING COLLABORATIVELY: PROPOSE, EXPLAIN, UPGRADE

In collaborative practice, try eliminating the concept of "counterproposal." It implies positional bargaining and opposition. Words matter; words shape thought. Instead of counterproposals, think of the steps in negotiating a challenging issue or working on resolution with challenging clients this way:

- PROPOSE: When the time is right (but not before), put together a concept for settling one, many, or all issues, and present it at (but not before) a four-way meeting intended for that purpose. The idea is to develop a concept that addresses the reasonable concerns and interests of both parties to the maximum extent possible, or that allocates deficiencies equitably if that is not possible. But do not become attached to the proposal. Present it as a discussion concept.

- EXPLAIN: At the same or the next meeting (depending on the capacities of the clients), the agenda is limited to answering all questions from the other client and other lawyer that they may have about the proposal. No attacks, critiques, or defenses; no alternatives. The agenda consists solely of continuing to ask and explain until the shape and content and rationale of the proposal are fully understood by all.

- UPGRADE: At the next four-way meeting, the lawyer and client who did not make the initial proposal respond by offering their improvements, or upgrades. The upgrades consist of ideas that will make the original proposal work better in meeting the legitimate needs of both clients and/or allocating deficiencies equitably.

- The process continues with explanations and upgrades, until agreement is reached or a new proposal is offered for consideration.

GETTING THE MOST OUT OF THE LAST FOUR-WAY

Resist the temptation to skip the final four-way meeting by circulating the agreement for execution by mail. That is wasting an important opportunity to provide the clients with closure and a forward look. Use the last four-way to:

- Highlight acts of generosity, grace, and growth that occurred during the process.

- Express appreciation to the other party and the other lawyer for a job well done.

- Remind the clients of their enhanced problem-solving skills learned during the process.

- Review with the clients the important points of the settlement agreement and acknowledge the accomplishments it represents.

- Help clients anticipate and normalize future speed bumps when they may need to review and revise the terms of their agreement; discuss the steps they will take when that happens.

- Sign the settlement agreement and the other necessary divorce papers and explain when the divorce will be "over."

- Review and evaluate the collaborative law process.

- If appropriate, include a closing ceremony of some sort—small gifts to the clients (books about personal growth, shared parenting or travel are good) or toasts to a job well done.

Notes

1. The author's work with clients is now limited to collaborative cases, second opinions, and consultations. This form is used to screen out and refer cases obviously unsuited to collaborative practice (e.g., cases with active domestic violence), and to highlight points needing to be discussed as the client considers selecting collaborative law (e.g., spouse already represented by gladiatorial counsel). For example, a client may indicate that there is a custody motion about to be heard and yet want collaborative law representation, or may live in a distant state but want remote collaborative services. These situations, though difficult, are not impossible to handle collaboratively but it is likely that these clients have an imperfect understanding of how the model works when they first contact you with such situations. Any client who expresses interest in a collaborative divorce merits at least a serious discussion of whether it might be a realistic option.

2. Assume nothing about your client's understanding of conflict-resolution options. Unless he or she is a collaborative professional, you need to spend time ensuring that the client makes a fully informed process choice. It is not uncommon for clients to assert that they know "all about" collaborative law, and in the next breath ask why the lawyer cannot represent both parties, or whether there is any problem about the other party proceeding without counsel. With clients who have some basic knowledge of collaborative practice, consider offering a pre-consultation copy of Tesler and Thompson's book, Collaborative Divorce: The Revolutionary Way to Restructure Your Family, Resolve Legal Issues, and Move on with Your Life (2006). Clients who read this book generally choose collaborative representation.

3. See Appendix II for useful diagrams and tables that you can incorporate into this stage of your work with potential clients.

4. Some commentators suggest that practitioners of collaborative law and other innovative conflict-resolution modalities should have a duty to ensure "super-informed" consent on the part of the clients. Putting aside the question of how to differentiate "informed" from "super-informed" consent, or whether it is appropriate to legislate such matters, a better idea in terms of consumer protection would be for all lawyers to embrace such a responsibility. No apparent basis exists for assuming that clients come to lawyers well-informed about the risks of conventional litigation-matrix advocacy, which can be considerable. Any persuasive rationale for requiring "super-informed" consent only in collaborative cases would need to begin with a showing that (a) clients do not generally understand what they are choosing when they elect collaborative representation, and (b) they *do* have a full and accurate understanding of the risks, benefits, and costs of conventional representation. No such showing has yet been made.

5. Like nearly every statement about mediation, this one has exceptions—for instance, co-mediation by two mediators. The term "mediation" covers a very broad range of models and styles, and takes significantly different forms from one locale to another. Even professionals may mean widely divergent things when they refer to mediation. The term embraces mediation that is court-annexed and private, mandatory and voluntary, evaluative and facilitative, transformative and narrative, pre-litigation and eve-of trial. It can be conducted by lawyers, mental health professionals, accountants, or laypeople. Sessions may extend to marathon lengths or be strictly time-limited, may include or preclude caucusing with the mediator, and many other variables. Speaking accurately about mediation is difficult when it is not known who will be the service provider. *See* Joan B. Kelly, *A Decade of Family Mediation Research: Some Answers and Questions*, Fam. & Conciliation Ct. Rev., 34, (3), 373–85. Nonetheless, there are some general characteristics associated with mediation that can be discussed with clients—the characteristics that differentiate it from collaborative practice.

6. These comparisons of structural features of mediation and collaborative law relate to inherent aspects of the processes. Obviously, a very talented mediator will be able to

accomplish a great deal within the mediation structure, as compared to a less talented mediator, and the same is true for the relative ability of talented and less talented collaborative lawyers to make maximum use of the structural advantages of collaborative law.

7. In jurisdictions like California that have a statutorily mandated duty to disclose all financial facts during divorce, the collaborative disclosure phase tends to be a more efficient and complete method of satisfying that obligation than is generally achieved in conventional representation. Where the obligation does not exist per statute, it is customary for it to be embraced voluntarily by the clients as a component of the collaborative participation agreement. Without it, good-faith collaborative negotiations would be difficult or impossible.

8. Clients, in the author's experience, worry far less about termination short of agreement than critics do. Practitioners usually estimate that roughly 90–95% of collaborative cases reach full resolution. Empirical research so far is consistent with those estimates. *See, e.g.*, William H. Schwab, *Collaborative Lawyering: A Closer Look at an Emerging Practice*, 4 Pepp. Disp. Resol. L. J. 351 (2004); David Hoffman, *Colliding Worlds of Dispute Resolution: Towards a Unified Field Theory of ADR*, 2008 J. Disp. Resol. 11, 33.

9. *See* Julie MacFarlane, *The Emerging Phenomenon of Collaborative Family Law (CFL): A Qualitative Study of CFL Cases* (2005), http://www.justice.gc.ca/en/ps/pad/reports/2005-FCY-1/index.html, at 34–39, for a discussion of differences in lawyers' and clients' perceptions about the collaborative law model and implications for informed consent.

10. Some collaborative lawyers engage in what might be called "minimal" collaborative lawyering, in which the only real change in their mode of practice when they undertake a collaborative case is that they cannot threaten or participate in litigation. In all other significant respects, their negotiations resemble conventional litigation-matrix settlement efforts. Such lawyers may intentionally or as a matter of habit engage in positional bargaining and treat legal rights as the measure and boundary of negotiations. The author is not aware of any trainers or commentators who advocate this approach. Apart from the narrowed and impoverished scope of problem solving possible with this approach, it cannot be regarded as "client-centered," inasmuch as the lawyers exert a high degree of control over disclosures, negotiations, and outcomes. Nor is there a high likelihood of success using such an approach. If predictions about what a judge would do are the context for reaching resolution there would seem to be little reason why, when impasse arises, clients would not want to terminate the process and find out for themselves what the judge will do.

11. It cannot be said often enough that the collaborative lawyers do not make decisions for the clients about what goals are important or what interests will be pursued. The lawyer's job is to help the client figure out why a particular goal matters, why a particular interest is important, so that it can be explained at the table in a way that the spouse might be willing to accept as reasonable and therefore might make an effort to accommodate. The lawyer also helps the client see whether there could be more than one way to achieve the goal or satisfy the interest, because this is the doorway to developing a range of options rather than one binary, "yes/no" demand. Doing this work well with the client is the essential first step in successful interest-based bargaining. It is a best practice not because it is morally better for clients to think this way, but rather because this is the most practical way to help a client achieve what he or she wants in a good-faith consensual process. If after working this way with the client, there appears no reasonable explanation for a goal or interest, the likeliest explanation is that it is arbitrary and perhaps unreasonable. Again, the lawyer does not say to the client, "I think your goal is unreasonable and so you should not have it as a goal." The lawyer says, in effect, "So far I still don't understand the reasons for this goal being on your main priority list. If I don't yet understand it after all our conversation about it I am skeptical that your spouse and her lawyer will be able to appreciate why it matters and why it is worthy of efforts on their part to achieve it. I don't know how to present it in a way that will make sense. If they don't see your goal as reasonable and achievable, it's not likely that your spouse is going to say 'yes' to it in a settlement. So, what shall we do about this problem?" If

the client's goals seem to his or her own lawyer to be arbitrary and unreasonable, it might be a good time to discuss whether collaborative law is a process in which the goals are achievable. The process may need to terminate if the goal is both a high priority for the client and unlikely to be achievable in the collaborative process.

12. This may be necessary for tax or other reasons but unilateral filing and service of the petition is not generally the best way to start a collaborative representation. Best practice in most communities is for the timing of filing the divorce petition to be discussed during Act One (opening moves) meetings and agreed to by the parties.

13. Some lawyers will not sign on to a formal collaborative representation under such circumstances because of the higher risk of a failed representation. Others point out that these very same problems will be present with a troubled or dishonest spouse, whatever dispute-resolution mode is selected, and believe that so long as the client is fully advised of the risks, it may make sense to give collaborative law a try if the client wants to. Utilization of an interdisciplinary team and stipulations for audits and asset tracing can be posited as threshold requirements for collaboration in such cases.

14. This is an increasingly popular technique, in which the two lawyers agree that if either of them considers the other to be creating rather than helping to resolve problems, they will on request of either lawyer engage in mentoring sessions with a designated trusted colleague, at their own expense. Some practice groups include the responsibility to provide this kind of mentoring to colleagues as one of the expectations of membership.

15. If the clients decline to work with coaches at this stage, the subject can be revisited later if it becomes apparent that this resource is essential.

16. For example, a dependent spouse who is anxious but willing to work on career development with a vocational consultant may feel more comfortable and engaged if the person is brought in as her personal consultant rather than as someone who will be accountable to and reporting to both parties. Or, if the earning spouse is sophisticated about finance and the homemaker spouse is not, sometimes the process works better if the financial consultant works intensively with the homemaker to review documents and fill in missing information. The key here is for the consultants to be instructed to conduct the work as if it were a joint retention rather than as a positional advocate, to avoid polarizing the process. Another situation arises when a client is not satisfied with what seems to be the best achievable outcome in a negotiation. Among the techniques for addressing the situation can be a consultation between the client and another lawyer for a second opinion. Failing to disclose this consultation could give rise to legitimate suspicion that "shadow counsel" is preparing for litigation (something inconsistent with the good-faith undertakings of collaborative law), but if the reason for the consultation is disclosed, second-opinion consultations with a lawyer familiar with client-centered, interest-based negotiations as well as litigation can support the integrity of the collaborative process rather than undermining it.

17. Illustrations of information clients have produced in response to this kind of homework assignment range from "John sees himself as always responsible and someone who always keeps his word, so don't suggest that he would ever fail to honor commitments—instead, say things like, 'I know from talking with Alice that it is quite important to you to follow through with your promises and so we need to understand better what you feel you committed yourself to do,'" to "She is a careful reader of body language; be sure to make direct eye contact when you speak to Mary; talk to her, not about her; and lean forward comfortably so she feels you are relaxed rather than tense and coiled to attack."

18. The term "brainstorming" has a specific meaning in conflict resolution: it is a structured lateral thinking mode. The point is to encourage every possible idea that could address a problem, no matter how crazy or impractical it may sound. The single most important rule in brainstorming is: no criticism, no evaluation. All ideas are listed and later they can be reviewed to consider which of them might spark useful approaches to resolution.

19. Many excellent trainings focus on interest-based techniques for averting or dealing with apparent impasse. A good introductory collaborative law training will include at least

some such techniques. Taking a full 30- or 40-hour course is an excellent way to strengthen these important skills and is a component of the IACP minimum standards for practitioners.

20. By this is meant a prolonged silence of the lawyers at the collaborative table, during which clients eventually will recall that unless someone comes up with an idea, this meeting and the process itself will terminate and new lawyers will have to be hired.

21. The collaborative process does not operate under the rules of evidence.

22. The collaborative process is not limited to justiciable issues within the jurisdiction of the family law court.

Chapter 7

Statutes, Rules, Standards, and Protocols for Collaborative Law Practice[1]

"The courts of this country should not be the places where resolution of disputes begins. They should be the places where the disputes end after alternative methods of resolving disputes have been considered and tried." —Sandra Day O'Connor

No presentation of collaborative law to a new audience of lawyers lasts long without someone asking questions like these:

- Isn't this unethical? What about the duty of zealous representation of the client?
- Am I allowed to do this? Isn't it an impermissible limitation on my professional responsibility to provide full and complete representation to my client?
- Will my malpractice carrier cover me for collaborative legal work? Is this work within the standard of care for family lawyers?

As collaborative lawyers, we work under the same licensure and ethical mandates as other lawyers. That is the starting point for talking about the ethics of collaborative practice. We are bound by the lawyer-client privilege exactly as other lawyers are. We must advocate for our clients' interests diligently as all lawyers must.

But there are important differences in how we interpret our ethical duties compared to how a gladiatorial litigator might. Collaborative lawyers do not agree to serve as their clients' alter egos or attack dogs. We come to the table as "engaged moral agents," not as disengaged (albeit hungry) barracudas. And, by contract with our clients we limit the procedural scope of our representation, in that our clients retain us solely to settle their issues and agree that if litigation is needed it will be done by other lawyers.

Thus, we make it clear to clients and they give their informed consent to the fact that there are several situations in which we might bow out of a representation before all the client's issues have been resolved. First, the case may reach impasse (or the client may believe that impasse has been reached) and the client may decide to terminate collaboration and proceed to court. Second, a client may behave in bad faith, leading to termination of the collaborative process by the other party, in consultation with his or her lawyer. Finally, a client's own collaborative lawyer may have to withdraw or proceed with constructive termination of the collaborative process if his or her own client is in persistent bad faith.[2] This could consist of purposely engaging in delaying or obfuscating tactics, violating or failing to follow through with interim agreements, taking unilateral action—such as vis-à-vis community assets or concerning children—that are inconsistent with collaboration, persistently behaving with disrespect toward other participants, or refusing to share information that a reasonable decision maker would require in order to make an informed decision on a particular subject. In all these cases, collaborative lawyers undertake with their clients and their colleagues that they will not continue the collaborative process.

Collaborative lawyers also take a somewhat different view of their duty of zealous advocacy than a gladiatorial litigator would. Although the job description of a collaborative lawyer is to work diligently to help the client achieve his or her goals, collaborative lawyers don't adopt the role of guns for hire. Helping the client reflect carefully about goals and priorities is a central part of the collaborative lawyer's work. In their capacity as wise counselors and engaged moral agents,[3] collaborative lawyers raise with their clients questions like these:

- How will achieving this goal make your life better in the future, long after the divorce chapter has closed?
- How will achieving this goal affect the long-term and/or immediate interests of your children?

- How will your extended family and friends be affected if you proceed in this manner?
- What is the likelihood that you will look back upon this decision years from now with a sense of satisfaction about how you conducted yourself?[4]

Collaborative lawyers working from this perspective look ahead to a day when the standard of care for family lawyers will require all of us to include ethical and moral considerations like these in our advice and counsel whenever we handle a divorce, collaborative or otherwise, because of the predictable collateral damage to clients and those they care most about when these dimensions of competent family law advocacy are overlooked or seen as optional.

The field of family law is undergoing a sea change in this regard, with collaborative law one of its most interesting current manifestations.[5] In the words of Andrew Schepard (co-chair of the Family Law Education Reform [FLER] Project, sponsored by Hofstra Law School and the Association of Family and Conciliation Courts), over the past quarter-century "[v]irtually everything about family law has evolved—the role of the family court, the procedure for resolving family disputes, the role of the family lawyer and the substantive law. . . . Today's family lawyer must be fully equipped to work with professionals from different disciplines and multiple dispute-resolution processes in an increasingly complex and differentiated system. The traditional full service adversarial model of lawyer representation is being increasingly challenged by emerging models that call for problem solving, collaboration, and unbundled (limited task) representation. Many argue that family lawyers should have different ethical responsibilities than lawyers in traditional civil and criminal cases, including a responsibility to discuss alternative dispute resolution with their clients and an obligation to 'do no harm' to their clients' children."

While collaborative practitioners welcome and are contributing substantially to this evolution in our understanding of what it means to be an ethical family lawyer, we also are obliged to understand the current status of collaborative legal practice from the perspective of existing ethics rules and their interpretation.

In the years since the first edition of this book was published, considerable material has emerged addressing ethical concerns, with more expected as collaborative legal practice moves further into the conflict-resolution mainstream. Many of these commentators have focused attention on the importance of fully informed client consent to all elements of the collaborative participation agreement, particularly the disqualification provision barring both lawyers from further representation if either party elects to litigate. Other concerns, ranging from significant to unpersuasive, have been raised in ethics opinions and academic debate.

This chapter presents an overview of current U.S. legislation, ethics rules and opinions, standards, protocols, and similar material, as well as a brief annotated bibliography of articles addressing the ethics of collaborative practice.[6]

Statutory Recognition of Collaborative Law

Three state legislatures in the United States have codified statutes recognizing collaborative law. Texas Family Code Section 6.603, enacted in 2001, provides for the use of collaborative law procedures in divorce cases without children; Section 153.007 authorizes the use of collaborative law in suits affecting the parent-child relationship, whether or not joined with a marriage dissolution action.[7] In 2003, North Carolina General Statutes §§ 50-70 through 50-79 were enacted, defining and recognizing collaborative law as a means of resolving issues other than by a court proceeding, and setting out procedural and evidentiary rules for the practice of collaborative law.[8] California has also enacted a statute recognizing collaborative family law, Family Code § 2013.[9]

Perhaps the most important indication of the status of collaborative law as an important feature of the legal landscape in the United States (as of the second edition of this book) is the creation of a Drafting Committee on collaborative law by the National Conference of Commissioners on Uniform State Laws (NCCUSL), which is responsible for drafting such uniform laws as the Uniform Commercial Code and Uniform Arbitration Act. In December, 2006, the NCCUSL announced the appointment of Professor Andrew Schepard of Hofstra University School of Law as reporter and Peter Munson, of Sherman, Texas, as chair. The Committee began drafting a model statute recognizing and defining collaborative law in 2007.[10]

Congruence of Collaborative Legal Practice with Ethics Rules

As of mid-2007, ethics opinions in six states (Kentucky, Minnesota, New Jersey, North Carolina, Colorado, and Pennsylvania) had addressed collaborative legal practice; of these, only one state (Colorado) has issued an unfavorable ruling.[11]

With the exception of the Colorado opinion (which focuses on a unique provision of the Colorado ethics rules that does not appear in the American Bar Association Model Rules), these ethics opinions have addressed state rules that are essentially the same as the ABA Model Rules. The opinions are as follows: Kentucky Bar Association Ethics Opinion KBA E-425, June 2005; New Jersey Advisory Committee on Professional Ethics Opinion 699; North Carolina State Bar 2002 Formal Ethics Opinion 1 (Cite as: 2002 WL 2029469 (N.C.St.Bar.); Pennsylvania Bar Association Committee on Legal Ethics and Professional Responsibility Informal Opinion 2004-24; May 11, 2004 advisory opinion letter dated March 12, 1997 from Office of Lawyers Professional Responsibility of Minnesota Judicial Center to Laurie Savran, Esq.; Ethics Committee of the Colorado Bar Association advisory opinion #115. The Model Rule that is discussed in each state ethics opinion is indicated below.

(a) Competence and diligence—Rules 1.1 and 1.2 (PA)
(b) Limited scope representation—Rules 1.2 and 1.5 (MN; NC; NJ; PA)
(c) Informed consent—Rule 1.0 (CO; KY; NC; NJ)
(d) Zealous representation—Rule 1.3 (KY)
(e) Confidentiality—Rule 1.6 (KY; NC)
(f) Loyalty to the client—Rule 1.7 (CO; PA)
(g) Withdrawal—Rule 1.16 (KY; MN; PA)
(h) Providing referral list to unrepresented party—Rule 4.3 (NC)
(i) Restriction on practice—Rule 5.6 (KY)
(j) Legal services organizations—Rule 6.3 (KY; NC)
(k) Communications and advertising—Rules 7.1 and 7.5 (NC)

Outside the United States, the collaborative law model has been recognized formally or informally in a number of jurisdictions. For example, the Law Society of Alberta, in Canada, has adopted a "Companion Code of Conduct for Collaborative Lawyers," which is in the nature of an addendum to the provincial Code of Professional Conduct. In the Irish Republic, the tax-funded Legal Aid Board of Ireland has been the leading proponent of collaborative legal services for divorcing couples in that country. And in Australia, Attorney General Philip Ruddock issued an official government report in 2006 favoring the broad availability nationally of collaborative law representation in family law matters.[12]

Standards for Collaborative Legal Practice

The International Academy of Collaborative Professionals adopted minimum standards for collaborative lawyers in 2004 and substantially revised them in 2007 to keep pace with the rapidly evolving refinement of collaborative legal practice. These are not "gatekeeper" standards; IACP does not verify whether individual members meet these standards, nor does it (or any jurisdiction or entity) presently engage in credentialing or certification. IACP members may, if they wish, affirm their compliance with IACP standards, both on their member page at the IACP website and elsewhere. The IACP Standards for Practitioners set out minimum expectations in terms of training and experience for the practice of collaborative law (including interdisciplinary team collaborative divorce practice). There are also standards for trainers, and for trainings, as well as Ethical Standards. The most recent version of these standards can be found on the IACP website, www .collaborativepractice.com. The IACP Ethical Standards for Collaborative Practice appear as Appendix I-I in this book.

Many local and statewide practice groups and collaborative organizations in the United States and elsewhere have adopted standards for their members. Generally these standards incorporate or parallel the IACP standards, and none is intended to conflict with them. Collaborative practice groups and organizations that are committed to maintaining high standards of excellence in collaborative practice are advised as a best practice to incorporate compliance with standards as part of their membership requirements and to consider either adopting or incorporating a version of the IACP standards. The emerging national and international consensus about standards for collaborative practice has benefits for practitioners and clients alike: consumer protection, clarity, consistency of models, malpractice prevention, and widespread elevation of quality of collaborative services.[13]

Protocols for Collaborative Legal Practice

It is so central to effective collaborative representation that the lawyers representing both parties hold the same expectations for how the process will unfold, that many collaborative practice groups and organizations have moved toward adoption of formal "protocols" for collaborative representation.[14] While the standards set out basic principles for competent, ethical collaborative legal practice, the protocols lay out, often in considerable detail, the order of events, the documentation that will be used, the good-faith commitments that will guide the work, and a host of other procedural matters both large and small that arise during the course of the collaborative case. Even where formal written protocols are not in place, one of the functions of an effective collaborative practice group is to provide a forum in which practitioners discuss and reach agreement informally as to the protocols by which they will do the work. The effect of having such protocols in place is to make the process management in a collaborative case smooth and seamless, and to avoid the misunderstandings and rough spots regarding procedural matters that can undermine effective conflict resolution.

Even though these understandings are typically called protocols (defined as a specific custom, practice, or procedure established by usage and widely accepted) and not standards (which suggest norms for measuring the quality of performance), it should be anticipated that where protocols exist, they might at some point be deemed part of the standard of practice in the community for purposes of malpractice litigation.

The Collaborative Law Institute of Texas published a particularly comprehensive set of protocols in 2005, entitled *Protocols of Practice for Collaborative Family Lawyers*, consisting of 13 chapters (21 pages) addressing virtually every aspect of the collaborative process in considerable detail. Their purpose is set out in Section 1.04 as follows:

COMPLIANCE WITH PROTOCOLS.

(a) These protocols are designed to be used by lawyers on a voluntary basis. The Collaborative Law Institute of Texas, Inc. strongly recommends that its members and other lawyers follow the protocols in good faith. The ultimate sanction against a lawyer who uses tactics or trickery to abuse or evade the collaborative law process, or condones or encourages such abuse by the client, is the diminution of that lawyer's reputation.

(b) The Collaborative Law Institute of Texas, Inc. urges adoption of these protocols by local practice groups as expectations and aspirations of membership.

(c) Because these protocols aspire to a level of practice above the minimum established in the Texas Disciplinary Rules of Professional Conduct, it is inappropriate to use these protocols to define the level of conduct required of lawyers for purposes of professional liability or lawyer discipline.

The Texas protocols cover a broad gamut of matters, from the use of forms, understandings about attorneys' fees, and the normal sequence of events in a case, through screening clients, expectations for good-faith participation, interest-based negotiations, and interdisciplinary collaboration, to matters such as confidentiality and informed consent that overlap with the explicit rules of professional ethics. The following passage illustrates the approach of the Texas protocols:

SECTION 2.03. FAITHFUL REPRESENTATION OF CLIENT.

(a) The collaborative lawyer should commit the time and resources necessary to gain a clear understanding of the client's values, assist the client in identifying and articulating the client's interests and goals in a manner consistent with the client's values, and explore with the client the means by which the collaborative law process can satisfy the client's interests and achieve the stated goals in a constructive manner.

(b) The collaborative lawyer should inform the client, as soon as feasible, about interest based negotiation and the priority that collaborative law gives to preserving an ongoing relationship between the parties through the nonjudicial resolution of the client's matter.

(c) The collaborative lawyer should at all times be faithful in the representation of the client and zealously represent the client in pursuit of the client's stated goals. This faithful representation includes informing the client about the law and its application to the client's matter on an ongoing basis, preserving confidential communications, and assisting the client to develop approaches, collaboratively with the other participants, to resolving the matter without judicial intervention.

(d) The collaborative lawyer should explain to the client that the process allows settlement of the matter outside the limits of a judicially imposed solution, subject to securing court approval of the settlement.

CONFIDENTIALITY AND PRIVILEGE IN COLLABORATIVE LEGAL PRACTICE

The collaborative law process cannot work well unless lawyers can trust that their collaborative colleagues will insist upon voluntary production of all discovery documents and information that a reasonable decision maker would want to know before deciding an issue.

What if your client discloses relevant and material information to you, but prohibits its disclosure to the spouse and the other lawyer? IACP ethical standards and most practice group protocols reach this conclusion: the collaborative lawyer is bound by the voluntary ethical undertakings of the collaborative process to refuse to go forward unless the information is disclosed. If the client refuses, the lawyer must withdraw, and/or terminate the collaborative process. But the lawyer—like all lawyers—remains bound by the attorney-client privilege and cannot disclose a client confidence under those circumstances unless state law provides otherwise.

Apart from questions of privilege, collaborative lawyers exchange a great deal of information that traditional lawyers probably would not offer to one another, and from the perspective of best practices as well as informed consent, clients should be made aware that this will be part of how the collaborative lawyers provide effective collaborative representation and should provide written acknowledgment of understanding and permission.

- Effective collaborative lawyers alert one another to emotional issues and concerns of their respective clients that could affect the tone or movement of a four-way meeting.

- They share information about personal events in the client's life and history that will help the other lawyer guide discussions in fruitful directions.

- The purpose of sharing such information always is to advance the interests of the client by streamlining the effectiveness with which the lawyers can manage agendas and guide negotiations to avoid conflict and move toward constructive solutions.

If clients request that information of an emotional or personal nature be kept confidential and there is no objective issue-related need to know on the other side, the collaborative lawyer keeps the information confidential. Never does the lawyer disclose something that a client has directed him or her to keep confidential.

But the collaborative lawyer ought to discuss with the client whether the collaborative process should continue if, despite the lawyer's best efforts, the client is impeding the lawyer's ability to collaborate effectively by needlessly constraining effective communications between counsel.[15] The lawyer is the guardian of the process; the client is the guardian of the substance. If the client cannot accept this division of responsibility, it is unlikely that he or she is going to be served well by collaborative representation.

Another well-considered set of protocols is that adopted by the Collaborative Law Institute of Minnesota. Their *Collaborative Law Institute Protocols* is an 18-page compilation that is "intended to be a roadmap to consistency among practitioners, but should not be utilized inflexibly, as the process needs in each case will vary depending on circumstances." Couched less formally than the Texas protocols, the Minnesota protocols use bullet points rather than the language of legal rules to guide the practitioner from the beginning to the end of a collaborative representation, not only in terms of what to do and in what order, but also in terms of the special role and responsibilities that a collaborative lawyer assumes in undertaking this model of representation. While less formal in tone than the Texas protocols, these protocols are extremely detailed. For example, here is the protocol for the first conversation between collaborative lawyers at the start of a new case:

   B. Commencing the Case—At the outset of a case, Collaborative Law attorneys meet or talk by telephone:
   1. To introduce themselves to one another and establish a tone for a good working professional relationship throughout the case;
   2. To reaffirm the requirement of full disclosure of all legally relevant facts and matters regarding the case;

3. To identify issues or matters unique to each Client relevant to the dissolution process, such as:

Emotional/Physical issues
- Anxiety/anger
- Depression/mental illness
- Chemical dependency
- Physical, verbal or emotional abuse
- Infidelity or other marital misconduct

Learning Styles/Process Needs
- Need to move slowly or quickly
- Need for more or less professional assistance to understand relevant facts and issues
- Preference for auditory or visual communication

Practical Matters
- Payment of fees—financial resources of each party to do so
- Restrictions on either party affecting time and place for four-way meetings

4. To discuss means to accommodate each Client, such as:
   a. Use of coaches or child specialists;
   b. Tools to use in four-way meetings (i.e., visual aids, software programs);
   c. Whether caucusing during four-way meetings should be permitted to occur, or, under certain circumstances, whether Clients should be in different rooms;
   d. Location of four-way meetings. (Location is usually alternated between the attorneys' offices or takes place at some other "neutral" location.);
   e. Seating arrangements at four-way meetings; and
   f. Time requirements (length of meetings, time of meetings, time between meetings, amount of time to complete the dissolution process).

5. To identify pressing needs of each Client, such as:
   a. Need to establish parenting arrangements;
   b. Need for financial support; and
   c. Need for exclusive occupancy of home.
   (A pressing issue is a matter that must have a temporary solution in order to permit the parties to carry on until the next four-way meeting. It is not intended to be anything other than a temporary solution.)

6. To identify issues and matters not in dispute;

7. To discuss and agree on an agenda for the first four-way meeting; and

8. To discuss which Collaborative Law attorney will:

   a. Prepare the Participation Agreement;

   b. Draft the Joint Petition;

   c. Prepare and circulate the agenda; and

   d. Draft and circulate minutes following each four-way meeting.

Perhaps the most extensive protocols currently in use as of mid-2008 are those of the Collaborative Council of the Redwood Empire (Sonoma County, California), consisting of a 275-page bound manual with chapters entitled: Initial Steps, Agreements, Process Framework, Information Gathering, Four-Way Meetings, Negotiations, and Completing the Case.

Collaborative Law in the Larger ADR Context

Those new to collaborative law or skeptical about it sometimes worry that the collaborative contract itself, involving a commitment to stay out of court and disqualification of both lawyers if the process breaks down, might run afoul of lawyers' professional responsibility to provide full and complete legal advice and counsel to our clients. This concern is addressed in certain ethics opinions (see *supra* in this chapter) as well as in the protocols discussed above. These concerns may be expected to diminish as collaborative practice expands, and as the anticipated uniform model collaborative law statute becomes available, recognizing and authorizing the practice of collaborative law.[16]

Meanwhile, practitioners in states lacking a statute or ethics opinion may find the legal underpinnings of other conflict resolution modalities to be relevant and of interest. For some decades now, there has been movement in civil conflict resolution generally and family law specifically toward so-called "alternative" (more felicitously named "appropriate") dispute resolution as the first and favored resort, rather than litigation. For instance, many state codes impose mandatory mediation or arbitration requirements on family law and civil litigants before they are permitted access to the trial courts. The federal court system has embraced both mediation and early neutral evaluation to assist parties to resolve disputes out of court.[17] The California Family Code (§ 271) allows the family law court to "base an award of attorneys' fees and costs on the extent to which the conduct of each party or attorney furthers or frustrates the policy of the law to motivate settlement of litigation and, where possible, to reduce the cost of litigation by encouraging cooperation between parties and attorneys." And no less an authority than Supreme Court Justice Warren Burger urged lawyers to become "healers, not warriors."[18]

In light of this growing mandate that litigation be treated as a last rather than a first resort for dispute resolution, appellate decisions in many jurisdictions have scrutinized carefully contentions of litigants that would undermine the ability of lawyers to provide effective alternative dispute-resolution services.[19] That being so, there is reason for some confidence that (provided lawyers do their job carefully and well) collaborative law, too, will be treated favorably by the courts should disputes arise about whether collaborative contracts will be enforced, or whether this work lies within or outside the family lawyer's standard of care.[20]

Although no reported decisions yet exist relating to collaborative law,[21] a well-reasoned 1999 ethics opinion from the Los Angeles County Bar Association[22] concerning unbundling of legal services addresses many of the same concerns being raised by some cautious lawyers embarking on collaborative practice. The conclusion of that ethics opinion is that a lawyer who contracts with a client to limit significantly the scope of representation of a client must make the limitations clear and explicit. The opinion warns that the lawyer should be careful to advise the prospective client of any risks associated with the limitations on the lawyer's scope of representation, and remains under a duty of care to advise the client about his or her rights, the alternatives available under the circumstances, the consequences of each, their cost, and their likelihood of success (citing Nichols v. Keller, 15 Cal. App. 4th 1672, 1684–87, 19 Cal. Rptr. 2d. 601 (1993). Further, as asserted in dicta in *Nichols,* although "the attorney may still have a duty to alert the client to legal problems which are reasonably apparent, even though they fall outside the scope of representation . . . [t]he attorney need not represent the client on such matters. Nevertheless, the attorney should inform the client of the limitations of the attorney's representation and of the possible need for other counsel." 15 Cal. App. 4th at 1684.[23]

Informed Consent: How Much, and About What?

Both in terms of ethical responsibilities and in terms of standards of practice, it is apparent that informed consent is vital. In "no fault" divorce jurisdictions, the informed-consent process that is undertaken at the start of a collaborative case will focus primarily on ensuring that the client understands the specific characteristics of the collaborative process itself as compared to other conflict-resolution models: the disqualification agreement, the client's direct participation in all negotiations, the way that reactive or emotion-fueled thinking on the part of the client will be handled, the focus on long-term as well as short-term interests, the need to have goals beyond narrow economic self interest for the process to work, the kind of process information the lawyers will share, the nature of interdisciplinary team involvement, and so forth.

The informed-consent process is more complicated where the very choice of the collaborative model may alter the ability of the client to pursue certain legal avenues or expose the client to legal risks. Examples include: disclosure risks in jurisdictions where fault-based divorce is still an option, or where domestic violence or other marital torts may exist between the couple; where reportable child abuse may be involved; where (as in the United Kingdom) lawyers have a duty to report certain kinds of criminal economic malfeasance by the client; or where choice of forum has a major impact on rights (e.g., where Hague Convention or other custody jurisdictional and/or substantive rights, or substantive laws regarding economic rights, substantially differ between possible forums).

Collaborative lawyers have an ethical duty to advise clients about potential direct or collateral substantive claims under their own state laws that cannot be addressed within the collaborative process. For example, in a state that permits clients to elect between fault and no-fault divorce, the collaborative lawyer would be obliged to advise clients about any differences in rights and remedies, as well as the potential costs, benefits, and risks of each approach, and to make it clear that in electing collaborative law the client is choosing not to pursue any fault-based claims, perhaps irrevocably. Similarly, in states where it is possible to pursue civil claims for adultery or other tort claims arising out of the marital relationship, the client should be advised about the potential existence of those claims, the costs and benefits and risks associated with pursuing them, the fact that it is not possible to pursue such fault-based claims within the collaborative process, and the possibility that disclosures within the collaborative process could affect the viability of such claims should the collaborative process terminate. Also, one party may have information as yet unavailable to the other spouse that if disclosed could give rise to civil or criminal consequences outside the collaborative process (e.g., tax fraud). And, in the procedural realm, where more than one state or nation might colorably exercise jurisdiction, how jurisdictional issues will be handled where collaborative law is being considered by a client can give rise to serious consequences with regard to substantive legal rights. Informed consent implicates all these matters.[24]

In the end, highly risk-averse lawyers may decide to wait until there are formal ethics opinions, statutes, or appellate decisions within their own jurisdictions specifically addressing these concerns in the realm of collaborative practice.

Malpractice Claims and Collaborative Legal Practice

Family lawyers know that practitioners in our field face a comparatively high exposure to malpractice claims from disgruntled clients, particularly as a defense to fee-collection efforts.[25] Maintaining adequate malpractice insurance is important to us, and making sure that the legal work we do falls within our policy coverage is equally important.

It is not possible to assure readers that collaborative law representation falls within the scope of coverage of all their malpractice insurance policies. Each reader can answer that question for himself or herself by writing to the malpractice insurance carrier, describing simply but fully the elements of collaborative law practice, and asking two questions of the carrier. First, is this work the practice of law for purposes of inclusion with the scope of coverage of the existing policy? And second, if not, is there a rider that can be purchased, similar to a mediation rider, that will provide coverage for that work? To date, the author is aware of no major carrier that has determined collaborative practice to fall outside the realm of covered services. In other words, when asked, carriers appear to conclude that collaborative practice is not different in essence from the other kinds of work lawyers do.[26] That conclusion appears eminently sensible. Any reader who is concerned about this issue should satisfy himself or herself about questions of coverage, and should not rely on the author's views.

From a logical viewpoint, there is no obvious reason to regard the work of a collaborative lawyer as anything but good legal advocacy, counsel, and negotiation—old wine in a new bottle. The collaborative lawyer has a responsibility, like any lawyer, to advise and counsel the client fully, to advocate diligently on the client's behalf, to abide by the attorney-client privilege, and the like. In some circumstances, adhering to the terms of the collaborative participation agreement may require that the collaborative lawyer terminate the collaborative process or withdraw, and help the client make the transition to new counsel. Lawyers do this from time to time in conventional representation as well. While the collaborative lawyer will not take the client's case to court, the collaborative lawyer may have to advise the client to do so, and help the client find a lawyer to conduct the court proceedings. Doing these aspects of the collaborative work carefully is just as much a part of the collaborative lawyer's responsibility as conducting skillful negotiations. Careful attention to informed consent before the participation agreement is signed, and performing the work of transitioning the client to other counsel where necessary, will be important areas for collaborative lawyers to attend to.

Might a collaborative lawyer be sued for malpractice? Of course. However, to the author's knowledge, this has yet to occur at the time of the writing of this second edition, 18 years after the first collaborative representations concluded. Any professional can be sued at any time by an unhappy client. Malpractice insurance carriers often advise lawyers that the best protection against a malpractice suit is attention to the human dimension of the lawyer-client relationship—for example, answering client inquiries promptly, keeping the client well-informed of the progress of the case, billing regularly and providing detailed billing explanations, and apologizing sincerely when errors or annoyances happen.[27] Lawyers are also advised by their malpractice carriers to avoid the unreasonable client, the client who is on a crusade for abstract justice, the client who moves from lawyer to lawyer, and other inherently difficult people.[28] By all these measures, collaborative lawyers have good reason to believe that they are at significantly lower risk for malpractice claims than their adversarial colleagues. The clients who choose the collaborative mode of representation are not on a quest for revenge or abstract justice, nor do they tend to lawyer-shop or to identify highly unrealistic objectives. The nature of collaborative representation makes it easy to connect on a more human level with the client than in litigation practice, particularly since four-way meetings with a great deal of direct client participation constitute the core of a collaborative representation. By definition, recalibrating the expectations of the client to a reasonable range, proceeding at a pace the clients are comfortable with, and arriving at agreements that both parties consider reasonable, are at the heart of collaborative practice and are not likely to result in angry, frustrated clients consumed with buyer's or seller's remorse.[29]

The greatest risk of malpractice suits against collaborative lawyers probably lies in that small percentage of cases that terminate short of agreement, where the parties end up in court represented by litigation counsel. If the case ultimately goes poorly, the client may point the finger of blame at the collaborative lawyer as well as the divorce trial counsel, claiming that participation in the collaborative process somehow prejudiced her interests. Other risks for the collaborative lawyer include one party or the other seeking to attack in subsequent litigation elements of the collaborative contract (e.g., the disqualification stipulation, or the insulation of documents from admissibility in court); and one party attempting to claim that the collaborative participation agreement somehow gives rise to a duty that the lawyer for the *other* party owed him—and breached.

The best protection for the collaborative practitioner against these and other risks of engaging in a still-new mode of conflict resolution remains best practices like these:

- ensuring that the engagement letter and collaborative participation agreement that will be signed by the client are comprehensive, well-drafted, and clear
- spending ample time at the start of the representation ensuring that the unique aspects of collaborative representation and negotiations are fully explained and understood by the client
- avoiding acting as a cheerleader or huckster for collaborative law, instead providing balanced information about both the advantages and disadvantages of all conflict-resolution choices, including collaborative law
- making sure that clients understand exactly what kind of collaborative services will and will not be provided in their specific case
- making sure that clients understand how you will bill for your services and helping them assess realistically whether they can afford the services you contemplate providing before you begin
- making sure that clients understand the timing and pacing of a typical collaborative case and do not have unrealistic expectations of speed
- making sure that the prospective client is not seeking collaborative representation for purposes of manipulation, delay, or other bad-faith reasons
- making sure that clients understand and agreed in writing about how confidentiality and privilege issues will be handled in the collaborative representation
- making it clear to the client that a unilateral decision to litigate by the other party will cause you to have to terminate your lawyer-client relationship
- declining to undertake collaborative representation where there is no confidence that the lawyers can work together effectively to guide negotiations and manage conflict
- declining to undertake collaborative representation where there is reason to believe the client or the spouse will not be able to participate fully, intelligently, and in good faith
- ensuring that in situations where interdisciplinary collaborative team resources seem essential for the clients to be able to participate effectively, those resources are on board—or if they are not, declining to represent collaboratively

- Working with your colleagues in your practice group to elevate standards of practice and to develop and adhere to sound protocols for practice
- Becoming familiar with all local and national standards for collaborative practice and implementing them in your own work

Conclusion

The ethical practice of law requires, at a minimum, the informed consent of the client and the loyalty of the lawyer to the client's interests. The meanings of "informed consent" and "loyalty" are not fixed; these concepts change with the times, a fact that is evident as one reviews the evolution of the ABA Model Code and its predecessors, and the academic literature about legal ethics.[30] At any moment in time, reasonable lawyers can easily disagree about how much information is required for fully informed client consent, and in any event, the amount of the information that is required varies from client to client, depending upon the client's sophistication, knowledge, and even psychological state. The question of a lawyer's loyalty to the client's interests is also not a fixed or static standard, but depends in large measure on a full understanding of what the client's interests actually are.

Rather than adopting an automatic and somewhat circular view that a client's interests must necessarily be identical with the lawyer's own view of those interests—an approach that puts the rabbit in the hat by defining client interests in terms of the lawyer's own preconceived ideas about advocacy and the lawyer's proper role—collaborative lawyers spend a great deal of effort during the initial stages of the representation working with the client to identify the client's own interests as the client sees them. Collaborative lawyers also as a "best practice" spend considerable effort ensuring that the client understands the collaborative practice processes and goals in the context of the menu of conflict-resolution options available to the client. In this author's experience, the widely shared understanding that the collaborative lawyer has an obligation to explore client interests carefully and to explain conflict-resolution options thoroughly at the start of the representation causes collaborative practice to stand out as distinctly different from other types of legal representation, which do not necessarily operate with a shared baseline expectation that responsible and ethical legal representation begins there.[31]

It can be said with confidence that this is the consistent message of those providing leadership in the collaborative movement. In collaborative trainings and writings and in the collaborative practice standards and protocols that have been published, there is a clear and consistent emphasis on the importance—resulting from the newness of collaborative practice and the lack of widespread awareness of its elements—of ensuring that the client becomes as fully informed as reasonably possible before entering into a participation agreement and proceeding with a collaborative process in his or her own case. Not only is the lawyer expected to do this privately with the client in the early stages of representation, but further, the consistent practice protocol is for the first four-way meeting to be devoted entirely to confirming, face-to-face, both clients' understanding of and commitment to the specific terms of the collaborative process.

What about the lawyer's loyalty to the client? It has been argued—unpersuasively, in the author's view—that when a collaborative lawyer signs the participation agreement and agrees to withdraw if either party takes the dispute to court, the lawyer thereby assumes a duty of loyalty or obligation to the opposing party such that the attorney's loyalty to his or her own client potentially becomes compromised. Those who have advanced that argument fail to appreciate the "paradigm shift" that lawyers are taught to make if they are to do effective work in a collaborative practice representation. The commitment of each lawyer to withdraw if either party breaches his or her commitment to a respectful, good-faith, negotiated resolution of the dispute (regardless of how impassioned and forceful the negotiations might be), is at the heart of collaborative practice, and is the commitment that each lawyer makes to *his or her own client in the first instance*. Each lawyer promises each client—at the client's request and direction—that everything ethically permissible will be done to resolve the dispute without resorting to the path of litigation, with all the risks and harms that the litigation path is well-known to entail, and that the highest and best motives, desires, hopes, aspirations, feelings, needs, and responsibilities of each party will be recognized, acknowledged, and responded to in the process.

If your client understands and embraces that commitment and asks you to do the same, and if you, as a lawyer, make that commitment to your client after satisfying yourself that the client is making a fully informed and reasonable choice, can it be said that you are not fully loyal to your client and your client's interests? Surely the professional ethics of our profession should not be read so narrowly as to deprive a fully informed and competent client of the right to choose collaborative conflict resolution and legal representation. Any competent lawyer can envision some theoretical situations in which difficult challenges could arise under a collaborative participation agreement. But surely a balancing of the advantages of collaborative representation against the known risks of litigation, particularly in a family law context, and particularly given our growing awareness of the predictable damage to children in litigated family matters, weighs heavily in favor of allowing our clients to choose collaborative representation and to allow collaborative lawyers to do this work—work that has not been shown to have harmed any clients and that seems to serve remarkably well the interests of those who have chosen it. That is the view that nearly all ethics opinions take, the view that predominates in the academic literature, and in the state legislatures that have enacted collaborative statutes.

Collaborative practice opens the door to a new way of seeing the lawyer-client relationship. Family lawyers know that most of our clients come to us wanting the counsel and advocacy of a lawyer who will guide them toward the resolution of disputes in a way that preserves the client's integrity while reaching an outcome that is equitable, reasonable, and satisfactory in terms of the client's own perceived needs and interests. On difficult days—which clients encounter with some regularity during any divorce conflict-resolution process—there is a certain appeal to the idea of revenge. But when lawyers provide wise counsel to their clients, the idea rarely has lasting appeal. We are not only advisors about the law; we are also, necessarily, the wise counselors to our clients about the nature of conflict and conflict resolution, and about the nature of the divorce transition itself, and we are the only professionals who are likely to be in a position to provide that wise counsel to people going through immensely stressful but temporary life changes. Since the Greek poets and playwrights, it has been clear that vengeance is not nearly as sweet as it appears during moments of anger or jealousy, and that even when achieved, it has a short shelf life and long collateral consequences.[32] Preserving personal integrity, and helping a client achieve the satisfaction that he or she behaved with dignity and fairness in reaching resolution, can have a powerful effect in satisfying the actual needs and interests of the client going through divorce—as distinct from achieving maximum outcome defined solely in terms of the legal rights that can be pursued in litigation.

Clients surely have the right to be informed fully by their legal counselors, not only about their legal rights—though that is essential information—but also about the other powerful human needs and interests of both adults and children that are implicated in the life passage that is divorce. Lawyers who capably provide that perspective and that kind of legal representation surely have their client's interests at the forefront of their work, while lawyers who cannot see this are in a real sense substituting their own views for those of their clients as to what really matters and what does not.

A PRACTICE GROUP MEMBERSHIP AGREEMENT

This membership agreement represents an approach a practice group might take to ensure that all its members are well trained, participate in the activities of the group, and follow best practices, including standards and protocols. This isn't the only way to do it, nor necessarily the best way to address every concern, but it touches nearly all the important bases in a way that looks as if it might succeed in its goals.

INDEPENDENT COLLABORATIVE ATTORNEYS OF CENTRAL PENNSYLVANIA MEMBERSHIP AGREEMENT

I, _____, hereby agree to become a member of the Independent Collaborative Attorneys of Central Pennsylvania (ICACP). I understand that my membership is subject to the terms and conditions set forth in this Agreement and such other terms and conditions as may hereafter be adopted by the ICACP.

1. I certify that I have met, or will meet as indicated, the following mandatory criteria for membership in the ICACP:

   A. I am now an active member of the Pennsylvania Bar.

   B. Prior to my initial application for membership in the ICACP, I successfully completed a two (2) day training in Collaborative Law which was at least twelve (12) hours in length.

   C. I will be a member of IACP while I am a member of ICACP.

   D. I have completed or will complete on or before December 31 of the year that I joined ICACP, a minimum of twenty-four (24) hours of mediation training. I understand that if I do not complete the training by the end of the current year, I will not be a member of ICACP as of January 1 of next year and my name will be removed from all materials and the web-site of ICACP, as well as the ICACP listing on the IACP website.

   Please initial the appropriate statement:

   _____ I have completed the required mediation training.

   _____ I have not yet completed the required mediation training, however, I will complete this requirement by December 31 of this year and will notify the Chair of the Policy and Procedure Committee as soon as my training is complete.

   E. I have malpractice insurance coverage in the minimum amount of $200,000.00 per incident and agree that I will continuously maintain such minimum coverage throughout the course of my membership in the ICACP.

2. I understand that the following criteria are recommended for all members of ICACP:

   A. The attendance at the monthly ICACP General Membership meetings.

   B. The participation in committee meetings and activities of ICACP.

3. I acknowledge that the ICACP has adopted the following conditions to maintain membership in good standing and agree that I will comply with each of these conditions:

   A. All of my collaborative family law cases with other members of ICACP will be conducted in accordance with all rules and protocols of the ICACP as may be adopted from time to time, including without limitation utilization of the ICACP Collaborative Law Participation Agreement and other forms developed and adopted by the ICACP for use in collaborative cases.

   B. I will follow all of the standards of practice adopted by the ICACP for collaborative family law cases including the following:

      i. Prompt production of full and fair discovery.

      ii. Advance preparation with client and counsel for all four-way meetings.

      iii. Timely preparation of four-way meeting agendas and meeting session minutes as allocated between counsel.

      iv. Prompt debriefing with client and counsel following four-way meetings.

   C. I have paid or will pay to the ICACP a nonrefundable initiation fee of Three Hundred Dollars ($300.00), and an annual nonrefundable membership fee as established by ICACP, prorated quarterly for the first year of membership based on the date of my initial application for membership. I understand that the amount of the annual dues will be adopted each year by the ICACP and I agree to make payment of such within thirty (30) days of the adoption.

   D. Upon adoption by the ICACP for an additional assessment during any calendar year, I agree to make payment of the assessment within thirty (30) days of the adoption.

4. I acknowledge that my membership in the ICACP must be renewed each calendar year no later than January 31 and that my current membership ends on December 31 of this year.

5. I agree that I will hold myself out as a member of the ICACP only while my membership is in good standing.

6. I understand that I may terminate my membership in the ICACP by notification of such in writing to the chair of the Policy and Procedure Committee and that upon such termination my name may be removed from the ICACP member list, brochure, website, and any other IACP or ICACP marketing or education materials.

7. I acknowledge that my membership in the ICACP may be terminated by the ICACP, upon recommendation of the Policy and Procedure Committee, if I fail to meet the criteria or conditions for membership as set forth in this Agreement or hereafter adopted by the ICACP and in the event my membership is terminated by the ICACP, my name may be removed from the ICACP member list, brochure, website, and any other ICACP marketing or education materials including the ICACP listing on the IACP website.

8. I agree that any dispute related to my membership shall be submitted to the Policy and Procedure Committee for resolution in accordance with guidelines and procedures adopted by the ICACP.

By signing this Membership Agreement, I certify that the statements made herein are true and correct.

Date: _____

[revised December 8, 2006] Signature of Member

Notes

1. For assistance with portions of the material that appears in this chapter, I am grateful to Peter Sandmann, David Hoffman, Sonia Song, and Diane Diel.

2. The sample form retainer or engagement letter provided in Appendix I-A and discussed in Chapter 8 includes a provision for constructive termination of the collaborative process where the client is in bad faith. The IACP Ethical Standards, Section 9, address termination by the lawyer. (See Appendix I-I.)

3. *See, e.g.,* Deborah L. Rhode, *Ethical Perspectives on Legal Practice,* 37 Stan. L. Rev. 589, (1985); Richard Wasserstrom, *Lawyers as Professionals: Some Moral Issues,* 5 Hum. Rts. 1, (1975); Gerald J. Postema, *Moral Responsibility in Professional Ethics,* 55 N.Y.U.L. Rev. 63, 1980; Monroe H. Freedman, *Moral Responsibility in a Professional System,* 27 Cath. U. L. Rev. 191, 1978; Rand Jack & Dana Crowley Jack, Moral Vision and Professional Decisions: The Changing Values of Women and Men Lawyers (1989); Pauline H. Tesler, *Collaborative Law: What It Is and Why Family Law Attorneys Need to Know About It,* 13 Am. J. Fam. L. 215, 1999.

4. American Bar Association Model Rules of Professional Conduct, Rule 1.14, amended pursuant to recommendations set forth in ABA Ethics 2000, guides lawyers in representing clients with diminished capacity (formerly termed "disability" under the rules); Model Rule 2.1 allows a lawyer to counsel a client not only about the law, but also about moral, economic, social, and political considerations. The American Academy of Matrimonial Lawyers' *Bounds of Advocacy* goes so far as to advise that a lawyer need not follow even a competent client's irrational or potentially harmful directives. These ethical guidelines speak with particular cogency to collaborative lawyers. *See* David Walther, *The Ethics of Advocacy,* 23 Fam. Advocate 37 (Winter 2001).

5. Legal scholars place this shift in the context of larger transformations in the legal profession's understanding of effective advocacy. *See, e.g.,* Julie MacFarlane, The New Lawyer (2007); Susan Daicoff, Lawyer, Know Thyself: A Psychological Analysis of Personality Strengths and Weaknesses (2004); Dennis P. Stolle, David Wexler, & Bruce Winick, (eds.), Practicing Therapeutic Jurisprudence: Law as a Helping Profession (2000); and Marjorie Silver (ed.), The Affective Assistance of Counsel: Practicing Law as a Healing Profession (2007).

6. This chapter is not intended to be a comprehensive treatise on the ethics of collaborative law, but rather an introduction and overview as of mid-2008. A lawyer who has serious concerns about the ethics of collaborative practice will find the information in this chapter useful as a starting point for legal research. The public sections of the IACP website offer additional information, with more resources available in the members-only section. It is likely that the web pages for the Dispute Resolution Section of the American Bar Association will provide further resources. The IACP Ethics Task Force plans to publish a comprehensive White Paper on the ethics of collaborative legal practice sometime in 2008.

7. The text is available at http://tlo2.tlc.state.tx.us/statutes/docs/FA/content/htm/fa.001 .00.000006.00.htm.

8. The text is available at http://www.ncga.state.nc.us/gascripts/Statutes/StatutesTOC .pl?Chapter=.

9. The text is available at http://www.leginfo.ca.gov/cgi-bin/calawquery?codesection= fam&codebody=collaborative&hits=20.

10. The October 2007 discussion draft of a proposed Uniform Collaborative Law Act (National Conference of Commissioners on Uniform State Laws) can be found at www .collaborativepractice.com/lib/PDFs/CollLaw_Draft_Oct07.pdf. For a discussion of the need for state legislation, *see* Elizabeth K. Strickland, *Putting "Counselor" Back in the Lawyer's Job Description: Why More States Should Adopt Collaborative Law Statutes*, 84 N.C.L. Rev. 979 (2006).

11. On February 24, 2007, the Ethics Committee of the Colorado Bar Association issued an advisory opinion—the first and only such opinion in the 12 or more nations where collaborative law is currently practiced—concluding that Colorado attorneys cannot sign a collaborative law participation agreement that both lawyers and both clients execute without violating the Colorado Rules of Professional Conduct. In an important footnote, however, the opinion notes that the clients themselves could sign the collaborative participation agreement, and could also enter into retainer agreements with their own lawyers for legal representation in a manner consistent with the principles of collaborative law as well as Colorado ethics rules. Interestingly, §§ 50-72 of the North Carolina collaborative law statute mandate that lawyers do precisely what the Colorado advisory opinion considers unethical: "Agreement requirements. A collaborative law agreement must be in writing, signed by all the parties to the agreement and their attorneys, and must include provisions for the withdrawal of all attorneys involved in the collaborative law procedure if the collaborative law procedure does not result in settlement of the dispute." The Texas statute has a similar provision specifying an agreement executed by both lawyers and both clients ("§ 6.603. COLLABORATIVE LAW. (a) On a written agreement of the parties and their attorneys, a dissolution of marriage proceeding may be conducted under collaborative law procedures.").

The Colorado opinion has been widely criticized for its narrowly legalistic reasoning and for its unpersuasive conclusions, most definitely in Formal Opinion 07-447 of the ABA Standing Committee on Ethics and Professional Responsibility (August 9, 2007). The opinion appears in Appendix I-K. *See also The Ethics of the Collaborative Participation Agreement: A Critique of Colorado's Maverick Ethics Opinion* (2007), http://www .collaborativepractice.com/documents/IACPEthicsTaskForcearticle.pdf.

12. The report, entitled *Collaborative Practice in Family Law: A Report to the Attorney-General prepared by the Family Law Council*, can be found at: http://www.ag.gov.au/ agd/WWW/flcHome.nsf/Page/Publications_Reports_to_the_AG_All_Reports_Collaborative_ Practice_in_Family_Law. It begins,

> Recommendation 1: The Family Law Council and the Law Council of Australia should establish a working group to develop national guidelines for collaborative practice in family law. The working group should comprise members and observers of the Family Law Council and nominees of the Law Council of Australia, who will in turn consult with representatives of each State and Territory together with community-based service providers involved in the new family law system. In undertaking this task, the working group should:
>
> (a) further disseminate for discussion the draft Guidelines attached in Appendix A to this report
>
> (b) explore how cross-sector professional relationships may be strengthened to facilitate collaborative practice, and
>
> consider how best to develop specialist accreditation to ensure a consistent standard of collaborative practice in Australia.

The IACP website, www.collaborativepractice.com, expects to post a selected resource bank of ethics rules and opinions from U.S. and non-U.S. jurisdictions relating to collaborative law sometime in 2008.

13. Legal malpractice claims involve allegations that a lawyer failed to practice with the knowledge and skill that lawyers of ordinary skill possess. Widespread adoption of congruent minimum standards for collaborative legal practice should enable clients across the international collaborative community to expect, as a matter of law, that collaborative lawyers will comply with those standards, to the benefit of both clients and collaborative colleagues.

14. The IACP Ethical Standards (see Appendix I-I for text) include (in Section 9) protocols on two centrally important matters: the sharing of information among members of the professional team, and provisions for withdrawal of counsel or termination of the collaborative process where bad faith participation occurs.

15. *See* ABA Model Rules of Professional Conduct, Rule 1.6 (a lawyer may reveal confidential information if "the disclosure is impliedly authorized in order to carry out the representation . . .").

16. Two treatises slated for publication in 2008 should provide resources for those wishing to delve more deeply into ethics questions. One is a white paper from the Collaborative Law Committee of the ABA Dispute Resolution Section. The second is an academic study being written pursuant to a grant from the International Academy of Collaborative Professionals through its Ethics Task Force.

17. *See, e.g.,* United States District Court, Northern District of California, Local Rules, ADR Rule 5 (Early Neutral Evaluation), ADR Rule 6 (Mediation)[both adopted in substantially their present form in 1995].

18. http://www.u-s-history.com/pages/h2022.html.

19. For instance, *In re* Jensen, 966 S.W.2d 850, 851 (Texas); *In re* Acceptance Ins. Co., 33 S.W.3d 443, 451 (Texas); Gibson v. Bobroff, 57 Cal. Rptr. 2d 235, 239 (California); *Matter of Marriage of A.,* 860 S.W.2d 590, 592 (Florida); Brucker v. McKinlay, 557 N.W.2d 536, 540 (Michigan).

20. In California, for example, well before a collaborative statute went into effect in 2007, it was clear that a lawyer and client could agree to limit the scope of the lawyer's representation of the client, so long as (1) the lawyer advises the client fully about the limits of the lawyer's role in the case and (2) the client consents expressly to the limited role. *See, e.g.,* Joseph E. DiLoreto, Inc. v. O'Neill (1991) 1 Cal. App. 4th 149, 158, 1 Cal. Rptr. 2d 636, 641. Cf. Rule 5.70 (a), California Rules of Court (concerning unbundled legal services); Rules of Professional Conduct of the State Bar of California 3-400 (acknowledging in the discussion of the rule that it is permissible for members of the California bar ethically to reasonably limit "the scope of the member's employment or representation"). Similarly, see American Bar Association Model Rules, Commentary to Rule 1.2 ("The scope of services to be provided by a lawyer may be limited by agreement with the client or by the terms under which the lawyer's services are made available to the client.") and Massachusetts Rules of Professional Conduct, Commentary to Rule 1.2 ("the terms upon which representation is undertaken may exclude specific objectives or means.") In other words, lawyers and clients can agree in advance not to seek outcomes that a court could award, and can agree to exclude litigation entirely as a means. This is what collaborative lawyers and clients do.

21. As of mid-2008, 18 years after the first collaborative lawyer began practicing in this model, the author is aware of no malpractice suit alleging professional negligence in delivery of collaborative legal services in any jurisdiction within or outside the United States.

22. Los Angeles County Bar Association Formal Ethics Opinion 502 (1999).

23. Theodore Schneyer sees the emphasis on informed consent as the criterion for ethical practice of collaborative law as an illustration of a pendulum swing in ethics opinions toward favoring client autonomy over client protection where those interests are in tension. Theodore Schneyer, *The Organized Bar and the Collaborative Law Movement: A Study in Professional Change,* 50 Arizona L. Rev. 289, 316 (2008).

24. Collaborative lawyers in European Union jurisdictions are taking the lead in developing protocols and strategies for satisfying ethical obligations to the client with respect to choice of forum while still maintaining collaborative representation as a viable option. For instance, clients might establish jurisdiction with the assistance of a conventional family law-

yer, with the understanding that the intent thereafter will be to shift to collaborative counsel if the spouse is willing.

25. "Experience has shown us that a cross-complaint for malpractice is not an unusual concomitant to a fee dispute between lawyer and client." 10 Lawyers Mutual Ins. Co. Bull. (1995). "[R]eal estate attorneys, divorce lawyers and personal injury lawyers have a higher likelihood of being sued" than those in other specialty areas of practice, according to an article in the National Law Journal, *How Small Firms Can Ward Off Malpractice Suits* (April 18, 2005). Because traditional family law clients so often experience disappointment with the results of trial or settlement, because they so often cannot afford the fees and costs of representation, and because the gladiatorial lawyer creates high expectations and often is the most obvious person in the picture to blame for failing to make it all better, many litigators operate with one eye on the opposing party as the immediate adversary, and another eye on the client as a potential future adversary.

26. For example, the Lawyers Mutual Insurance Company, which provides coverage for many California lawyers, responded affirmatively in the early 1990s when lawyers in the Silicon Valley area queried whether their regular insurance policies would cover their collaborative work. Private correspondence between the author and Jonnie Herring, Certifed Specialist in Family Law, State Bar of California, 1994.

27. *See, e.g.,* 9 Lawyers Mutual Ins. Co. Bull. No. 5 and No. 7; http://www.ilead .com/ilead/malpractice_tips.htm.

28. *See, e.g.,* Lawyers Mutual Ins. Co. Bull. on these subjects: Vol. II, No. 2; Vol. 12, No. 6; Vol. 14, II.; Shannon B. Jones, *Seven Steps for Avoiding Legal Malpractice,* http://www .landy.com/download/misc/avoid_legal_malpractice.pdf ["Although communicating with a client seems like elementary advice, it is amazing how many attorneys do not adhere to it. In fact, a majority of all legal malpractice suits arise out of an attorney's failure to communicate with a client. If attorneys communicate effectively with their clients, they can avoid a lot of problems and improve client satisfaction. Communication includes asking and listening to what the client wants from a matter. Sometimes a client's interests or motivations are not what the attorney expects."]

29. Malpractice insurance underwriters may be waiting for empirical research data before we see this reality widely recognized by carriers in the terms of coverage for collaborative practitioners. But the trend is beginning. "In Minnesota, we have been working with Minnesota Lawyers Mutual, a cooperatively owned local insurer that provides the malpractice insurance for the overwhelming majority of attorneys in our state. They have been very interested in providing a discount to Collaborative practitioners. This past year, for the first time, their online application asked whether the applicant's family law practice was Collaborative." Private correspondence between the author and Ron Ousky, President-Elect (for 2008) of the International Academy of Collaborative Professionals, July 2007. Ousky believes that discounts may currently be in effect for Minnesota collaborative lawyers.

30. For an extended academic analysis of the ethics of collaborative legal practice in terms of existing ethics rules, *see* John Lande, *Principles for Policymaking about Collaborative Law and Other ADR Processes,* 22 Ohio St. J. on Disp. Resol. 619 (2007).

31. Obviously, different practitioners will display differing levels of skill and accomplishment as they undertake these tasks. But a review of collaborative practice protocols and writings shows that best practices consistently emphasize the need to start with educating the client about conflict resolution choices, ensuring that an informed process choice is made by the client, and exploring actual client interests with care at all stages of the representation. This is not characteristic of conventional legal practice. For example, the Bar Plan Mutual Insurance Company of Missouri, when asked about potential risks of collaborative legal practice, provided an opinion letter to a practitioner in 2003 which emphasized the importance of informed consent to the terms of the collaborative retention for purposes of risk minimization, and went on to note, "but of course, if lawyers had long, extensive counseling of clients in every instance, malpractice risks would be minimized in every type of representation. The problem is that lawyers routinely do not." Letter to Hugh F. O'Donnell, III, from

Christian A. Stiegemeyer, Director of Risk Management, The Bar Plan Mutual Insurance Company, October 10, 2003.

32. Theodore Schneyer refers to this aspect of the collaborative lawyer-client contract as a "Ulysses" proviso. In the ILIAD, Ulysses ordered his crew to lash him to the mast so that when he heard the sirens' song, which no man could resist, he would be unable to steer toward it—and to shipwreck on the twin rocky hazards, Scylla and Charybdis. Schneyer, *supra*, n. 142.

Chapter 8

Documents and Useful Forms

"Everything should be made as simple as possible, but not simpler."
—Albert Einstein

A set of complete, well-crafted documents forms the armature on which you will build a successful collaborative representation. These documents serve a number of procedural functions. They explain clearly and comprehensively what the responsibilities of each party and each collaborative lawyer will be and how the collaborative process works, and they confirm each step of the process that will take place. The clients will refer to these documents again and again to orient them when they become confused. The lawyers will use them as conflict-management tools. They constitute the baseline protection against any potential claims that a lawyer breached professional responsibilities in providing collaborative law services. In this chapter you will learn the purpose served by each of the basic collaborative law documents. A form for each document—one that has been used by other collaborative lawyers—is provided in Appendix I for you to use or adapt.

These forms are works in progress, reflecting ongoing contributions from many hundreds of collaborative lawyers over more than 15 years, integrating the thinking of many experienced practitioners and many well-established collaborative practice groups. You and your collaborative practice group will have many discussions about the precise wording of the basic documents your group will use—the participation agreements that both clients and both lawyers will sign to initiate a collaborative process. State law and local rules may require certain adaptations to the basic documentation forms provided in this book. They are the fundamental documentation used in collaborative representation.

Appendix I provides a representative set of collaborative practice documents and forms, some essential for the practice of collaborative law, and others optional internal forms in use in the author's practice or adapted from other models. This chapter addresses the use of each document and form. If you decide not to use these models, you and your colleagues will need to adapt or craft your own basic practice documents very carefully to meet the purposes served by each of the essential forms. You will also probably want to create your own form letters and checklists that will help you manage your collaborative practice effectively.

Other resources provide sample collaborative practice forms. Updated sample forms in use in various collaborative practice communities are posted from time to time at the IACP website, www.collaborativepractice .com, and also at the privately maintained collaborative listserv, collablaw@ yahoogroups.com (admission to this very lively listserv is open to all interested professionals, by application). You can also view variants of these documents in use throughout the collaborative community by going to the websites for particular practice groups. Links to many such practice group websites can be found on the IACP website. Some practice groups post their basic collaborative practice forms on the public section of their websites so that clients can become familiar with them. Some groups post them in the members section of the website, while others include them in protocols adopted by the group. Those groups that have adopted protocols will generally provide them on request, either for free or for a reasonable purchase price.

Several cautions: First, be aware that there is no single standard set of collaborative forms in use everywhere. Some versions are much are better than others and it is worth taking time to put together the best forms you can, and then to review them regularly to incorporate improvements. Second, you should not assume that the version of a basic collaborative practice form that you find either in this book or via web sources represents the best version currently available. An e-mail query to the collaborative listserv will usually yield information about the most current versions of basic forms being used by various groups. The forms are constantly updated and adapted to meet concerns as they arise.

You will find each of the forms discussed in this chapter in Appendix I and also in a CD-ROM in the inside back cover of this book. They may be freely used and adapted. Sharing improvements to these forms with the international collaborative community can be accomplished by uploading them to the collaborative listserv, collablaw@yahoogroups.com.[1]

Comments on the Use of These Forms

The forms provided in Appendix I and in the accompanying CD-ROM fall into four categories: intra-office forms for managing a collaborative practice effectively; documents establishing and supporting a collaborative case; documents ending a collaborative representation; and data-gathering forms.

Intra-Office Forms

Initial Telephone Screening Form

This telephone screening form is used in the author's office. (Review this form at Appendix I-A(1).) Support staff complete the form whenever a potential new client calls. It ensures that information about the collaborative law process is always offered to clients at their first inquiry, tracks necessary follow-up with the client, and provides basic information for the lawyer prior to the first lawyer-client conversation. You should adapt this form to include all points that you want your support staff to cover with potential clients during the first telephone contact. You can also augment it to include office administration checklists (e.g., notations for sending information packets, opening files, sending a retainer/engagement letter, etc.).

New Client Basic Information Form

This longer information form is filled in by new clients immediately before beginning the initial consultation with the lawyer. (Review this form at Appendix I-A(2).) It is a convenient and economical way for very basic information about the family to be gathered in one place without the lawyer billing for the time. It can be a comfortable springboard to begin the first conversation between the potential collaborative client and lawyer.

The Collaborative Retainer Agreement

The retainer agreement (sometimes called "engagement letter") is the basic contract between lawyer and client.[2] A good collaborative retainer agreement will do what all such documents do—lay out clearly what the lawyer's duties and responsibilities are, specify what is not included within the contract for representation, and describe the lawyer's charges and financial policies. (Review this form at Appendix I-A(3).) In addition, it is important that your collaborative retainer agreement clearly advise your client about the differences between retaining a conventional lawyer and retaining you, a collaborative lawyer. It will recite that this is a "limited-purpose retention" and emphasize that you will not under any circumstances represent the client in court proceedings—that you will cease representing the client at all if the matter should go to court.

The retainer should also educate the client about key differences between collaborative and adversarial legal proceedings from the client's perspective, including the facts that both lawyer and client commit to good-faith bargaining and voluntary discovery and that the lawyer will withdraw or terminate the collaborative process (a "constructive termination" by the client) if the client should abuse the collaborative process.[3]

The sample retainer letter offered in this chapter includes a section containing those disclosures, as well as other provisions required in retainer agreements under California law. It reflects contributions from many California collaborative practitioners.

Sample Letters to Prospective Clients, Spouses of Clients, and Lawyers for Spouses

The sample letters offered in Appendix I-A(4) meet a need that will arise as soon as your collaborative practice develops momentum. When potential clients want information about the collaborative law process, you will find it convenient to use a form letter that your secretary or assistant can be directed to send out with a book or information packet (or two packets if you are using the version of the letter that advises the client to share the information with the spouse). You can file copies of these letters in a designated alphabetical and cross-referenced folder for convenience when you need to do conflict checks.

Your clients and potential clients may ask that you send an information packet to the other party rather than doing so themselves. The form letter that you use for this purpose is very important because it may be the other party's first introduction to collaborative law and the first introduction to you as the spouse's lawyer. The letter needs to make clear that you are writing as counsel for the other spouse. It should be informative and courteous, but should not address any specifics of the particular case other than to advise the party to select collaborative counsel if he or she agrees that is a good way to proceed. (Bear in mind that you are sending an unsolicited letter to someone who may not have understood that a divorce is about to begin until your letter arrives.) This communication is an opportunity to educate the spouse and to lay groundwork for an effective collaborative process. Make sure you do it well.

If you have been retained by a client who has filed a divorce petition *in propria persona* (or *pro se*) and who is very eager to get started, under some circumstances you might be mailing the divorce petition to the spouse at the same time that you provide information about collaborative law. A sample letter for that purpose includes not only information about collaborative law but also information about service of the petition. Make clear in that letter to the other party whether you will be handling the conventional divorce process for your client if the recipient does not elect collaborative law, or whether you are going to be involved only provided both parties elect collaborative law.

At the point when the other spouse has retained collaborative counsel, whether as the first or as the second to do so, the next step is for the lawyers to make initial contact with one another. Ordinarily the first contact between collaborative lawyers would be by telephone, but included here is a sample first communication by letter with a collaborative lawyer you haven't worked with before who may be new to the process. You should have a good reason for initiating contact via letter; if there isn't one, use the telephone.

Financial Disclosure Forms

These financial disclosure forms have evolved from the statutory requirement in California that all divorcing parties complete both preliminary and final declarations of disclosure in connection with divorce. (Review this form at Appendix I-A(5).) In litigated divorces, information is often treated as a strategic weapon or resource, but in collaborative practice, we encourage our clients to expand, annotate, and in general to provide as much information as possible, in an organized way. These forms help clients do that task in cases that do not have a neutral financial consultant participating as part of an interdisciplinary collaborative divorce team. Your practice group might consider developing agreed-upon forms that will be used by all members in collaborative cases, or you can simply adapt this or a similarly complete form for use with your own clients. When a neutral financial consultant assists in a collaborative case, he or she normally gathers financial disclosure documents under the guidance of the two lawyers and prepares draft spreadsheets and budgets for both parties, which are then used in the Act One disclosure phase of the collaborative process.

Documents Establishing and Supporting a Collaborative Case

The forms described in this section should be discussed and adopted by each practice group, with an understanding or protocol that all group members will use these forms and that they will be adapted regularly over time as needed. In some communities, form documents are adopted at a statewide level (e.g., Texas).[4]

Principles and Guidelines for the Practice of Collaborative Law

The *Principles and Guidelines for Collaborative Law/Collaborative Divorce* set out the plain English statement of what collaborative law is and is not, and the good-faith undertakings that both clients and both lawyers (and any other professionals who become involved in the process) agree to honor. (Review this form at Appendix I-B(1).)

While this document originally came into being as a more accessible restatement of the binding commitments set out in the formal participation agreement (or Stipulation and Order) that is described below, its importance as the embodiment of the clients' informed consent to the collaborative process has grown to the point where the Principles and Guidelines is thought by many to be the most significant of all documents used in collaborative legal practice. This document still does what was originally envisioned: it clarifies the meaning of the more legalistic participation agreement (see below) that will be signed by the lawyers and the clients. But in addition, this document is the road map for educating clients about what they can and cannot expect from the collaborative process, and about the roles and responsibilities of the lawyers and clients in the collaborative process. As a matter of sound practice, to ensure compliance with emerging ethics opinions and rules, as well as to protect against potential malpractice and other claims, it is wise for the practice group to review and update the terms of the *Principles and Guidelines* (and retainer agreements) used by members on a regular basis.

The *Principles and Guidelines* are usually reviewed first between lawyer and client, and then again reviewed and signed by all at the first four-way meeting. This document is often attached to the formal stipulation and order filed with the court in the divorce action, and sometimes also to the marital settlement agreement, to make clear what process was used in reaching the agreement and to confirm the clients' informed consent to that process. A sample of such a document is included here. This version was originally developed by lawyers in the San Francisco Bay area in the early 1990s. It has been widely adapted since then and is in use in revised form in most communities where collaborative law is practiced. The form provided in this chapter is a comprehensive one that can be used where only collaborative lawyers are involved, as well as in cases involving other collaborative divorce professionals and neutral consultants and experts.

The form provided here emphasizes fully informed consent by the clients, and addresses ethical concerns about informed consent to the limited-purpose retention of the collaborative legal process that have been raised by commentators through early 2007. Other versions of this document can be found on practice group websites and elsewhere. Practitioners are advised to ensure that the Principles and Guidelines or equivalent document in use in their locale addresses all ethical issues that are important for clients' fully informed consent to collaborative representation.

Participation Agreement, or Stipulation and Order

In some collaborative practice groups, the formal document that defines the commencement of a collaborative law case is referred to as a "participation agreement," while other groups call it a "stipulation and order for collaborative divorce," or a "disqualification agreement." Whatever it is called, this vital document sets out the binding commitments of both parties and the undertakings of the collaborative lawyers. (Review this form at Appendix I-B(2).) It includes the core definitional element of a collaborative representation: the binding agreement that neither lawyer will participate in any subsequent contested proceedings between these parties after the document is executed. Whether contractual or issued as a court order, the participation document is the legally binding document that all participants in the collaborative process discuss and sign at the start of the case.

The participation agreement can include a description of the expanded collaborative divorce team, with space for each collaborative professional involved in the process to sign on to the fundamental commitments contained in the participation agreement. The participation agreement also specifies in detail who can terminate the collaborative process, under what circumstances, and how. It is the procedural road map and bible for a collaborative law representation, and the form that will be used should be discussed very carefully by your practice group before you take on collaborative clients.

Where the document is in the form of a stipulation, it is intended to be filed in the parties' divorce action, and often includes space for the judge to render the document an order of court. Where there are state statutes recognizing collaborative legal representation, and particularly if the statute sets out procedural rules specific to collaborative cases, use of a stipulation (with or without appended order) is appropriate and may be required.

Many lawyers take the view that a stipulation and order is important in any event, to put the court on notice that the case is collaborative, to have an order in the divorce file that the lawyers and other collaborative professionals are disqualified from participation in subsequent litigation, to approve provisions in the document that may relate to privity-of-contract concerns, to exempt the matter from certain procedural requirements triggered by the opening of a divorce file, and for other reasons. Issuance as a court order lends a certain gravitas to the collaborative process and the disqualification agreement, reinforcing for clients the significance of the documents being signed. Nonetheless, in some communities practice groups prefer to keep the participation agreement contractual and outside the divorce file.

A considered discussion in the practice group regarding which approach to take with respect to this essential document would be wise. It is also important to distinguish carefully those undertakings that are intended to be enforceable (whether by contract or by court order) from those that are precatory and aspirational in nature, and those that are important for purposes of clients' informed consent but that you do not regard as enforceable contractual undertakings of the professionals who sign the document. You and your colleagues should agree in advance on a form you all can accept.

When used, a stipulation and order is ordinarily the second or third court paper filed in the divorce action, after the divorce petition and response. It is reviewed, discussed, and executed at the first four-way meeting, but if there is no divorce action yet on file, it is held and filed when appropriate. In the form shown in this chapter, it is signed by the parties, the collaborative lawyers, and the judge, issued as a stipulated court order, and filed as a pleading.

This document is normally reviewed privately between lawyer and client, then again at the first four-way meeting, where it is signed. Signing this and the Principles and Guidelines together at the first meeting is an important ceremonial confirmation of the serious good-faith undertakings contained in those documents. Reading them out loud together and agreeing in one another's presence to abide by their terms can have powerful positive effects on future behavior. The discussion of the participation agreement at the first four-way meeting can also be an educational tool in your work with collaborative lawyers who are new to the process and will be learning to master their craft on the job.

The point is not simply that signatures be appended to these documents. The signatures matter greatly, but the conversation preceding execution is even more vital. In this sense the participation documents confirm that an educational and trust-building event took place: the meeting at which all participants in the collaborative process confirmed face-to-face a shared understanding and commitment regarding how they intend to conduct themselves during the divorce, and why. Do not let an impatient client or couple persuade you to skip over this face-to-face discussion for reasons of imagined efficiency or cost reduction; you will regret it if you do.

Sample Letters Retaining Collaborative Neutral Experts/Consultants

It is important that every consultant, expert, and other professional involved in a collaborative matter understands and affirms commitment to the basic principles of collaborative conflict resolution: good-faith, evenhanded, constructive efforts to reach interest-based consensual resolution, and a binding agreement never to participate in court proceedings between the parties if the process terminates. It is also important that the job description of the consultants and experts be reasonably well defined, and that communications understandings be set out clearly.

You and your practice group colleagues can use the sample forms provided in Appendix I-B(3) as a basis for developing similar retention letters that match the particular needs of your community and legal culture.

Sample Recitations Re: Collaborative Representation and Informal Discovery to Include in Marital Settlement Agreements

Lawyers generally include in their marital settlement agreements a provision that recites what kind of advice and legal counsel each party had in the negotiating and drafting of the marital settlement agreement. (Review sample recitations at Appendix I-B(4).) Since the parties will ordinarily be filing their court papers *in propria persona,* it is especially important for the divorce agreement to recite that each party was advised and represented in the negotiations and drafting by collaborative counsel of his or her choice, and to recite the absence of coercion and duress. As a matter of prudence, attaching the *Principles and Guidelines* or participation agreement to the marital settlement agreement may also be a good idea, so that professionals coming into the matter later will understand the genesis of the settlement agreement. For instance, it can happen that parties enter into a binding contract at the end of the collaborative process settling the terms of their divorce without any divorce action yet on file. In such cases it could be some time before the agreement ever is submitted to a court for approval and incorporation into a divorce judgment; the judge reviewing the papers at that time might be unfamiliar with the model. Or a death and probate proceeding could intervene before a divorce judgment is entered. Or there could be post-judgment proceedings that would be handled by someone other than you. Similarly, proceedings to end nonmarital relationships and domestic partnerships may or may not involve court action; a contract could be the sole embodiment of the agreements at the end of the collaborative process. And, of course, the collaborative process can also be used in negotiating prenuptial and postnuptial agreements, surrogate parenting contracts, and other domestic relations matters that do not involve court proceedings. In all such situations the more information provided in the agreement about the collaborative process that led to the settlement terms, the better.

Sample Provision Re: Resolving Future Disputes to Include in Marital Settlement Agreements

Helping clients to understand that future issues may arise as a normal consequence of the passage of time and changing circumstances is an important element of collaborative representation. It is wise to include in the settlement agreement a provision setting out the steps to be followed by the clients when future issues arise, as this will help guide them and perhaps avert conflict in the future. (Review this form at Appendix I-B(5).)

Documents Ending a Collaborative Representation

A collaborative representation can end in more than one way. Most commonly, in roughly 90 percent of cases, the collaborative legal negotiations result in a complete settlement agreement, with the collaborative lawyer at some point acknowledging the end of the work through withdrawing as counsel. Occasionally, there can be reasons for a collaborative lawyer to withdraw from representation while negotiations are still going on, with a new collaborative lawyer signing on and continuing to work collaboratively with the client and the other participants. On rare occasions, the clients decide that collaborative law is not working but elect to try mediation, neither engaging in nor terminating the collaborative process and without either firing their collaborative lawyers or retaining conventional counsel to take over their representation.[5] And, on relatively rare occasions, the collaborative process must terminate entirely, either because one or both parties wish to retain conventional counsel, or because someone seeks orders of court, or because a client is unable to participate in good faith in the collaborative process. In each of these instances, it is prudent as a matter of best practice and professional responsibility to clarify the status of the collaborative representation with a written document. If your state has a collaborative statute, it may include procedural requirements relating to filing participation agreements, notices of withdrawal or termination, or other forms.

Amendment of Participation Agreement When Clients Elect Mediation

Included in the estimated 10 percent of collaborative cases that do not result in a settlement agreement resolving all issues is a small percentage of matters in which the clients decide that they do not want to continue with collaborative four-way negotiations but would prefer to work with a single neutral mediator as the primary conflict-resolution mode. It is customary for ethical mediators to advise clients of the need for independent legal counsel during a mediation process. In that situation, where no resort to litigation is contemplated, there is no inherent reason why the two collaborative lawyers could not continue in a different role, as independent consulting lawyers for clients proceeding with mediation as the primary conflict-resolution mode.[6] However, as with all terms of engagement, the prudent collaborative lawyer in this situation will be attentive to informed consent, making it clear that the role of the lawyer has now changed in a significant way. It is important to explain in detail how the role of the consulting lawyer is different from the role of a collaborative lawyer where collaborative representation has previously been the primary conflict-resolution mode for the client. The prudent lawyer will again emphasize that it is not possible, once the original collaborative participation agreement is executed, for the collaborative lawyer ever to resort to litigation or threaten to do so—even as a consulting lawyer in a mediation. This is a significant difference as compared to the role of a conventional lawyer who serves as a consulting lawyer in a mediation process and it is essential that the client understand fully that the collaborative lawyer whose role changes to consulting attorney in a mediation is still precluded from ever taking matters to court. It is also prudent to clarify in an amendment to the retainer agreement the new, and presumably diminished, responsibilities of the lawyer as consulting independent counsel in a mediation rather than collaborative lawyer.[7]

The sample language suggested in Appendix I-C(1) is intended to be adapted for use in amendments to retainer/engagement letters and in amendments to collaborative participation agreements. Explaining why these amendments are necessary, ensuring that your client understands and agrees, and that the informed consent is memorialized in a document the client signs, is basic good practice.

Final Letter at Time Divorce Is Concluded

When your work with a client to resolve all divorce-related issues has been completed, a written confirmation to that effect is prudent. This lets the client know that you have no further tasks needing completion and informs the client of tasks he or she must attend to.

At the same time, collaborative lawyers should bear in mind that the entry of judgment in the legal divorce action is an arbitrary point that may or may not represent the end of a client's need for advice and counsel from the collaborative lawyer. Mental-health professionals working in the area of divorce note that the period of most rapid and challenging changes for many couples takes place not between separation and entry of judgment, but rather for about 18 to 24 months following entry of judgment.[8] Unlike conventional modes of reaching resolution of divorce-related issues, collaborative divorce negotiations can include express recognition of that reality and an expectation that the collaborative professionals will continue to assist after entry of a divorce judgment until the stresses of divorce transition and immediate post-divorce consolidation have had time to settle down. For that reason, collaborative lawyers may sometimes defer the formal end of representation (reflected by service of a notice of withdrawal of collaborative counsel) for some period after entry of judgment.

If all issues have been resolved within the collaborative process (which is the way roughly 90 percent of collaborative cases end), you may want to make use of a form letter to your client like the sample provided in this chapter. It informs the client that you have completed the legal work associated with the divorce and alerts the client to paperwork he or she must attend to. The letter may—but does not necessarily have to—be accompanied by a notice of withdrawal. The form supplied in Appendix I-C(2), obviously, should be adapted to the specific requirements of the client and case, so that the specific client is alerted to all matters requiring attention after your own work is finished.

Notice of Withdrawal of Collaborative Counsel

If the collaborative case ends in a complete settlement agreement, it is wise at some point, in addition to sending a final letter to the client (described above), to also send out a form notice of withdrawal to the client, the other lawyer, the other collaborative professionals if any, the other party, and possibly the court, informing all that your representation has ended. (Review this form at Appendix I-C(3).) When a lawyer withdraws in this manner, the client has the option of retaining the lawyer in the future for further collaborative services if post-agreement or post-judgment matters arise for which the client wants collaborative legal representation.

The notice of withdrawal sent out at the end of a successful collaborative representation puts your own client on notice that he or she is now fully responsible for divorce-related matters and you are not. And it notifies the other participants that future communications about divorce-related matters that would have been sent to you should now be directed to your client. In some jurisdictions such a notice starts time running for filing of malpractice claims.

There is a second situation in which the notice of withdrawal is used. If a collaborative lawyer withdraws prior to the end of the collaborative case, whether for personal reasons or because of differences with the client, without either the client or the lawyer wishing to terminate the process, the collaborative case can continue. In that situation, the client has the option of retaining new collaborative counsel who will take over representation, sign on to the participation agreement, and continue efforts to reach resolution with the other party and his or her collaborative counsel. In such situations, a notice of withdrawal should be sent to the client, the other party, and the other lawyer as part of transitioning the file to the new collaborative lawyer.

Notice of Termination of a Collaborative Case

A collaborative case can end in a termination of the process before the parties have been able to reach agreement. A termination means that the entire collaborative process ceases, and the role of both collaborative lawyers is thereafter limited to transitioning the file to conventional counsel. This occurs if either party initiates any contested proceedings. Termination also occurs if either party decides to end the collaborative process and retain traditional rather than collaborative successor counsel. And finally, constructive termination can occur in circumstances of client bad faith or misuse of the collaborative process (so long as the lawyer-client engagement letter includes a constructive termination provision).

Whenever the intention is to end the collaborative process—or to put in place a written confirmation that it has already ended—the termination notice should be used. (Review this form at Appendix I-C(4).)

It is prudent for a collaborative lawyer to make sure that either a notice of withdrawal or a termination notice is in place if the lawyer's work on the case has ended. If a stipulation and order was filed with the court in the parties' divorce action at the start of the collaborative representation, it may be appropriate to file the notice of withdrawal or termination with the court as well.

Data-Gathering Forms

As the collaborative legal model enters the conflict-resolution mainstream, there is increasing interest in gathering data that can be used for research and public education purposes. Data is being gathered in local and state-wide practice groups, on the collaborative listserv, and by the IACP.

Your collaborative practice group may want to adopt forms to be completed by all members when a collaborative case ends. Whether or not it does so, individual lawyers may want to use their own data-gathering forms when closing collaborative cases, to evaluate marketing strategies and referral sources and to improve quality of collaborative professional services and office procedures. Some examples from the author's practice and from several practice groups are included for you and your colleagues to adapt and use.

Internal Data-Gathering and Evaluation Form

A data-gathering and evaluation form given to clients at the end of a collaborative case is an opportunity that should not be overlooked. The useful information you can elicit with such a form includes:

- where your clients are learning about collaborative law and collaborative divorce
- which referral sources are currently sending clients to you for collaborative representation—and which are not yet doing so
- how effectively your web and print advertising of collaborative services is reaching potential clients
- how well your office staff is meeting the needs of collaborative clients
- where your own services to clients could be improved
- what the client appreciated about your representation
- your client's view of how well the process worked, and why
- whether this client would be willing to be interviewed by journalists interested in collaborative divorce

The internal information form provided in Appendix I-D(1) can be readily adapted to elicit other information and to further practice group data-gathering needs.

Practice Group Data-Gathering and Evaluation Forms

The practice group data-gathering and evaluation forms provided in Appendix I-D(2) are illustrative examples, one from Dallas, Texas, and one from

Niagara Falls, Canada.[9] Many practice groups now ask members to complete forms like these at the conclusion of every case, both for practice group purposes and to assist the IACP in gathering national and international statistics for public education purposes. With a data-gathering program supported by forms like these, the practice group will have reliable information about the experience of clients in collaborative divorces available for members to use in writing, speaking, and public education efforts.

IACP Survey Form

Since 2006, the International Academy of Collaborative Professionals has asked members to submit survey forms after completing collaborative cases. Participation in the quarterly surveys is voluntary. The IACP collates and publishes the survey data for public education purposes and to provide an informational basis for its ongoing efforts to keep standards of practice high. (Review this form at Appendix I-D(3).)

Notes

1. Membership in the privately owned collaborative listserv is open to all professionals with a legitimate connection to collaborative practice, by application to carlMichael rossi, lhdragon@ameritech.net.

2. Your state may have specific rules governing when a retainer agreement (or engagement letter) is required, and what it must contain, and you of course need to adapt the collaborative retainer document to comply with those rules. Beyond that, your retainer agreement with your client is the evidence that you have met your ethical responsibilities to ensure that your client understands and agrees to all elements of the collaborative process. A well-drafted retainer letter protects both your client and you.

3. In the report on her case-study research project, Julie MacFarlane notes some discrepancies between lawyers' understanding of collaborative law and their clients' expectations and experiences during the process. Her observations provide a road map for a number of matters that a good collaborative retainer agreement should in some fashion address. Julie MacFarlane, *The Emerging Phenomenon of Collaborative Family Law (CFL): A Qualitative Study of CFL Cases,* http://canada.justice.gc.ca/en/ps/pad/reports/2005-FCY-1/2005-FCY-1.pdf, especially pp. 25–27.

4. The forms provided here, in the author's view, represent good models for establishing informed consent and good-faith commitments at the start of a collaborative matter. However, practitioners should not rely on these forms. It is important that each practitioner and practice group ensure that the basic documents establishing the collaborative case that are in use in the community meet any unique state or other requirements for informed consent, limited-purpose retentions, and other matters pertaining to legal ethics and standards of practice.

5. In such a situation, the collaborative work of the lawyers has as a practical matter ended because the conflict-resolution functions of the collaborative lawyers have been assumed fully by the mediator. This should be distinguished from the more common situation in which collaborative lawyers working with particularly challenging clients or issues might bring in a "meta-mediator" to assist at the collaborative legal table. This technique is in use in many communities. Incorporating the assistance of a mediator into a collaborative

process in this manner allows each collaborative lawyer to devote more concentrated attention to the needs of their respective clients, while the mediator becomes responsible for managing conflict or strong feelings at the table and for helping to facilitate the interest-based negotiation process at the table. Many collaborative retainer agreements and participation agreements specifically refer to this as one of the ways that other professionals may become involved in the collaborative process. Utilizing the services of a meta-mediator in this way is a tool within the collaborative process and does not require any supplemental documentation, while collaborative lawyers changing their role and responsibilities to become consultants to a mediation should be documented.

6. Indeed, mediators have embraced with some enthusiasm the idea of collaborative lawyers serving as consulting lawyers in mediations because of their greater alignment with client-centered, out-of-court conflict resolution, and there is no reason why the collaborative lawyers could not be brought in for that purpose when mediation is the clients' initial conflict-resolution process choice. The lawyers can adapt their customary retainer agreements and participation agreements to create a second layer of intentional commitment to resolving matters out of court, as consulting lawyers to the mediation. *See Mediators and Collaborative Lawyers*, 4 COLLABORATIVE REV. at 12 (October 2002), by Pauline H. Tesler with commentary by Gary Friedman.

7. A form for that purpose has not been included because it will need to be tailored to the recitations in the original collaborative retainer or engagement letter that specify the lawyer's role and responsibilities.

8. Collaborative settlement agreements can recognize this reality and help clients handle predictable change constructively by building into the agreement a schedule of periodic follow-up reviews with the collaborative lawyers and other collaborative professionals, if any, during that post-judgment period of rapid change. Such reviews can focus on fine-tuning parenting plans, and/or adjusting support arrangements in light of anticipated or unexpected changes in needs or income.

9. The two forms reproduced in Appendix I-D have been adapted slightly for purposes of clarity. They are intended only as illustrations, not as exemplars of what should be contained in evaluation or data-gathering forms. They are a good starting point for a practice group discussion of what kind of information to gather, and how, and what uses it will be put to.

Chapter 9

Developing and Marketing Your Collaborative Practice

"The pessimist sees difficulty in every opportunity. The optimist sees the opportunity in every difficulty."—Winston Churchill

Once you have embraced the collaborative law model and have embarked on your personal paradigm-shift journey, your next questions are likely to be, "Where do I find colleagues, and how do I get clients?" This chapter offers tested, successful ideas for developing and making the best use of a community of collaborative colleagues, and for educating potential clients and referral sources about collaborative law.

Practice Groups: The Sine Qua Non for Practice Development

Stuart Webb, the originator of the collaborative law concept, tells the old story of the lawyer who moved to a small town that had no other lawyers, and hung out a shingle. No clients came. The lawyer met people, networked, joined organizations, shook hands—still, no clients came. Finally, he called a lawyer friend and persuaded her to move to the town and open a second law office there. From then on, both lawyers had all the legal business they could handle. There is a moral here for new collaborative lawyers: the more skilled collaborative lawyers there are in your community, the more collaborative law business there will be, because every case requires two collaborative lawyers.[1] If you market your own collaborative practice effectively, you will be increasing not only your own collaborative caseload, but also the caseloads of your colleagues, who will be providing representation for your clients' spouses.

When your first collaborative client comes to you, you simply cannot do your job unless there is a critical mass of other competent collaborative lawyers in your community. That is because the other spouse will need to select collaborative counsel with whom you are able to work effectively. What can you do to build this resource in your community? Plenty. The way to begin that has proved effective in communities both large and small wherever collaborative legal services are offered is to gather together a cadre of like-minded lawyers and to "hit the ground running," by building your skills in an introductory training that you attend together and by working collectively afterward to present the collaborative conflict-resolution model to your community as a group.

Let us assume that you are the first lawyer in your area to discover collaborative law. How do you call forth this essential practice group of colleagues? Here is a well-tried sequence of steps you can take to make that group a reality. There may be other effective ways to reach the goal; this is a plan that has worked in many communities.

1. First, learn how collaborative practice groups in communities that are demographically similar to yours[2] got launched, and take advantage of their experience and resources. There are now many collaborative practice groups in the United States and elsewhere, many of which have websites where you can find materials and resources as well as contact information for practice group leaders. The International Academy of Collaborative Professionals' website has pages listing nearly 200 practice groups as of 2008. The members' section of the website includes information about how to organize an effective practice group. Learn as much as you can before you begin contacting other lawyers.

2. Consider whether your group will start out as an interdisciplinary collaborative practice group (including not only lawyers but also mental-health and financial professionals) or whether you will begin with lawyers and expand into an interdisciplinary group later.[3] Obviously, your core group should reflect the professions you intend to include in the practice group.

3. Next, form a small core organizing group, consisting of from two to six or seven other family lawyers (and other professionals if you intend to include them from the start) whom you like and respect and who share your philosophy of family law. This generally will include the shortlist of the lawyers you most like seeing on the other side of a case. It can be very helpful to include in your core group

at least one or two highly respected family lawyers who are well-liked and considered "opinion makers" in your locale. Take them to lunch one or two at a time, give them information packets about collaborative law, tell them what you know about it and why it excites your imagination, refer them to the websites you think are most informative, and ask them to read the materials and consider helping you create a collaborative law presence in your locale. If they are not enthusiastic once they've read the materials, don't try to persuade them; try again with the next likeliest lawyers you can identify. Don't settle for lukewarm responses. You will be able to find at least a few others who are as enthusiastic as you are; seek them out.

4. Spend some time with your core group learning more together. Consider going together to a collaborative law or interdisciplinary collaborative divorce training program.[4] You are going to be the leaders in your own community; you may be more effective in that role if you can present yourself as already fully trained and knowledgeable about the collaborative model. Whether you get your initial

LEVELS OF COLLABORATIVE ORGANIZATION AND INFRASTRUCTURE

The Individual Practitioner

The Local Practice Group

Regional Organization of Individuals or Groups

Statewide or Provincial Organization

National Organization

International Academy of Collaborative Professionals

collaborative training at this stage or later (in your own community after the practice group has been formed), be sure to seek out the best training you can find, as that will be an invaluable investment in your future collaborative practice.

5.   Discuss with your core group what kind of collaborative practice group you would like to form: Will it be open-ended or close-ended in membership? How big? Invitation only, or open announcement? Affiliated with a bar association or other organization, or new and independent? How broad a geographical area will it cover? Do you envision it as one of many "affinity groups," or as an umbrella organization for all collaborative practitioners in the locale?[5]

6.   Once you are all reasonably confident about what kind of group you envision, and reasonably knowledgeable about collaborative legal practice, it is time to organize the practice group. If you have opted for a small, invitational group, you and your core group will decide how big it will be, and who will be invited to the kickoff meeting. If you opt for an open-ended group, you will decide how to announce it, and where, and whether you will form the entity

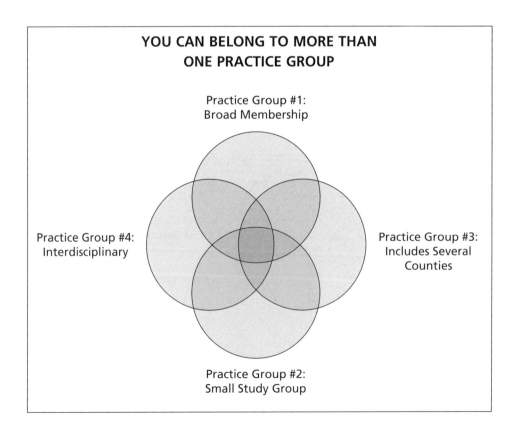

YOU CAN BELONG TO MORE THAN ONE PRACTICE GROUP

Practice Group #1: Broad Membership

Practice Group #4: Interdisciplinary

Practice Group #3: Includes Several Counties

Practice Group #2: Small Study Group

(perhaps a nonprofit corporation, perhaps an unincorporated association, perhaps a committee of the local bar association) before or after calling the first meeting. It is wise, before the first meeting, to have in place a procedure for joining, and membership rules. These can be amended later but having them in place at the start can be an important protection for the integrity of the group. For instance, it is wise to have already in place rules about training requirements and ongoing professional development, attendance expectations, a membership fee, a membership term—generally one year—or alternatively a procedure for dealing with removal of members, and the like, and a form on which those deciding to join commit to abide by those rules.

SIX WAYS YOUR OFFICE STAFF CAN SUPPORT THE COLLABORATIVE PARADIGM SHIFT AND BUILD YOUR COLLABORATIVE PRACTICE

1. Teach all support staff what collaborative family law is and how it differs from other forms of family law practice and from mediation so that they can incorporate those understandings when they talk about you and your practice.
2. Help each staff person who speaks with potential clients to develop an "elevator message"—a one- or two-sentence punchy description of what collaborative law is—and encourage each to make use of it liberally in the office and in the community.
3. Train staff members to include in the office telephone-answering protocol an explanation of the range of family law services you provide, with particular emphasis upon your collaborative family law services.
4. Encourage your staff to adopt an engaged, helpful, sympathetic manner when speaking with clients and colleagues.
5. Work up an information packet about collaborative law and about collaborative practice in your community and train your staff to send it out to anyone who calls or e-mails as a potential new client.
6. Use an intake protocol for new clients in which your staff sends a detailed follow-up information packet when the first consultation is scheduled, with a request that the client read the material before the consultation in order to use the consultation time most efficiently. Consider including a complimentary copy of a general readers' book such as Tesler and Thompson's *Collaborative Divorce: The Revolutionary New Way to Restructure Your Family, Resolve Legal Issues, and Move On With Your Life.*

7. Either before or at the first large group meeting, you will need to decide upon an organizational structure and purpose. Consider the advantages of providing your group with an already-formed structure—perhaps one that provides for reconsideration after a year or two. Having a structure already in place at the time of the first large-group meeting makes it unnecessary for the practice group to do these organizational tasks during its first year. Many a practice group has dissipated irreplaceable enthusiasm and energy for collaborative legal practice by getting its members bogged down at the start in tedious large-group discussions of bylaws, board structure, and the like. Those matters can be decided initially by your core group and reconsidered later by a committee, without siphoning off vital group energy in its formative stages. There are plenty of other organizational tasks that the larger group does need to address at the first or second meeting. Your members need to agree on a schedule of meetings, and form committees for such essential tasks as: brochure development, practice protocols, and documentation; public education; advertising; education of the judiciary[6] and adoption of local procedural rules; investigation of malpractice insurance issues; case conferencing; substantive programs for practice group meetings; mentoring; training and skills development; retreats; networking and marketing to referral sources; and data gathering, to name a few.

    Sponsoring good introductory training is an important early priority, as members should not take on collaborative representation without first attending a training that meets IACP standards. Do your homework, and bring in the best possible trainer—one whose introductory trainings have led to flourishing collaborative practice communities. Consider whether the initial training should be for lawyers only, or for interdisciplinary collaborative divorce teams.[7]

8. Brochures can be the most valuable as well as the simplest of marketing and practice development tools. The International Academy of Collaborative Professionals now has a high-quality set of brochures for clients and for referral sources that can be purchased in bulk by individual members and practice groups, which make it unnecessary for the practice group to incur the cost of professional design services, and which also ensure that a congruent message about collaborative law and collaborative divorce is being put forward nationally and internationally. Many practice groups now allocate funds to develop brochure inserts or covers that interface

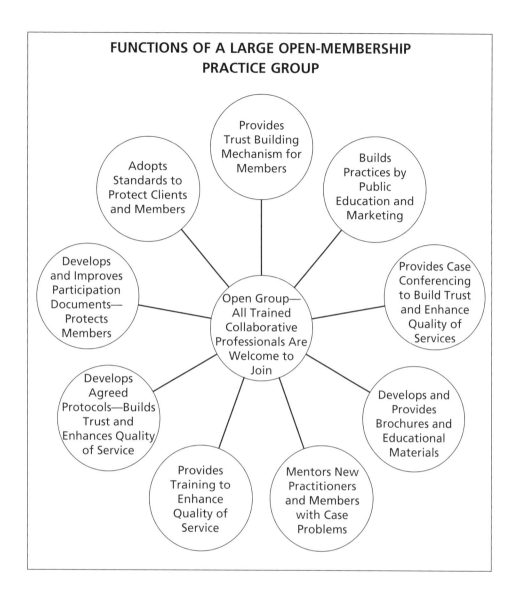

FUNCTIONS OF A LARGE OPEN-MEMBERSHIP PRACTICE GROUP

Open Group—All Trained Collaborative Professionals Are Welcome to Join

- Provides Trust Building Mechanism for Members
- Builds Practices by Public Education and Marketing
- Adopts Standards to Protect Clients and Members
- Develops and Improves Participation Documents—Protects Members
- Provides Case Conferencing to Build Trust and Enhance Quality of Services
- Develops Agreed Protocols—Builds Trust and Enhances Quality of Service
- Develops and Provides Brochures and Educational Materials
- Provides Training to Enhance Quality of Service
- Mentors New Practitioners and Members with Case Problems

with the IACP brochures and that provide the additional local information that your group will want to put out for potential clients and referral sources. Usually these brochure supplements include a current list of practice group members with addresses, telephone numbers, and perhaps e-mail and web addresses. Some brochure cover formats permit insertion of individual business cards or brief individual professional biographies. Once your group has decided how it will customize its brochure, you will use the brochure in a variety of ways. You and your colleagues can display them in your office waiting room and you can mail them as part of a standard information/orientation packet to potential new clients. You, or

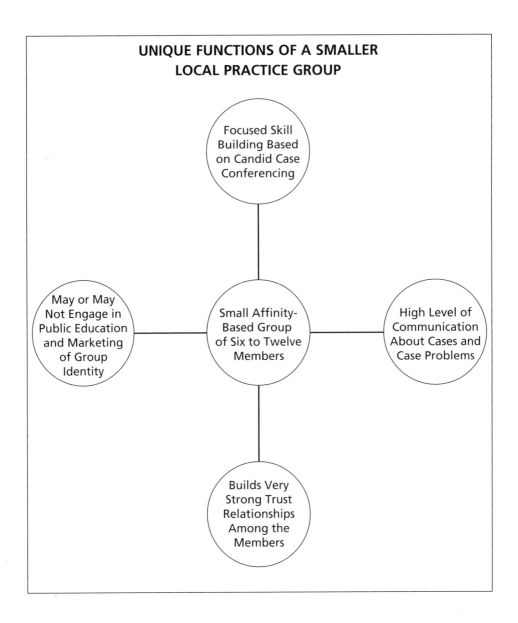

**UNIQUE FUNCTIONS OF A SMALLER
LOCAL PRACTICE GROUP**

Focused Skill Building Based on Candid Case Conferencing

May or May Not Engage in Public Education and Marketing of Group Identity

Small Affinity-Based Group of Six to Twelve Members

High Level of Communication About Cases and Case Problems

Builds Very Strong Trust Relationships Among the Members

your practice group, can send targeted mailings to potential referral sources, such as psychotherapists, clergy, accountants, or estate-
planning lawyers. You and your colleagues can hand them out at
public appearances and meetings. You can distribute them as part
of your press packet for inclusion with press releases. You can leave
bundles in places where potential clients can pick them up: doctors' offices, hair salons, health clubs. Keeping the membership list
current is obviously important, and being on that list is a motivation for less-committed members to meet annual group membership
renewal requirements.

JUDGE'S LETTER TO PEOPLE
FILING FOR DIVORCE

Your local family law judge can be a powerful ally for the growth of collaborative practice in the community. Here is an example of what a judge committed to the idea of collaborative law can do. Hon. Donna J. Hitchens, as presiding judge of the San Francisco Superior Court family law department, enacted a local rule that the following letter be given to everyone filing a family law proceeding in the county.

To Divorcing Spouses:

If you have a copy of this letter, you are probably getting divorced or having problems working out a custody plan regarding your children. You may also be angry or hurt. Before you rush into court, take a deep breath and think about what you really want to accomplish. The court system will not meet any need you have to punish or feel supported. In fact, it often does the opposite and is not the best way to solve family and personal issues.

There are many ways to resolve your disagreement without fighting through the courts. A number of effective alternative dispute-resolution methods are available to you. One of the best methods is to work things out by participating in collaborative law.

In collaborative law, two lawyers specially trained in negotiations and conflict resolution represent you and your partner or "ex," but only for the purpose of helping you settle your case. These two lawyers can never go to court for you. If you and your spouse or partner cannot reach an agreement, you can terminate the collaborative process and go to court, but these collaborative lawyers cannot go to court with you. They are out of a job if they cannot help you reach a mutually satisfactory settlement.

Please think carefully about the choices that are available to you. Litigation is an adversarial approach. It is expensive, tends to fan the flames of conflict, results in very personal attacks among the parties, and is often limited to "winners" and "losers" by the end of the case. On the other hand, mediation or collaborative law can result in an agreed-upon resolution that is less expensive, less hostile, and more creative. The choices you make now can have an enormous impact on you and your children for the rest of your life.

More information about collaborative law is available in brochures that can be found in Rooms 103 and 4012 of the Civic Center Courthouse.

Sincerely yours,
Donna J. Hitchens
Supervising Judge
Unified Family Court

KNOWLEDGE IS POWER

Consider creating case report systems within the practice group for gathering data in an organized manner about the cases members are handling. Find out the number of cases handled by each member, the outcomes, the time required, the fees charged, the involvement of interdisciplinary team professionals, the referral source, client satisfaction, and anything else you and your colleagues would like to know about. You could use the IACP survey form provided in Appendix I-D(3), or you could adapt and expand it.

What would you do with that kind of data? It could inform your group about matters such as these:

- Where are clients finding out about collaborative law?

- Where could the group do a better job of public education about collaborative law?

- Are some members getting most of the cases? What could or should be done about that?

- Are some members having disproportionate numbers of unhappy clients? Would mentoring be useful? Additional training?

- Are there any patterns for why clients are dissatisfied, or why cases terminate short of full resolution? How could those patterns be addressed in training and mentoring?

QUALITY ASSURANCE
IN THE COLLABORATIVE COMMUNITY

The Individual Practitioner:

- Obtains basic and regular additional training to meet and exceed IACP minimum international standards

- Deserves trust, expects trust, builds trust

- Learns from each case through case conferencing

- Seeks mentoring if problems arise

- Participates actively in the local practice group

- Joins and participates in the international collaborative community

The Practice Group:

- Adopts international standards of practice

- Has high expectations of quality service delivery

- Requires and provides breadth and depth of training
- Requires and provides mentoring and case conferencing
- Provides content-rich meetings
- Requires attendance at meetings
- Regards problem members as a group issue
- Facilitates and encourages communicating congruent core messages about collaborative practice to the community
- Develops and updates participation documents
- Develops and updates protocols of practice
- Mentors and trains new members
- Provides regular trust-building experiences, formal and informal
- Conducts strategic planning to identify challenges, and set and meet goals

This information can enrich your press releases about collaborative law. You will have reliable data that journalists often want to know about: the number of cases completed, the percentage that end in full settlement, the percentage that terminate and go into litigation, the reasons clients identify for choosing collaborative law, the typical cost of a collaborative case, the typical elapsed time from beginning to end, and much more. And, these forms can identify clients who are willing to speak to journalists about their experiences with collaborative law.

NINE RULES FOR MAGNETIC AND EFFECTIVE PRACTICE GROUPS

1. Keep administrative business to a minimum at large group meetings
   a. Use committees
   b. Have an executive committee
   c. Spend a maximum of 10 minutes on administration unless more is *essential*
2. Honor the rule of size for a hunter-gatherer species: find ways to utilize working groups of 8 to 12 members (committees, task forces, multilevel infrastructure, study groups—whatever works)
3. Every meeting must have a purpose and an agenda
   a. Honor the agenda and purpose
   b. Keep to time commitments
   c. Rotate program committee chair?
   d. Rotate meeting location and agenda responsibility?

4. Learn something important at every meeting
   a. Make the agenda as vibrant and fascinating as possible
   b. What do members need? Supply it!
5. Enhance quality of services to clients at every meeting
   a. Case conferencing
   b. Mentoring and troubleshooting
   c. Presentations and trainings
   d. Study group discussion topics and readings
   e. Development of collaborative referrals and panels
6. Build trust relationships at every meeting
   a. Do not permit factionalization
   b. Do not permit resentment
   c. Do not permit passengers
7. Require attendance and make it easy to attend
   a. Find out preferences about when, where, how often
   b. Consider alternating schedules
   c. Reward and penalize
8. Membership should not be automatic
   a. Open membership is good
   b. Requirements for membership are important
   c. Set the bar high
   d. Insist on continuing education and training
   e. Consider a point system
   f. Require affirmation of compliance every year
   g. Consider occasionally closing membership and then announcing
      reopening to applications
9. Have fun, but canvass and respect preferences of members about timing
   a. Socialize first? Afterward?
   b. Retreats? Mandatory?

9. When your group is ready for it (after most members have handled 5 to 10 cases and most members have participated in intermediate and advanced collaborative trainings), consider sponsoring a practice development workshop for your group. This kind of workshop teaches members a more powerful and consistent way of speaking about collaborative law, and includes strategic planning of how to get information about collaborative conflict resolution into the community more effectively, identification of obstacles to broaden expansion of the collaborative model in the community, identification of challenges within the practice group, and strategic planning of solutions that address the challenges.

10. Once you have your practice group launched, keep it lively and active. Make sure your rules permit only fully participatory, committed collaborative lawyers to remain members. Make sure you have

realistic continuing education and training and mentoring requirements, and that the members meet those requirements. Use your
meetings for skills development, case conferencing, trust-building,
protocol improvement, and mutual troubleshooting assistance. Bring
in speakers and trainers.

MAKING PRACTICE GROUP MEETINGS IRRESISTIBLE (IDEAS FOR CONTENT-RICH MEETINGS)

- Develop a group protocol about how to explain collaborative divorce most effectively to clients.

- Educate support staff in how to offer collaborative divorce information packets and brochures to prospective clients: discussion, or brief skills training session.

- Educate support staff in how to reinforce the concepts behind collaborative divorce practice in their contacts with clients: discussion, or brief skills training session.

- Develop a group protocol about how to present collaborative divorce to the other spouse.

- Develop a group protocol for offering collaborative divorce where the other party may already have consulted a traditional divorce lawyer.

- Present committee recommendations for agreed participation documentation; discuss improvements to agreed documents.

- Discuss how to address problems that arise in the "information-gathering stage"—discussion or brief skills training.

- Practice using formal brainstorming techniques at four-way meetings— either group discussion or facilitated workshop format.

- Explore techniques for developing and presenting appraisal results in collaborative cases—discussion or brief skills training.

- Invite presentations by accountants, business appraisers, career counselors, and others who may be "groomed" as collaborative professional resources.

- Practice techniques for handling impasse at the four-way meeting— discussion or brief skills training.

- Learn to make the best use of the final four-way "signing"meeting— discussion or brief skills training.

- Learn to recognize the difference between normal divorce stress and psychiatric disturbances in clients—presentation by mental-health professional.

- Provide communication skills training

- Play the "prisoner's dilemma" and other negotiation games.
- Develop protocols for domestic violence, alcoholism, and other challenges in a collaborative practice.
- Learn to integrate "meta-mediators" into a difficult collaborative case—discussion and/or presentation.
- Hold case-conferencing sessions whenever members complete a case.
- Plan a day-long or two-day practice group retreat.

Other Practice Development Ideas

As an individual there is much you can do to develop your own collaborative practice, once there is a strong community of collaborative lawyers in your locale for clients to draw upon for representation. The goal is simple: You want clients to hear about collaborative law not just from you, but from as many separate reliable information and referral resources as possible, so that the model appears well-established and generally accepted in the community as a way of divorcing.

Here is a short list of public education ideas, to which you will undoubtedly add others of your own:

- Create an information packet that is ready to be sent to clients and to professional referral sources. These may be the same packet, or may differ in content. At a minimum include the group brochure, information about yourself, informative web links, and perhaps an article or two about collaborative law. Add to this packet as you find newspaper or magazine articles or other resources that would be of interest and that show collaborative law in a positive light.

- Take a therapist, a clergyperson, an accountant, or a lawyer to lunch on a regular schedule to let them know about collaborative law and your availability for collaborative divorce representation. Commit yourself to do this every week or every month. Follow up with an information packet.

- Create and use a client evaluation form that clients fill out at the end of each collaborative representation.[8] In it, ask questions such as whether the client would or would not recommend the model to others, and how effectively the collaborative model addressed the client's needs in the divorce. Ask for written permission to quote from the form in publicizing collaborative law. Construct a quote sheet of favorable client comments that can be included in your information packet and on your website or blog.

- Learn how to write and distribute press releases.[9] Make a press-release template, containing boilerplate information about your collaborative law practice. Adapt it, with a new title and first paragraph, any time you do anything at all noteworthy. Send it out often to your local newspapers. Whether or not the specific press release produces any media coverage, eventually your name will become familiar and an editor may decide to do a feature on your practice.

- Volunteer to speak wherever people will listen. Do presentations about collaborative practice at bar events and conferences. Offer to speak at church and civic groups. Offer to do workshops or presentations at local or statewide meetings of accountants and psychotherapists.

- When people ask what you do, answer in terms of your collaborative practice. Learn how to express this in a powerful "elevator message" (a one-sentence description in dynamic language of what you do as a collaborative lawyer—e.g., "I help divorcing people get their legal issues resolved out of court in a way that allows them to be good parents to their children after the divorce is over").

- Write a short piece for your local bar newsletter or for the chamber of commerce newsletter. Write about your collaborative work for your college or law school alumni magazine. Write a piece and submit it to newsletters of other professions, such as psychotherapists and accountants.

- List yourself in the yellow pages as a collaborative lawyer.

- Create a website and a blog for yourself and use them both for publicity and as client education tools. Post information about yourself and about collaborative law, and include the web and blog addresses on your business card and letterhead. Provide links to related sites for your practice group and other appropriate organizations.

- Join the International Academy of Collaborative Professionals, make use of their public education and marketing resources, and attend their annual meeting to learn more about developing strong collaborative practices and practice groups.

PUBLICIZING COLLABORATIVE LAW:
LEARN TO USE "THE HOOK"

If you send out enough press releases about collaborative legal practice to the right editors and feature writers in your community, eventually you'll be regarded as an expert and you'll get calls from journalists who need comments from experts to add to their stories. Whatever they ask, link your answer to collaborative law.

If you are really lucky, one of your local journalists may do a feature piece about you or about the collaborative practice group. How can you help journalists see good feature stories? Learn to hook your press releases to events that journalists already want to write stories about: holidays and breaking news stories.

For instance, here are some natural links to stories about collaborative practice—point them out to your local editor or features writer in good, timely press releases:

- Valentine's Day: In collaborative divorce, Valentine's Day does not have to be a painful reminder. Some divorcing couples in the collaborative process manage to send appropriate valentines to the soon-to-be ex, or otherwise find ways to continue as friends or extended family.

- Mother's and Father's Day: In conventional adversarial divorces, battling spouses may try to deprive one another of the children's company on these holidays. Not in collaborative divorce! Ask some of your clients how they feel about the children being with the appropriate parent on such days, and use those quotes in your press release about the virtues of collaborative divorce.

- Spring break and other school holidays: Again, contrast the battle between warring spouses over who gets the kids in conventional nasty divorces with the focus on children's needs and the effort to support a good relationship with the other parent that is characteristic of most collaborative divorces.

- Thanksgiving and Christmas holidays: A surprising number of divorced couples with children who have divorced collaboratively will find ways to celebrate these holidays together, even with new mates and blended families, long after the divorce. This is newsworthy.

- News stories of violence associated with divorce: There are dismayingly regular incidences of shootings at divorce courts and violence against estranged spouses and even children. A counterbalancing "good news" item about collaborative divorce as a mode that helps reduce stress and anger might seem appealing to a features editor if you provide such a press release promptly and hook it to the bad news story in the headlines.

Conclusion

In summary, keep in mind a few key concepts for effective public education and practice development. First, you need a critical mass of capable, enthusiastic, well-trained collaborative law practitioners as colleagues in your locale. Second, you and your colleagues need to let the professionals who may be making divorce referrals in your community know about collaborative law in an organized, persistent way. Third, you need to ensure that potential clients hear about collaborative law from multiple reliable sources when they are looking for divorce representation. Fourth, you need to ensure that the standards for collaborative practice in your practice group start high and remain high so that clients will be satisfied and will tell their friends.

Notes

1. Thus, while from a market-share perspective, an increase in the number of mediators can both increase competition for mediation clients and also diminish the amount of work available for domestic relations lawyers in that locale (because one neutral professional does the dispute-resolution work previously performed by two lawyers), an increase in the number of family lawyers who shift to collaborative law will generally result in more work for the other collaborative lawyers in the community over the long term, provided the lawyers are functioning at a competent skill level and handling cases effectively so that the positive reputation of the model grows in the community. Experience tells us that word-of-mouth client satisfaction is one of the most effective marketing tools available. Thus, not only does each collaborative case require two collaborative lawyers, each successful case yields future referrals.

2. The challenges associated with launching collaborative practice in a large urban area are similar in some ways, and differ in some ways, from the challenges that typically exist in small and medium-size communities. Trainers (such as the author) who offer practice development workshops can help practice groups tailor their public education and practice group development plans to the specific needs of their own communities. Broadly speaking, in rural areas challenges often focus on the low population density, small number of professionals (and thus greater need for most or all to become trained in collaborative law), and large distances. Those same factors also present opportunities: in rural areas it is not difficult for nearly all divorce lawyers to offer collaborative law, and thus for many clients and many referral sources to become familiar with it quickly and for a substantial percentage of divorcing clients to choose it relatively soon. In large urban areas, the challenges focus on the very large number of family lawyers and thus the difficulty of reaching a critical mass of trained collaborative lawyers, and the corresponding difficulty of getting a congruent, consistent message about collaborative law out to a substantial number of divorcing clients and referral sources. On the other hand, in large urban areas it is often easier to build effective practice groups with many members from whom clients can choose representation, to mount trainings and other events that enhance the quality of practice in the community, and to develop protocols and other practice resources for members.

3. Some communities and states have launched themselves into collaborative practice by offering interdisciplinary collaborative professional services from the start—for instance, Collaborative Divorce Vancouver (British Columbia); Collaborative Family Law

Group of San Diego (California); Collaborative Divorce Professionals of Arizona; Collaborative Law Institute of Georgia. Others have grown from lawyers-only to include all professions in their practice groups—for instance, Collaborative Practice San Francisco (California); Collaborative Council of the Redwood Empire (California); Collaborative Law Institute of Minnesota; and Massachusetts Collaborative Law Council. Some still (as of early 2008) include only lawyers as practice group members—for instance, The Association of Collaborative Lawyers of Rockland-Westchester, New York; Collaborative Family Law of Utah; Portland (Oregon) Collaborative Law Group; Wake County (North Carolina) Collaborative Family Law Practice Group. In nearly all communities, however collaborative legal practice begins, there is an inevitable evolution toward interdisciplinary collaborative practice simply because it meets the needs of a broader spectrum of divorcing clients and their children than lawyers alone can.

4. There are now many trainers (including the author) who offer both lawyer-only and interdisciplinary trainings at introductory, intermediate, and advanced levels, as well as practice development workshops and seminars. Contact the author at teslercollaboration@lawtsf .com for schedules and check her blog for descriptions of current trainings, mentoring, and case-conferencing services, www.collaborativedivorcenews.com. The IACP website has pages where both new and experienced trainers can list forthcoming trainings, but the IACP does not screen or approve trainers or trainings and their presence on the website is not a guarantee of excellence. IACP has adopted excellent voluntary aspirational standards for trainers and trainings [see http://www.collaborativepractice.com/t2.asp?T=Resources], but not all trainers/trainings available in the growing marketplace meet those standards. Make sure you and your colleagues get training that does. Further, make sure that you check out the trainer's reputation: Talk with sponsors of prior events and compare several before deciding on who will offer your first training. Practice groups that choose well get off to an excellent start. Communities whose initial trainings are less than inspiring may find it more difficult to get collaborative practice off the ground.

5. These can be challenging questions to resolve and will shape how the collaborative model develops in your community. Some believe that it is better for the first collaborative practice groups in a community to be close-ended and small, consisting of lawyers who already work well together and who have excellent reputations as family lawyers in the community. Limiting membership to a small number makes self-training and quality control easier, as it is possible to demand high levels of attendance at meetings as a condition of membership. Also, pre-existing respect and trust make it likelier that early collaborative representations will go well, even before a high level of skill at collaboration has been developed. Existing relationships of trust and respect, together with small group size, make it possible to conduct candid case conferencing about problems that will arise in cases, enhancing the collective level of practice in your group. Including highly regarded practitioners in the membership enhances the early public relations efforts of your group, and helps to establish credibility for your efforts among judges, therapists, and other key referral sources. Other communities opt for starting with as large a group as possible. Large open-ended groups offer the advantage of getting many divorce lawyers trained in collaborative law who then will offer it to their clients, spreading the word about collaborative law more broadly than a small group can. Also, clients will have a large spectrum of lawyers from whom to choose representation. On the other hand, large groups can have difficulty forging trust and collegiality because of the sheer number of members and the tendency in a large group for individual attendance and participation to be more sporadic—a situation that reduces the quality of case conferencing and self-training, and can thus make uniformly high quality service delivery hard to achieve. Now that collaborative law is visible on the mainstream spectrum of legal conflict-resolution options, open-ended practice groups can attract practitioners looking for business wherever they can find it, who may have little commitment either to the group or to excellence in collaborative practice. Such members will generally not do well in their cases, a situation that can result in more botched cases at the vulnerable early stages of public knowledge of

the model. Bear in mind that while the initial choice of group size matters, the decision can change over time. A small group can elect to expand, while members of a large group sometimes also participate in smaller invitational study groups. As time goes on and collaborative practice becomes well-established in the community, the impact of a less-than-committed or less-than-skilled collaborative lawyer on the reputation of the model diminishes and these considerations may become less significant. If you opt for the small, invitational group, you can still encourage broad involvement in collaborative law among family lawyers in your community by sharing information freely and encouraging other lawyers to start similar affinity groups in the locale, without diluting your own ability to form a group of like-minded, competent collaborative colleagues. Even a small invitational group should be large enough to allow each spouse plenty of good choices for collaborative representation. Fifteen to 20 is a good size for a small group, though there is nothing to prevent larger or smaller groups from working well. If you and your colleagues opt for broad open membership, it will be very important to anticipate and devise methods for dealing with the predictable problems—those described above in this note, and others—before they happen, in the rules for membership and in the programs conducted by the group.

6. The judiciary can provide important support for collaborative practice, especially once they understand that collaborative practice reduces docket congestion and averts many cases from high-conflict proceedings and post-judgment recidivism. For instance, in San Francisco, Superior Court Judge Donna Hitchens, the presiding family law judge, announced early on that her courtroom would be the "Collaborative Law Department," where any cases that went to litigation concerning the enforceability or scope of the collaborative law contracts or agreements would be heard, and motions regarding misuse of the collaborative process would be assigned. She has expressed strong support for the model. *See* Pauline H. Tesler, *Donna J. Hitchens: Family Law Judge for the Twenty-First Century,* 2 THE COLLABORATIVE Q. I (Oct. 2000). Other judges who have provided vital support for the development of collaborative practice in their communities and states include: Hon. Ross Foote (retired), (Louisiana); Hon. Roderic Duncan (retired), (California); Supreme Court Justice Bobbe Bridge (Washington); Hon. Bruce Peterson (Minnesota); and Hon. Anne Kass (New Mexico).

In some jurisdictions, collaborative lawyers will need to work with local judges to craft exceptions to local rules that could thwart effective collaborative practice. For instance, in certain counties, filing a divorce petition leads quickly to setting a trial date. The looming trial date would inevitably cause family lawyers to worry about prejudice to their clients if trial preparation efforts did not commence promptly, and would therefore impair the ability of collaborative lawyers to do their work. Judges need to be made aware that without that specter of a forthcoming trial, the great majority of collaborative cases would be likely to settle, without consuming any judicial or administrative resources. That is an excellent reason for exempting collaborative cases from rules designed for adversarial practice. A statewide or province-wide collaborative statute is the most efficient way to address statewide procedural problems; the National Conference of Commissioners on Uniform State Laws (NCCUSL) has appointed a committee to draft a model collaborative statute and for that reason, it would be sensible to postpone state legislative efforts until the forthcoming model statute is available.

7. One argument for beginning with a lawyers-only training is the generally acknowledged reality that lawyers have a lot of learning—and unlearning—to do before they can be very good at collaborative law. There is also a second substantial learning curve for lawyers before they can collaborate with other professionals very effectively; we lawyers have a tendency to regard other professionals as secondary, and ourselves as primary, a viewpoint that does not lead to mutual respect and collegiality in interdisciplinary collaboration.

These are big steps for lawyers, and there is much to be said for taking these steps one at a time. Once the lawyers know how to practice collaborative law effectively, and begin to encounter the limitations of their ability to work on their own as collaborative lawyers with more challenging clients, then interdisciplinary collaboration generally can take root quickly in the practice group. (The mental-health and financial professionals who choose collaborative practice need to learn new skills and interdisciplinary practice protocols too, but do not typically have to unlearn adversarial habits in the way that lawyers generally do.)

Where interdisciplinary collaboration is launched from the outset in a community, the nonlawyer professionals sometimes complain about lack of collegiality on the part of the lawyers within the practice group, and unhelpful adversarial behavior with the clients. In the author's view, lawyers benefit from some additional time learning the art and craft of collaborative legal practice before they expand their horizons to interdisciplinary work, and the expanded interdisciplinary practice groups tend to experience fewer of the problems described in the preceding sentence when the lawyers have more collaborative experience prior to undertaking interdisciplinary work.

8. See Appendix I-D(2)(d) for sample client evaluation forms.

9. An excellent manual for this purpose is DAVID E. GUMPERT, DO IT YOURSELF PUBLIC RELATIONS: A SUCCESS GUIDE FOR LAWYERS (1995), published by the American Bar Association. A wealth of information about press releases—how to write them and what to do with them—is available on the Internet.

Chapter 10

Collaborative Law Beyond Family Law[1]

"Win/win is an attitude, not an outcome"   —Don Boyd

The early years of the 21st century have seen growing interest among civil and commercial lawyers in extending the availability of collaborative legal representation to civil and commercial clients. While there have been few such collaborative cases completed at the time of this second edition, there is a considerable amount of writing, teaching, speaking, and other activity directed toward answering these questions:

- In what areas of civil and commercial practice might collaborative law be attractive to clients?
- What challenges stand in the way of widespread use of collaborative law in civil/commercial disputes?
- How can those challenges be addressed?
- What is the current state of development of civil/commercial collaborative practice, and what steps should be taken next?

In what areas of civil and commercial practice might collaborative law prove attractive to clients?

It is generally accepted that for a dispute to be amenable to collaborative conflict resolution, there must be some ongoing interests present that are of significant importance to the disputing parties—perhaps even more important to the long-term mutual welfare of the disputants than marginal advantage in the immediate dispute. When such factors are present, attention to the larger web of connections potentially linking the parties to their mutual advantage can put the immediate dispute into a broader perspective that facilitates settlement, can contain transactional and other costs, and can also expand the pie to include options for settlement not available in litigation.[2]

**SEVEN REASONS WHY COLLABORATIVE CONFLICT
RESOLUTION SHOULD BE APPEALING TO CIVIL
AND COMMERCIAL CLIENTS**

1. Collaborative conflict resolution maximizes privacy. Clients can maintain substantial control over whether and to what degree the dispute is aired in public records.
2. Clients have maximum control over the quality and shape of the outcome. Because results are fully consensual, the solutions are "owned" by the clients. No third-party decision maker dictates the resolution of the dispute, nor do adversarial lawyers jockey for position with mediators or settlement judges.
3. The entire universe of areas of potential cooperation and mutual advantage can be brought to bear in expanding options for settlement, in sharp contrast to litigation, which is constrained by limits: limited jurisdiction, limited time, and limited attention of third-party decision makers.
4. Collateral damage, in the form of destruction of potential areas of future mutual benefit, does not occur in collaborative legal practice.
5. The cost of collaborative conflict resolution is far lower than the cost of litigating the same set of issues, and is generally much speedier.
6. The face-to-face collaborative negotiations, with good-faith disclosures and real-time deliberations involving clients and lawyers in face-to-face multi-party communications, lead to creative out-of-the box thinking and superior solutions as compared to the two-way communications characteristic of litigation (and litigation-matrix mediation) in which lawyers control the inflow and outflow of information for strategic and tactical advantage.
7. Because clients generate and own the solutions to their disputes, post-judgment conflicts about the dispute tend to be rare and are more readily resolved than in litigated resolution of disputes.

It was thought that probate law might be the first nonfamily area of practice to offer collaborative conflict resolution, because of the ongoing extended family relationships that can be placed at risk when such matters are litigated rather than resolved in a manner that values the context in which the dispute takes place. That prediction has proved accurate. Several collaborative practice groups, most notably the Collaborative Council of the Redwood Empire (Santa Rosa, California), have offered trainings aimed at adapting family law collaborative protocols to the needs of probate practice. Practitioners have provided collaborative representation in cases involving business succession planning, will contests, and estate planning. Lawyers doing this work confirm that much of the appeal to clients lies in the reality that extended families may be fractured or healed depending on how the lawyers view the long-term relational interests of their clients as compared to immediate bottom-line distributive economic gain. These longer-term relational interests provide motivation for electing collaborative law, and for staying with it when negotiations are challenging. Because of the intense emotion associated with the death of a family member, and the not-infrequent presence of longstanding patterns of family dysfunction, as well as the need to marshall assets, pay debts, and allocate appropriate shares of the estate to beneficiaries, involvement of interdisciplinary collaborative teams is a logical next step for lawyers engaging in probate collaboration. Trained collaborative coaches can facilitate communications and difficult conversations, as well as help with planning terms of guardianship of children, while collaborative financial consultants can help avert squabbling over the nature, value, and disposition of estate assets and debts.

IN CONFLICT RESOLUTION, AS IN SHOW BUSINESS, TIMING MATTERS

While mediation has become commonplace in commercial and civil litigation, it often takes the form of mandatory court-annexed mediation, required by the courts as a way to clear dockets and conserve judicial resources.

This kind of mediation bears little resemblance to the client-centered conflict resolution that collaborative lawyers are trying to bring to their clients. Here are some of the chief differences:

- Mandatory court-annexed mediation generally takes place late in the litigation process, after positions have polarized and the parties and lawyers have devoted considerable time and expense to discovery and pretrial motions. In Dallas, for instance, the court's standard mediation referral order states that mediation will take place 30 days prior to the date of trial. With trial impending and trial preparations in high gear, litigation lawyers frequently approach a pretrial mediation as just another opportunity for positional advocacy, controlling the negotiations as they would in a judicial settlement conference. So late in the process, with so much time and money already invested, it is common for both lawyers and clients to perceive little downside risk associated with holding firm and taking the matter before the judge or jury.

- Collaborative legal representation takes place entirely outside the framework of litigation, generally before any complaint has been filed and before hard lines have been drawn in a dispute. When the process is engaged early, the savings in time and expense can be considerable, and the openness of the parties to creative conflict resolution is optimal.

- Transactional lawyers who practice collaborative law can move the initiation of collaborative conflict resolution even earlier, by recommending or engaging in collaborative advocacy as soon as it is apparent that a problem may be developing. Clients benefit when potential conflicts are addressed before they become full-blown legal disputes.

- Transactional lawyers can build into contracts and other documents an expectation of collaborative conflict resolution in the event of difficulties, so that clients will think of collaborative resolution as soon as they become aware of an impending problem.

Collaborative law also offers potential benefits in commercial disputes when the parties have long-term potential for ongoing or new commercial relationships. While many commercial disputes ultimately end in a settlement forged by litigation counsel, the conventional litigator's short-term focus on resolving the immediate dispute tends to constrain settlement discussions to predictions about how a judge will resolve the matter. In such litigation-matrix settlement discussions, the universe of potential resolution is bounded by the jurisdiction and substantive law of the local court. Future business opportunities do not lie within that universe of discussion, and may not only be overlooked, but may be destroyed, in the course of settling or litigating the immediate dispute.

In contrast, such potential business opportunities can enrich the development of settlement options in a collaborative, "expand-the-pie" approach to dispute resolution—in ways that commercial mediation often cannot.[3]

Other advantages to business clients of the collaborative conflict-resolution process include:

- Reducing transactional costs (lawyers' fees, expert witness and litigation consultant fees, litigation costs)
- Reducing the negative impact on business operations of the uncertainty associated with unresolved disputes
- Reducing or eliminating negative publicity associated with litigated business disputes
- Maintaining privacy of business records, plans, and trade secrets by avoiding motions, hearings, trials, and appeals on the public record
- Reducing the drain on time, energy, and attention of principals, executives, managers, bookkeepers, board members, and key employees—and the resulting negative impact on the business bottom line—that litigation involves

- Reducing emotional stress associated with participating in depositions, testimony, and cross examination
- Enhancing quality of outcomes by ensuring that knowledgeable employees and managers participate directly in designing solutions

For these and other reasons, lawyers engaged in advancing collaborative practice beyond family law envision that clients with disputes in many areas of civil and commercial practice can be shown the advantages of collaborative conflict resolution. Specifically, efforts are being made to educate potential clients in areas such as these:

- Construction defects disputes
- Business and commercial contract disputes of all kinds
- Professional practice dissolutions
- Nonprofit corporation board disputes
- Elder law matters
- Environmental disputes
- Franchise disputes
- Claims against health-care providers
- Insurance claims and bad-faith disputes
- Intellectual property claims
- Employment and labor disputes
- Personal injury claims
- Homeowners' and condominium association disputes
- Probate and estate-planning matters
- Mergers and acquisitions
- Professional errors and omissions
- Real property transactions
- Securities and antitrust matters

Finally, in disputes where institutional behavioral change is a goal for one or both of the parties, collaborative problem solving may in some instances be better suited to achieving that goal than litigation, which can lead to entrenched positions that are harder to change than was the case before the litigation. Some employment and civil rights disputes and some immigration disputes involve institutional change objectives like these. Political asylum advocates, for example, have worked with federal officials to implement sweeping changes in immigration policies and procedures that affect large groups of asylum applicants, to the benefit of both asylum applicants and the agency.[4]

10 QUESTIONS FOR BUSINESS CLIENTS WONDERING WHETHER TO CHOOSE COLLABORATIVE LAW

1. Is it necessary or potentially useful for you or your business to have future dealings with the other disputant(s) or their officers, directors, employees, or consultants?
2. Is it the best use of your time to go to court, depositions, and litigation meetings from time to time over the next few years?

   a. Will your attention and energy be distracted from the business of your business?

   b. Will your employees (assistant, secretary, managers, bookkeeper) be taken away from their work for periods of time that will interfere with productivity or efficiency?

3. Did the lawyer(s) advising you about this dispute say that you will achieve a complete win in court? Do you believe that?
4. Are you confident that your current legal adviser(s) understands and appreciates the broader business context in which you operate and in which this dispute is taking place? Or are they focused primarily on the outcome of the immediate issues?
5. Would your reputation or the interests of your business potentially be harmed by a public airing of this matter—or by a public defeat in this dispute?
6. Do you believe that a neutral third party (whether a settlement facilitator or a judge or arbitrator) would be able to devise an optimal outcome for your business in the context of litigating this dispute—an outcome better than, or even as good as, you could devise yourself?
7. Would you derive more personal satisfaction from your lawyer(s) winning a litigated victory sometime in the future (perhaps years from now, after trial and appeal) or from working out your own solution now, while the issues are fresh and relevant to your current business activities?
8. What impact would result to your business from having the current dispute remain unresolved for a protracted period of time?
9. Even if you were to achieve a complete victory in litigation, would you also risk incurring significant unrecovered financial costs, such as litigation costs, attorneys' fees, expert witness fees, and consultant fees?
10. Is the person (or persons) advising you about these questions looking dispassionately at the business consequences of how and when you resolve this dispute, or are you being advised by someone who is angry or bitter, or who feels that the other disputant(s) should be punished for some reason?

Adapted from *Ten Questions for Clients Weighing Litigation v. Collaborative Law*, by Peter B. Sandmann and Pauline H. Tesler, CPR Alternatives, Vol. 21, No. 1, p.11 (January 2003).

What challenges stand in the way of widespread use of collaborative law in civil/commercial disputes?

For some years now,[5] civil and commercial lawyers across the United States and Canada—and now in England and Australia—have been sharing thoughts about specific challenges in advancing collaborative practice outside the area of family law. Some consistent themes emerge from the dialogue, including these:

- While some types of disputes—e.g., medical malpractice, will contests, and business partnership disputes—can involve high levels of emotion as well as a desire for continuing connection, or at least a need to minimize the damage to reputation, many commercial disputes lack these elements. Where the dispute is about little more than money, it can be difficult for clients to find the requisite common ground, or even the motivation for respectful, timely resolution.

- Most mid-size and large cities have a specialist family law bar whose members come to know one another and to have repeated encounters on cases over time. It is easier for these lawyers to develop trust relationships and to know whom to invite into a new collaborative practice group than it is for civil and commercial lawyers in urban areas, who report that it is uncommon to encounter the same lawyer repeatedly on different cases. The challenges for civil and commercial lawyers who want to build collaborative practice groups and achieve visibility in the community are different and perhaps greater than for family lawyers in the same communities.[6]

- While most divorcing spouses sooner or later share a common desire to finish the divorce process and move on with life, impersonal business disputes may lack this dimension, resulting in unbalanced or even nonexistent motivation to reach resolution. In many such disputes, one party may benefit from the matter languishing without resolution, while the other party suffers from delay. In such cases the role of the collaborative lawyers is complex, and more attention may need to be paid to techniques and protocols for moving negotiations forward appropriately.[7]

- Family law matters generally involve only two stakeholders, the divorcing couple, at the negotiating table.[8] Multiparty civil litigation, in contrast, is commonplace, and both disclosed and undisclosed alignments of parties' interests may exist. Collaborative work in such cases will be highly complex and may require new structural devices and protocols in order to proceed smoothly.

- Family lawyers tend to practice most commonly in small firms or as solo practitioners, and repeat business is rarely a significant factor in a family law business model. Commercial and civil lawyers interested in collaborative law include practitioners in large firms whose repeat-business clients are extremely important to the economic interests of the firm. The principle that a collaborative lawyer must be disqualified from further involvement in litigation between the parties if they resort to third-party decision making is consequently difficult for large-firm lawyers to accept. The debate continues as to whether a "Chinese Wall" would suffice, permitting the litigation department of the firm to continue to represent the client in litigation in a matter in which the "collaborative law department" was disqualified. Most lawyers argue that this is a slippery slope and that the integrity of the collaborative model requires that the same rules should govern with respect to disqualification as are applied to determine conflict for representation purposes. It is unlikely that collaborative law will be embraced to any significant extent by large firms if the conclusion is that the Chinese Wall is an insufficient protection for the integrity of the collaborative process. Whether this is a serious obstacle, or simply a reason for focusing attention on developing collaborative practice among smaller boutique firms and solo practitioners, remains a subject of debate.

How can those challenges be addressed?
Most lawyers who have been wrestling with the foregoing challenges for some years now would agree that no single answer is correct, and that multiple trial-and-error efforts should continue, with the measure of success being the choice by increasing numbers of clients to use collaborative law for conflict resolution. By that measure, the right configuration of strategies has not yet emerged.

Among the approaches being taken as of 2008 that appear promising are these:

- Continuing education efforts aimed at civil and commercial lawyers, delivered through bar associations and professional organizations, at conferences, and in law schools.
- Outreach efforts to lawyers who are "gatekeepers"—who manage litigation and conflict resolution for large corporations, and who contract with litigation departments of outside law firms to handle

specific disputes. These outreach efforts focus on educating gate-keepers about the advantages to their company of starting with collaborative conflict resolution before turning to litigation. Among the possibilities that can be explored with gatekeeper lawyers are both referral to small collaborative firms as an initial step, and also utilizing trained in-house counsel for the collaborative phase of conflict resolution.

- Educating small and medium-size business owners and professionals about collaborative law, through articles in professional journals, conference presentations, speaking engagements and workshops at local business and public service organizations, and similar activities.

- Exploring models for limited representation and reciprocal referrals between large firms and boutique or solo collaborative practices, so that valuable large-firm clients can benefit from collaborative representation as an early conflict-resolution intervention, while remaining with or returning to the large firm for ongoing representation.

- Developing presentations and articles targeted for homeowners' associations, health-care organizations, elder-care organizations, environmental groups, and the like.

- Working closely with interested judicial officers to develop local rules and policies favorable to collaborative law.

YOUR LOCAL JUDGE CAN RAISE AWARENESS OF CIVIL AND COMMERCIAL COLLABORATIVE LEGAL PRACTICE

A supportive judicial officer can be a strong ally in giving collaborative law visibility and credibility. For example, Hon. Mary L. Murphy, of the 14th Civil District Court in Dallas, includes the following in the policies and procedures for her department posted on her website, www.judgeMaryMurphy.com.

"Mediation/ADR/collaborative Law

". . . It is the Court's policy to require mediation of all cases, but not to force parties to mediate if good reason exists not to mediate. If the file does not reflect that a mediator has been selected at the time the Court Administrator sends the 30-day trial notice, the Court will appoint a mediator. Judge Murphy also encourages use of the collaborative law process for appropriate cases. Information regarding collaborative law may be found at http://www.collaborativelaw.us/."

What is the current state of development of civil/commercial collaborative practice, and what steps should be taken next?

As of mid-2008, no lawyer has yet reported completing more than two civil/commercial collaborative cases, and most who wish to do this work have yet to begin one. However, a significant number of lawyers in major cities across the United States, Canada, England, and now Australia, are devoting sustained efforts to changing this picture, and most observers believe that these efforts are starting to bear fruit.

U.S. lawyers from Texas (including Larry Maxwell and Sherrie Abney) have delivered presentations on civil and commercial collaboration at Oxford University, England, and a Massachusetts collaborative lawyer, David Hoffman, made a similar presentation in Australia in 2007. Brad Hunter, in Saskatchewan, Canada, has completed two collaborative cases involving estate planning and probate, and Bill Andrews, of Santa Rosa, California, reports similar success in the same area of law. Stacey Langenbahn and Gay Cox, of Texas, and Karen Fasler, of Washington, are having success at educating organizations of medical professionals about the advantages of collaborative conflict resolution. In Boston, a pilot program for collaborative resolution of employment discrimination cases is under development; in Saskatchewan, efforts are under way to implement a similar pilot program in the area of insurance disability claims.

While cases so far have involved estate matters and small to medium-size business and professional practices, there is evidence that larger corporations are beginning to take notice of the potential advantages to them of considering collaborative conflict resolution at the start of a matter rather than automatically referring cases to traditional litigation counsel. For example, Debra Branom, an executive with Electronic Data Systems Corporation, has taken an interest in making EDS a pioneering leader in bringing collaborative law to the world of international corporate conflict resolution. The internal EDS litigation group she works with is implementing a program to include collaborative law as the first step in an escalating tree of conflict-resolution options for contract disputes. She notes, "Our litigators want EDS to be a pioneer in this area by resolving disputes in a way that maintains and hopefully strengthens the business relationships that are key to successful outsourcing arrangements." (COUNSEL TO COUNSEL newsletter, page 7, September 2006.) Branom has picked up on an approach that collaborative lawyers have long assumed would be a key to implementing collaborative conflict resolution in large corporate contexts: rather than waiting for outside litigation counsel to begin offering collaborative law to her firm, she is treating this as a matter of importance in the first instance to the client, and appears to have no intention of waiting for outside litigation firms to decide whether they want to offer collaborative representation to EDS. Branom points out by way of analogy that while mediation is still far from universally accepted, it is nonetheless a key conflict-resolution tool that EDS builds into its contracts. Using that as a model, and taking leadership to protect the interests of her company, she wants to incorporate collaborative law as the first conflict-resolution tool in contract disputes with outsourcing partners, building in mediation or arbitration as a later step to be taken if a solution is not reached via collaboration. This project is in its "infancy," Branom notes, but she is clearly not waiting for outside litigation counsel to take the lead. At EDS, she says, "We view education as the first, and most important, step in utilizing this concept. Our [internal] litigators are educating our commercial contract lawyers and legal professionals about collaborative law. From there, it's a matter of educating our internal deal teams and our external clients."

There is reason to believe that Branom's counterparts in upper management of other national and multinational corporations would share her enthusiasm for adding collaborative law to the front end of the conflict-resolution menu, to be built into their agreements with business partners and outsourcing contractors.

EDS: A PIONEERING MULTINATIONAL CORPORATION

Our litigation group is exploring a nonadversarial dispute escalation and resolution process known as "collaborative law." Although we still use informal dispute escalation/resolution, mediation, and arbitration provisions because they are well understood by clients and are common in the outsourcing industry, we are in the process of determining how and in what context to incorporate a collaborative law process into our contracts. Its use would be voluntary and, if chosen, it would be the initial dispute escalation/resolution vehicle, to be followed by mediation and/or arbitration only if unsuccessful.

Potential benefits of a collaborative law approach include:

- Having representatives of the parties (rather than their lawyers) drive the process and be actively involved in negotiations that take place through a series of meetings with jointly prepared agendas;

- Conducting interest-based negotiations focused on each party's business goals, objectives, and interests rather than positional bargaining based on legal and contractual rights, duties, liabilities, and claims;

- Reducing expenses associated with pretrial discovery, motion practice, and "battles of the experts" by focusing on what is necessary to resolve the dispute and by jointly engaging experts and consultants as needed;

- Having flexibility in conducting the process and in exploring resolution options that are not available to courts and arbitrators, including nonmonetary options; and

- Restoring and maintaining relationships based on transparent, honest, confidential, face-to-face, respectful, and good-faith negotiations.

Debra Branom, Manager, U.S. and Latin America Business Support for Electronic Data Systems Corporation.

BUSINESS ROUNDTABLE EXECUTIVES WANT COLLABORATIVE LAW—BUT JUST DON'T KNOW IT YET!

Listen to what corporate executives identify as key conflict-resolution priorities and concerns.

"The biggest cost-benefit is to resolve a case as early as possible."

"Our business is not litigation. One of the goals we have is to ensure that the litigation does not disrupt the company."

"[T]hey [outside litigation counsel] wouldn't even know about these alternatives if we hadn't brought them to the table and described the downsides of litigation."

Kathleen A. Bryan, Director of Litigation
Motorola, Inc.

"The idea is to get away from the on-the-one-hand, on-the-other-hand legal analysis and focus on the broader business context."

". . . fees and expenses are the tip of the iceberg. We all know that in complex cases the management disruption and lost-opportunity costs can dwarf these expenses."

"It requires more than just experience, because every litigator has been on the litigation treadmill. . . . [T]he question is: Are these collaborative kinds of people? Are these good communicators? Are these people who can look beyond the pure legal issue to the broader business context? These are hard people to find. But for the way we do things, these are the kinds of people we have to have."

Paul J. Ehlenbach
The Boeing Co.

"But on very large, complex cases, a separate settlement counsel on the outside can be very helpful. . . . When you have a trial lawyer . . . negotiating, you have a lot of posturing. An outside settlement counsel eliminates that because you have somebody who says: 'Look, I'm not going to try this case. I'm here to resolve this.'"

Peter M. Lieb
International Paper Co.

"Our mediation of commercial disputes generally has involved at least a couple of sessions where all the parties are in one room. It's helpful, because ultimately it's the business managers who are present who will initiate imaginative settlement options, such as the purchase of products or other ways of continuing to do business."

J. Lawrence McIntyre
The Toro Company

"There have been many situations where we settle a case without getting trial lawyers involved."

"The more buy-in you have from the business side, the more creative solutions you will get as to how to resolve the litigation."

Jeanine Marie Jigante
Caremark Rx, Inc.

FURTHER INFORMATION ABOUT COLLABORATIVE LAW FOR CIVIL, BUSINESS, AND COMMERCIAL CLIENTS

ARTICLES

Sherrie R. Abney, *Collaborative Resolution of Civil Disputes: New Opportunities for Mediators,* ALTERNATIVE RESOLUTIONS, pp. 7–11 (Summer 2005).

Debra E. Branom, *Business Relationships: Exploring Collaborative Law,* COUNSEL TO COUNSEL, p. 7 (September 2006).

Gay G. Cox, *Avoiding the Trauma of Courtroom Drama,* JOURNAL OF ONCOLOGY PRACTICE, pp. 155–56 (July 2006).

Karen S. Fasler, *Combining Collaborative Law and Patient Safety Programs: A Proposal For The Use of Parallel Processes to Facilitate Early Detection of Safety Issues and Early Reparation for Injury-Causing and Near-Miss Episodes,* ALTERNATE RESOLUTIONS, pp. 11–20 (Winter 2007).

R. Paul Faxon, *Resolving Real Estate Disputes: The Case for Collaborative Law,* MASS. COLLABORATIVE L. J., Vol. 2, No. 2, p. 23 (Winter 2004).

David Hoffman, *Collaborative Law in the World of Business,* Collaborative Rev. (Winter 2004).

R. Bradley Hunter, *Preventative Collaborative Law* (paper presented at IACP 2004 Forum, and at Boston Family Firm Institute; copies available from author, brad.hunter@collabcan.com).

Nicole T. LeBoeuf, *The Front Edge of the Wave,* Professional Liability Underwriting Soc. J. (February 2007).

Lawrence R. Maxwell, *A New Way of Doing Business: Collaboration* (paper presented at 5th Annual Institute for Responsible Dispute Resolution, South Texas College of Law, 2004).

Douglas C. Reynolds and Doris F. Tennant, *Collaborative Law—An Emerging Practice,* Boston Bar J. (November 1, 2001).

Pauline H. Tesler, *Collaborative Law Neutrals Produce Better Resolutions,* Alternatives (Journal of the CPR Institute for Dispute Resolution), Vol. 21, No. 1 (January 2003).

BOOKS

Sherrie R. Abney, Avoiding Litigation: A Guide to Civil Collaborative Law (2005).

WEBSITES

Collaborative Council of the Redwood Empire: www.collaborativecouncil.org
Massachusetts Collaborative Law Council: www.massclc.org
Texas Collaborative Law Council: www.collaborativelaw.us

Notes

1. I wish to thank the following people for their generous assistance with portions of the material that appears in this chapter: Larry Maxwell, Peter Sandmann, Brad Hunter, Bill Andrews, and David Hoffman.

2. For more extended explanation of these ideas, see Mnookin, Peppet & Tulumello, Beyond Winning: How Lawyers Help Clients Create Value in Negotiation (1999).

3. Litigation-driven mediation is a very common mode of mediation in the commercial sector, where it can be undertaken at any point in the conflict-resolution process, including in the shadow of trial, long after the complaint has been filed and discovery is close to completion. Many of the potential benefits to clients that collaborative lawyers consider most valuable are no longer available to the disputants when mediation occurs so late in the litigation process, guided by lawyers who have no special investment in achieving settlement.

4. This is not to suggest that collaborative law is always the best strategy for achieving institutional change. There are situations involving the public interest in which class action or test case litigation with reported appellate decisions is clearly the better choice. *Brown v. Board of Education,* 347 U.S. 483 (1954), would not have had large-scale impact if the plaintiffs had negotiated a private deal with the institutional defendant.

5. Beginning with informal conversations in the late 1990s, lawyers began to write exploratory articles for local and state dispute-resolution journals and newsletters, such as the ones listed at the end of this chapter, followed soon afterward by speeches, conference presentations, workshops, and eventually trainings aimed at applying concepts and protocols

developed by collaborative family lawyers in the civil and commercial areas of practice. Some collaborative practice groups founded in the late 1990s included civil and commercial lawyers from the start, such as the Massachusetts Collaborative Law Council and the Collaborative Law Center of Cincinnati, Ohio. The latter group received support from a magistrate of the federal court, and devoted considerable effort to developing civil/commercial collaborative practice, but apparently is now focused exclusively on family law collaboration. Massachusetts collaborative lawyers continue to be leaders in efforts related to civil and commercial collaboration, leading workshops and training programs, and writing articles on the subject.

In recent years, Texas lawyers have been particularly visible in this effort. Their statewide organization, the Texas Collaborative Law Council (TCLC), has developed protocols for civil and commercial collaborative practice, and has been the source of training programs that have been offered both in Texas and elsewhere. A first collaborative training for nonfamily lawyers took place in Texas in 2005, and annual trainings of this kind continue in Dallas (sponsored by the Texas Collaborative Law Council and the Collaborative Law Section of the Dallas Bar Association) and in Houston (sponsored by the Collaborative Law Section of the Houston Bar Association, with particular leadership from Norma Trusch). TCLC lawyers have spoken and trained on this subject in other states in America as well as in England on this subject. TCLC members have written numerous articles as well as the first full-length book. In addition, the Dallas and Houston bar associations have established Collaborative Law Sections that include lawyers handling civil as well as family disputes. Hon. Mary L. Murphy, of the 14th Civil District Court in Dallas, is currently working with Collaborative Law Section officers to develop procedures for removing collaborative cases from the docket to give the parties an opportunity to settle their disputes without court intervention. And in 2006, 24 Dallas lawyers with diverse practices (including probate, construction, professional errors and omissions, employment, real estate, and insurance) formed The Civil Collaborative Practice Group, modeled after family law practice groups, and chaired by Hon. Ted Akin, retired Justice of the Court of Appeals, Fifth District of Texas. Active efforts continue among civil and commercial collaborative lawyers in Texas as of 2007 to secure passage of the first nonfamily collaborative law statute.

Another practice group that is taking a leadership role is the Collaborative Council of the Redwood Empire, an interdisciplinary organization of practitioners in Sonoma County, California, formed in 2007, that sponsored the first nonfamily law collaborative training, for probate practitioners as one of its earliest projects. Presently, the organization is offering short workshops in conflict resolution techniques for businesspeople, at Chamber of Commerce and similar gatherings, as a way of publicizing civil and commercial collaborative law.

The IACP has included programs on civil and commercial collaborative practice in its annual forum since 2004. And, in 2007, the ABA Section on Dispute Resolution established a Collaborative Law Committee, thanks to the efforts of David Hoffman.

6. On the other hand, family lawyers in large urban areas have also found it more difficult to reach critical mass than in smaller cities, simply because there are so many lawyers representing so many divorcing clients that it can be challenging to achieve the goal of making every divorcing couple in the community aware that collaborative legal representation is available to them. It may be that methods urban collaborative family lawyers have used with success may be adaptable to the needs of civil and commercial lawyers.

7. As with family law matters, civil and commercial collaborative lawyers will need to develop screening criteria to identify the characteristics that make a matter appropriate for collaborative law and should not assume that all clients and all cases are amenable to effective collaborative conflict resolution.

8. While the children, if any, are stakeholders in a family law collaborative process, they do not ordinarily participate directly in the collaborative process. New mates or extended family members may on occasion be brought to the collaborative table, but this is a relatively rare occurrence.

Chapter 11

Frequently Asked Questions About Collaborative Law

"Conflict is inevitable, but combat is optional."—Max Lucade

In this chapter, you will read answers to the most commonly recurring questions about collaborative law—those raised by lawyers at trainings and workshops worldwide, and some that clients often ask. The answers amount to the pooled wisdom of many experienced collaborative practitioners. You may eventually come up with different ideas; treat these as suggestions for how to start thinking about these issues—suggestions that you may decide to accept, reject, or amend.

a. How can a client's need for temporary orders be met in the collaborative process in light of your advice to defer difficult issues until the clients have developed some negotiating competency and have experienced some success in early four-way meetings?

Answer: The collaborative process is fluid and adaptable. Although starting the first four-way meeting with tense negotiations about the amount of temporary support to be paid is a mistake, there are other ways to get money flowing from the higher to the lower earner, or to get a retainer paid to the homemaker-spouse's lawyer, while preserving potential deductibility or claims about ultimate characterization of the payments. To do so requires that the lawyers think their way out of the box of motions and orders, which are merely the litigation-template approach to solving such immediate problems. Skilled counsel can present ideas to their clients for interim short-term solutions to obvious cash flow and similar problems that won't inter-fere with building a strong foundation for collaboration, saying something like this: "John, you know Mary hasn't got any money coming in and she needs to buy food and pay rent and so forth. We don't know yet what the regular amount of support is going to be for her and the children, but we can't even get to the meeting where we will discuss that unless she has some money for necessities. You aren't giving up your right to negotiate about the amount, but we need a gesture of good faith so that Mary will know this collaborative process is not going to be unsafe for her. Tell me what you have coming in this month, and how much you think she'll need for the basic monthly bills, and we'll write up a quick short-term agreement that protects your legal rights to get credit for the payment once we figure out later what the support should really be. Then we can focus the nego-tiations on looking at the big picture about support instead of you paying lawyers to work on urgent solutions that will only last for a few months."

A client who has resources but rejects his lawyer's advice to advance suf-ficient money to the dependent spouse to tide her over until the second or third four-way meeting (subject to reservation of all rights to claim a differ-ent amount should have been paid, and subject to an agreement in writing that the payment will be deductible) probably does not belong in a collab-orative representation. Similarly, a spouse who will not honor the thres-hold understanding set out in the participation agreements to the effect that both collaborative lawyers need to be paid might not be a good candidate for this process. From that perspective, the degree to which your client can respond appropriately and somewhat informally to these threshold needs may be a good indicator of how good a fit collaborative law is for that client.

Such interim agreements can be reduced to stipulated court orders at any time. However, the speed and efficiency with which the collaborative process sometimes reaches comprehensive frameworks for settlement can lead experienced collaborative lawyers to prefer moving directly into nego-tiations about long-term support rather than devoting costly lawyer time to negotiating temporary support. In those cases the parties and their lawyers often agree early on that the long-term support numbers that are ultimately reached (whether collaboratively or in court after a potential termination) will also apply retroactively to sums advanced in the early phases of the col-laborative representation.

b. What if one of the parties to a collaborative representation is secretly act-ing in bad faith and misusing the process to gain time, advantage, informa-tion, or leverage?

Answer: If a party is misusing the collaborative process by not participat-ing in good faith in negotiations, voluntary discovery, or follow-through with interim agreements, the bad faith will become apparent to that party's lawyer fairly soon as well as to all the other participants, because there is nowhere to hide in collaborative negotiations. Either documents are pro-duced or they are not. Either money is paid as agreed or it is not. Either stipulated restraining orders are honored or they are not. If they are not, it will not take very long to recognize the fact, and either the client will mend his or her ways or the process will move toward termination. A collabora-tive lawyer vouches for the client's good faith by his or her continued par-ticipation in the process. If the lawyer suspects the client of bad faith and efforts to bring the client around do not succeed, the collaborative retainer and participation agreements provide that the lawyer must withdraw or ter-minate the collaborative process. A lawyer who does not follow through on this undertaking to collaborative colleagues may get away with covering up for a bad-faith client once, perhaps even twice, but will in all likelihood have a short career as a collaborative lawyer. Colleagues will not advise cli-ents to participate in collaborative processes with a collusive lawyer whom they cannot trust. Of course, if the bad faith is apparent to all, then the spouse's counsel will recommend terminating the process and going into the traditional litigation model, if the spouse hasn't already reached that conclusion on his or her own.

Since there is always some risk that a dishonest party could gain some advantage before the other collaborative participants catch on, the real ques-tions for the collaborative lawyer are: (1) Is there really any better protection for my client available in court? (2) Is maximum protection against all poten-tial risks of this kind right from the start as important to my client as what surely will be lost on the relational side if risk-avoidance trumps all other concerns? and (3) Whose decision should that be, mine or my client's?

c. How can a collaborative lawyer satisfy the duty of due diligence in the discovery phase of the process if all discovery is voluntary in collaborative law?

Answer: A collaborative lawyer can use all the discovery tools that are avail-able to the litigator, excluding only those that are unilateral or inherently coer-cive. For instance, it is perfectly consistent with collaborative law to use interrogatories or requests for admission if there is a perceived need to do so. Third-party subpoenas may also be used. It would be contrary to the spirit required for effective collaborative negotiations (though not barred specifically by most participation agreements) to conduct a deposition of a party, though it would not be impossible to depose a third party. Motions to compel, however, would be unavailable, and collaborative lawyers electing to use formal rather than informal discovery methods during a collaborative representation would be well-advised to enter into stipulations that preserve the right to file motions to compel should the process terminate short of agreement and enter the litigation mode. In all but very rare instances, however, collaborative lawyers find that written authorizations for third-party release of documents and declarations under penalty of perjury attesting to the accuracy and completeness of voluntary discovery provide a more economical, quicker, and more constructive form of disclosure than formal discovery and many collaborative lawyers and clients prefer to use such voluntary methods. Moreover, the good-faith undertakings of the collaborative process and the interest-based negotiations that are at its core lead good collaborative lawyers to produce very complete voluntary discovery, because the fuller the information, the better-informed the decision making.

Litigators know that a determined liar may succeed in concealing assets, income, and other relevant information even after vigorous formal discovery, and they know that ferreting out all possible information about assets and income is expensive and time-consuming and not always worth the costs. It is always wise to explain the risks and benefits of each approach (voluntary vs. formal discovery) and to let the clients decide which route they prefer.

A useful perspective is to consider whether a fear of possible malpractice claims is causing you to push clients into more costly discovery than they really need under the circumstances of their particular cases. Placing responsibility for informed decision making on the client's shoulders is more consistent with collaborative practice than allowing fears about malpractice claims to drive up the financial and emotional costs of dispute resolution.

d. How can you be sure assets or income are not being concealed?

Answer: You cannot be sure, any more than you can be sure of nonconcealment in litigated cases. Exhaustive discovery, audits, and private investigation are very costly, and in the end, collaborative lawyers should expect their clients to make informed cost-benefit decisions about how much should be spent to verify the representations made by the spouse, rather than dictating to the client that exhaustive discovery must be done simply because it can be done. The client, not the lawyer, should decide how much investigation is needed for the client to be satisfied with the information base. The lawyer needs to advise the client fully, and hand over the decision. Indeed, this is a sensible approach even in noncollaborative cases.

e. How can I answer a client who says that she cannot possibly trust her husband to participate honestly in collaborative law after all the lies he told her during the marriage?

Answer: It is never wise to persuade a client to use the collaborative process if she has reservations about it. What you can do is counsel her about putting her perceptions about her spouse into perspective. This might include helping her to compare what might happen during the collaborative process with what is very likely to happen if she elects conventional representation. A good starting point is to distinguish the emotional betrayals and dishonesty that often accompany the unraveling of the intimate marital relationship from the kind of lies associated with tax fraud or embezzlement. The latter is a serious contraindication for collaborative representation, but the former may not in fact be a problem. One might ask the client whether she believes her husband has ever lied on an income tax return, or whether she thinks he would lie if asked whether he had a safety deposit box. Most spouses have a fairly clear sense of their partner's fundamental fiscal honesty and can with some thought accept the possibility that a spouse could be honest about income, assets, and debts despite having committed seemingly unforgivable personal betrayals. If this process of reflection leaves your client still uneasy about collaborative law, then collaborative law isn't the right choice.

It also can be useful to remind clients that the spouse they are divorcing will have the same basic character and proclivities whether the divorce proceedings are collaborative or adversarial. Invite clients to consider which process is likely to elicit the spouse's "better self," if there is a better self. From this perspective, a client could rationally decide that even with a fundamentally dishonest spouse, the overall outcome might be better, and probably wouldn't be worse, in a collaborative process than in highly conflicted court proceedings.

In short, don't let your knee-jerk gladiatorial reactions put you on a white horse unless your client has made a fully informed decision that she wants a costly warrior and a black-and-white court battle, even if you are itching to teach her spouse a lesson. The decision should be hers, not yours. Your job should be to give her all the accurate information she needs to make that decision.

f. If my client does behave dishonestly or in bad faith in a collaborative representation, do I terminate the collaborative process or do I merely withdraw as counsel?

Answer: Different lawyers and different practice groups have come up with different answers to this question. Your group needs to discuss the issue carefully and if possible reach a decision collectively, so that you and your colleagues will know what to expect from one another if this situation arises. Your policy on this point should be stated in writing in the retainer agreements, stipulations, and ground rules that everyone signs at the start of the process. Some practice groups have expressed concern that if the lawyer treats the client's misfeasance or nonfeasance as cause for constructive termination of the process, that is tantamount to publicly accusing one's own client of dishonesty or bad faith. They allow the clients to terminate the process but permit the lawyers only to withdraw.

A more prevalent view is that the clients, in signing the collaborative documentation, are agreeing in advance that bad faith will be cause for one's own lawyer to terminate the collaborative process. These groups believe that their retainer agreement and participation agreement provisions stating that persistent dishonesty or bad faith constitutes a constructive termination by the client would be enforceable as a knowing and intelligent waiver of any objection to the lawyer terminating the process under those circumstances. Few collaborative lawyers believe that courts would be inclined as a policy matter to protect a client's knowing misuse of the collaborative process under these circumstances, particularly since no facts are divulged by the lawyer, the client retains full access to the courts, and no trial date will have been set. The sample forms in Appendix I contain alternatives with regard to constructive termination of the collaborative process. The IACP Ethical Standards permit termination by the lawyer if not inconsistent with applicable rules of practice in the jurisdiction.

g. What do you do if one client in a collaborative representation has speed as a priority, but the other client insists on moving forward very slowly?

Answer: This is a fairly common situation, because the "leaver" spouse generally has moved further through the emotional stages of grieving about the end of the marriage than the "left" spouse has, and may want to be done with it all quickly. The skillful collaborative lawyer does not simply act as alter ego for this wish, because the lawyer's job includes guiding the negotiations so that the clients have the best possible circumstances for reaching a comprehensive win-win agreement. Pushing a grieving, confused, frightened spouse faster than he or she can go will not achieve the goal. To put it metaphorically, both clients need to cross the finish line at the same time in a collaborative case. The lawyer needs to be a counselor for his or her own client, explaining (probably more than once) that the leaver's own self-interest will be best served by slowing down, so that the left spouse can recover emotionally to the point of being able to participate effectively in the collaborative process. The lawyer also should explain the direct connection between pushing an emotionally distraught spouse too hard and the evolution of a litigated high-conflict bad divorce. To counsel one's client about this requires that the collaborative lawyer understand and explain the divorce grieving process and the psychodynamics of high-conflict divorce litigation to the client. The lawyer also needs to help the client put the issue of speed into perspective, comparing the overall speed and costs of the collaborative process (even if it needs to begin quite slowly) with the overall speed and costs (including relational ones) of the litigation process. Few clients fully understand the "hurry up and wait" pacing of litigation. The lawyer does.

h. What do I do if my client tells me something in confidence that I believe the other side needs to know in order to negotiate on a sufficiently informed basis in the collaborative process, but my client forbids me from disclosing it?

Answer: If you have done a good job of explaining the collaborative process at the front end, and if your documentation (retainer agreement, participation agreement, *Principles and Guidelines*) is complete and accurate on this point, there should be no confusion on your part or the client's about what must happen at this point. You tell the client that in your professional judgment, the information must be disclosed or the integrity of the collaborative process would be compromised. You further confirm to the client that you are bound by the attorney-client privilege and will not disclose the information without the client's permission. And then you remind the client that as provided in your retainer agreement you will have to either withdraw, or terminate the collaborative process (depending on the approach your practice group has decided is required) if the client does not give you permission to disclose. The IACP Ethical Standards confirm the obligation of a collaborative lawyer to proceed in this manner.

i. Suppose that a case reaches an impasse on a financial issue. Are there any techniques other than using a private judge or arbitrator that collaborative lawyers have used to help get through the impasse?

Answer: In my experience it is rare in collaborative practice that apparent impasses fail to spark creative solutions where the lawyers have had sufficient training in interest-based conflict resolution. The process is fluid enough that creative lawyers have already thought of many imaginative ways to help clients get past impasse in the rare instances when the creative silence of the four-way meeting proves insufficient. Collaborative lawyers and clients have agreed to bring in a "meta-mediator," creating a "five-way" meeting. They have agreed to resort to some authority (such as a CPA or venture capitalist) for a neutral advisory opinion. They have agreed to conduct an informal auction within the collaborative process. Lawyers have taken a fearful or resistant client for a private second-opinion consultation with the potential successor litigation counsel so that the risks and benefits of terminating the collaborative process and going to court can be explained by the lawyer who would be responsible for litigating the matter rather than by the collaborative lawyer. Lawyers have taken fearful or resistant clients for second opinions from other collaborative lawyers. (Best practice is for the fact of a second-opinion consultation and the reason for it to be disclosed to your collaborative counterpart, to avoid the risk of inadvertent disclosure with consequent sowing of seeds of mistrust. Make sure you and your colleagues understand the practice group protocols on this point.) Creative new approaches to surmounting apparent impasse emerge constantly in collaborative practice.

IMPASSE: THE MAGIC MOMENT

For litigators, even in settlement mode, impasse means the end of creativity. When the going gets tough in negotiations, the litigator says, "We'll see you in court." Or, "No problem—we'll just let Judge Jones resolve it."

In other words, litigators' creative problem-solving efforts short-circuit and come to a halt when impasse arises. The availability of court limits their conflict-resolution capacities.

Psychologist Abraham Maslow put it this way: "If your only tool is a hammer, all problems will look to you like a nail."

For collaborative lawyers, in the words of collaborative law originator Stu Webb, "Impasse is simply the moment when we roll up the sleeves and get to work."

At moments of apparent impasse in a collaborative four-way meeting, when everyone has said everything they can think of, a silence will descend. Everyone looks around the table and the realization takes shape in each mind:

"If we can't figure out a way around this problem, this is our last collaborative meeting—we four will never again gather together around this table; the process ends here."

If the lawyers have enough experience and self-discipline to *keep quiet and allow the silence to do its work, it almost invariably happens that one party or the other will say, "Well, maybe . . . ," "I guess . . . ," "Well, perhaps I could. . . ."*

And in that moment lies the remarkable power of the collaborative law process. The creative juices begin to flow. Idea builds upon idea, concessions take shape, and often the resolution of the issue occurs in a kind of creative "hyperspace" that the participants enter only after sitting for some time with the apparent impasse.

The clients in a well-managed collaborative case will always have more information about facts, goals, priorities, and interests than any judge will, and therefore will always have an ability superior to the judge's to craft individualized solutions that can work well for their own situation.

It is the distribution of risk of failure to the lawyers that allows the collaborative process to enter the creative hyperspace where those solutions can be devised.

If the lawyers can go to court as a way of resolving impasse, then when impasse arrives, the lawyers, eager to resolve the problem, will take it to court.

If the lawyers cannot go to court, they will do all they can as problem solvers to help their clients find solutions to the impasse. It's that simple!

j. Can a lawyer make a living doing only collaborative law? Won't my income fall if I do very much collaborative work?

Answer: A lawyer can make a very comfortable living doing collaborative law. There are only so many billable hours in a year, and you can ethically fill them only once. As the collaborative model becomes more popular, more and more former family law litigators are limiting their practices to collaborative representation and other nonlitigated modes of representation. They find they can readily fill their billable hours without needing to take on litigated matters. The benefits in terms of satisfaction, stress reduction, and calendar control are obvious. But if maximizing income is the priority, collaborative law is probably not the best choice for you, because litigation—especially high-conflict litigation—is the source of the greatest number of billable hours for a family lawyer. When in trial one bills from eight to 12 or more hours a day, sometimes for weeks at a time. Few collaborative lawyers would choose to work so intensively.

However, while the absolute billable hours per year may be lower in collaborative practice, collection problems diminish dramatically. First, happy clients tend to pay their bills, and collaborative clients tend to be satisfied with the results of their lawyers' work. Second, since a collaborative lawyer is not counsel of record, and no motions or trials are scheduled during the collaborative process, it is unusual for unpaid fees to mount very high during a collaborative representation and it is generally easy for the lawyer either to work out a payment schedule or to withdraw. Third, since parity of payment to the lawyers is one of the basic hallmarks of collaborative representation, usually agreed to in writing by both clients and both lawyers, it is as a practical matter much easier to achieve payment of the nonemployed spouse's fees in collaborative practice than it is in litigated proceedings. In short, high-conflict litigators tend to have high fee write-offs, while collaborative lawyers almost always get paid for the hours they work.

k. I practice family law in an area distant from any big cities. There are only a few family lawyers in our region, and we can't afford to bring in costly trainers to help us develop our collaborative lawyering skills. Any suggestions about how we can learn this new skill set?

Answer: You can learn on the job, but the process will be slower without training and you will inevitably be reinventing some wheels. One alternative is to travel together to a collaborative law or interdisciplinary collaborative divorce training. (Be sure that the training includes role plays and critique and the other elements of a training that meets IACP standards.) Doing that together is likely to have a more potent effect on the level of practice once you return home than if each lawyer tries to master collaborative skills alone. Another alternative is to find a collaborative lawyer who has experience training other lawyers in collaborative law, and contract with that person for private small group consultation time at that person's office about how to do collaborative law effectively. A third option is to contract for mentoring/coaching with an experienced collaborative law or collaborative divorce trainer, using telephone or video conferencing. The author and some other experienced trainers are available for coaching, consultation, and mentoring at our customary hourly billing rates. You can do this on your own, or with your practice group, or you can use the mentoring/coaching relationship for help in case conferencing and troubleshooting with the other collaborative lawyer if a particular case runs into problems. Finally, the International Academy of Collaborative Professionals is developing a bank of presentation materials that are intended for self-teaching use in communities that are too small to be able to bring in trainers.

l. Is my collaborative client's spouse limited to selecting collaborative counsel from my practice group? If not, what if the other spouse selects the "lawyer from hell" as his or her supposedly collaborative lawyer? Do I go along with it? Or do I refuse?

Answer: It is important ethically to make it clear that each party to a collaborative representation is free to choose any competent collaborative lawyer and is not restricted to any one practice group. At the same time, it is appropriate to provide all potential collaborative clients and their spouses with the accurate information that an important predictor of a successful collaborative process (provided both spouses are equally committed to reaching a negotiated outcome) is for them to retain two skillful collaborative lawyers who respect and trust one another. It would be unwise to try to restrict your clients' spouses to your own group if there are other groups in the locale whose members have the necessary training. If there is more than one collaborative practice group in your locale there is no reason why a spouse could not select competent counsel from outside your practice group. However, if the spouse chooses someone you have no experience with, it would be important to meet with the lawyer prior to starting the case to establish a basis for mutual trust and cooperation, and to make explicit agreements about the ground rules and documentation that will be used in the case. Agreeing on a designated experienced mentor to assist if the lawyers run into difficulties at the professional level is a responsible and prudent step in such situations.

The "lawyer from hell" is a thornier problem. Most experienced collaborative lawyers will not sign the formal participation agreement for a collaborative case if they distrust the capabilities or bona fides of the other spouse's lawyer, because of the higher risk that one's own client will lose his or her lawyer if it becomes necessary to terminate the collaborative process. A second risk is that the other lawyer may be more likely to collude with the client to misuse the collaborative process, whether intentionally or because of poor understanding of the collaborative process or poor collaborative skills; this may not be apparent until well along in the collaborative process. Another viewpoint—at this juncture, it is a minority view—is that if your client's spouse has retained the lawyer from hell, your client is better off having that lawyer working in a collaborative process than in court. People who hold this view observe that either you will be able to inspire that lawyer to work more or less effectively within the collaborative process, or at worst, if you are disqualified because of terminating the collaborative process, the other lawyer will be disqualified as well. Lawyers who are willing to collaborate with all comers report some success in winning even very contentious lawyers over to a more positive mode of practice within the collaborative model.

Cautious lawyers are well advised to wait until they have some experience under their belts before attempting collaboration with lawyers known to be difficult. If you refuse to engage in formal collaboration because of the spouse's choice of counsel, there is no reason not to explain your reasons to your own client. You do not need to make directly critical comments. Try this: "I've learned that collaborative law works best when both lawyers have at least some training or experience in how to do this work well. I'll describe to you my own experience and training, and tell you which collaborative lawyers I work particularly well with. You may want to suggest that your spouse ask his or her lawyer to do the same, and the two of you could share that information before making your final decisions, to make sure you both retain counsel who can do this work effectively with one another." Sometimes the spouse will have been unaware that the lawyer he or she chose has no prior experience with collaborative law and will rethink the choice of counsel. If not, you will have to decide whether to opt out altogether, or whether to do the best job you can in the situation without signing the formal collaborative agreements.

COLLABORATING WITH ATTILA THE HUN

What if your client's spouse retains Attila the Hun, or even Darth Vader, as collaborative counsel? What do you do then?

Some of us simply withdraw from combat. We advise our client that the chances that we could succeed in collaboration with Attila or Darth are too low for us to be willing to sign on to a disqualification stipulation. Others of us, braver souls, move forward and try to educate, mold, and seduce Darth and Attila into the kinder, gentler ways of collaborative law.

If one of these guys shows up in a case of yours, or even if it is simply a lawyer you don't know well, here is an idea that protects the clients and the integrity of the process—not to mention yourself:

Speak with this lawyer before the first four-way and before you have committed to going forward collaboratively. Discuss collaborative practice, and candidly explain your concern that you haven't yet got a collegial track record established together. There is a risk, you can explain, that the lawyers could slip into adversarial behaviors and inadvertently become the problem, rather than the problem solvers. In order to deliver to the clients what the lawyers are promising, propose that the two lawyers enter into a side agreement

> designating a facilitator or mediator that both trust. In the event either of you feels that the lawyers are becoming the problem, on request both of you will make use of the designated facilitator, at your own mutual expense, to help you move back to positive problem-solving mode. It is a good idea to insist on this, politely but firmly, as a condition of working collaboratively with Mr. or Ms. Attilla.

m. My collaborative practice group includes mental health and financial professionals as well as lawyers. I haven't yet had a case in which my client was interested in the extra expense of coaches and a financial consultant, though I think the interdisciplinary approach has merit. How can I persuade my clients to include the other collaborative professionals?

Answer: Never try to persuade your client to choose a conflict-resolution approach that he or she is hesitant about. Your job is to inform and to insist that the client take responsibility for making an informed choice. It is to be expected that clients may have heard little or nothing about interdisciplinary collaboration when they first consult you. Given that reality, why is it that clients of other lawyers in your community choose interdisciplinary collaboration, but yours do not? Your own degree of conviction about the value of interdisciplinary professional services is very likely being mirrored in your clients' lack of interest. You do not need to tell a client that it is the right choice for his or her own divorce in order to explain with enthusiasm how this integrated professional collaborative approach can help families in ways that lawyers alone cannot. Also, you should be prepared to explain clearly how the use of interdisciplinary team services paradoxically can help contain the cost of professional services by providing the right professional assistance at the appropriate fee. It always costs more when lawyers try to do work they are not trained for: mental-health coaching, child-development consulting, or financial analysis. In many communities where interdisciplinary collaboration is available, the protocol is for the lawyers to make a firm and reasoned request that the clients have one exploratory interview with collaborative divorce coaches so as to make an informed decision about whether and when to involve them in the divorce process. Few clients refuse a preliminary informational session, and most clients who meet with coaches decide to make use of that resource. Clients generally see the utility of one financial neutral preparing financial disclosures rather than having the two lawyers prepare potentially duplicative or incomplete disclosure packets; the lawyers' recommendation in this regard rarely meets with opposition from clients. One exception is the client who has complex finances and already has an accountant who is fully familiar with the financial information. The question in that instance is whether the accountant is sufficiently evenhanded in relation to both spouses to serve as a neutral. If not, this accountant can still provide well-organized data to the neutral financial consultant.

Tools and Resources for Lawyers

Appendix I-A

Intra-Office Forms

1. Initial Telephone Screening Form

New Client Phone Screen

❏ CALL PARTY TO SCHEDULE CONSULTATION
[who should call?_____]
❏ PARTY WILL CALL BACK AFTER REVIEW OF MATERIALS

Name _____

Address _____

Telephone Numbers _____

E-mail Address _____

Nature of Call _____

How did you hear about our office? _____

How did you hear about Collaborative Law? _____

Urgent? Yes/No/Why? _____

Name of Other Party _____

Represented by Attorney? _____

Spouse's Attorney _____

Used Google? _____

Referred by _____

Call Taken by _____

Date/Time of Call _____

CL Info Packet Sent?   Book Sent?   Date: _____

Appointment Date? _____

Scheduled by _____

Notes

2. New Client Basic Information Form

Initial Consultation

Please fill out as completely and accurately as possible. Date:

YOU

Your Full Name: _____   Date of Birth: _____

Home Address:

Own or Rent: Home Phone: Home Fax:

Cellular Phone: E-mail:

Employer Name:

Employer Address:

Work Phone: Work Fax: Job Title:

How long employed there?

Which address shall we use as your mailing address?

Social Security No. _____ Driver's License No.

YOUR SPOUSE

Full Name: Date of Birth:

Address: Phone:

Own or Rent?   Employer:

Work Address:

Work Phone: Job Title:

How long employed there?   Social Security No.

Does your spouse have a lawyer for this matter? If so, who?

Was either of you in the armed forces? If so, branch, rank/rate, station, entry date, separation date:

CHILDREN OF THIS MARRIAGE

Name	Sex	Date of Birth	Place of Birth

Has any minor child lived outside this state? If so, give dates and addresses:

_____

_____

_____

Which parent are children living with at present?

Are adult children or stepchildren of another marriage living in your home?

Date of Marriage: _____   Still living with spouse? ___ yes

___ no

If "no," who moved out and on what date?

Years in state: _____ Years in county: _____

You are requesting: Information and consultation only _____
                        Divorce
                        Other (specify):_____

If divorce is sought:

Do you have a former name that you wish restored?

Request regarding parenting arrangements for children:

Additional Comments:

_____

For office use only:

Fee Rates:

Retainer Amount: Client File Number:

3. The Collaborative Retainer Agreement

[A Sample Form Consistent with California Rules of Practice]

Date

[*Client Name*]
[*Client Address*]
PERSONAL AND CONFIDENTIAL

 Re: <u>Retainer Agreement</u>

Dear Mr./Ms. _____:

Introduction

You have retained our firm to advise you in connection with your Collaborative Law/Collaborative Divorce process in which you and [*name of spouse or partner*] each has your own lawyer, and all have a shared commitment to avoid litigation. The process primarily entails informal discussions and face-to-face conferences for purposes of settling all issues. Each party and his or her lawyer agrees to adhere to honesty, constructive problem-solving efforts, and mutual respect for the integrity of the people and the process.

Scope and Duties

Assuming your spouse agrees to proceed via the collaborative process using a trained collaborative lawyer, I will represent your interests through the final settlement and filing of a judgment of dissolution. *My representation of you as a collaborative lawyer differs in some important respects from conventional representation by a litigation lawyer. Please read particularly carefully* the following section describing my responsibilities, and yours, in collaborative representation under this agreement.

 Your retention of me as your Collaborative Divorce lawyer is a "limited-purpose retention." You are retaining me specifically to assist you in reaching a comprehensive agreement with your spouse or partner, and for no other purpose. You retain the right to terminate the Collaborative Divorce process at any time and go to court, *but doing so ends my representation of you.*

 If your spouse should elect to go to court, this also terminates the Collaborative Divorce process, and you would need to retain litigation counsel to assist you in court. Accordingly, my representation of you and your retainer agreement with this firm are subject to the following:

- I will not be your lawyer of record, except for purposes of filing the Judgment.
- I will not represent you in any adversarial proceedings except to the extent that both parties agree within the scope of the Collaborative Divorce Stipulation to submit selected issues to a private judge or arbitrator for resolution. My representation is terminated by any party's decision to litigate, *whether or not it was your decision.*
- I will not represent you or assist in any litigation against [*name of spouse or partner*] should the Collaborative Divorce process end before complete settlement. However, I will cooperate with you in transferring your file to new counsel.
- I will not be called by you to give evidence in any family law litigation against [*name of spouse or partner*], nor will I testify if called as a witness.
- I will keep you fully informed about the collaborative settlement process and will not negotiate a settlement of any issue without your participation and consent. I will promptly respond to your inquiries.

You acknowledge and agree that for so long as you elect to participate in the Collaborative Divorce process, you are—for that time only—giving up your right to unilateral advocacy in the process by your own expert(s), and your access to the court system for resolution of issues. However, you may terminate the Collaborative Divorce process at any time if you wish to seek remedies from the Court.

You acknowledge and agree that for so long as you elect to participate in the Collaborative Divorce process, you are—for that time only—giving up your right to formally object to producing any documents or to providing any information to the other side, if in my professional judgment the document(s) or information is relevant, material, nonprivileged, and the kind of information a reasonable decision maker would want to have available in order to make an informed decision on an issue in your family law matter.

To this end, you agree to make full disclosure of the nature, extent, value of—and all developments affecting—your income, assets, and liabilities. You authorize me to fully disclose all such information that in my discretion must be provided to your spouse and his or her lawyer. If you should decline to make disclosures I regard as necessary, I am bound by the lawyer-client privilege to keep such information confidential. However, I will, in my discretion, withdraw as your lawyer, or terminate the Collaborative Law process in that situation. *In signing this agreement, you agree that a persistent failure and/or refusal by you to make disclosures that I regard as necessary will constitute your decision to terminate the collaborative process–in other words, will constitute a "constructive" termination of the process by you.*

Your spouse is not a party to this Agreement, and is not a "third-party beneficiary" of this Agreement, nor are you a third-party beneficiary of any collaborative agreements between your spouse and his or her collaborative counsel. This means that although both clients and both lawyers will sign documents undertaking adherence to the good-faith principles of collaborative negotiations, the commitments to make full disclosure contained in this Agreement and in those documents do not give either you or your spouse rights to sue the other party's lawyer for breach of contract or as a "third-party beneficiary." My legally enforceable professional obligations are to you alone; the legally enforceable obligations of your spouse's or partner's lawyer are to him or her alone; and the signing of the Collaborative Divorce participation documents do not create new professional obligations enforceable by a party who is not represented by the lawyer.

The Collaborative Law/Collaborative Divorce process (those terms are used interchangeably in this document) depends upon good-faith participation by both parties. *A dishonest or unscrupulous party could take advantage of the Collaborative Divorce process for delay or advantage in litigation.* Neither I nor any collaborative lawyer can guarantee that their client will in fact adhere to the good-faith undertakings that are made formally in writing at the start of the process. Remedies against your spouse or partner for bad faith might possibly be available subsequently in court under relevant family law provisions, but might or might not actually remedy the consequences of bad-faith behavior in the Collaborative Divorce process. My commitment to you is that I will alert you to any suspicion of bad faith and recommend termination of the process if I suspect bad faith. Similarly, I will either withdraw as your counsel or terminate the Collaborative Divorce process, at my election, if it appears to me that you are unwilling or unable to meet your good-faith commitments in the Collaborative Law process. In signing this agreement, you are authorizing me to withdraw or terminate the Collaborative Law process if, in my judgment, you are failing and refusing to participate in good faith. *In signing this agreement, you agree that a persistent failure and/or refusal by you to participate in good faith will constitute* your *decision to terminate the collaborative process—in other words, will constitute a "constructive" termination of the process by you.*

I may recommend that you and your spouse work with Collaborative Divorce coaches, and/or a collaborative financial consultant. Where emotion runs high or where there are minor children, collaborative coaching may be essential in order for the Collaborative Divorce process to work effectively. Occasionally it is necessary to bring a mediator in for a time to assist if an impasse persists. In signing this Agreement you acknowledge your understanding that if such additional professional resources are in my professional judgement necessary, you have the right to decline to retain such additional collaborative professionals. You also acknowledge and agree that should you so decline, it may not be possible to continue the Collaborative Divorce process if in my judgment collaborative negotiations without such professional assistance are unlikely to be successful.

No collaborative lawyer can guarantee that this process will be effective in resolving your issues. Success in collaboration is possible only if you and your spouse share a commitment to respectful, honest, efficient, and direct consensual resolution of all issues. While most couples who elect the Collaborative Divorce process arrive at a full resolution of all issues, some do not. *If overall resources (yours and your spouse's) are strained, you should consider carefully whether to allocate limited resources to the Collaborative Divorce process if doing so would impair your ability to retain conventional legal counsel in the event you and your spouse were not able to reach full agreement using the collaborative process.*

You and I both retain the right to withdraw from this contract if either of us feels we cannot abide by the principles of Collaborative Divorce or that the collaborative process is not functioning satisfactorily, by notifying the other in writing. I agree to give you fifteen (15) days' notice of my intention to withdraw.

If your spouse declines to proceed in a Collaborative Divorce process, this retainer agreement will be null and void. In that event I will assist you to locate appropriate conventional divorce representation.

Financial Provisions

It is understood that our firm utilizes a team approach, involving partners, associates, associated counsel, and legal assistants where appropriate when their participation will in our judgment facilitate highest-quality, efficient, and most cost-effective representation of our clients. We reserve the right to, and you agree that we may, bring in associated counsel to assist in your case when in our judgment it is appropriate to do so.

For our services you agree to pay for time devoted to your dissolution at our current rates for 2008, which are $_____ per hour for myself and my partners. Our paralegal's services will be billed to you at $ _____ per hour. We also bill for certain services of our case manager (who handles scheduling of meetings and certain file management tasks) at $ ____ per hour. These rates are subject to adjustment, and in signing this letter you agree that after written notification is sent to you of such a fee adjustment, you will be responsible for payment for services rendered, at the adjusted rate.

You are billed for all time we spend associated with your case, including telephone time, regular lawyer supervision of the work of paralegal and case manager on your case, file review and updating, travel time, preparing for and attending meetings, and the other tasks involved in advising and representing you and managing the paperwork associated with your representation. We are not able to quote a fixed lawyer fee or to predict what your total fee will be because each case is unique and it is impossible to predict just how much time will be required. In addition, you will be charged for actual costs for such expenses as service of process, filing fees, photocopies, messengers, and telephone charges out of our local area.

Also, it may be necessary to retain the services of an accountant, appraiser, actuary, or other expert to value certain assets. Such experts are ordinarily retained jointly in a neutral capacity in collaborative law cases. If we deem it advisable to retain a neutral expert, we will recommend an expert to you and your spouse's collaborative counsel, and will obtain full consent of all prior to engagement of his or her services. Consultants may also be retained to advise you or me regarding financial or other matters. Once you have agreed to retain such an expert or consultant, payment for your share of those services and other costs is your sole liability. We may, at our election, *either* advance payment on your behalf (in which case you agree to reimburse us in full) *or* require that you provide payment in full within fifteen (15) days of our transmitting to you a bill for expert services, *or* pay the expert from funds on deposit in your retainer account with us, *or* require that you provide your share of a deposit retainer for such services. You agree to notify us promptly if you wish to terminate the services of any such expert or consultant. Any disputes that may arise between you and any expert or consultant about billings or services rendered are matters to be resolved between you and that expert or consultant. You agree that notwithstanding any such dispute, bills that are directed to this office for services rendered in your case will be paid by us and reimbursed fully to us by you if your retainer account is insufficient for the payment. *We are not able to contract on your behalf for services from any experts or consultants without the aforesaid agreement.*

In certain cases, we make use of highly specialized computer programs to assist us in analysis of issues. If such a program is used in your case, you will be billed a flat fee for the program use, ranging from $75 to $250, in addition to lawyer time. Also, we maintain an inventory of complex documents, which we adapt for individual cases. If we utilize such a document in your case, you will be charged a minimum of one to four hours' time in addition to the time expended by your lawyer. Lawyer time is normally billed in increments of tenths of an hour; the minimum unit charge for lawyer time is 0.20 hours (12 minutes). You are billed for all time we spend associated with your case, including travel time to meetings, telephone time, file review, and the very numerous other tasks involved in preparing your case to reach resolution.

In certain instances, one party agrees to pay some of the other party's lawyer fees and costs. *Where appropriate, we will seek such agreements on your behalf; however, the obligation to pay fees and costs to us remains your own, regardless of any such agreements.*

Before proceeding, we request an initial retainer of $_____. We require that you pay any outstanding charges and replenish your initial retainer so that your trust account balance is restored to $ _____each month. Any retainer balance remaining after we complete our services to you is refundable. We will send you itemized bills on a monthly basis for all fees and costs. You agree to pay any balance due thereon *within twenty-five (25) days* of billing. Unless you advise us within fifteen (15) days of the billing that you have questions about the bill, you agree to accept the bill as correct. A late charge of one percent (1%) per month (12% per annum) will be added to the balance on any amounts owed to this office for more than thirty (30) days. This is not a finance charge; we do not extend credit. Bills are payable in full each month. This late payment charge is intended as damages for failure to pay fees when due, and also represents payment for reasonable administrative costs of collecting and accounting for unpaid fees. By signing this letter, you agree and acknowledge that separate calculation of actual damages for each instance of late payment would be extremely difficult and impracticable, and you agree that the foregoing provision for liquidated damages is reasonable under the circumstances existing as of the date of this agreement.

If any dispute should arise between us as to whether any legal services rendered to you under this contract were unnecessary, or unauthorized, or excessive, or were improperly or negligently rendered, you and we agree that any such dispute will be determined by submission to arbitration as provided by California law (pursuant to the California Arbitration Act, Code of Civil Procedure §§1280–1296), and not by a lawsuit except as California law provides for judicial review of arbitration proceedings. Any controversy concerning the interpretation or scope of this arbitration agreement shall also be submitted to arbitration as provided above. Both parties to this agreement (you and our firm) are giving up their constitutional right to have any such dispute decided in a court of law before a jury, and are instead accepting arbitration. This arbitration agreement applies to all legal services provided by any lawyer working on your case for or with our firm.

If there should be a dispute between us regarding any bill for services, you and we agree that the dispute will be submitted to arbitration upon request for arbitration by either you or us.

You and we agree that the arbitration of any of the foregoing matters shall be conducted under the auspices of one of the following entities, the choice to be at the election of our firm:

The Marin County Bar Association
The Bar Association of San Francisco
The American Arbitration Association, San Francisco
Judicial Arbitration and Mediation Services (JAMS)

Any fees and costs charged for the services of the arbitration panel will be paid in equal shares by you and by our firm except for initial filing fees, which shall be paid by the party seeking arbitration.

You agree to pay for all legal services rendered in your case until such time as our lawyer-client relationship is ended. In the event that the retainer is not replenished promptly as agreed above and/or any bill is not paid within thirty (30) days, we reserve the right to cease providing any further legal services to you, or on your behalf, until payment is received, or other satisfactory arrangements are made and confirmed in writing. In the alternative, we reserve the right to withdraw as your lawyer, and you agree to sign any documents necessary for us to withdraw, upon our request.

Please note that because of necessary processing delays, the statement date shown on your monthly bill is ordinarily up to a week later than the actual date of services, which will be recorded on the statement. Since your subsequent monthly bill may include services that were actually rendered during the prior billing period, you should not assume that a statement contains *all* charges incurred up to the statement date.

If for any reason we are compelled to commence collection efforts on any outstanding bill, then in addition to the above, you agree to pay us actual lawyer's fees and costs incurred (whether our own time or that of other lawyers employed) in connection with that collection effort.

You agree that our firm is entitled to be fully compensated for all reasonable lawyers fees and costs incurred or paid by us in the course of collecting fees and costs owed by you to this firm per this retainer agreement. Accordingly, in the event that we must retain collection counsel to represent us in collecting unpaid fees and costs owed to this firm by you, it is understood and agreed that you will be responsible for payment of all reasonable fees and costs payable by this firm to collection agencies and/or collection counsel, including any contingent fees withheld by them from payments made by you, and you agree that the court will have jurisdiction to make such an award against you in connection with proceedings to enforce or collect a fee arbitration award against you. The court will also have jurisdiction to, and you agree that it should, determine a reasonable amount to compensate me and my staff for fees and costs at our usual hourly rates, for time that we spend preparing for and in the course of any fee arbitration proceedings against you.

You are encouraged to consult with a legal advisor of your own choosing if you have any concerns or hesitancies about any of these provisions with respect to fees and costs, as it is important that we have a very clear understanding with you about your responsibility for payment of your lawyers fees and costs before we can agree to represent you.

We make every effort at this point to acquaint you with our firm's philosophy and procedures, and with the parameters within which we are able to assist you. Should there occur a change in your needs and expectations that are incompatible with our views regarding the conduct of your case, or should there arise a substantial disagreement between us, we reserve the right to withdraw from your employment. Should that occur we will provide you with at least fifteen (15) days' notice so that you may have the opportunity to employ other counsel.

Please read this letter carefully, and if you are in agreement with its terms, sign the copy that is enclosed and return it to me. *This agreement is a legally binding contract between us, which you are free to have reviewed by another lawyer before signing.* We encourage you to do that if you have any uncertainty about entering into any part of this agreement with us. Should you have any comments or questions concerning this letter of agreement, please contact me at your convenience. We feel it is very important that we have a clear understanding about fees and costs because we want to devote our efforts and attention to the substance of your case and to avoid any possible future misunderstanding about our financial arrangements with you.

Sincerely,

[Lawyer]

Enclosure: Duplicate copy of retainer agreement for your records

I understand and agree to the terms of the foregoing letter.

Dated: _____
          [Client]

4. Sample Letters to Prospective Clients, Spouses of Clients, and Lawyers for Spouses

(a) Initial Letter to Client Providing Information about Collaborative Law

(Lawyer Offering Both Collaboration and Mediation)

Date
Name
Street Address
City, State, Zip

Dear Mr./Ms. _____

I appreciate your inquiry regarding mediation and collaborative law. I am enclosing some information that will help you decide on the best divorce conflict resolution approach for you and your partner, including:

- Two Collaborative Law Group brochures, one for you and one for your spouse. This brochure describes the process and includes a list of independent family lawyers, colleagues of mine who are committed to using the collaborative family law process. It includes information about both mediation and collaborative law. If you select collaborative law, your spouse can choose a lawyer from this list or can find a lawyer through his or her own inquiries who is able and willing to work effectively in the collaborative law model. The enclosed list includes only practitioners who have training and experience in both family law and the collaborative process. I can work well with any lawyer on that list.

- A copy of the Principles and Guidelines for the Practice of Collaborative Law, a statement prepared by the lawyers in the Collaborative Law Group. This document is signed by both parties at the start of a collaborative divorce.

- A packet of articles and press clippings about collaborative law and collaborative divorce.

- Printouts of information from web pages from my own and other websites about collaborative law and collaborative divorce, as well as about mediation.

In addition to offering the collaborative law model, I am also a trained mediator and could work with you and your spouse in that mode as a neutral. However, you need to be aware that in order for a mediated agreement to reflect the full informed consent of each of you, nearly all mediators strongly recommend that each partner have their own independent family lawyer as a source of advice and counsel about the law during the mediation process, who will also review the final agreement. Without that legal advice, the resulting agreement can be flawed in ways that could make it vulnerable down the road.

For that reason, I do not recommend that clients make their decision between mediation and collaborative law on the assumption that mediation is necessarily cheaper because only one professional conducts the process. Normally three professionals are involved in a mediation, not one. The selection should be made based on a judgment as to which mode has the best likelihood of effectively guiding you and your spouse to an optimal agreement on all points. For some people this is mediation and for many people this is collaborative law. Please note that my own practice with clients is limited to these modes of out-of-court conflict resolution and to second opinions. I no longer handle litigated family law matters.

If you are interested in collaborative law or mediation, you may want to schedule a preliminary meeting with me to get more information or advice about those processes before deciding whether collaborative law or mediation looks like a better choice for you. I can meet with both you and your spouse—for that purpose only—if you are both comfortable with the fact that should you select collaborative law rather than mediation, I will be representing only one of you in that process. The person I do not represent would need to sign a consent and waiver if you both attend our preliminary informational meeting. If you both attend this meeting, we will not discuss issues in your own situation but will focus solely on which conflict-resolution process would be the most appropriate choice.

Once you and your spouse have selected either mediation or collaborative law, the next step would be to schedule a first meeting to begin the process. If you and your spouse select collaborative law, one of you would then select another collaborative lawyer as counsel and would have a first meeting with that person to get the collaborative process started.

The enclosed brochure provides further information about beginning the collaborative law process. I look forward to hearing from you if you are interested in meeting with me for either purpose.

Sincerely yours,

Enclosures: as stated

(b) Initial Letter to Client Providing Information about Collaborative Law

(Lawyer Offering Only Collaborative Representation)

Date
Name
Street Address
City, State, Zip

Dear Mr./Ms. _____

I appreciate your inquiry regarding collaborative law. I am enclosing some information that will help you decide whether this is an appropriate divorce conflict-resolution approach for you and your partner, including:

- Two Collaborative Law Group brochures, one for you and one for your spouse. This brochure describes the process and includes a list of independent family lawyers, colleagues of mine who are committed to using the collaborative family law process. If your partner is interested in collaborative law, he or she can choose a lawyer from this list or can find a lawyer through his or her own inquiries who is able and willing to work effectively in the collaborative law model. The enclosed list includes only practitioners who have both training and experience in both family law and the collaborative process. I can work well with any lawyer on that list.
- A copy of the Principles and Guidelines for the Practice of Collaborative Law, a statement prepared by the lawyers in the Collaborative Law Group. This document is signed by both parties at the start of a collaborative divorce.
- A packet of articles and press clippings about collaborative law and collaborative divorce.
- Printouts of information from web pages from my own and other websites about collaborative law and collaborative divorce, including how it differs from other kinds of legal representation in conflict resolution.

If you both agree that this is how you wish to proceed, the next step would be for each of you to schedule a first meeting with your respective lawyers. Alternatively, you could schedule an informational meeting with me first, before discussing this option with your spouse if you would like to have more information or advice before deciding whether collaborative law looks like a good choice for you. I look forward to hearing from you if you are interested in meeting with me.

Sincerely yours,

Enclosures: as stated

(c) Extended Letter to Client after Initial Consultation Re: Collaborative Representation

(An Educative Document Intended to Be Shared with Nonclient Spouse)

Re: Marriage of _____

Dear Dr. _____:

I enjoyed speaking with you yesterday and I am delighted that you are interested in exploring collaborative law as an alternative to the traditional court-based litigation system of divorce.

In a collaborative case, each party selects an independent lawyer of his or her own choosing who is trained and experienced in the collaborative process as well as in family law. It is particularly helpful if the two lawyers have handled collaborative divorces together before, or are members of the same collaborative practice group, as a professional relationship based on trust and respect between the two lawyers benefits the divorcing couple greatly. In collaborative divorces, the lawyers and clients sign an agreement that the lawyers are hired solely to help the two spouses reach agreement. Neither lawyer can ever take matters to court in your divorce case once the collaborative agreement has been signed. You and your spouse, of course, have the right at any time to end the collaborative process and take issues to court if you wish, but in that event each of you will be assisted to hire litigation counsel, and both collaborative lawyers' involvement will end, regardless of how or why the collaborative process was terminated.

A collaborative case proceeds via a series of four-way meetings attended by both spouses and their lawyers. No one ever goes to court except for the filing of papers or other administrative/bureaucratic matters. All negotiations take place in these face-to-face meetings. The lawyers never negotiate terms of settlement without both of you present and participating. The lawyers ensure that no decisions are made until both of you fully understand all the financial and other relevant facts, and then help you develop a broader range of possible options for resolution than would be available in court. Instead of "one size fits all," which happens frequently when judges make the decisions, in collaborative divorces couples are able to design individualized solutions that fit their own priorities, values, and needs.

If the four-way settlement process should break down and either of you elects to go to court on a contested issue, the two collaborative lawyers must bow out after helping you transition to a litigation lawyer. Thus, unlike all other legal models, the consequences of failure to achieve settlement out of court are experienced by the collaborative lawyers as well as the divorcing couple.

This distribution of risk is a very powerful tool. It is a fact of life that in negotiations where the option of going to court has been reserved by all parties and their counsel, lawyers frequently threaten to go or actually do go to court as part of the negotiating process. Unfortunately for their clients, those very lawyers who could not help their clients bring the settlement process to a constructive solution, also end up being financially rewarded as a direct consequence of their settlement efforts failing. This is because when a case goes to trial, the lawyers generally earn far more in fees than they would have earned if a pretrial or out-of-court settlement had been reached. I am not suggesting that a conventional lawyer deliberately sabotages settlement efforts; that would be unethical. But while a trial is stressful and expensive for a client, there is no downside for a conventional lawyer if the case goes to trial rather than settling, and lawyers often enjoy the challenge of trial practice as well as being financially rewarded for it.

In the collaborative process, however, positive consequences for the lawyers occur only if they can succeed in the job they were hired for: to help you and your partner reach optimal terms of settlement. If the collaborative settlement efforts fail, both lawyers must resign and will inevitably feel that they were unable to do the job they were hired for. While it would be unethical for a collaborative lawyer to keep the process going if no progress were being made, and also unethical for a collaborative lawyer to try to persuade a client to accept terms of settlement that are unsatisfactory, the fact that your collaborative lawyer will not take matters to court means that collaborative lawyers put in the extra effort to help you and your spouse find solutions that might work, if that is achievable. Their desire to do a good job as lawyers is aligned with their clients' stated desire to reach an out-of-court settlement, in a way that does not exist outside collaborative law. They don't threaten to go to court, and they recommend terminating the collaborative process only if further negotiations would be a waste of time or otherwise not in your interests. They do not leap hastily to the conclusion that litigation is necessary, or would be a clever strategic move, as conventional lawyers too often do.

As you can imagine, the public has been embracing collaborative law with a great deal of enthusiasm. Lawyers have been offering collaborative family law representation since the idea first emerged in 1990, and the number of family law attorneys in this community who have been trained in the process and have developed the new set of skills required to manage such cases effectively is growing each year. The lawyers who do collaborative work tend to prefer this model over other practice/settlement modalities because of how satisfied most collaborative clients are with this process. That is the reason that the field is growing very rapidly. Your spouse should have no difficulty locating experienced, well-trained collaborative counsel in this locale with whom I can work effectively.

In this community, it is also possible to proceed using not only collaborative lawyers, but also other specially trained collaborative professionals who can work in a coordinated way to assist you and your spouse and any children with the emotional and financial issues that almost always accompany divorce. These interdisciplinary collaborative divorce teams represent the cutting edge of professional help during divorce—the "Rolls Royce" of professional divorce help, at Honda or Toyota cost. When a full collaborative divorce team is involved, the work that is done at the legal negotiating table almost always goes even more smoothly and efficiently than when collaborative lawyers alone are facilitating the settlement process. Involving these other professionals would be discussed with you, your partner, and your partner's collaborative lawyer early in the process.

Collaborative divorce is well suited to situations where both parties are intelligent and have some degree of emotional maturity, where both parties share a commitment to preserve the ability to co-parent children optimally after the divorce and to protect them from avoidable divorce-related conflict, where there are shared values about parting with respect and dignity, and where both parties value active participation in the design of the settlement process itself. It is also necessary if the process is to work most effectively for you and your spouse that both partners retain capable collaborative lawyers with not only training but also mutual respect and trust, who have talents as facilitators of high-quality settlements.

Enclosed for your attention are two identical information packets that describe the collaborative process and also provide the names and contact information for a group of experienced family lawyers in the area who have been trained as collaborative lawyers and with whose participation I know I can provide the highest quality collaborative representation. The enclosed packets also contain web links that provide a great deal more information about collaborative divorce and collaborative law. One packet is for your partner.

I also have enclosed a copy of my collaborative retainer agreement, setting out the terms under which I would represent you if you wish me to. As I explained when we [met/conferred by telephone], whether you elect to retain me or not, I will be billing you at the end of this month for the time I spent consulting with you.

Divorce is rarely easy. In a well-managed collaboration, each spouse plays a primary role in the creation, design, and implementation of high-quality, lasting, future-oriented solutions to the challenges associated with all divorces, in a contained and emotionally safe process. In contrast, in the traditional court process, judges who know very little about your case, who are under-informed as to the facts, and whom each of the parties and their counsel are actively seeking to persuade at the expense of the other side, ultimately impose solutions upon both parties. In my experience, these solutions never are better than solutions the parties themselves would have designed had they known beforehand where that traditional system was likely to lead both of them and what the emotional and financial costs would be.

I sincerely hope that you and your spouse conclude it is appropriate in your situation to make the effort to resolve your differences collaboratively. From what you have shared with me regarding your situation, I believe collaborative law may be a good choice for you.

Please advise me how you wish to proceed.

Very truly yours,

[Lawyer]

Enclosure: Two information packets

(d) First Letter to Nonclient Partner or Spouse

(Lawyer Provides Collaborative Representation Only)

Date
Name
Street Address
City, State, Zip

Dear _____ :

Your [wife/husband/partner] has retained me to assist [her/him] in obtaining a marital dissolution. I will be participating as a collaborative lawyer. Collaborative law is a new way of reaching agreement in divorce that involves specially trained lawyers whose only job is to help the two partners reach the best mutually acceptable agreements they can devise—regardless of whether a judge could have ordered those terms or not. If the lawyers cannot do this, they are "out of a job."

I am enclosing an information packet for you—the same one that I send to my clients—which should help you decide whether collaborative law might be a good choice for your situation.

If you are interested, then the next step is for you to find and confer with your own collaborative lawyer. The enclosed packet includes a list of lawyers in this area who have made a commitment to collaborative law, all of whom I have worked successfully with before. You are of course free to choose your own lawyer, whether from this list or elsewhere. Many lawyers are now becoming interested in collaborative law because it is such a powerful tool for reaching optimal agreements in divorce.

I encourage you to locate a collaborative lawyer experienced in family law matters who has both experience and training in the new skills needed to do this work well. All else being equal, both you and your spouse benefit when the two lawyers have a professional working relationship of mutual respect and trust. The lawyers on the enclosed list have worked hard to build that kind of professional relationship with one another and with me, for the benefit of their clients.

My own legal practice at this time is limited to collaborative divorce and for that reason I will be representing your [husband/wife/partner] only if you also wish to proceed with this divorce as a collaborative matter. If it is for some reason not of interest to you, your [husband/wife/partner] will be represented by a traditional family lawyer.*

Sincerely yours, [Lawyer]

Enclosures: As stated

Copy: Client

*This paragraph can be omitted or adapted if you will represent the client regardless of whether the matter is collaborative or not.

(e) First Letter to Nonclient Partner or Spouse

(Divorce Petition Already Filed)

Date
Name
Street Address
City, State, Zip

Re: Marriage of _____

Dear _____ :

Your [wife/husband] has retained me to assist [her/him] in obtaining a marital dissolution. I enclose a brochure, which I have also given [her/him], describing a new process for reaching mutually acceptable divorce agreements called "Collaborative Law." This process is highly regarded by clients, lawyers, and judges, and is both a powerfully effective and a civilized method for resolving the issues involved in a divorce. Your [wife/husband] would like to proceed this way, and I urge you to consider selecting Collaborative Law yourself.

The enclosed brochure includes basic information about the process, and a list of experienced family lawyers who understand the Collaborative Law process and have the necessary new skills, from whom you could select a collaborative attorney to represent you. These lawyers, who share a commitment to helping clients reach settlements, but who are not affiliated in law practice with one another, are knowledgeable about both the collaborative and the conventional divorce process. (You are, of course, free to select your own lawyer from this or any other source.)

A divorce petition has been filed by your spouse. The next step is to "serve" the petition, which is the event that starts this state's waiting period for a divorce. I would like to discuss with your chosen lawyer when and how to accomplish service of the petition, in a way that does not inconvenience or embarrass you at all. This can easily be done once you have chosen a lawyer to represent you.

Alt. A: (Whether or not you agree that it would be appropriate to use the collaborative law process in your divorce, I ask that you let my office know who you will be retaining as your lawyer, or alternatively that your counsel contact us, sometime during the week of _____, so that the two lawyers can arrange for the petition to be served, and can begin assisting you and _____ through the divorce process.)

Alt. B: (I will be representing your [husband/wife] only if you also select collaborative law and choose a collaborative lawyer to represent you. Please let my office know whom you retain as collaborative legal counsel sometime during the week of _____ , so that we can begin assisting you and _____ through the divorce process. If you decide not to elect collaborative law, you will be contacted by your spouse's litigation counsel regarding next steps in the divorce process.)

Sincerely yours,

[Lawyer]

Enclosures: As stated

Copy: Client

(f) First Letter to Nonclient Partner or Spouse

(A Polite Request to Begin the Collaborative Process)

Date
Name
Street Address
City, State, Zip

Re: Marriage of _____

Dear _____:

Your [wife/husband] has retained me to assist [her/him] in obtaining a marital dissolution. [She/He] informs me that you are familiar with the Collaborative Law process for divorces and are interested in handling this matter through that process. [She/He], too, wishes to proceed via the collaborative process.

I would appreciate it if you either would let my office know whom you will be retaining as your collaborative counsel, or would request that your counsel contact us, sometime during the week of _____, so that we can begin assisting you and (_____) to reach an agreement.

Sincerely yours,

[lawyer]

Copy: Client

(g) Initial Letter to Other Collaborative Lawyer

(First Collaborative Case Together)

Re: Marriage of [_____]

Dear [_____]:

I will be representing [_____] in [his/her] divorce proceedings. I understand you may be representing [_____], the other party to this divorce. My agreement with [_____] is that I will represent [him/her] only as a collaborative lawyer.

   This will be my first collaborative case with you. Although I know you are familiar with collaborative practice, I thought it might be useful to send you a copy of the information packet that I send to my clients who are interested in collaborative law, so that you can see what my client's expectations about this process may be, and what [he/she] may be sharing with your client about collaborative law.

   I would like to meet with you very soon to talk over how we will be working together in this matter. I will call to schedule a lunch, if that is agreeable to you. And, of course, please let me know if I am mistaken—if you are not actually going to be representing [**], or if your client has not in fact elected collaborative law. I look forward to working with you on this matter.

Sincerely yours,

[Lawyer]

cc: client

5. Financial Disclosure Form

Property Data Worksheet

The items that are starred (**) require documents.

I.   **Real Estate.** Attach the following for each property:
  **1. Copy of the original closing escrow statement and any refinance closing statements
  **2. Copy of the original deed to you and any subsequent deeds and deeds of trust
  **3. Copy of latest lender's statement and second mortgage/secured credit line statements

	PROPERTY #1	PROPERTY #2
Address:		
How title held (exact):		
Purchase Date:		
Purchase Price:	$	$
Down Payment:	$	$
Source of down payment (your funds or your spouse's or other funds):		
Dates of all refinances of this property since original purchase:		
Estimated present market value:	$	$
Loan balance:		
1st trust deed:	$_____	$_____
2nd trust deed:	$_____	$_____
Secured line of credit:	$_____	$_____
Monthly payments:		
1st trust deed:	$_____	$_____
2nd trust deed:	$_____	$_____
Secured line of credit:	$_____	$_____
To whom payable:		
1st trust deed:	_____	_____
2nd trust deed:	_____	_____
Secured line of credit:	_____	_____

If you do not have these documents, a copy of any recorded document (such as a deed) can be obtained at the County Recorder's office. Your lawyer can get them for you, but it will be less expensive if you do so yourself.

II. **Furniture**
  **Attach a list of furniture, specifying those items you believe to be separate property, and your opinion of the value of each item if it were going to be sold by you.

III. **Jewelry, furs, collectibles, antiques, and other valuable items**

**Attach a list of valuable items and specify those items you believe to be separate property, and your opinion of the value of each item if sold by you.

IV. **Vehicles**

	Vehicle #1	Vehicle #2	Vehicle #3
Year			
Make			
Model			
Mileage			
"Extras"			
Condition			
How title held			
Purchase Price			
Loan balance			
Monthly payments			
To whom payable			
Date acquired			
Source of down payment			
Mid-point Kelly Blue Book Value			
Who usually drives this car?			

V. **Cash assets**

Deposits (indicate amount, location, account number, in whose name held and where the money came from.) **For each account for which you have a passbook, statement, or other document, attach a copy of the latest statement and statement as of date of separation.

	Account #1	Account #2	Account #3	Account #4
Institution name, Location, Account #, Account type				
Account balance [If cash, give location.]	$	$	$	$
How account is titled				
Explain the origin of deposits				
Date opened				
Separate, community, or mixed property?				
Comments				

VI. Life insurance policies

**Attach a copy of the declaration page for each policy. For each policy set forth: [Use additional sheets if necessary.]

	Policy #1	**Policy #2**	**Policy #3**
Institution name			
Name of insurer			
Policy number			
Type of insurance:			
Explain the benefits (or attach copy of policy) Cash value?			
Date acquired			
Beneficiary			

VII. Stocks, mutual funds, brokerage accounts

For all stock held indicate name of company, number of shares, whether common, preferred, or other, cost of acquisition, date acquired, present value, how title is held, source of purchase price.

**ATTACH A COPY OF THE STOCK CERTIFICATE OR THE LATEST STATEMENT FROM YOUR BROKER. [Use extra sheets if necessary.]

	Stock/Fund/ Brokerage #1	**Stock/Fund/ Brokerage #2**	**Stock/Fund/ Brokerage #3**
Name of company			
Title holder			
Number of shares Common Preferred			
Cost of acquisition			
Date acquired			
Present value			
Source of purchase price			
Community, separate, mixed, property?			

VIII. Bonds

For all bonds held indicate date of acquisition, issuer, type, date of maturity, face amount, how title is held, source of purchase price.

**PLEASE ATTACH A COPY OF THE BOND OR THE LATEST STATEMENT FROM YOUR BROKER. [Use extra sheets if necessary.]

	Bond #1	Bond #2	Bond #3
Issuer			
Type			
Date of maturity			
Face amount			
Date of acquisition			
Title			
Source of purchase price			
Community, separate, mixed property?			

IX. **Retirement, pension, profit-sharing, annuities, IRAs, deferred compensation**

    **ATTACH COPY OF LATEST PLAN SUMMARIES AND LATEST BENEFIT STATEMENT.

    **A. Pension rights of you and/or spouse
    **B. Profit-sharing plans
    **C. IRAs (Individual Retirement Accounts)/401Ks/Sep-IRAs
    **D. Annuities

Retirement Accounts:

	Account #1	Account #2	Account #3	Account #4
Institution name				
Type of account				
Account number				
Title holder				
Date acquired				
Source of funds				
Explanation of origins of deposit				
Current account value as of____				
Community, separate, mixed property?				
Comments				

X. **Receivables**
    Does anybody owe you any money? If so, indicate amount, date acquired, name of debtor, and payment provisions. **ATTACH A COPY OF THE PROMISSORY NOTE.

XI. **Business interests of you or your spouse**
    **ATTACH COPY OF MOST CURRENT K-1 FORM AND/OR SCHEDULE C.

	Interest #1	Interest #2
Name of interest		
Type of business		
Corporation, partnership, LLC, sole ownership		
Percentage owned		
Name in which title is held		
Annual net income		
**Partnership/Shareholder/Buyout agreements [attach copy]		

XII. Miscellaneous

Do you or your spouse have any of the following:	Yes	No
1. Stock options?		
2. Oil royalties?		
3. Investment interests not otherwise listed?		
4. Club memberships?		
5. Option rights?		
6. Trusts (settlor, trustee, beneficiary, principal and income; if you or spouse are the settlor, state date of trust set up, source of funds, date of termination)?		
7. Legacies or bequests receivable from probate estates?		
8. Personal injury causes of action?		
9. Copyright ownership (literary, musical, etc.)		
10. Patent ownerships?		
11. Licensing agreements as licensor?		
12. Licensing agreements as licensee?		
13. Rights to receive royalties?		
14. Other contractual rights?		

If the answer to any of the above is "yes" please describe on additional sheets.
**Documents required.

XIII. Separate Property
A. Did you have any money or property at the time of your marriage? If so, where is it now? Set forth detailed list if still in existence.
B. Did your spouse have any money or property at the time of your marriage? If so, where is it now? Set forth a detailed list.

XIV. Taxes
**ATTACH COPIES OF THE PAST FIVE YEARS' TAX RETURNS.

	Yes	No
Do you expect a tax refund this year?		
If so, how much?	$	
Are any back taxes due to either the state or federal government?		
If so, how much and for what years?	$	
Are there any significant losses that are being carried forward onto tax returns not yet filed?		
Has either spouse been including income or losses from separate property sources (real estate or other investments) on joint income tax returns?		

XV. **Debts and Liabilities**
** ATTACH A COPY OF THE STATEMENT OR BILL OF EVERY CREDITOR AT THE DATE CLOSEST TO SEPARATION.

Creditor	Purpose Incurred	Amount Due at Separation	Balance Due Now	Monthly Payment
1				
2				
3				
4				
5				
6				
TOTALS		$	$	$

XVI.   Unpaid loans for school tuition (either spouse)?

Documents Establishing and Supporting a Collaborative Case

1. Principles and Guidelines for the Practice of Collaborative Law/Collaborative Divorce

I. INTRODUCTION

1.01 The essence of Collaborative Law and Collaborative Divorce is the shared belief of the participants that it is in the best interests of the parties and their family to avoid adversarial legal proceedings and to adopt a conflict-resolution process that does not rely on a court-imposed resolution. Collaborative Divorce relies on an atmosphere of honesty, cooperation, integrity, and professionalism geared toward the future well being of the parties and their children.

1.02 One of the major goals in choosing Collaborative Divorce is to minimize, if not eliminate, the negative economic, social, and emotional consequences of the traditional adversarial legal process to the parties and their family. The divorcing parties in signing this document commit themselves to the Collaborative Divorce process and undertake to devote all their efforts to resolving their differences constructively, justly, and equitably.

II. NO COURT OR OTHER INTERVENTION

2.01 By electing to treat this matter as a Collaborative Divorce case, the parties and their Collaborative Divorce professionals commit to the purpose of resolving all divorce-related issues without court intervention. The parties agree to give complete, full, honest, and open disclosure of all information having a material bearing on the case, whether requested or not, and to engage in informal discussions and conferences for the purpose of reaching resolution of all issues. All legal, financial, and mental-health professionals working as a team in this matter pursuant to this document, as well as any appraisers, evaluators, and other consultants retained by the parties to assist in this Collaborative Divorce, will likewise be directed to work in a cooperative effort to resolve issues constructively, without resort to litigation or any other third-party decision-making process.

III. LIMITATIONS OF COLLABORATIVE PRACTICE

3.01   In choosing Collaborative Divorce, we—the divorcing couple—each understand that there is no guarantee of success. We also understand that we cannot eliminate concerns about disharmony, distrust, and irreconcilable differences that have led to the current circumstances. While we all are intent on reaching a cooperative and complete resolution of all issues, we understand that our actual experience in our Collaborative Divorce may fall short of that goal.

3.02   Even though we have chosen Collaborative Divorce, we—the divorcing couple—understand that each of us is still expected to protect his or her respective interests and not to lapse into a false sense of security in the assumptions and expectations each holds about the other, the collaborative lawyers, or the Collaborative Divorce process. Subject to the requirements of applicable law and the good-faith commitments of these Principles and Guidelines, each of us may and should continue to act in our own respective best interests, even where those interests may diverge from the other party's interests. We both understand that we should not lapse into a false sense of security. These good-faith undertakings address how we will conduct ourselves during these negotiations and are not a substitute for attending carefully to our own respective interests and concerns during all phases of the collaborative process.

3.03   Each of us understands that while both of us, both our lawyers, and the other professionals signing this document are all affirming our good-faith undertakings about how we will and will not behave during this Collaborative Divorce, this document does not give either of us enforceable legal rights that we did not already have, to hold anyone legally accountable for failing to meet the commitments set out in this document. We both understand that these good-faith undertakings set out in this document are affirmations of intention, and not legally enforceable contractual obligations. We also understand that other documents will be signed in the Collaborative Divorce process that *are* legally enforceable documents, including the Stipulation and Order for Collaborative Divorce, and the retainer agreements we sign with our lawyers and other Collaborative Divorce professionals, if any.

IV. PARTICIPATION WITH INTEGRITY

4.01   As participants in the Collaborative Divorce process, all signatories to these Principles and Guidelines affirm their commitment to respect the dignity of all participants, including parties, lawyers, and if applicable, collaborative coaches, financial specialists, child specialists, and any consulting professionals. Further, each of us will uphold a high standard of integrity. We ourselves undertake, and we direct all Collaborative Divorce professionals working with us, not to take advantage of inconsistencies, misstatements of fact or law, or others' miscalculations, but rather to disclose them and seek to have them corrected at the earliest opportunity. In the event a Collaborative Divorce professional discovers inconsistencies, misstatements of fact or law, withheld information, or miscalculations by a party or by any other professional, the Collaborative Divorce professional is expected to inform that person of the discovery and remind him or her of the obligations under these Principles and Guidelines to make the required disclosure. In the event a Collaborative Divorce professional discovers that she or he has made a misstatement of law or a miscalculation, he or she is expected to disclose and correct the same. In the event a Collaborative Divorce professional discovers that another Collaborative Divorce professional has made a misstatement of law or a miscalculation, she or he is expected to inform the other Collaborative Divorce professional of the discovery and request disclosure and correction.

V. COLLABORATIVE DIVORCE TEAM AND OTHER PROFESSIONALS

5.01   We, the parties, understand that each of us must be represented by a Collaborative Lawyer and we understand that we are each expected to retain or at minimum to have a preliminary consultation with a Collaborative Divorce Coach. Where appropriate, we understand that (with the advice of the Collaborative Lawyers) we may be expected to retain a Collaborative Financial Consultant to assist in gathering and evaluating financial information and, if we are parents, we understand that we are expected to retain a Child Specialist (with the advice of the Collaborative Divorce Coaches) to give support and a voice to our children during the divorce process. These professional helpers are referred to collectively as the Collaborative Divorce professionals.

5.02   In addressing questions about sharing the enjoyment of and responsibility for our children, we, the parents, and all Collaborative Divorce professionals assisting us are expected to make every reasonable effort to devise amicable and well-informed solutions that promote the children's best interests. We undertake to act quickly to resolve all differences related to our children in a manner that will promote a caring, loving, and involved relationship between the children and each parent.

5.03 In securing additional professional assistance where needed, we, the parties, understand that we are expected ordinarily to retain joint neutral experts and specialist consultants as recommended by the Collaborative Lawyers and/or Collaborative Divorce Coaches. While neither of us and and neither Collaborative Lawyer is precluded by these Principles and Guidelines from consulting privately with separate experts or consultants, each such expert or consultant is expected to follow the spirit of these Principles and Guidelines, and when appropriate to collaborate with each other, meet and confer, and, if practicable, render joint statements on the matters in question. Each of us undertakes not to retain separate experts or specialist consultants without advising our respective Collaborative Lawyers of our intent to do so, during this Collaborative Divorce process.

VI. DUTIES OF CLIENTS AND LAWYERS REGARDING NEGOTIATION IN GOOD FAITH

6.01   We, the parties, and our Collaborative Divorce professional helpers will sign these Principles and Guidelines, and such other documents as the Collaborative Divorce professionals request, including but not necessarily limited to fee agreements, a Coaching Agreement, and a Stipulation and Order Re: Collaborative Divorce, and we, the parties, and our Collaborative Divorce professionals affirm our intent to act in accord with the letter and spirit of their terms and provisions. However, these Principles and Guidelines themselves do not give rise to any right of either of us for legal claims against any signatory.

6.02 We, the parties, understand that even with full and honest disclosure, the Collaborative Divorce process will involve vigorous good-faith negotiation. Each of us will be expected to take a reasoned and constructive approach on all disagreements and disputed matters in the interests of reaching consensus, for so long as the collaborative process continues, and if such approaches differ, or if negotiations appear stalled, each of us will be encouraged to consider whether modifying his or her approach would be appropriate in order to reach a resolution of all disputed matters. At the same time, we understand that throughout the Collaborative Divorce process each of us has the responsibility for asserting—constructively—our respective needs, interests, goals, and priorities, with the help of our respective Collaborative Lawyers and other Collaborative Divorce professionals.

6.03 While we understand that our Collaborative Lawyers will inform us fully about applicable law and about the litigation process, neither of us and no Collaborative Divorce professional will use threats of going to court, or any other threats, as a way of forcing settlement. Our purpose during the collaborative divorce process is to seek mutually acceptable solutions that meet the reasonable needs of each of us and any children, and not to pressure either of us into accepting terms of agreement that do not serve that purpose.

6.04 We, the parties, understand that although our Collaborative Lawyers undertake to adhere to the letter and spirit of these principles and guidelines, each lawyer represents only his or her own client and has a professional obligation solely to that client. We each have instructed our respective lawyers that they are retained solely to help both of us, the parties, to reach an acceptable agreement resolving all our issues without court proceedings. We understand and confirm that the job of each lawyer is to help his or her respective client to achieve his or her goals and priorities within the collaborative process, in accord with these Principles and Guidelines, and to provide appropriate advice and counsel if it appears that our respective goals and interests are not being met within the Collaborative Divorce process. We both affirm our understanding that neither lawyer has a legal duty in this process except to his or her own client. Both of us understand that the Collaborative Lawyers each represent only one of us and not both of us. Both of us understand and acknowledge that neither Collaborative Lawyer owes a legal duty to a party he or she does not represent. We both understand and agree that nothing in these Principles and Guidelines or in any of the documents establishing this as a Collaborative Divorce should be interpreted by either of us, or by any court, to mean that either of us could ever have a claim against the other party's lawyer with respect to any aspect of Collaborative Divorce, including, without limitation: disclosures, negotiations, and/or terms of settlement. Each lawyer's duty is to his or her own client to provide advice and counsel aimed at constructive resolution of all divorce-related issues in a manner consistent with these Principles and Guidelines, and to provide appropriate advice and counsel if it appears that our respective goals and interests are not being met within the Collaborative Divorce process.

VII. ABUSE OF COLLABORATIVE PROCESS

7.01   Each of us expects and directs our own Collaborative Lawyer immediately either to withdraw from or terminate a Collaborative Divorce case upon learning that her or his client is knowingly withholding or misrepresenting information having a material bearing on the case or otherwise acting so as to undermine or take unfair advantage of the Collaborative Divorce process. Examples of such behavior include: the secret disposition of marital, quasi-marital, or nonmarital property, failure to disclose the existence or the true nature of assets and/or obligations, ongoing emotional or physical abuse by either party, secret preparation to engage in litigation while appearing to participate in a Collaborative Divorce process, or withholding a secret plan or intention to leave the jurisdiction of the court with their children.

7.02   Each of us understands the need to clarify separately, in writing, with his and her respective Collaborative Lawyers whether the lawyer will withdraw from or terminate the Collaborative Divorce process in the event his or her client abuses the process.

7.03   We, the parties, and all signing Collaborative Divorce professionals, understand that while other remedies may exist, the ultimate sanction against professionals who abuse the Collaborative Divorce process, or condone and/or encourage such abuse by clients, is the diminution of that professional's reputation in the legal community, including the judiciary.

VIII. DISQUALIFICATION BY COURT INTERVENTION

8.01   We, the parties, understand that the collaborative lawyers' representation is limited to the Collaborative Divorce process. Thus, while each Collaborative Lawyer is a counselor and advocate bound by all professional obligations of a lawyer practicing in this state, we, the parties, have entered into a binding agreement with one another and with our respective lawyers that neither lawyer can ever represent either of us in court in proceedings against the other spouse, nor be named or remain as lawyer of record on any document filed with the court in our divorce proceedings.

8.02   We understand and direct that none of our Collaborative Divorce professionals, including the Collaborative Lawyers, Collaborative Divorce Coaches, Collaborative Financial Consultant, and Child Specialist, and none of the other jointly retained experts and specialist consultants participating in our Collaborative Divorce, may ever assist either of us in court proceedings against the other, nor give evidence in such a matter.

8.03   In the event one of us ever files adversary documents with the court, we, the parties, understand that all Collaborative Divorce professionals will be disqualified from further representing or assisting their respective clients, and the Collaborative Divorce process will automatically terminate. We understand that this means actions by *one* of us can cause *both* collaborative lawyers to be disqualified from further participation. Upon termination of the Collaborative Divorce process, all Collaborative Professionals will be disqualified as witnesses and their work product and the work of all other jointly retained experts and consultants will be inadmissible as evidence in any adversarial court proceeding.

IX. WITHDRAWAL OF LAWYER

9.01   If a Collaborative Lawyer deems it appropriate to withdraw from the case for any reason, we understand and direct that he or she will do so by a written Notice of Withdrawal to the parties, their coaches and lawyers, and the financial and child specialists, as well as any other participants and, if a Stipulation and Order has been filed, to the court. This may be done without terminating the status of the case as a Collaborative Divorce case.

9.02   The party losing her or his collaborative lawyer by virtue of withdrawal may continue in the Collaborative Divorce process by retaining a new collaborative lawyer who will agree in writing to be bound by these Principles and Guidelines and by the separate collaborative stipulation and order or participation agreement that we have signed.

X.   ELECTION TO TERMINATE COLLABORATIVE PROCESS

10.01   If either of us, the parties, decides that the Collaborative Divorce process is no longer appropriate and elects to terminate the status of the matter as a Collaborative Divorce case, she or he agrees to do so by sending a written Termination Notice to all other parties, Collaborative Professionals, and other participants, and, if a Stipulation and Order has been filed, to the court. Similarly, if either of our Collaborative Lawyers deems it necessary to terminate the Collaborative Divorce process, we understand and direct that he or she will send a written Termination Notice to the recipients noted in the preceding sentence.

10.02 We, the parties, understand that termination of the Collaborative Divorce proceeding will occur automatically in the event either of us initiates an adversarial court proceeding against the other.

XI. PROFESSIONAL FEES AND COSTS IN COLLABORATIVE DIVORCE

11.01   We, the parties, understand that all Collaborative Divorce professionals are independent of one another and have no financial connections, fee-setting, fee-sharing, or referral fee arrangements with one another. We also understand that each Collaborative Divorce professional must be paid separately for his and her services in this Collaborative Divorce pursuant to the terms set out in separate fee agreements we each will sign with each professional helper. Those financial terms are worked out separately with each professional and the fee arrangements with our respective lawyers and coaches may or may not be the same for each of us, the parties.

11.02   We, the parties, understand that imbalance in payment to our respective coaches or lawyers can adversely affect one party's access to advice and counsel as compared to the other party. For that reason we both undertake to keep payment of all coaches' and lawyers' fees current. The Child Specialist and Collaborative Financial Consultant and other jointly retained neutral expert consultants will also be paid in a timely manner. Any disagreements between us about ultimate responsibility for payment of such fees will be resolved as and when other financial issues are resolved. Each of us understands that no Collaborative Divorce professional can continue to provide services without being paid.

11.03   We, the parties, understand that the Collaborative Divorce professionals will confer with one another from time to time by telephone, in person, and via e-mail, in service of ensuring full and complete disclosure of material information and in service of ensuring an effective Collaborative Divorce process. Each professional will bill for time spent in such communications as set out in his and her separate fee agreements.

11.04 We, the parties, understand the importance of clarifying with our respective Collaborative Divorce coaches and lawyers at the start of this process how private confidential communications will be handled by that professional.

XII. SELECTION OF NEW LAWYER; ADDITIONAL FEES

12.01 We, the parties, understand that if our Collaborative Divorce matter terminates short of full resolution, our respective Collaborative Lawyers will assist each of us in the selection of new lawyers.

12.02 We, the parties, understand that if it should be necessary to retain new lawyers in the event of the termination of the Collaborative Divorce matter prior to full resolution, we each will incur further professionals' fees—including but not necessarily limited to lawyers' fees—that may equal or exceed those paid during the Collaborative Divorce process. We understand that there is no guarantee of complete resolution of all our issues in the Collaborative Divorce process. We are aware that if our financial resources are scarce we may have difficulty retaining litigation counsel should the Collaborative Divorce process terminate short of full resolution.

XIII. PLEDGE

13.01 We, the parties, hereby affirm our understanding of and agreement with the letter and spirit of this document and affirm our intention to proceed in a manner consistent with it. Moreover, by our signatures we direct each lawyer, coach, financial consultant, child specialist, and other expert professional consultant who has signed below, to proceed in a manner consistent with the letter and spirit of this document.

Parties:

Dated: _____
                                                Wife

Dated: _____
                                                Husband

Collaborative Lawyers:

In signing below, each of us confirms that the foregoing document conforms to the agreement of our respective clients, and each of us affirms our intent to proceed in a manner consistent with the letter and spirit of this document.

_____   _____
Collaborative Lawyer for Wife   Collaborative Lawyer for Husband

Other Collaborative Divorce Professionals:
In signing below, each of us affirms our intent to proceed in a manner consistent with the letter and spirit of this document.

_____   _____
Collaborative Divorce Coach for Wife   Collaborative Divorce Coach for Husband

_____   _____
Collaborative Financial Consultant   Child Specialist

Other Expert Professional Consultants:
In signing below, each of us affirms our intent to proceed in a manner consistent with the letter and spirit of this document.

_____   _____
Real Estate or Other Appraiser   Actuary

_____   _____
Vocational Consultant   Certified Public Accountant

_____   _____
Other   Other

[Rev. 7/24/07]

2. Participation Agreement or Stipulation and Order

John Doe, *in propria persona*
c/o [Law firm]
[Address]
[Phone]
[Fax]

Respondent *in propria persona*

SUPERIOR COURT OF CALIFORNIA

COUNTY OF MARIN

In re the Marriage of:	Case No. ******
JANE DOE,	**STIPULATION AND ORDER RE: COLLABORATIVE LAW/ COLLABORATIVE DIVORCE**
Petitioner,	
and	
JOHN DOE,	
Respondent.	

Petitioner JANE DOE, *in propria persona*, and Respondent JOHN DOE, *in propria persona*, each agree as set forth below, and further stipulate that orders shall be entered as follows which shall remain in effect until and unless modified by written agreement signed by both parties or further court order, whichever first occurs. This stipulation is intended to be a binding court order upon being signed by the parties; it shall thereafter be filed with the court in the parties' action for Marital Dissolution.

LAWYER REPRESENTATION

1. _____ has been retained by John Doe to advise Respondent during the course of this proceeding as his collaborative lawyer and __ _____ has been retained by Jane Doe to advise Petitioner during the course of this proceeding as her collaborative lawyer. Neither lawyer is lawyer of record in this proceeding. Each lawyer named above and any successor collaborative lawyer who later subscribes to this Stipulation shall be bound by the terms and provisions of this Stipulation and Order. Each lawyer named above, and any lawyer in association with such lawyer, and any successor collaborative lawyer who later subscribes to this Stipulation

is forever disqualified from appearing as counsel of record for either party named above in this proceeding or in any other family law matter involving both parties, including but not limited to proceedings or actions for dissolution, parentage, modification, enforcement, writs, and/or appeals. This disqualification shall survive the term of this Stipulation and Order and cannot be altered by subsequent agreement to the contrary between the parties. A lawyer shall be deemed "in association" if, at any time during the pendency of these proceedings or future family law proceedings between these parties, such lawyer is the employer or employee of, or co-employee with, or shares a relationship of independent contractor status with any lawyer named above.

Notwithstanding the above, the lawyers named above may appear as counsel of record for purposes of filing the final judgment and/or other final documents reflecting the agreement of the parties, upon the entry of which they are immediately authorized to withdraw.

COLLABORATIVE LAW MATTER

2. This matter shall be treated as a Collaborative Law Case. Each party and each lawyer whose signature appears below acknowledges that he or she has read and understands the document entitled Principles and Guidelines for Collaborative Law/Collaborative Divorce, and shall act in good faith to comply with the undertakings set forth in that document.

3. Neither party shall be a third-party beneficiary of any agreements made between the other party and his or her lawyer, or of the undertakings of the other party's lawyer set forth in this Stipulation and/or in the Principles and Guidelines.

4. For so long as this Stipulation and Order is in effect, the parties and lawyers shall devote all of their efforts to a negotiated settlement in an efficient, cooperative manner pursuant to the terms of this Stipulation, and agree that neither party nor lawyer named in this Stipulation will file any document requesting intervention by the court, including, but not limited to, a Request to Enter Default, Notice of Motion, Order to Show Cause, or At-Issue Memorandum, except as otherwise specifically permitted below. The filing of any of the aforesaid documents by either party shall constitute automatic termination of the status of this matter as a collaborative law matter. The provisions regarding disqualification of collaborative counsel from further representation, as set forth in Section 1, above, shall survive the termination of this as a collaborative law matter.

5. Both parties agree that commencing immediately:
    *   Each is restrained from removing their minor child(ren) from the state of California without the prior written consent of the other or order of court;
    *   Each is restrained from borrowing against, canceling, transferring, disposing of, or changing the beneficiaries of any insurance or other coverage including life, health, automobile, and/or disability held for the benefit of the parties or their minor child or children;
    *   Each is restrained from transferring, encumbering, hypothecating, concealing, or in any way disposing of any property, real or personal,

whether community, quasi-community, or separate, without the written consent of the other party, or an order of court, except in the usual course of business or for the necessities of life.

- Each party will notify the other of any proposed extraordinary expenditures at least five business days prior to incurring these extraordinary expenditures and account to the court for all extraordinary expenditures made after these restraining orders are effective. However, nothing in this Stipulation and Order precludes either party from using community property to pay reasonable lawyer's fees in order to retain and maintain legal counsel in the action.

6. Neither party will incur any debts or liabilities for which the other may be held responsible, other than in the ordinary course of business or for the necessities of life.

PROFESSIONAL ASSISTANCE IN COLLABORATIVE LAW CASE

7. Any person or firm retained by either or both parties or collaborative lawyers, or whose work product is used by either or both parties or lawyers, during the term of this Stipulation and Order, is forever disqualified from appearing as a witness for either party to testify either as a percipient witness, or as an expert witness with regard to any matter related to such person's or firm's work product in the collaborative law process. All expert notes, work papers, summaries, and reports shall be inadmissible as evidence in any proceeding involving these parties unless the parties agree otherwise in writing, but shall be furnished to successor counsel and shall be available for nonevidentiary use in litigated proceedings. Such persons or firms include, but are not limited to, accountants, lawyers, financial consultants, psychotherapists, mediators, coaches, child specialists, personal or real property valuation experts, vocational consultants, private investigators, doctors, or any other persons retained or employed in connection with the Collaborative Law process. No such person shall be called as either an expert or a percipient witness with respect to any matters relating to the Collaborative Law process nor shall testimony from any such person be admissible in any proceedings in this action.

DISCLOSURE AND DISCOVERY

8. Both parties shall timely serve their respective Preliminary and Final Disclosure Declarations as provided under the California Family Code and shall provide each other with any written authorizations requested that may be required in order to obtain information or documentation, or to prepare a Qualified Domestic Relations Order or other orders facilitating agreements reached. The parties and lawyers acknowledge and understand that honesty and the full disclosure of all relevant information is an integral factor in the success of a Collaborative Law case.

9. All discovery requests shall be made informally. No motion to compel or for sanctions is available for any discovery requests made during the Collaborative Law process. Responses to any discovery requests should be made within the time limits prescribed by applicable statute or local rule

unless otherwise agreed by the parties. All responses to discovery requests shall be under penalty of perjury or verified by the party responding unless otherwise agreed by the parties.

CUSTODY MEDIATION

10. In the event the parties agree to refer any issue to any mediator during the term of this Stipulation and Order, no action beyond mediation shall occur and no custody evaluation report or other report shall be prepared for use in connection with any court proceeding in this matter.

LAWYERS' FEES

11. The Court may award lawyers' fees and impose sanctions under any applicable Family or Code of Civil Procedure section in the event any party or any lawyer has (i) used the Collaborative Law process in bad faith for the purpose of unilateral delay, or (ii) engaged in any concealment, misrepresentation, or perpetuation of the same in any way that materially and adversely affects the rights of the other party.

STATEMENTS OF PARTIES AND LAWYERS

12. All documents prepared for use in the Collaborative Law process and all communications made during the course of the collaborative process shall be deemed inadmissible for any purpose in any subsequent proceeding except as may be otherwise agreed specifically in writing between the parties, and no communications made within the process shall be deemed a waiver of any privilege of any party. Nonetheless, statements by any party that indicate an intent or disposition to endanger the health or safety of the other party, or of the children of either party, or to conceal or unilaterally change the residence of the child, or to commit irreparable economic damage to the property of either party, are not privileged. However, neither collaborative lawyer, and no experts or consultants retained within the collaborative law process, may give testimony in any court proceedings between the parties regarding any communications made within the collaborative process.

TERMINATION OF COLLABORATIVE STATUS

13. Either party may unilaterally and without cause terminate this Stipulation and Order by giving written notice of such election to all other parties ("Termination Election" hereafter) and by filing a Termination Election with a proof of service of a copy of such Termination Election to all other parties in the proceeding.
14. Either lawyer may withdraw from this matter unilaterally by giving fifteen (15) days' written notice of such election to other parties and lawyers. Notice of Withdrawal does not terminate the Collaborative Law process. The party whose lawyer withdraws may retain a new lawyer who will agree in writing to be bound by this Stipulation and Order and the above-referenced Principles and Guidelines. Alternatively, the party may proceed without counsel. The other party's collaborative lawyer may continue to represent his or her client and to facilitate negotiations under those cir-

cumstances without termination of the Collaborative Law process. However, both parties understand and agree that such negotiations are not Collaborative Law as contemplated by this Stipulation and Order and the Principles and Guidelines, because of the need for two collaborative lawyers in a Collaborative Law matter. In the event that either party files any document requesting intervention by the court, including, but not limited to, a Request to Enter Default, Notice of Motion, Order to Show Cause, or At-Issue Memorandum, the filing of any of the aforesaid documents by either party shall constitute automatic termination of the status of this matter as a Collaborative Law matter.

15. In the event either lawyer believes his or her client is acting in bad faith, or otherwise misusing the Collaborative Law process, the lawyer may elect whether to withdraw or to terminate the Collaborative Law process, but in no case shall the lawyer continue to represent the party under such circumstances.

16. Upon termination of the process or withdrawal of any counsel, each collaborative lawyer so affected will promptly cooperate to facilitate the transfer of the client's matter to successor counsel.

17. The parties do not waive their right to seek the assistance of the Superior Court named above; however, any resort to litigation, including any appeal of any order made by a private judge, results in the automatic termination of the Collaborative Law process, on the date any application to the Superior Court for its orders or notice of intent to appeal is signed or otherwise made.

Dated:

_____

JANE DOE,
Petitioner, *in propria persona*

Dated:

_____

JOHN DOE,
Respondent, *in propria persona*

Approved as conforming to the agreement of the parties:

Dated:

_____

XXX
Collaborative Lawyer for Petitioner

Dated:

_____

YYY
Collaborative Lawyer for Respondent

/ / /

ORDER

Good cause appearing therefor, and the parties having stipulated thereto, the foregoing IS SO ORDERED. Each party and each collaborative lawyer is ordered to comply with all of the foregoing terms and provisions.

Date: _____   _____
                                       Judge of the Superior Court

[Rev. 7/24/07]

3. Sample Letters Retaining Neutral Collaborative Experts/Consultants

(a) Real Estate Appraiser

Date

Name of appraiser
Address

     Re: *Marriage of [_____]*

Dear _____:

     As you and I discussed in a telephone conference earlier today, [names of clients] would like to retain you jointly to perform a fair-market appraisal of their residence [or other real property] located at _____ , California. This appraisal is for divorce purposes. I represent [name of client] in [his/her] divorce case. [Name of other party] is represented by [name, address, phone, fax, and e-mail of other counsel].

     [Name of other counsel] and I have agreed that in making your appraisal, you should be governed by the following "ground rules":

1. You are not being asked to prepare an appraisal that favors or disfavors either spouse's position. Rather, each party wants you to render an opinion as to what a ready, willing, and able purchaser who is fully informed as to all material facts would pay for this property assuming the property was currently listed for sale by ready, willing, and able sellers on a nondistressed basis who have both sufficient time and sufficient financial resources so as to be able to market and sell their house in a professional manner for full value.

2. There will be no "confidential" communications between you and me, you and [name of other counsel], or you and either of the parties. Anything one of us says to you may be reported to the others without restriction. When your report is issued, we ask that it be sent simultaneously to both lawyers.

3. [Option A: Before you render any final valuation opinion, I encourage you to receive input from both owners to the extent either or both wish to provide you with information that may have an impact on the fair-market value of the property. [Name of client] can be reached at [client's phone no.]. [Name of other party] can be reached at [telephone number of other party]. You can contact either party to arrange access to the property.]

   [Option B: The parties have agreed that it is best if they do not communicate directly with you about factors that either believes could have an impact the value of their house. My office will contact you to arrange a time for a telephone conference with me and [name of other lawyer] to give you that information, and to arrange your access to the property.]

4. If a range of values rather than a single specific number would accurately reflect the fair-market value of this property, we encourage you to provide us with your opinion of that range rather than a specific dollar value. If you prefer to provide a specific dollar value, that is acceptable. Either way, we ask that you include in your valuation report a narrative explanation

of the significant features of this property that have guided your opinion, as well as a narrative explanation of the degree to which comparable sales relied upon by you do, or do not, closely resemble this subject property.

5. If there have been few sales of comparable properties in the vicinity of this subject property during the past six months, we would appreciate a narrative explanation of how the lack of recent sales has or has not affected your opinion of value.

6. This is a "collaborative law" representation. Neither the lawyers nor any neutral experts we retain (including yourself) can ever participate in litigation regarding this case. You will not be deposed, called as a witness in court, or otherwise be asked to participate in any adversarial proceedings, and in accepting this assignment, you agree that under no circumstances will you participate in any such proceedings, even if a party should ask you to do so.

You have told me you require a retainer of $_____, which is your anticipated fee for this appraisal. [Name of other lawyer] and I will arrange for payment by the parties this week so that you can begin your work. We look forward to having your assistance in this matter. Please call either me or [other counsel] with any questions regarding this assignment.

Sincerely,

[Lawyer]

cc: [client]
    [other counsel]

(b) QDRO Specialist

Date

Name
Address

Re: *Marriage of [_____]*

Dear _____:

[Names of clients] would like to retain you jointly to prepare their Qualified Domestic Relations Orders (QDRO) in the above-referenced dissolution action.

I represent [name of client] in [his/her] divorce case. [Name of other party] is represented by [name, address, phone, and fax of other counsel]. The parties have reached terms of settlement of all issues, and a marital settlement agreement is being prepared at this time. There are _____ deferred compensation plans in which the parties own interests to be divided per one or more qualified domestic relations orders.

This is a "collaborative law" representation. Neither the lawyers nor any neutral experts we retain (including yourself) can ever participate in litigation regarding this case. You will not be called as a witness in court or otherwise be asked to participate in any adversarial proceedings. Assuming you are able to assist with this work, we will ask that you sign the collaborative Principles and Guidelines document for this case.

Please let counsel know what you will require to begin your work, by way of information releases and retainer, and how soon you can begin.

Sincerely,

[Lawyer]

cc: [client]
[other counsel]

4. Sample Recitations Re: Collaborative Representation and Informal Discovery to Include in Marital Settlement Agreements

Collaborative Legal Representation and Agreement. This Agreement was arrived at through the Collaborative Law process, which is described more fully in the Stipulation and Order re: Collaborative Law filed by the parties in their marital dissolution action and in the Principles and Guidelines executed by the parties, a copy of which is appended to this Marital Settlement Agreement as an exhibit. Both parties have been represented throughout the process by their respective collaborative lawyers, neither of whom is counsel of record in the dissolution proceeding. At the commencement of the Collaborative Law process and through it, the parties agreed to work toward a comprehensive settlement of all of their property support rights and parenting issues, and this Marital Settlement Agreement reflects their comprehensive resolution of all such issues. In arriving at the terms of settlement set out in this Marital Settlement Agreement, Husband and Wife have applied their individual standard of fairness and have been advised throughout their negotiations by their respective collaborative attorneys. The conclusions they have reached are based in part on their respect and regard for each other.

Informal Discovery and Disclosures in Collaborative Divorce Process. Husband and Wife represented to one another throughout the Collaborative Law process leading to this Agreement that their negotiations were in good faith and that each had fully and completely disclosed all information necessary or requested in order to resolve the parties' property and support rights appropriately and equitably. Husband and Wife each affirm their understanding that under California law, each of them owes a fiduciary duty to the other with respect to all financial issues until all their property has been fully divided and each of them affirms that his and her disclosures have been made consistent with that fiduciary duty. The Parties understand that the law provides procedures for formal discovery, which includes taking depositions, submitting interrogatories, obtaining documents, requesting admissions, and using subpoenas. They have chosen not to conduct formal discovery or investigation beyond that already performed. The parties acknowledge that no independent investigation has been made by counsel for the parties or other experts or consultants of the character or the value of the parties' property, the extent of debt, or the amount of income of the parties, other than an inspection of income tax returns. The parties have instructed their respective counsel that they desire to make this Agreement without such investigation. The parties understand and acknowledge that they are relying on their mutual disclosures, including their preliminary Declarations of Disclosure, in making this Agreement and that they are not relying on their counsel for any independent verifications of the accuracy or completeness of those disclosures. Each party acknowledges that he or she has made such investigation of assets and obligations of the parties and of the value and amount thereof as each party has deemed sufficient and necessary for their own purposes in negotiating this Agreement.

5. Sample Paragraph Re: Resolving Future Disputes to Include in Marital Settlement Agreements

It is possible that in the future we may have disagreements with one another concerning the interpretation of this Agreement and the resulting decree or Judgment based on the Agreement, or concerning modification of support or parenting provisions of this Agreement. We do not wish resort to the court before reasonable noncourt alternatives have first been attempted. We agree therefore that it is in our best interests to try to resolve informally, outside the court system, any disagreements that may arise in the future using the steps set forth below, except in the case of urgent or emergency situations that would prevent us from taking such steps or would make them impracticable or inappropriate:

(a) As a first step in resolving future differences, if any, we first will attempt in good faith to confer with one another face-to-face or telephonically.

(b) If that is unsuccessful, then as the second step we will try to achieve resolution in writing, with each of us to present to the other a proposed modification to and/or implementation of this Agreement.

(c) If there is no resolution at the end of the second step, then as a third step we agree to each retain collaborative counsel and reconvene the collaborative process pursuant to the Principles and Guidelines previously signed by us in this proceeding, a copy of which is attached hereto and incorporated herein by reference.

If there is no resolution at the third step, either party may commence contested court proceedings.

Documents Ending a Collaborative Representation

1. Amendment of Participation Agreement When Clients Elect Mediation
[An Example That Can Be Adapted as Needed]

The signatures below on this document acknowledge the signatories' understanding of and agreement to the following:

- On or about [date] [lawyer] was retained to represent [husband] and on or about [date] [lawyer] was retained to represent [wife] as their respective collaborative counsel in a collaborative law process.

- On or about [date], the parties and their respective collaborative lawyers signed a participation agreement [and Principles and Guidelines] confirming that the lawyers were retained solely to provide collaborative legal representation and could never participate in any litigated proceedings between the parties, and setting out some parameters for the work of the lawyers within the collaborative process.

- The parties now wish to suspend the collaborative process and to work instead with [name of mediator] as their neutral mediator for purposes of continuing their efforts to resolve their divorce-related issues.

- Each party wishes to have independent consulting counsel to advise him or her and to provide legal counsel in connection with the mediation process.

- Both parties wish to have their respective collaborative lawyers continue to assist by serving as independent consulting counsel during the mediation process, and both collaborative lawyers have agreed to serve in that role.

- The lawyers' signatures below confirm their willingness to serve as consulting counsel, with the express understanding that they cannot and will not under any circumstances participate in any litigation between these parties.

- The parties acknowledge by their signatures their understanding that their respective collaborative lawyers will now serve solely as consulting counsel to the mediation and that as of the date this addendum is executed the lawyers will no longer act as collaborative lawyers. They further acknowledge that neither lawyer under any circumstances will participate in any litigation between the parties, whether as counsel, consulting counsel, or percipient witness.
- The parties further understand and agree that if either of them retains a lawyer who has not signed a collaborative participation agreement that bars him or her from participating in litigation, **both lawyers whose signatures appear below will cease to serve as consulting counsel to the mediation** and each will promptly assist in transitioning the client to representation by a noncollaborative lawyer.
- To the extent that there are any inconsistencies between them, this amendment modifies the terms of the retainer/engagement letter between each party and his or her collaborative lawyer, as well as the terms of the collaborative participation agreement referenced above.

Date: [signature of Husband]
Date: [signature of Wife]
Date: [signature of Husband's collaborative lawyer]
Date: [signature of Wife's collaborative lawyer]

2. Final Letter at Time Divorce Is Concluded

Date
Name of Client
Address

Dear _____:

Now that the Final Judgment has been entered with the court, I want to take this opportunity to remind you that you need to attend to the following details if you have not done so already. This letter does not address support payments or other obligations delineated in the Marital Settlement Agreement. Please note that some of these points may not apply to your situation; if so, please disregard them.

Transfer of Ownership

You and [name of spouse] should sign the pink slip for the other's vehicles, removing each name from the registration records of the other's automobile. You should also contact your automobile insurance agent and inform him or her which spouse is to receive and continue to drive which vehicle.

If you have not already done so, you should either remove [name of spouse]'s name from all bank accounts, IRAs, etc., awarded to you, or, in the alternative, open new accounts in your name alone. You should also either remove [name of spouse]'s name from any credit card accounts awarded to you, or open new accounts. Be sure that your name does not remain on any credit card accounts for which [name of spouse] is responsible, if possible. If you have not already done so, notify the creditors on all joint credit card accounts on which you remain liable that you and [name of spouse] are divorced and you are no longer responsible for charges made by [name of spouse].

Tax Matters

It is particularly important that you keep the IRS and other taxing authorities apprised of your current address and request that all notices come to you directly. This is because your tax returns are linked to the first social security number listed on the return. If any deficiency notice or like assessment is mailed to [name of spouse], and he or she does not provide you with a copy, you could face significant liability when the IRS finally locates you.

Important Support Issues

If you are paying support and for *any reason* find yourself unable to make the payments (your income has dropped, you have a new family, you become disabled, etc.), you need to take steps promptly to modify the support amount in writing. If you do not modify the amount, the obligation keeps running. In other words, you cannot modify a support order retroactively. You should have advice of legal counsel if a support modification is needed.

Miscellaneous MSA Provisions

If you have not already done so, you and [name of spouse] need to address the following remaining tasks outlined in your MSA:

- Section 1. A. Community Property Accounts: divide any remaining community property accounts listed in Exhibit A to the MSA.
- Section 1. C. [name of business] Stock Options: if legally possible, transfer [name of spouse]'s portion of options to her.
- Section 1. D. Family Educational Account: establish and fund family educational account according to terms of this section.

Insurance

Unless ordered to do otherwise by the terms of the Judgment, you should contact your insurance agent and remove [name of spouse]'s name as beneficiary on any policies except pertaining to assets she will own. Likewise, unless ordered otherwise by the terms of the Judgment or QDRO, you should instruct your employer to remove [name of spouse]'s name as partial owner or beneficiary of any employee benefits.

Wills and Trusts

You must execute a new will or a codicil to your existing will with new directions regarding the disposition of your property in the event of your death. This may be of particular importance because of your children, and because of the need to create a trust so that the person you wish to be the trustee will manage their estates after your death. Any living trust you created with your former spouse must be revoked and the trust assets must be divided as provided in your Judgment.

Notice of Withdrawal

To complete the process, enclosed is a Notice of Withdrawal of Collaborative Counsel, which I have also sent to your former spouse's counsel. This is a routine document that causes any future correspondence from your former spouse's lawyer to be sent directly to you in the future rather than to me.

This document does not in any way mean that I am no longer interested in your situation. I very much enjoyed working with you and would be pleased to assist you in the future should you wish to consult or retain me. We wish you the very best.

Very truly yours,

[Lawyer]

3. Notice of Withdrawal of Collaborative Counsel

Name of Lawyer
Address
Telephone
Fax

E-mail address

Collaborative Lawyer for _____

NOTICE OF WITHDRAWAL AS COUNSEL

To: _____ and _____ Esq. collaborative counsel for **:
PLEASE TAKE NOTICE that effective immediately, [name of lawyer] withdraws as collaborative counsel for _____. The current address, telephone number, and e-mail address for _____ are as follows:

Date: _____

                                         [Lawyer]

                                         Collaborative Counsel for _____

4. Notice of Termination of Collaborative Case

Name of Lawyer A
Address
Telephone
Fax

E-mail address

Collaborative Lawyer for [Name of Client A]

NOTICE OF TERMINATION OF COLLABORATIVE CASE

To: [Client A], [Client B], and [_____, Esq.] collaborative counsel for [Client B]:

PLEASE TAKE NOTICE that effective immediately, [*choose either* (1) (*lawyer*), or (2) (*client A*)] terminates the above Collaborative Law/Collaborative Divorce matter. As provided in the Stipulation and Order for Collaborative Divorce executed by the parties and their collaborative lawyers, both [Lawyer A] and [Lawyer B] are from the date of this notice disqualified from any further participation in this matter, except to assist our respective clients to retain litigation counsel upon the client's request. All experts, consultants, and other collaborative professionals who have participated in this collaborative process are also disqualified from further participation in this matter, except to assist the parties in obtaining other professional help.

The current address and telephone number for [*client A*] are as follows:

Date: _____

                                                    [Lawyer A]
                                                    [Collaborative Counsel for Client A]

Appendix I-D

Data-Gathering Forms

1. Internal Data-Gathering and Evaluation Form

(a) Letter to Client Re: Evaluation of Collaborative Process

Dear (Client) _____ :

I would be grateful if you would take the time to complete and return the attached evaluation questionnaire. You may sign your name or complete it anonymously, as you prefer, and you may elaborate or comment wherever you like. The purposes of this questionnaire are:

- to help improve the quality of services my staff and I provide to our clients.
- to assess the strengths and weaknesses of the collaborative model itself, so that it can be improved where needed.
- to generate data for purposes of comparing satisfaction with process and outcome in collaborative and noncollaborative cases.
- to help identify areas where research and training are needed to enhance delivery of collaborative legal representation.
- to assist in educating the public and the judiciary about collaborative law.

You have participated in a conflict-resolution process that is transforming the field of family law. Your thoughtful comments will help advance that transformation.

Sincerely,

[Lawyer]

Enc.

(b) Evaluation of the Collaborative Process

Date: _____

I. Personal

   1. Your age _____   Spouse or partner's age _____
   2. Your sex _____
   3. Length of marriage or relationship at time collaborative representation commenced _____.
   4. Who decided to end the relationship or marriage?
       You [ ]   Spouse [ ]   Mutual [ ]
   5. If there are children of relationship
       How many? _____

       Their ages at commencement of collaborative representation:
       _____

II. Entry into Collaborative Law Process

   1. How did you learn about Collaborative Law/Collaborative Divorce, and about me specifically as a Collaborative Lawyer?
       _____
       _____
       _____
       _____

   2. What were your reasons for selecting Collaborative Law/Collaborative Divorce as your conflict-resolution process?
       _____
       _____

   3. Did you and your spouse/partner make any coordinated effort to select collaborative lawyers who had a prior history of successful settlements?
       _____
       _____
       _____

III. The Collaborative Process

   1. How many legal four-way meetings took place in your case? _____
   2. Did a signed settlement agreement result from the Collaborative Law process?
       Yes [ ]   No [ ]

3. How long did the Collaborative Law/Collaborative Divorce process take, from the first four-way meeting to the end of the process?

___less than four months
___less than six months
___less than 12 months
___less than 24 months
___longer than that

4. Were any other collaborative professionals involved? [Check those that apply]

___Collaborative divorce coaches
___Child specialist
___Neutral collaborative financial consultant
___CPA
___Vocational consultant
___Real estate or other appraiser
___Neutral mediator
___Other [Explain]:

5. On a scale of 1 to 10 (10 = very satisfied, 1 = very disappointed) please rate

a) your own lawyer   _____
b) your spouse's/partner's lawyer   _____
c) the other professionals, if any   _____

If you were less than fully satisfied with any of the professional helpers, please explain why.

6. How well did the Collaborative Law/Collaborative Divorce process meet your expectations?
(Using the same 1-to-10 scale) _____
(Please comment) _____
_____

7. How well did the Collaborative Law/Collaborative Divorce process meet your needs?
(Using the same 1-to-10 scale) _____
(Please comment) _____
_____

8. Was the cost of your own lawyer's services in your divorce (or other legal matter) reasonable, considering the issues and personalities involved in your situation?
___Yes
___No
(Please comment) _____
_____

9. Was the cost of the other professionals' services in your divorce (or other legal matter) reasonable, considering the issues and personalities involved in your situation?
___Yes
___No
(Please comment) _____
_____

10. Was the length of time involved in reaching resolution reasonable, considering the issues and personalities involved in your situation?

___Yes

___No

(Please comment) _____

_____

11. Is there anything about your experience with Collaborative Law/Collaborative Divorce that you think could be improved? (Please explain)_____

_____

_____

_____

_____

12. Is there any statement you can make about Collaborative Law/Collaborative Divorce that might assist other people who are deciding on which conflict-resolution model to use for their own divorces? _____

_____

_____

_____

_____

_____

13. May I share your comments about the Collaborative Law/Collaborative Divorce process at my trainings and in public/professional education efforts?

[ ] Yes, you may quote me

[ ] Yes (but keep it anonymous)

[ ] No

14. Sometimes journalists interested in Collaborative Law/Collaborative Divorce want to interview people who have experienced the process. May we notify you about such requests if in our view the journalist is responsible and professional, would respect your privacy requests, and would be likely to produce an accurate report? Yes [ ] No [ ]

(We will never release your name to a journalist without your specific consent.)

Your signature below is optional, but we need it if we have your permission to quote you (item 13) or to contact you regarding journalist inquiries (item 14).

_____   _____

Signature (optional)   Printed Name (optional)

2. Practice Group Data-Gathering and Evaluation Forms
(a) Data-Gathering Report for Lawyers Only
(An Example Focusing on Objective Facts)

Joint Case Report

[Adapted from a Form Devised by the Niagara Collaborative Law Group]

Date: _____ /_____/_____ (dd/mm/yy) Case Report Number _____(TBA)

Part 1. Information That Applies to Both Parties

1.1 Demographic Information

    1.1.1 Couple's status: (check one)
        ( ) married   ( ) common-law   ( ) never cohabited
        ( ) divorced   ( ) other (specify) _____

    1.1.2 Ages of dependent children involved in the case: _____
    _____

    1.1.3 Years of cohabitation with this partner: _____

1.2 Case-Related Information

    1.2.1 Nature of case/application:
        ( ) separation   ( ) divorce   ( ) other (specify) _____

    1.2.1.1 If separation or divorce, was it:
        ( ) an original agreement
        ( ) an order/agreement variation (modification)

    1.2.2 First 4-way date : _____/_____/_____ (dd/mm/yy)
        End date: _____/_____/_____

    1.2.3 How many 4-way meetings? _____ How many total hours
    spent in 4-way meetings?_____

1.3 Settlement and Closure Information

    1.3.1 Settlement reached
        ( ) yes   ( ) no   ( ) partial

    1.3.1.1 If *partial settlement,* which issues were *not* settled?
        ( ) custody   ( ) child support   ( ) spousal support
        ( ) access   ( ) third-party support ( ) property
        ( ) other (specify) _____
        _____

    1.3.1.2 If *partial settlement* or *no settlement,* what do parties intend to do?
        ( ) start new CL process ( ) go to mediation ( ) work it out alone
        ( ) go to court   ( ) other (specify): _____

    1.3.1.3 If *no settlement,* who terminated the process?
        ( ) client(s)   ( ) lawyer(s)

1.3.1.4 What was the reason/issue for the termination? _____

_____

1.3.2 Did any issues arise during the case that were not identified at the outset?
( ) yes   ( ) no

1.3.2.1 If yes, what other issues were identified?

1.3.2.2 _____

_____

1.3.3 Were any joint or neutral experts retained?   ( ) yes   ( ) no

1.3.3.1 If yes, for what issue(s)?

_____

1.3.3.2 What did the expert(s) cost? _____

_____

1.4 Particular Challenges in the Case:

1.4.1   Were there notable problems or issues involved that made this case particularly challenging?
( ) Concerns of abuse or fear for safety
( ) Power imbalance between parties
( ) Alcohol, drugs, or other addictions
( ) Other (please specify) _____

_____

Part 2. Information for Partner 1

2.1 General Information:

2.1.1 Gender: ( ) male   ( ) female
2.1.2 Age of the client: _____
2.1.3 Approximate annual income: $ _____
2.1.4 Relation to children involved in the case:
( ) biological parent   ( ) adoptive parent   ( ) step-parent
( ) other (specify): _____

2.2 Case-Specific Information:

2.2.1 Issues for partner 1 (rank in order all that apply)
( ) custody   ( ) child support   ( ) spousal support
( ) access   ( ) third-party support   ( ) property
( ) other (specify): _____

2.2.2 What was the approximate number of hours logged for this case?

_____

2.2.3 How many hours for lawyer-client communication?

_____

2.2.4 How many hours for third-party communication, research, and drafting? _____

2.2.5 What were the legal fees for partner 1? (approximate; before tax)
( ) under $2,500   ( ) $12,500 to $15,000
( ) $2,500 to $5,000   ( ) $15,000 to $17,500
( ) $5,000 to $7,500   ( ) $17,500 to $20,000
( ) $7,500 to $10,000   ( ) over $20,000
( ) $10,000 to $12,500

2.2.6 Are there any comments you would like to make about this case?

_____

_____

_____

_____

Part 3. Information for Partner 2

3.1 General Information:

3.1.1 Gender: ( ) male   ( ) female

3.1.2 Age of the client: _____

3.1.3 Approximate annual income: $ _____

3.1.4 Relation to children involved in the case:
( ) biological parent   ( ) adoptive parent
( ) step-parent   ( ) other (specify): _____

3.2. Case-Specific Information:

3.2.1 Issues for partner 2 (rank in order all that apply)
( ) custody   ( ) child support   ( ) spousal support
( ) access   ( ) third-party support ( ) property
( ) other (specify): _____

3.2.2 What was the approximate number of hours logged for this case?
_____

3.2.3 How many hours for lawyer-client communication? _____

3.2.4 How many hours for third-party communication, research, and drafting? _____

3.2.5 What were the legal fees for partner 2? (approximate; before tax)
( ) under $2,500   ( ) $2,500 to $5,000
( ) $5,000 to $7,500   ( ) $7,500 to $10,000
( ) $10,000 to $12,500   ( ) $12,500 to $15,000
( ) $15,000 to $17,500   ( ) $17,500 to $20,000
( ) over $20,000

3.2.6   Are there any comments you would like to make about this case?

_____

_____

_____

4.1 SUBMITTED:

Lawyer for Partner 1:

_____

Date:

Lawyer for Partner 2:

_____

Date:

(b) Client Evaluation Questionnaire
(An Example Focusing on Client Satisfaction)

[Adapted from a Form Devised by the Dallas Alliance of Collaborative Family Lawyers]

I invite you to evaluate my performance and that of other members of your collaborative professional team. Please answer the following questions and return your responses to my law office at your earliest convenience. My colleagues and I will use this information to improve the services we provide in collaborative representation.

1. How did you learn about me and my firm?
   ___Telephone book
   ___Internet
   ___Advertisement
   ___Prior case
   ___Referral
   Name/relationship to you of person making referral _____
   ___Book, magazine, or other media [specify]:_____
   ___Other [specify]:_____

2. How did you learn about collaborative law/collaborative divorce?
   ___Telephone book
   ___Internet
   ___Advertisement
   ___Referral
   Name/relationship to you of person making referral _____
   ___Book, magazine, or other media [specify]: _____
   ___Other [specify]:_____

3. Were there other professional helpers involved in your collaborative divorce, in addition to the collaborative lawyers?
   ___No
   ___Yes
   What other professional helpers? [specify] _____

4. Did the collaborative professionals show respect for you personally and for your point of view, feelings, and concerns during the collaborative process?
   Did I ? __Yes
        __No
   Did your spouse or partner's collaborative lawyer?
   __Yes
   __No
   Did the other collaborative professional helpers?
   __Yes
   __No

5. Did the collaborative professionals listen to what you had to say and take time to understand your viewpoint?
   Did I ? __ Yes
        __ No

Did your spouse or partner's collaborative lawyer?

__Yes

___No

Did the other collaborative professional helpers?

___Yes

___No

6. Did the collaborative professionals explain matters so that you and your partner or spouse understood what was happening during each stage of the process?

Did I ? ___Yes

        ___No

Did your spouse or partner's collaborative lawyer?

___Yes

___No

Did the other collaborative professional helpers?

___Yes

___No

7. Overall, did the collaborative professionals handle our work for you and your partner or spouse in a satisfactory fashion?

Did I? ___Yes

        ___No

Did your spouse or partner's collaborative lawyer?

___Yes

___No

Did the other collaborative professional helpers?

___Yes

___No

8. Was the cost of the collaborative process reasonable considering the people and issues?

Was mine? ___Yes

        ___No

Was your spouse or partner's collaborative lawyer's?

___Yes

___No

9. Would you consider retaining me to handle a future legal matter?

___Yes

___No

10. Would you refer a friend or family member to me?

___Yes

___No

11. Would you refer a friend or family member to your spouse's or partner's collaborative lawyer?

___Yes

___No

12. Would you recommend the collaborative process to a friend or family member who wanted a civilized and respectful process for handling a divorce or other legal matter?

___Yes

___No   If no, why not? _____

13a. What do you like best about the collaborative process and/or the manner in which your case was handled?

_____

_____

_____

_____

13b. What do you like least about the collaborative process and/or the manner in which your case was handled?

_____

_____

_____

_____

14. Is there anything you think I or any of my professional colleagues should know about our behavior, personality, style, mannerisms, or office, in order to improve our collaborative services to clients?

_____

_____

_____

15. May I share your responses with the other collaborative lawyer?
   ___ Yes
   ___ No
   May I share it with others?
   ___ Yes
   ___ No

16. May I use your name when communicating this information to others? If so, please sign and date:

_____

[Name]

_____

[Date]

3. IACP Survey Form

Lawyer Worksheet for IACP Survey of Collaborative Practice Process***

What hourly fee did you charge in this matter? $_____

Check here if you received basic (noninterdisciplinary) collaborative training. ___

Check here if you received interdisciplinary collaborative training. ___

What functions did you as the lawyer or your staff perform in this case? (Check all that apply)

___ assist client(s) to identify their highest prioritized needs, considering moral, economic, social, and other factors relevant to each client's situation

___ serve as a process guide to ensure adherence to basic Collaborative principles (transparency of the process, full disclosure, client self-determination, resolving issues out of court, etc.)

___ create an environment for client(s) that is safe and conducive to settlement

___ empower client(s) to actively participate in the process and "find their voice"

___ assist client(s) in preparing for settlement meetings by helping clients with effective and strategic communication

___ educate client(s) about the legal process

___ educate client(s) about the law generally

___ give legal and decision-making advice

___ help client(s) recognize legal consequences of choices

___ conduct legal research

___ assist client(s) with determining what additional professionals should be retained, if any

___ assist client(s) with gathering together necessary documents

___ assist client(s) with preparing budgets

___ assist client(s) with preparing cash flow analyses

___ assist client(s) with developing list of assets and liabilities

___ give feedback and "reality checks" to client(s)

___ make an effort to understand the family dynamics and the needs of the children

___ assist client(s) with developing a parenting plan

___ assist client(s) with negotiating and reaching agreements that satisfy each party's interests and, if there are children, that are best for their children

___ facilitate creative problem solving

___ draft agendas and minutes

___ draft legal documents

___ review and revise legal documents drafted by other collaborative lawyer

What is your view of the order of your responsibility to the following? (1 means greatest responsibility is owed; 3 (or 4) means the least responsibility is owed)

___ Your client
___ The Collaborative Process
___ The family
___ Other _____

Indicate the face-to-face joint hours/meetings involving you and *both clients*.

- Indicate the date of your face-to-face meetings involving both clients in column 1.
- Indicate the length of the meeting rounded to the nearest one-half hour in column 2.
- Identify the professionals present at the meeting by putting a check in columns 3 through 7.

1. Dates of face-to-face meetings	2. How long the meeting lasted (rounded to closest one-half hour)	3. MHP who worked with the adults and not with the children	4. MHP who worked with the children	5. FP	6. Lawyers	7. Mediator

What total legal fees did you or your firm charge? _____

Dated:_____   _____
                                              Name

A Collaborative Divorce Case History

Parties: Henry and Ruth, ages 45 and 50, married 25 years, with a son Joe (age 15) and a daughter Marie (age 19)

Team Members: Two Lawyers (Pauline and John); Two Coaches (Joan and Brad); One Child Specialist (Sam); One Financial Consultant (Kevin)

September

1. Ruth telephones Pauline's office and is sent a collaborative law information packet.
2. Ruth schedules first consultation with Pauline.
   Content of consultation:
   Exploration of Ruth's situation and needs
   Presentation and discussion of conflict-resolution process options
   Recommendation of Collaborative Divorce Team
   Decision to proceed as collaborative case if Henry agrees
3. Henry retains John, a collaborative lawyer with whom Pauline has worked well previously.
4. Pauline has "pre-meeting" via telephone with John:
   First legal four-way meeting is scheduled.
   Lawyers share insights about clients.
   Lawyers begin to identify priorities and "hot buttons."
   Lawyers discuss and agree about preliminary conflict-management approaches.
   Lawyers agree that client exploration of team model will be an expectation.
5. Pauline and Ruth meet; Henry and John meet.
6. First four-way meeting is held:
   Collaborative documents are discussed in detail and signed.
   Interest-based conflict resolution is explained.
   Legal divorce process is explained.

Agreements about document exchange are made.

Homework: preparation of financial disclosures with financial consultant (Kevin); initial consultations with coaches (Joan and Brad).

Agenda for next four-way meeting is agreed.

Schedule of four more four-way meetings is set.

October

7. Post-meeting conferences (Henry and John; Pauline and Ruth) to discuss client satisfaction with process and to move forward with clarification of goals, interests, priorities, concerns.

8. Post-meeting conference (Pauline and John) via telephone to discuss what worked, what needs improvement, and agenda considerations for next meeting.

9. Second and third four-way meetings: similar process of pre-meetings and post-meetings.

> Financial consultant, Kevin, attends second meeting to explain and walk through financial disclosure spreadsheets.
>
> Henry and Ruth agree that divorce petition will be filed by Ruth, and served at third four-way meeting.
>
> At second meeting, Henry and Ruth each express highest intentions for divorce (in terms of both process and outcome).
>
> Further documents are exchanged and reviewed at third meeting.
>
> Problems with Joe's possible drug abuse are discussed and John and Pauline advise that coaching and child specialist involvement is essential.

10. Henry's Response to the Petition is prepared and served by mail so that waiting period for divorce can begin to run.

11. Coaching proceeds and adolescent child specialist (Sam) is involved. Sam confers with Joe and brings information about his experience of the divorce and his concerns and needs into the coaching process.

November

12. Fourth four-way/five-way meeting: Pauline and John together present information about state law with regard to child and spousal support, as another kind of information Ruth and Henry need before making decisions. With Kevin's assistance, a final agreement is reached about amount and duration of long-term spousal support, with agreement to review amount after one year, after Ruth confers with vocational consultant.

13. Fifth four-way meeting: draft parenting plan prepared by coaches, Joan and Brad, is reviewed with the lawyers, who make a few suggestions to be discussed further with coaches before final plan is signed. Final agreement about amount of child support, primary residence of Joe, and percentages of financial responsibility for college expenses of Marie is reached. Agreement to "take a break" until January to allow for peaceful holiday season.

January

14. Clients contact lawyers about Joe's growing substance abuse and emotional problems that reached a crisis over the holidays. They have some new ideas about how to change the draft parenting plan to switch primary custody from Ruth to Henry. They want to revise support, plan for property division, and other related matters in light of change in primary parenting arrangements for Joe. Lawyers refer Henry and Ruth back to coaches and to financial consultant for further discussion of implications of their ideas for changes.

15. By end of month, coaches, child specialist, and financial consultant have had several more meetings with Henry and Ruth and have conferred with one another and with Pauline and John. Joe is in a residential detox/adolescent treatment program.

16. A sixth legal four-way meeting is convened and a new property division and child support arrangement is agreed upon in light of changed parenting arrangements.

February

17. Pauline prepares first draft settlement agreement, which Ruth reviews and approves. The coaches facilitate signing of the final parenting plan, which is attached to the draft settlement agreement. It is sent to John.

18. John confers with Henry, proposes minor changes.

19. Final text of divorce settlement agreement is approved by all.

20. Final legal four-way meeting: lawyers and clients gather together for signing of settlement agreement and dissolution papers. Terms of agreement are reviewed and client satisfaction is verified. Provisions for collaborative approach to later modifications or disagreements are confirmed. Documents are signed and notarized. Fruit juice toasts to future co-parenting relationship. (Ruth does not drink alcohol). Henry and Ruth thank lawyers.

21. Divorce papers are submitted to court for no-fault marital dissolution. John and Pauline completed related paperwork (title transfers, retirement plan transfers).

June

22. Henry and Ruth return to coaches for planned review and "tune-up" of parenting plan for Joseph. No changes are needed.

November

23. Henry and Ruth each confer with their respective lawyers about whether any adjustment in the amount of Ruth's support is warranted. Ruth reports small increase in earnings but no luck in finding a better job; Henry tells John he feels no change in the amount of support is needed unless Ruth is able to find a better-paying job. All decide not to reconvene in a four-way meeting at this time.

December

24. Second planned review of parenting plan with coaches. All agree that child specialist should meet with Joe to see how the arrangement is working for him. Minor changes made in plan based on Joe's concerns. Revised parenting plan sent to Pauline and John, approved by them, and signed by Henry and Ruth.

Comments

The foregoing represents a reasonably typical scenario for a collaborative divorce involving some moderately challenging facts and some moderately difficult personalities. It is based on an actual case, with identifying facts changed.

Had Henry and Ruth not chosen collaborative divorce, the following facts about the clients could easily have led this case into a high-conflict dispute-resolution mode (i.e., intense litigation):

   a.   Ruth left Henry during the process of discovering that she was a lesbian.
   b.   Both Ruth and Henry have abused alcohol when stressed.
   c.   Henry did not want a divorce.
   d.   Henry and Ruth differed about how to handle Joe's problems. Henry's approach is more authoritarian; Ruth's approach is to make use of twelve-step techniques and resources as well as occasional "tough love."
   e.   Henry had unrealistic beliefs about Ruth's ability to become self-supporting at the marital standard of living.

Conventional litigation counsel would typically begin such a case (as Ruth's counsel) by filing a motion for child custody, child and spousal support, and temporary use of the family residence, supported by declarations under penalty of perjury reciting reasons why Ruth should have custody of Joe and use of the house. Starting this way polarizes the parties, triggers fear, anger, and defensiveness, and reduces trust and willingness to compromise.

Had they begun in that manner, they could easily have spent more money on the attorneys' fees and costs involved in obtaining temporary orders than they actually spent for the entire interdisciplinary collaborative team process. Their case would most likely have taken from 14 to 24 months to conclude in litigation, perhaps longer. They would have hired adversarial experts for the following issues: child custody evaluation, real property appraisal, vocational evaluation. They would have fanned mutual resentment by virtue of the allegations made by each of them in the course of preparing those issues for trial, and would have exacerbated Joe's emotional problems. They would have been left on their own by their professional helpers at the conclusion of the legal divorce process with poor prospects for effective parenting of a difficult, at-risk teenager. They would probably have returned regularly to court on motions to modify custody and support provisions.

By proceeding in the collaborative mode, Ruth and Henry were able to let their concerns about their son take priority, and to organize use of the residence and child support to conform to the agreements about who would provide a residence for Joe. These agreements changed over the period of the collaborative representation, and as a result, Ruth and Henry changed their agreement several times regarding which of them would buy the other out of the family residence. Recognizing that their ultimate decision about this could change again before their agreement was final, both agreed to a low market value for the home, not knowing for certain which of them would "buy" it from the other. Henry was able in the coaching process to come to terms with why the marriage to Ruth was ending, and ultimately to accept the reality of her sexual identity. Their experience of being reasonable with one another during the four-way meetings and in communicating clearly during coaching sessions and financial consultant sessions increased their confidence about their ability to negotiate directly with one another, a confidence that served them well when their child began acting out over the holidays. By the end of the process, Henry and Ruth carved out several issues that they preferred to handle themselves rather than involving the lawyers (division of the marital furniture and collectibles, and division of life insurance policies), issues that can be problematic where distrust and anger predominate.

Henry and Ruth left the collaborative divorce process satisfied, on much better terms with one another than when they began the process. They took with them improved communication and problem-solving skills. They had access to ongoing professional help from their coaches and the child specialist, and a built-in expectation that their arrangements for parenting Joe should be regularly reviewed and adjusted where necessary. They had a means for hearing Joe's views that was safe for him and nonpolarizing for them. Their prospects for co-parenting a difficult teenager seemed good. Their situation was still very challenging but their experience with collaborative divorce improved their ability to handle it effectively.

Lawyer Conference Checklist

First Meeting between Lawyers

1. Agree on how billings to clients for professional conferences will be billed. Identical? Not necessarily?
2. Agree on process anchors and understandings so that lawyers support one another
   a. First meeting is only about educating clients and confirming commitments—no negotiation
   b. Attorneys control process/clients control outcome
   c. Discuss warning signs, such as: client wants to skip reading the documents or wants to do "homework" before first meeting or already has a plan, or believes there is already an agreement, and wants to focus on that for efficiency reasons
   d. Impasse management: Private judge? Arbitration? Super-mediation?
   e. Bad news, criticism, behavior management delivered by own lawyer; good news, appreciation, congratulations delivered by other lawyer.
3. Discuss client "hot buttons" and priorities as you believe them to be, share perceptions of what strengths and challenges clients bring to process
4. Discuss team components
   a. Coaches mandatory if kids?
   b. Who decides if child specialist should participate, who chooses?
   c. Would a financial professional be helpful? Who chooses?
   d. Should clients see any of the nonlawyer professionals before the first legal four-way?
   e. Should team members have conference call or face-to-face meeting before first legal four-way?
5. Agree on documents for first four-way meeting
   a. Stipulation for collaborative law, or contract? Agree on form
   b. Principles and Guidelines or Statement of Understanding for Team? Agree on form
   c. Educational documents for clients?
   d. Discovery forms: What format will disclosures come in?

6. Agree on how to handle communications
   a. Ban on written communications except for minutes and transmittals?
   b. FYI communications between lawyers OK?
   c. E-mails from clients: when if ever can they copy spouse and spouse's lawyer? Scheduling? Corrections to minutes?
   d. Minutes
      i. How complete should the minutes be?
         1. Set out commitments and goals on every set of minutes?
         2. Agreements, tasks, and agenda for next meeting?
         3. Agreements, tasks, discussions, and agenda for next meeting?
      ii. Who gets first draft?
         1. Professionals in the room first, then clients?
         2. Sent to all?
      iii. Sent to all professionals in case or just lawyers?
7. Process amenities
   a. Food at every meeting? Hosted by person whose office the meeting is in or alternated?
   b. Alternate offices for meetings or always meet wherever convenient for clients
   c. Alternate minutes?
   d. Billing protocol for e-mails setting up meetings?
   e. Whether or how to bill for travel time?
8. Structure first meeting agenda
   a. Introductions, congratulations, expressions of support and respect for other lawyer, disclosure of experience with other lawyer in collaborative cases
   b. Have clients state goals and priorities
   c. Review documents with clients
      i. Agree on how to do this: Read line by line? Summarize?
      ii. Lawyers alternate paragraphs?
      iii. Review both documents or just one of them, referring to the other when not redundant?
   d. Describe stages of collaborative process:
      i. Commitment: Why are we here? What brought us to collaboration?
      ii. Explore hopes and concerns: What is important to us? What questions do we want to answer? What would success look like, for each member of the restructuring family?
      iii. Gather and organize information: What information do we need?
         1. Agreeing upon neutrals, gathering further information, getting reports, etc.
      iv. Brainstorm and evaluate choices: What choices do we both have? What are the advantages and disadvantages of each of these options, for both of us and for our children and others?
      v. Reach agreement: what choices can we both accept?
      vi. Closing: reviewing successful process, highlighting certainty of change and planning for it, closing ceremony of some kind?
   e. Describe legal divorce process
   f. Explain basics of interest-based negotiations
   g. Discuss interdisciplinary team involvement
   h. Questions?

       i. Ask clients what their interim financial arrangement is, and if they are comfortable with it while they are in collaboration. If they aren't, need to prioritize this item for next meeting.

       j. Agree on agenda for next meeting

       k. Homework: disclosure forms and worksheets—and with whom clients will work to prepare them

       l. Set two meetings

9. Agree on time spent at meeting so that billings to clients reflect similar entries.

[Adapted from San Francisco Bay Area Collaborative Practice Group protocols, with thanks to Jennifer Jackson, who drafted them.]

Appendix I-G

First Four-Way Meeting Checklist

Date:

Case:

Attendees:

1. DISCUSSION OF COLLABORATIVE PROCESS AS PART OF ADR CONTINUUM: WHERE IT FITS AND HOW IT WORKS IN COMPARISON TO OTHER CONFLICT-RESOLUTION PROCESSES
    * Seriousness of good-faith commitments.
    * Ethical commitments of lawyers and parties.
    * Comparison with mediation and with conventional representation.
    * Comparison with litigation-template representation. Comparative speed, cost, benefits, risks.
    * The three estates: separate, marital, and "invisible" or "relational."
    * The role of the lawyers: specialists in conflict management and guided negotiations, not gladiators.
    * The role of the clients: experts in facts and needs; responsible for all ultimate decisions made in process and responsible for helping to generate settlement options.
    * Discussion of how collaborative lawyer's role is different from conventional lawyer's.
    * Discussion of potential risks of collaborative process (including possible termination by other party and loss of lawyer).
    * Discussion of costs, speed, etc.
    * Discussion of interdisciplinary collaboration.

2. ROAD MAP OF COLLABORATIVE PROCESS [LEGAL SIDE ONLY, NOT INTERDISCIPLINARY TEAM PROCESS]
    * Map of legal divorce process in this state, and interface with collaborative process.
    * Sequence of probable agendas for four-way meetings:

First Four-way: introduction, setting container, signing documents, scheduling future meetings.

Second Four-way: "Walk around the Estate," statement of highest intentions and goals for the collaborative process, begin list of interests and goals, agree on schedule for sharing documents and information, attend to interim cash-flow and other urgent matters, plan agenda for third four-way.

Third and Subsequent Four-ways: Exchange information, bring in neutrals as needed, brainstorm and evaluate settlement possibilities, negotiate terms of agreement, assign responsibility for preparation of draft agreements.

Final Four-way: Review and sign divorce agreement and procedural divorce papers, review and evaluate collaborative process, discuss likely future "road bumps" and how they will be addressed, closing "ceremony" if any.

3. DISCUSSION OF CORE PRINCIPLES AND GUIDING METAPHORS FOR COLLABORATIVE PROCESS
    - Transparency and accountability.
    - The "shadow client" and the agreement to remind client of stated highest intentions and goals rather than being alter ego for shadow client.
    - Flooding and its impact on clear thinking.
    - The sack race: We go at the pace of the slowest person in the room.
    - Whitewater rafting: There will be rough spots, and the guides (the lawyers) are the experts in how to navigate them.
    - Mountain climbing.
    - The arena for training horses.
    - Crossing the dark forest, and avoiding cutting down trees.
    - The topographical map.
    - A peculiar kind of race: The goal is that everyone crosses the finish line at the same time.
    - Medical analogies: The court as intensive care unit or emergency room; preventive and primary care best delivered elsewhere.

4. ORIENTATION TO INTEREST-BASED VS. POSITIONAL BARGAINING AND NEED FOR PEELING THE ONION. THE PLACE OF THE LAW IN THE COLLABORATIVE PROCESS. ENLIGHTENED SELF-INTEREST RATHER THAN GREED OR ALTRUISM
    - No threats of court.
    - Win-win, or "good enough," as the goal.
    - Avoiding concept of "fair," substituting concept of "acceptable."
    - Cartoon sketch of disfavored bargaining styles: Scandinavian, Soviet Cold War, Mediterranean Marketplace.
    - Deconstructing the law: Where it comes from, what it can and cannot do, what it is and is not. Legal rights as the default setting if clients can't come up with something more tailored to their needs.
    - Interest-based bargaining model: The story of the orange.
    - The goal is not the quickest agreement, but the best and most lasting agreement.
    - We don't discuss resolution until we have completed exploring facts and expanding range of options to be considered.

5. BEHAVIORAL AND MODELING ISSUES
    - Lawyers are responsible for keeping the negotiating space safe and civilized.
    - Only constructive good-faith bargaining permitted.

- Caucuses OK to recover composure or confer with counsel.
- Easy issues first to build confidence in new, effective ways of problem solving to replace old habits.

6. REVIEW AND SIGN COLLABORATIVE DOCUMENTS

7. IDENTIFY IMMEDIATE URGENT ISSUES: E.G., TEMPORARY SUPPORT, HOUSE PAYMENTS, AND AGREE ON TIMING AND SEQUENCE FOR ADDRESSING THEM. AGREE ON INTERIM MEASURES WITHOUT PREJUDICE

8. ASSIGN HOMEWORK FOR SECOND FOUR-WAY
- Assign which lawyer prepares post-meeting memorandum.
- Clients to work on statement of highest intentions for collaborative process for self, other, and children, for next meeting.
- Clients to gather documents, prepare draft income and expense declarations, prepare draft schedules of assets and debts, if lawyers will facilitate disclosure phase. If financial neutral will assist, clients will work with that person.
- Clients to have preliminary informational meeting with collaborative divorce coaches.

9. AGREE ON AGENDA FOR SECOND FOUR-WAY MEETING

10. SCHEDULE THREE OR FOUR FOUR-WAY MEETINGS

Metaphors for Collaborative Practice

Metaphors are invaluable tools for shifting consciousness away from the adversarial "default setting" toward a new norm of collaborative, consensual conflict resolution. The metaphors that follow can be used in several ways in the collaborative process:

1. To help clients understand the nature of the divorce transition and the roles of all participants in the collaborative process by providing a readily understood image of the collaborative process that helps clients see where they are at any moment in relation to the process.
2. To help the collaborative lawyers build a container around the collaborative process, a simplified structure of shared understandings that can be used by the lawyers in moments of conflict or stress to remind their clients via shorthand references of the agreements and expectations that were confirmed early in the process.
3. To help lawyers remake their own internal archetype of the lawyer's role in the divorce process, shifting away from the old dominant paradigm of the gladiator to the new paradigm involved in collaborative law. The metaphors help one reset the internal default setting of warrior that often emerges unthinkingly when the collaborative process runs into a rough spot.

Use metaphors—these or your own—as an important element in your first meetings with the parties, so that you can then refer to them as needed during negotiations and at the end of the process.

Whitewater Rafting

A divorce is a common and normal life passage that can be likened to a whitewater rafting trip. There will be periods during the divorce process that will resemble floating down calm, slow-moving, smooth water, and there will also predictably be periods of dramatic white-water rapids and rocks; perhaps there will even be churning weirs and whirlpools that can pull the unwary under. Each lawyer is piloting a raft carrying the client and his or her possessions downstream. What the lawyer brings is knowledge of the river and how to navigate it. What the river brings is the unpredictable and the unforeseeable.

The task, for everyone, is to navigate the river successfully to its end, without overturning rafts, people, and possessions into the water, without losing people or things. A moment's thought makes it clear that there is no particular advantage in getting one's own raft to the bottom first, or in moving through any particular rapids first. Indeed, there is a good deal of risk to everyone involved in making "me first" your priority. Cooperating, yielding the right of way, and planning that takes into consideration the needs of the other rafters are the strategies that bring everyone to the bottom safe and dry.

The collaborative lawyers are the pilots of their respective clients' rafts, proceeding downstream to resolution. They know how to keep the boat upright and heading downstream; they know the river. But they cannot pilot the boat without the active paddling of the clients. They cannot avoid whitewater rapids entirely, nor can they completely eliminate the risks associated with the venture. They help each client through the legal journey, and also cooperate with the other raft and pilot for mutual benefit.

Mountain Climbing/Rock Climbing

The divorce passage can be compared to a mountain-climbing expedition where there will be ascents up steep rock-faces and over deep crevasses before reaching the top. At dangerous points, the entire party is roped together, for the safety of all. Any jostling, pushing forward, hanging back, lack of attention to the agreed rules, or other behavior that fails to take into account the safety of the entire party jeopardizes the entire venture, including the person behaving dangerously. Working within the agreed rules and behaviors attentively is not only best for the venture as a whole, but also serves enlightened self-interest.

The collaborative lawyers know the mountain, know the safe and unsafe routes up and down, know how to work with other professionals on the team (doctors, cooks, sherpas), and know how to move the team where it has to go, cooperatively. The clients, part of the team, bring their own strength, intelligence, and courage, and become vital parts of the team effort, not merely passengers. There are no passengers on a trip to the top of the mountain.

The Journey through the Deep, Dark Woods

Our clients generally come to us focused on what specific outcomes should be attained, and have almost no awareness of how many variables can be involved in how we will get to resolution, or how many different and perhaps better options for resolution can be developed if we stick with the process that works. If the ground to be covered in the divorce process is thought of as a forest, and the process of reaching agreement is thought of as finding a good, safe, efficient path through the forest, our job as collaborative lawyers is to be experienced, capable guides—i.e., guardians of the process.

We collaborative lawyers and our clients begin the journey at the top of a hill looking out over the expanse of forest ahead (as in a first four-way meeting). We point out to our clients the destination on the far side of the forest: a lovely green meadow extending to the horizon (i.e., their future after the divorce is over). The lawyers have guided clients on this journey many times, and while it is never easy, we know how to make the trip safely and efficiently. We know what kinds of equipment to bring along. There is more than one way to get through this forest. We know that the best pathways to take may look uninviting at places, or even appear to circle backwards at times, but paradoxically, these are the easiest and safest routes to the meadow. Others—though deceptively attractive—lead to swamps, quicksand, impassable rivers, and sudden deep crevasses. Some come to an end in the middle of the forest, where only trees can be seen ahead.

We as lawyers know that our clients have not made this trip before, and we take seriously our job of following the paths that work best; that's an important part of the collaborative process agreements that we make at the first meeting. We also know that our clients, out of fear, or confusion, or anxiety, sometimes turn off on an unpromising pathway, and end up with their noses pressed up against the nearest tree or their feet in a fast-moving stream (i.e., an anxiety-driven issue that is not yet ripe for resolution, such as "I've got to know right away how much support I'll get," or "I want us to talk about whether I get the house, at the next meeting.") Often clients with their noses pressed up against trees will demand that the tree be cut down immediately, and clients with their feet in the water want the guides to stop what they were doing and help them figure out how to ford the stream. Then, they think, the path will be clear and the journey can resume.

But we, the guides, know that if we yield to that anxiety-driven demand, we will spend a great deal of time and energy cutting down trees and fording rough streams, and there will be more trees or streams or other hazards to come in that direction. That is not the way to get through the forest. If the lawyers are allowed to do their job as guides, we won't have to cut down trees at all. (That is, when we address issues at the right time, after all process steps have been followed, they tend to be resolved far more easily than if they are put on the agenda because of clients' anxiety, before they can be addressed effectively.)

Divorce as a Trip from Here to There

If we imagine the divorce process as a trip from, let's say, San Francisco to New York, or Phoenix to St. Louis, we have a rich process metaphor for a collaborative divorce. Clients can take a road trip in their own car (i.e., self-help or pro per); they can hire a driver, or take the bus or train, or they can fly. On the bus, there might be a single driver (i.e., neutral mediator), while on the train or plane, there would be more, perhaps many more, involved in getting the vehicle and passengers from here to there.

Regardless of how they choose to go, it's very important to have a trip plan and maps if the intention is an orderly, efficient journey without unpleasant surprises, wrong turns, or getting lost. Maybe a travel agent will help, or maybe web information suffices. If there is a need for hotels or restaurants along the way, these are part of the plan. And it's just as important to know what kind of weather to expect, and to bring along what's needed: the right shoes, an umbrella, an overcoat, for instance. There are many ways to get from here to there, some slower and some quicker, some involving more planning and some less, some more efficient than others, some having many and some having few or no professional helpers involved to facilitate the journey. No two couples or families are likely to have exactly the same trip from Phoenix to St. Louis. They leave at different hours of the day, use different modes of transport, plan rest stops or drive day and night or take the red-eye, use interstate highways or back roads, travel in summer or winter, encounter sunshine or tornadoes or hail. But making a careful choice, planning well, and following the plan are the best guarantors of a safe and successful trip.

Airplane Travel as a Divorce Metaphor

Parents who are confused about how much to tell their children about the divorce process and the conflicts being addressed in it can be advised to think of their collaborative divorce as if they were the pilot and co-pilot of a small airplane that is traveling through a storm, with the children in the position of passengers. What the passengers want from the pilot in that situation is a calm and reassuring voice over the sound system, saying in effect, "Relax, we are passing through a bit of turbulence, but there is no problem here and we should be through it safely in about 15 minutes. Meanwhile, please stay in your seat with your seat belt buckled and we will update you again in a few minutes." The passengers do not want the co-pilot to come back into the cabin sweaty and anxious, to announce, "I am so angry at that pilot I don't ever want to see her again; I think she must have lost her mind driving us through this storm and I don't know when it's going to end or whether we're in big trouble or not. I think I'll just stay back here with the passengers." Or, "the pilot and I just can't agree on who should be flying this plane. All we do is argue and I'm sick of it. I think *you* should decide who should take over, and also whether we should continue to St. Louis or maybe take a detour to Denver to see if the weather's better there. Whatever you decide is fine with me; just tell me and I'll go tell the pilot that's what the passengers want."

Divorce as a Birthing Process

While this metaphor might more often be associated with psychotherapists, there is an aspect of midwifery in the collaborative lawyer's relationship with his or her client, and with the couple. What is being born in every transformational divorce process is a new sense of self as an unmarried person, and a new sense of family—the post-divorce restructured family. Some births are quick and almost painless. Some are not. The collaborative lawyer assists the client and the couple to maintain a perspective that sees the pain they may at times be experiencing as normal and leading potentially to something of value.

Durable Power of Attorney

In the collaborative process, we all agree that the lawyers are going to take their instructions from the highest-functioning member of the client's internal "committee," from what might be termed the "higher self." This is the part of oneself which aspires to behave with integrity and respect for the other spouse, to make decisions that serve long-term interests, to consider and meet the needs of the post-divorce restructured family, and to fashion outcomes that address all those concerns as important components of long-term enlightened self-interest—potentially as important for long-term satisfaction as marginal increments to the immediate personal "bottom line."

In effect, then, signing the Collaborative Divorce Stipulation and the Principles and Guidelines for Collaborative Law Divorce amounts to a metaphorical "durable power of attorney," in which the informed client directs the lawyer to take instructions from the client's higher-functioning self, and to politely disregard the instructions that may emerge from time to time during the divorce process when a more emotional and reactive self takes charge in the client. These lower-functioning selves may be termed the shadow. The shadow is present in all of us and at times will emerge and demand to be heard, especially during stressful passages such as divorce. The shadow is as present in a collaborative law divorce as in any other situation. What is different in a collaborative law divorce is the commitment in advance that while the lawyers will listen to, allow appropriate space for, and address the urgent needs presented by the shadow side, they will not permit the shadow side to direct the divorce process.

This does not mean that the lawyer substitutes his or her judgment for the client's on any issues whatsoever. This is a process agreement, not an agreement about arriving at terms of settlement. The client can decide at any time that the powerful negative emotions associated with the shadow are more compelling than the collaborative commitments and can terminate the process and proceed with conventional legal representation. The client is educated by the lawyer about the impact of strong emotion on cognitive thought, the shorthand term "shadow client" is identified with that information, and the client makes—or declines to make—an informed choice that he or she does not want the shadow client to make decisions—i.e., does not want to make decisions while experiencing a fight-or-flight cortisol surge that impairs rational thought. The client who chooses collaboration must understand that the choice includes an instruction to the lawyer that the client does not want the "shadow client" to be steering the boat and that he or she wants to be alerted when the shadow client is taking over control. The lawyer must clearly highlight both aspects of this "durable power of attorney"—both the reasons why it is an important part of the collaborative process, and the fact that the client can decide at any time to terminate the process and proceed in a manner that does not build in consideration of the impact of strong emotion on good decision making.

This differs dramatically from the common situation in an adversarial divorce, in which a lawyer usually hears from the client when the client is in a shadow state of fear, anger, or grief, and the strategies agreed to at that time may never be reconsidered at a later time when the client is in a clearer state of mind, able to consider the long-term interests of self and children.

Consider asking your client whether she wants to make long-term decisions for herself and loved ones while in a shadow state. She is unlikely to say yes. You can remind her of this conversation if the shadow emerges at an inconvenient time.

A Peculiar Sort of Marathon

If we compare the divorce and divorce-recovery process to a marathon run, we can see that some people run faster than others, for a variety of reasons, or just get off to a faster start. In a divorce, usually one person is ahead of the other in terms of emotional adjustment to the fact of the divorce, a grieving process that usually moves predictably through stages of shock, denial, anger, and bargaining, to acceptance. In a collaborative divorce we want to adjust the speed and timing of negotiations in light of that reality so that both spouses cross the finish line (i.e., reach closure on terms of agreement) at the same time. This may mean that the faster runner (the one who is further along in the stages of adjustment to divorce) may need to stop and slow the pace while the other spouse catches up.

The Sack Race

Timing can make the difference between a successful collaborative representation and a frustrating one. One aspect of timing involves respecting the fact that the clients are likely to be at different stages in coming to terms with the divorce. Another aspect of timing involves recognizing that everyone in the room—the lawyers as well as the clients—needs to build trust in the specific process unfolding in that unique collaborative representation, by experiencing successful negotiating together. The golden rule of timing is simple: Everyone must move at the pace of the slowest person in the room, whoever that may be at the moment. (Sometimes it is a lawyer.)

A useful metaphor for making vivid the critical importance of time is the childhood game called the "three-legged" or *sack race*. In a collaborative divorce, each lawyer and each client has one leg in a sack, the same sack. All are moving together toward the goal—a comprehensive, win-win agreement. All must move at a pace that each person can handle. If anyone becomes impatient and tries to rush the others, the likeliest outcome is that everyone will end up flat on their faces in the dust.

Training Horses

The functional importance of the disqualification stipulation in collaborative law practice can be communicated vividly to clients by comparing the collaborative law process to training horses in a fenced arena.

It is the nature of horses to spook easily, and to react automatically to fear with flight. That is the reason that trainers of horses work in a fenced arena with the gate closed. If the gate remains open, the horses may cooperate quite well with the training while they are calm, but as soon as something frightens them, they will bolt out the gate—perhaps back to the barn, perhaps further afield. The trainers must chase after them.

With the gate closed, the horses still will bolt, but they will remain in the arena and will be able to get back to work with the trainers far more quickly, with far less lost time, far less frustration, and far less risk of injury to the horses. When it is time for the horses to go, the gate is opened and all depart in a safe, controlled fashion.

Similarly, it is the nature of people experiencing divorce to become overwhelmed from time to time with strong emotions that may impel them to bolt from the collaborative law process. It also is common for conventional divorce lawyers engaged in settlement efforts to respond to upset clients (people who have become "spooked") with preparation of motions and other court papers (comparable to running out of the arena with the spooked horses). If there is a gate between the parties, their lawyers, and the courthouse, it will allow time for the clients to consider from a more balanced perspective whether they really want to terminate the collaborative process. They can always do so, opening the gate and leaving the collaborative arena, but the lawyers cannot pass through the gate with them. If the client does leave the collaborative arena, the disqualification stipulation (the closed gate) forces termination of the collaborative process to be the result of careful consideration rather than the hasty or impulsive consequence of transitory strong feelings.

IACP Ethical Standards

International Academy of Collaborative Professionals Ethical Standards for Collaborative Practitioners

[Adopted January 2007]

Preamble. Collaborative Practice differs greatly from adversarial dispute resolution practice. It challenges practitioners in ways not necessarily addressed by the ethics of individual disciplines. The standards that follow:

1) Provide a common set of values, principles, and standards to guide the Collaborative practitioner in his or her professional decisions and conduct,
2) Create a framework of basic tenets for ethical and professional conduct by the Collaborative practitioner, and
3) Identify responsibilities of Collaborative practitioners to their clients, to Collaborative colleagues, and to the public.

General Standards

1. **Resolution of Conflicts between Ethical Standards.**
   1.1 Any apparent or actual conflict between the Ethical Standards governing the practitioner's discipline and these Standards should be resolved by the practitioner consistent with the Ethical Standards governing his or her own profession.
2. **Competence.**
   2.1 A Collaborative practitioner shall maintain the licensure or certification required by the practitioner's profession in good standing and shall adhere to the Ethical Standards governing his or her discipline.
   2.2 A Collaborative practitioner shall have completed a minimum of 12 hours of Collaborative Practice/Collaborative Law training or Interdisciplinary Collaborative training consistent with IACP Minimum Standards for Collaborative practitioners, prior to commencing a Collaborative case or engaging in Interdisciplinary Collaborative Practice.
   2.3 A Collaborative practitioner shall practice within the scope of the Collaborative practitioner's training, competency, and professional man-

date of practice, as specified by the IACP Minimum Standards for Collaborative practitioners. The practitioner shall be mindful of the client's individual circumstances and the overall circumstances of the case that may require the involvement of other professionals, both within and outside of the Collaborative process.

Comment

As Collaborative practitioners experience a greater diversity in their client population they become confronted by more complexity in physical, psychological, and emotional factors affecting the client. It is important for the practitioner to be able to recognize these factors, as they will necessarily influence the Collaborative process and the client's decision making. It is even more important for the practitioner to recognize the limits of his or her ability to effectively deal with these factors and with the client's response to them. In fully addressing the client's needs, interests, and goals, the Collaborative practitioner must be willing to turn to other professionals both within and outside of the Collaborative process, such as mental health professionals, medical professionals, financial professionals, vocational specialists, and possibly rehabilitation counselors in the areas of physical disability, substance abuse, and domestic violence.

3. **Conflicts of Interest.**
    1.1 A Collaborative practitioner shall disclose any conflicts of interest as defined by the practitioner's respective professional guidelines and ethical standards.

Comment

Upon full disclosure of a conflict of interest, the party or parties affected may waive the conflict in writing consistent with the practitioner's professional guidelines.

4. **Confidentiality.**
    4.1 A Collaborative practitioner shall fully inform the client(s) about confidentiality requirements and practices in the specific Collaborative process that will be offered to the client(s).
    4.2 A Collaborative practitioner may reveal privileged information only with permission of the client(s), according to guidelines set out clearly in the Collaborative practitioner's Participation Agreement(s) or as required by law.

Comment

The rules of confidentiality are among the most important core values of the legal and mental health professions. Those standards may be modified by the terms of the Collaborative practitioner's fee and/or participation agreement with the client(s), so long as the modifications are consistent with the ethical standards of the practitioner's discipline. A competent Collaborative practitioner will be knowledgeable regarding the requirements of his or her professional standards pertaining to the necessity of obtaining a client's informed consent, and shall provide sufficient information to enable the client to give informed consent.

5. **Scope of Advocacy.**
    5.1 A Collaborative lawyer shall inform the client(s) of the full spectrum of process options available for resolving disputed legal issues in their case.

5.2 A Collaborative practitioner shall provide a clear explanation of the Collaborative process, which shall identify the obligations of the practitioner and of the client(s) in the process, so that the client(s) may make an informed decision about choice of process.

5.3 A Collaborative practitioner shall assist the client(s) in establishing realistic expectations in the Collaborative process and shall respect the clients' self determination; understanding that ultimately the client(s) is/are responsible for making the decisions that resolve their issues.

5.4 A Collaborative practitioner shall encourage parents to remain mindful of the needs and best interests of their child(ren).

5.5 A Collaborative practitioner shall avoid contributing to the conflict of the client(s).

Comment

This section highlights the special obligations undertaken by the Collaborative practitioner that specifically result from the unique nature of Collaborative Practice. Psychologists and social workers are free to recommend outcomes to their client(s) believed to be in the client(s') (or the clients' family's) best interest, provided that they take care to do no harm. The traditional model of lawyering is that the lawyer advocates for the client's position so long as that position is legally supportable. This section thus has particular impact for lawyers because it reflects the considerations underlying law society and bar association rules in a number of jurisdictions. For example, Rule 2.1 of the American Bar Association's Model Rules of Professional Conduct, which recognizes that the role of the attorney encompasses more than providing purely technical legal advice. As the Comment to Rule 2.1 explains, the attorney's advice can properly include moral, ethical, and practical considerations, and may indicate that there is more involved in resolving a particular dispute or even the client's entire case than strictly legal considerations. In Collaborative practice, the practitioner specifically contracts with the client(s) to provide advice that recognizes a full range of options for dispute resolution and takes into consideration relationship and family structures when looking at the possible outcomes for the client(s).

6. **Disclosure of Business Practices.**

   6.1 A Collaborative practitioner shall fully disclose to the client(s) in writing his or her respective fee structure, related costs, and billing practices involved in the case.

   6.2 A Collaborative practitioner shall be truthful in advertising his/her Collaborative practice and in the solicitation of Collaborative clients.

7. **Minimum Elements of a Collaborative Participation and/or Fee Agreement.**

   7.1 A Collaborative Participation Agreement and/or Fee Agreement shall be in writing, signed by the parties and the Collaborative practitioners, and must include provisions containing the following elements:

   A. Pertaining to Full Disclosure of Information

   1) No participant in a Collaborative case, whether a Collaborative practitioner or a party, may knowingly withhold or misrepresent information material to the Collaborative process or otherwise act or fail to act in a way that knowingly undermines or takes unfair advantage of the Collaborative process;

2) If a party knowingly withholds or misrepresents information material to the Collaborative process, or otherwise acts or fails to act in a way that undermines or takes unfair advantage of the Collaborative process, and the party continues in such conduct after being duly advised of his or her obligations in the Collaborative process, such behavior will be grounds for withdrawal of the Collaborative Practitioner and if such result was clearly stated in the Participation and/or Fee Agreement, the conduct shall result in termination of the Collaborative Process.

3) In the event of a withdrawal from or termination of the Collaborative process, the Collaborative practitioner shall notify the other professionals in the case.

B. Prohibiting Contested Court Procedures

1) Undertaking any contested court procedure automatically terminates the Collaborative process;

2) A Collaborative practitioner shall not threaten to undertake any contested court procedure related to the Collaborative case nor shall a Collaborative practitioner continue to represent a client who makes such a threat in a manner that undermines the Collaborative process.

3) Upon termination of the Collaborative process, the representing Collaborative practitioners and all other professionals working within the Collaborative process are prohibited from participating in any aspect of the contested proceedings between the parties.

Practice Protocols

8. **Consent.**

   8.1 Each Collaborative practitioner shall obtain written permission from his/her client(s) to share information as appropriate to the process with all other Collaborative professionals working on the case.

9. **Withdrawal/Termination.**

   9.1 If a Collaborative practitioner learns that his or her client is withholding or misrepresenting information material to the Collaborative process, or is otherwise acting or failing to act in a way that knowingly undermines or takes unfair advantage of the Collaborative process, the practitioner shall advise and counsel the client that:

   A. Such conduct is contrary to the principles of Collaborative Practice;

   B. The client's continuing violation of such principles will mandate the withdrawal of the Collaborative practitioner from the Collaborative process.

   9.2 If, after the advice and counsel described in Section 9.1, above, the client continues in the violation of the Collaborative Practice principles of disclosure and/or good faith, then the Collaborative practitioner shall:

   A. Withdraw from the Collaborative case; and

   B. Where permitted by the terms of the Collaborative practitioner's contract with the client, give notice to the other participants in the matter that the client has terminated the Collaborative process.

9.3 Nothing in these ethical standards shall be deemed to require a Collaborative practitioner to disclose the underlying reasons for either the professional's withdrawal or the termination of the Collaborative process.

9.4 A Collaborative practitioner must suspend or withdraw from the Collaborative process if the practitioner believes that a Collaborative client is unable to effectively participate in the process.

9.5 Upon termination of the Collaborative process, a Collaborative practitioner shall offer to provide his/her client(s) with a list of professional resources from the Collaborative practitioner's respective field from whom the client(s) may choose to receive professional advice or representation unless a client advises that he or she does not want or need such information.

Ethical Standards Specific to Particular Collaborative Roles

10. **Neutral Roles**

10.1 A Collaborative practitioner who serves on a Collaborative case in a neutral role shall adhere to that role, and shall not engage in any continuing client relationship that would compromise the Collaborative practitioner's neutrality. Working with either or both client(s) or with their child(ren) outside of the Collaborative process is inconsistent with that neutral role.

   A. A Collaborative practitioner serving as a neutral financial specialist in a Collaborative case shall not have an ongoing business relationship with a Collaborative client during or after the completion of the Collaborative case, but may assist the parties in completing the tasks specifically assigned to them by the parties' written, final agreement. Such assistance may not include the sale of financial products or other services.

   B. A Collaborative practitioner serving as a child specialist may assist the family in divorce-related matters for the child(ren.) Such assistance may not include becoming the child(ren)'s therapist.

   C. A Collaborative practitioner serving as a neutral coach may assist the family in divorce-related matters. Such assistance may not include acting as a therapist for one or both parties.

11. **Coaches/Child Specialists**

11.1 A Collaborative practitioner who serves in the role of coach on a Collaborative case shall not function as a therapist to the Collaborative practitioner's client after the case has ended. Coaches should remain available to continue to help the clients/family address specific divorce issues after the divorce is final. A therapist for a party shall not serve in the role of coach or child specialist on a Collaborative case involving a party with whom the therapist has acted in a therapeutic role.

11.2 A Collaborative practitioner acting as a child specialist shall inform the child about the child specialist's role and the limits of confidentiality as appropriate, taking into account the child's age and level of maturity.

When a Collaborative Case Is in Trouble

Communications	
Problem	**Try This**
People persistently fail to speak directly to one another—triangulating, speaking about rather than to a person.	Lawyers gently insist upon and model direct and straightforward communications.
People persistently misunderstand one another's words or intentions in ways that need to be addressed.	Lawyers use "pre" and "post" meeting conferences to share insights that can be brought by the attorney to the client.
	Clients are referred to Collaborative Divorce coaches for training in direct communication skills for negotiating more effectively.
Someone persistently fails to respect the boundaries of civility in four-way meetings; the lawyers fail to hold those boundaries effectively for the clients.	Lawyers share information about "hot-buttons," plan ahead for agenda management and conflict management, and do not permit their respective clients to "act out" in four-way meetings.

| Transference and Countertransference ||
Problem	Try This
Strong feelings (e.g., anger, fear, mistrust) or frustrating behavior (e.g., denial, irritability) are interfering with progress in collaborative negotiations.	Lawyer consults with mental health professional regarding transference/countertransference issues with client or collaborative counsel and uses awareness of countertransference as a creative tool in collaborative process.
A lawyer is behaving as the client's alter ego or hired gun, either overprotective or overaggressive.	Lawyers make use of a mediator or mental health consultant to shed light on how transference/countertransference issues or unexamined attorney role-definition may be interfering with effectiveness of collaborative process.
One or more persons are triggering unaccountably strong reactions in one another that interfere with the progress of negotiations.	Refer client(s) for Collaborative Divorce coaching (short-term and behaviorally focused).

| Need to Refer Client(s) for Treatment, Counseling, or Coaching ||
Problem	Try This
A client's emotional state with the attorney and/or in collaborative negotiations indicates a degree of grief, fear, depression, or anger that may require psychotherapy.	Lawyer requests counseling or psychotherapy for client as a condition of continuing the collaborative law representation, to ensure client is able to participate effectively.
A client is impaired physically or emotionally to a degree that prevents effective participation in the collaborative process.	Consider suggesting neurological or neuropsychiatric assessment of client. The attorney may be the only professional in a position to do so for the client.
A client reports that one or more children are at risk.	Work with the other collaborative attorney to encourage both clients to bring in immediate resources to stabilize and protect the children. (People don't function at their highest level when frightened about children's welfare.)
A client repeatedly behaves in ways that cause serious problems in negotiations or in the "real world" (e.g., alcoholism, drug abuse, overspending, inability to contain emotions sufficiently to listen accurately, refusal to participate fully in collaborative meetings, counterproductive "blaming" or "victim" stances in negotiations).	Collaborative attorneys share information in a positive, problem-solving way aimed joint recommendations for counseling, referrals (including possible Collaborative Divorce referral), behavioral change. Each attorney works with his/her own client; the other attorney is not the messenger.

A client lacks basic skills in money management, limit-setting (with spouse or with children), career planning, prioritizing goals and objectives.	Work with collaborative counsel to obtain financial resources for agreed counseling/training as needed: basic money skills, basic communication skills and assertiveness training, vocational counseling, etc., using Collaborative Divorce team if available.

Need to Terminate the Collaborative Law Process	
Problem	**Try This**
A client persistently refuses to behave honestly: refusal to disclose income or assets, refusal to disclose clearly pertinent life information such as planned remarriage.	Lawyer firmly demands adherence to Principles and Guidelines for Collaborative Law, explains need to withdraw as counsel if good faith honest is absent, and does so if behavior persists, or terminates Collaborative Law process, depending upon the retainer agreement and practice group protocols.
Persistent refusal to follow through on commitments to lawyer, collaborative process, or spouse.	Same response.
Extreme and persistent distrust between spouses that is inconsistent with the good faith commitment to meet the legitimate needs of both parties in the process, or with other elements of the "Principles and Guidelines for Collaborative Law."	If the distrust is well-founded, and it is one's own client who is dishonest, the lawyer withdraws as counsel, or terminates the collaborative law process, depending upon the retainer agreement and practice group protocols. If the distrust is well-founded and it is the other spouse who is dishonest, the lawyer advises the client to terminate collaborative law process and withdraws. If it may not be well-founded, the collaborative attorneys make appropriate referrals to other professionals to see whether distrust may dissipate as strong emotions about divorce resolve.
Fundamental need of client to have major decisions in divorce made by a third party; inability to take personal responsibility for necessary compromises.	Lawyer advises client to terminate collaborative law process, unless all can agree on limited-scope retention of private judge for case-management and/or decision-making.

A lawyer of client uses direct or implicit threats to gain advantage in the collaborative process.	The other lawyer advises his or her client to terminate collaborative law process. The threatening client's lawyer withdraws as collaborative counsel, or terminates the collaborative process if the behavior is likely to recur.
A lawyer or client uses delay to gain unfair advantage in the collaborative process.	

Appendix I-K

ABA Committee on Ethics Opinion

Standing Committee on Ethics and Professional Responsibility

Formal Opinion 07-447 August 9, 2007

Ethical Considerations in Collaborative Law Practice

Before representing a client in a collaborative law process, a lawyer must advise the client of the benefits and risks of participation in the process. If the client has given his or her informed consent, the lawyer may represent the client in the collaborative law process. A lawyer who engages in collaborative resolution processes still is bound by the rules of professional conduct, including the duties of competence and diligence.[1]

In this opinion, we analyze the implications of the Model Rules on collaborative law practice.[2] Collaborative law is a type of alternative dispute resolution in which the parties and their lawyers commit to work cooperatively to reach a settlement. It had its roots in, and shares many attributes of, the mediation process. Participants focus on the interests of both clients, gather sufficient information to insure that decisions are made with full knowledge, develop a full range of options, and then choose options that best meet the needs of the parties. The parties structure a mutually acceptable written resolution of all issues without court involvement. The product of the process is then submitted to the court as a final decree. The structure creates a problem-solving atmosphere with a focus on interest-based negotiation and client empowerment.[3]

Since its creation in Minnesota in 1990,[4] collaborative practice[5] has spread rapidly throughout the United States and into Canada, Australia, and Western Europe. Numerous established collaborative law organizations develop local practice protocols, train practitioners, reach out to the public, and build referral networks. On its website, the International Academy of Collaborative Professionals describes its mission as fostering professional excellence in conflict resolution by protecting the essentials of collaborative practice, expanding collaborative practice worldwide, and providing a central resource for education, networking, and standards of practice.[6]

Although there are several models of collaborative practice, all of them share the same core elements that are set out in a contract between the clients and their lawyers (often referred to as a "four-way" agreement). In that agreement, the parties commit to negotiating a mutually acceptable settlement without court intervention, to engaging in open communication and information sharing, and to creating shared solutions that meet the needs of both clients. To ensure the commitment of the lawyers to the collaborative process, the four-way agreement also includes a requirement that, if the process breaks down, the lawyers will withdraw from representing their respective clients and will not handle any subsequent court proceedings.

Several state bar opinions have analyzed collaborative practice and, with one exception, have concluded that it is not inherently inconsistent with the Model Rules.[7] Most authorities treat collaborative law practice as a species of limited scope representation and discuss the duties of lawyers in those situations, including communication, competence, diligence, and confidentiality. However, even those opinions are guarded, and caution that collaborative practice carries with it a potential for significant ethical difficulties.[8]

As explained herein, we agree that collaborative law practice and the provisions of the four-way agreement represent a permissible limited scope representation under Model Rule 1.2, with the concomitant duties of competence, diligence, and communication. We reject the suggestion that collaborative law practice sets up a non-waivable conflict under Rule 1.7(a)(2).

Rule 1.2(c) permits a lawyer to limit the scope of a representation so long as the limitation is reasonable under the circumstances and the client gives informed consent. Nothing in the Rule or its Comment suggest that limiting a representation to a collaborative effort to reach a settlement is per se unreasonable. On the contrary, Comment [6] provides that "[a] limited representation may be appropriate because the client has limited objectives for the representation. In addition, the terms upon which representation is undertaken may exclude specific means that might otherwise be used to accomplish the client's objectives."

Obtaining the client's informed consent requires that the lawyer communicate adequate information and explanation about the material risks of and reasonably available alternatives to the limited representation.[9] The lawyer must provide adequate information about the rules or contractual terms governing the collaborative process, its advantages and disadvantages, and the alternatives. The lawyer also must assure that the client understands that, if the collaborative law procedure does not result in settlement of the dispute and litigation is the only recourse, the collaborative lawyer must withdraw and the parties must retain new lawyers to prepare the matter for trial.[10]

The one opinion that expressed the view[11] that collaborative practice is impermissible did so on the theory that the "four-way agreement" creates a non-waivable conflict of interest under Rule 1.7(a)(2). We disagree with that result because we conclude that it turns on a faulty premise. As we stated earlier, the four-way agreement that is at the heart of collaborative practice includes the promise that both lawyers will withdraw from representing their respective clients if the collaboration fails and that they will not assist their clients in ensuing litigation. We do not disagree with the proposition that this contractual obligation to withdraw creates on the part of each lawyer a "responsibility to a third party" within the meaning of Rule 1.7(a)(2). We do disagree with the view that such a responsibility creates a conflict of interest under that Rule.

A conflict exists between a lawyer and her own client under Rule 1.7(a)(2) "if there is a significant risk that the representation [of the client] will be materially limited by the lawyer's responsibilities to . . . a third person or by a personal interest of the lawyer." A self-interest conflict can be resolved if the client gives informed consent, confirmed in writing,[12] but a lawyer may not seek the client's informed consent unless the lawyer "reasonably believes that [she] will be able to provide competent and diligent representation" to the client.[13] According to Comment [1] to Rule 1.7, "[l]oyalty and independent judgment are essential elements in the lawyer's relationship to a client." As explained more fully in Comment [8] to that Rule, "a conflict exists if there is a significant risk that a lawyer's ability to consider, recommend or carry out an appropriate course of action for the client will be materially limited by the lawyer's other responsibilities or interests. . . . The conflict in effect forecloses alternatives that would otherwise be available to the client."

On the issue of consentability, Rule 1.7 Comment [15] is instructive. It provides that "[c]onsentability is typically determined by considering whether the interests of the clients will be adequately protected if the clients are permitted to give their informed consent to representation burdened by a conflict of interest. Thus, under paragraph (b)(1), representation is prohibited in the circumstances the lawyer cannot reasonably conclude that the lawyer will be able to provide competent and diligent representation."

Responsibilities to third parties constitute conflicts with one's own client only if there is a significant risk that those responsibilities will materially limit the lawyer's representation of the client. It has been suggested that a lawyer's agreement to withdraw is essentially an agreement by the lawyer to impair her ability to represent the client.[14] We disagree, because we view participation in the collaborative process as a limited scope representation.[15]

When a client has given informed consent to a representation limited to collaborative negotiation toward settlement, the lawyer's agreement to withdraw if the collaboration fails is not an agreement that impairs her ability to represent the client, but rather is consistent with the client's limited goals for the representation. A client's agreement to a limited scope representation does not exempt the lawyer from the duties of competence and diligence, notwithstanding that the contours of the requisite competence and diligence are limited in accordance with the overall scope of the representation. Thus, there is no basis to conclude that the lawyer's representation of the client will be materially limited by the lawyer's obligation to withdraw if settlement cannot be accomplished. In the absence of a significant risk of such a material limitation, no conflict arises between the lawyer and her client under Rule 1.7(a)(2).

Stated differently, there is no foreclosing of alternatives, i.e., consideration and pursuit of litigation, otherwise available to the client because the client has specifically limited the scope of the lawyer's representation to the collaborative negotiation of a settlement.[16]

Notes

1. This opinion is based on the Model Rules of Professional Conduct as amended by the ABA House of Delegates through February 2007. The laws, court rules, regulations, rules of professional conduct, and opinions promulgated in individual jurisdictions are controlling.

2. We do not discuss the ethical considerations that arise in connection with a lawyer's participation in a collaborative law group or organization. *See* Maryland Bar Ass'n Eth. Op.

2004-23 (2004) (discussing ethical propriety of "collaborative dispute resolution non-profit organization.")

3. *See generally* Sherri Goren Slovin, *The Basics of Collaborative Family Law: A Divorce Paradigm Shift*, 18 AMER. J. FAM. L. 74 (Summer 2004), available at http://www.mediate .com/pfriendly.cfm?id=1684.

4. *Minnesota Collaborative Family Law FAQs*, available at http://www.divorcenet .com/states/minnesota/mnfaq01.

5. The terms "collaborative law," "collaborative process," and "collaborative resolution process" are used interchangeably with "collaborative practice." Although collaborative practice currently is utilized almost exclusively by family law practitioners, its concepts have been applied to employment, probate, construction, real property, and other civil law disputes where the parties are likely to have continuing relationships after the current conflict has been resolved.

6. *See* http://www.collaborativepractice.com/t2.asp?T=Mission.

7. Colorado Bar Ass'n Eth. Op. 115 (Feb. 24, 2007), *Ethical Considerations in the Collaborative and Cooperative Law Contexts*, available at http://www.cobar.org/group/display .cfm?GenID=10159&EntityID=ceth, is the only opinion to conclude that a non-consentable conflict arises in collaborative practice. Other state authorities analyze the disqualification obligation under Rules 1.2, 1.16, or 5.6. *See e.g.*, Kentucky Bar Ass'n Op. E-425 (June 2005), *Participation in the "Collaborative Law" Process*, available at http://www.kybar.org/ documents/ethics_opinions/kba_e-425.pdf; New Jersey Adv. Comm. on Prof'l Eth. Op. 699 (Dec. 12, 2005), *Collaborative Law*, available at http://lawlibrary.rutgers.edu/ethics decisions/acpe/acp699_1.html; North Carolina State Bar Ass'n 2002 Formal Eth. Op. 1 (Apr. 19, 2002), *Participation in Collaborative Resolution Process Requiring Lawyer to Agree to Limit Future Court Representation*, available at http://www.ncbar.com/ethics/ethics .asp?page=2&from=4/2002&to=4/2002; Pennsylvania Bar Ass'n Comm. on Legal Eth. & Prof'l Resp. Inf. Op. 2004-24 (May 11, 2004), available at http://www.collaborativelaw.us/ articles/ Ethics_Opinion_Penn_CL_2004.pdf. Several states have special rules for collaborative law practice. *See, e.g.*, CAL. FAM § 2013 (West 2007); N.C. GEN. STAT. § 50-70 to 5079 (2006); TEX. FAM. CODE ANN. §§ 6.603 & 153.0072 (Vernon 2005).

8. *Supra* note 6.

9. Rule 1.0(e).

10. *See also* Rule 1.4(b), which requires that a lawyer "explain a matter to the extent reasonably necessary to permit the client to make informed decisions regarding the representation."

11. Colorado Bar Ass'n Eth. Op.115, *supra* note 7.

12. Rule 1.7(b)(4).

13. Rule 1.7(b)(1).

14. Colorado Bar Ass'n Eth. Op.115, *supra* note 7 (practice of collaborative law violates Rule 1.7(b) of Colorado Rules of Professional Conduct insofar as a lawyer participating in the process enters into a contractual agreement with the opposing party requiring the lawyer to withdraw in the event that the process is unsuccessful).

15. *See Handbook on Limited Scope Legal Assistance: A Report of the Modest Means Task Force*, 2003 ABA Section of Litigation, at 27–29, available at http://www.abanet.org/ litigation/taskforces/modest/report.pdf.

16. *See* Lerner v. Laufer, 819 A.2d 471, 482 (N.J. Super. Ct. App. Div.), *cert. denied*, 827 A.2d 290 (N.J. 2003) (stating that "the law has never foreclosed the right of competent, informed citizens to resolve their own disputes in whatever way may suit them," court rejected malpractice claim against lawyer who used carefully drafted limited scope retainer agreement); Alaska Bar Ass'n Eth. Op. No. 93-1 (May 25, 1993) (lawyer may ethically limit scope of representation but must notify client clearly of limitations on representation and potential risks client is taking by not having full representation); Arizona State Bar Ass'n Eth. Op. 91-03 (Jan. 15, 1991) (lawyer may agree to represent client on limited basis as long as client consents after consultation and representation is not so limited in scope as to violate

ethics rules); Colo. Bar Ass'n Ethics Comm. Formal Op. 101 (Jan. 17, 1998) (noting examples of "commonplace and traditional" arrangements under which clients ask their lawyers "to provide discrete legal services, rather than handle all aspects of the total project").

AMERICAN BAR ASSOCIATION STANDING COMMITTEE ON ETHICS AND PROFESSIONAL RESPONSIBILITY, 321 N. Clark Street, Chicago, Illinois 60610-4714; Telephone (312)988-5300. CHAIR: Steven C. Krane, New York, NY; Elizabeth Alston, Covington, LA; T. Maxfield Bahner, Chattanooga, TN; Amie L. Clifford, Columbia, SC; Edwin L. Felter, Jr., Denver, CO; James Akio Kawachika, Honolulu, HI; Robert H. Mundheim, New York, NY; Arden J. Olson, Eugene, OR; Irma Russell, Tulsa, OK; Sylvia E. Stevens, Lake Oswego, OR. CENTER FOR PROFESSIONAL RESPONSIBILITY: George A. Kuhlman, Ethics Counsel; Eileen B. Libby, Associate Ethics Counsel.

Appendix I-L

Bibliography

Articles

Marshall J. Breger, *Should an Attorney Be Required to Advise a Client of ADR Options*, 13 Georgetown J. Legal Ethics 427 (2000).

Robert Cochran, Jr., *Must Lawyers Tell Clients About ADR*, Arb. J. (June 1993).

Jonathan R. Cohen, *Advising Clients to Apologize*, 72 S. Cal. L. Rev. 1009 (May 1999).

Susan Daicoff, *Lawyers, Know Thyself: A Review of Empirical Research on Attorney Attributes Bearing on Professionalism*, 4 Am. U.L. Rev 1337 (June 1997).

Roger Fisher, *What About Negotiation as a Specialty?* 69 A.B.A. J. 1220 (September 1983).

Ronald J. Gilson & Robert H. Mnookin, *Disputing Through Agents: Cooperation and Conflict Between Lawyers in Litigation*, 94 Colum. L. Rev. 2 (March 1994).

David Hoffman & Pauline H. Tesler, *Collaborative Law and the Use of Settlement Counsel*, The Alternative Dispute Resolution Practice Guide, Chapter 41 (West, 2002).

David Hoffman, *Collaborative Law in the World of Business*, Collaborative Rev. (Winter 2004).

Janet R. Johnston, Ph.D., *Building Multidisciplinary Professional Partnerships with the Court on Behalf of High-Conflict Divorcing Families and Their Children: Who Needs What Kind of Help?* 22 U. Ark. Little Rock L. Rev. 453 (Spring 2000).

Judge Anne Kass, *Clinical Advice from the Bench*, 7 J. Child & Adolescent Psychiatric Clinics of North America 247–57 (April 1998).

Steven Keeva, *Integrating Your Heart and Mind*, A.B.A. J. Vol. 82 (September 1999).

Joan Kelly, *A Decade of Divorce Mediation Research*, 34 Fam. and Conciliation Ct. Rev. 373 (July 1996).

John Lande, *Principles for Policymaking about Collaborative Law and Other ADR Processes*, 22 OHIO ST. J. ON DISP. RESOL. 619 (2007).

Lorraine Lopich, *Collaborative Law in Relation to Family Law*, 4 AUSTRALIAN FAM. L. (2007).

Julie MacFarlane, *The Emerging Phenomenon of Collaborative Family Law (CFL): A Qualitative Study of CFL Cases* (Department of Justice, Canada, 2005).

John V. McShane, *Is This All There Is? Specific Strategies for Becoming the New Family Lawyer*, 26th Annual Advanced Family Law 2000 Seminar, San Antonio, Texas (Aug. 21–24, 2000).

Gerald J. Postema, *Moral Responsibility in Professional Ethics*, 55 N.Y.U. L. REV. 63 (April 1980).

Marsha Kline Pruett & Tamara D. Jackson, *The Lawyer's Role During the Divorce Process: Perceptions of Parents, Their Young Children, and Their Attorneys*, 33 FAM. LAW Q. 283 (Summer 1999).

Stephen Reich, *California Psychological Inventory: Profile of a Sample of First-Year Law Students*, 39 PSYCHOL. REP. 871 (1976).

Douglas C. Reynolds & Doris F. Tennant, *Collaborative Law—An Emerging Practice*, BOSTON BAR J. (November 1, 2001).

Deborah L. Rhode, *Ethical Perspectives on Legal Practice*, 37 STANFORD L. REV. 589 (January 1985).

Diana Richmond, Esq., *Point of View: Collaborative Law*, 10 CALIFORNIA FAM. L. MONTHLY 244 (October 1995).

Elizabeth K. Strickland, *Putting "Counselor" Back in the Lawyer's Job Description: Why More States Should Adopt Collaborative Law Statutes*, 84 N.C. L. REV. 979 (2006).

Susan Sturm, *From Gladiators to Problem-Solvers: Connecting Conversations About Women, The Academy, and the Legal Profession*, 4 DUKE H. GENDER L. & POL'Y 199 (Spring 1997).

Pauline H. Tesler, *Collaborative Law: Practicing Without Armor, Practicing With Heart*, Chapter 8 in THE AFFECTIVE ASSISTANCE OF COUNSEL: PRACTICING LAW AS A HEALING PROFESSION (Marjorie Silver, ed., 2007).

Pauline H. Tesler, *Collaborative Law: What It Is and Why Family Law Attorneys Need to Know About It*, INTERNATIONAL FAM. L. 183 (2003).

Pauline H. Tesler, *Mediators and Collaborative Lawyers: Where We Are, Where We're Headed, And—Shall We Travel Together?*, FAM. MED. NEWS 6–8 (Summer 2003).

Pauline H. Tesler, *Collaborative Law Neutrals Produce Better Resolutions*, 21 ALTERNATIVES (J. CPR INSTITUTE FOR DISP. RESOL.) (January 2003).

Pauline H. Tesler, *A Peaceful Resolution*, DIVORCE MAGAZINE 49–52 (Spring 2002).

Pauline H. Tesler, *Collaborative Law: Achieving Effective Resolution in Divorce Without Litigation* (American Bar Association, 2001).

Pauline H. Tesler, *Collaborative Law: A New Paradigm for Divorce Lawyers*, 5 PSYCHOL. PUB. POL'Y & L. 967 (December, 1999).

Pauline H. Tesler, *The Believing Game, The Doubting Game, and Collaborative Law*, 5 PSYCHOL. PUB. POL'Y & L. 1018 (December 1999).

Pauline H. Tesler, *Collaborative Law: What It Is, and Why Lawyers Need to Know About It*, 13 AM. J. FAM. L. 215–225 (Winter 1999).

Pauline H. Tesler, *Collaborative Law: A New Approach to Family Law ADR*, 2 CONFLICT MANAGEMENT NEWSLETTER (American Bar Association, Summer 1996).

Richard Wasserstrom, *Lawyers as Professionals: Some Moral Issues*, 5 HUMAN RIGHTS 1 (1975).

Janet Weinstein, *And Never the Twain Shall Meet: The Best Interests of Children and the Adversary System*, 52 U. MIAMI L. REV. 79 (1985).

Books

SHERRY R. ABNEY, AVOIDING LITIGATION: A GUIDE TO CIVIL COLLABORATIVE LAW (2005).

DANIEL BOWLING & DAVID HOFFMAN, BRINGING PEACE INTO THE ROOM (2003).

JANET P. BRUMLEY, DIVORCE WITHOUT DISASTER: COLLABORATIVE LAW IN TEXAS (2004).

NANCY J. CAMERON, COLLABORATIVE PRACTICE: DEEPENING THE DIALOGUE (2004).

HELENA CORNELIUS & SHOSHANA FAIRE, WITH ESTELLE CORNELIUS, EVERYONE CAN WIN: RESPONDING TO CONFLICT CONSTRUCTIVELY (2d ed., 2006).

SUSAN SWAIM DAICOFF, LAWYER, KNOW THYSELF: A PSYCHOLOGICAL ANALYSIS OF PERSONALITY STRENGTHS AND WEAKNESSES (2004).

EDWARD DE BONO, DE BONO'S THINKING COURSE (1985).

ANN HALL DICK & TOM BALLANTINE, THE ART OF FAMILY LAW: SKILLS FOR SUCCESSFUL PRACTICE (2001).

ROGER FISHER & SCOTT BROWN, GETTING TOGETHER: BUILDING RELATIONSHIPS AS WE NEGOTIATE (1988).

ROGER FISHER & DANNY ERTEL, GETTING READY TO NEGOTIATE: THE GETTING TO YES WORKBOOK (1995).

Roger Fisher, Elizabeth Kopelman & Andrea Schneider, Beyond Machiavelli: Tools for Coping with Conflict (1994).

Roger Fisher & William Ury, Getting to Yes: Negotiating Agreement Without Giving In (3d ed., 1991).

Debbie Ford, Spiritual Divorce as a Catalyst for an Extraordinary Life (2001).

David E. Gumpert, Do It Yourself Public Relations. A Success Guide for Lawyers (1995).

Sheila M. Gutterman, Collaborative Law: A New Model for Dispute Resolution (2004).

David Hall, The Spiritual Revitalization of the Legal Profession: A Search for Sacred Rivers (2005).

Rand Jack & Dana Crowley Jack, Moral Vision and Professional Decisions: The Changing Values of Women and Men Lawyers (1989).

Janet R. Johnston & Vivienne Roseby, In the Name of the Child (1998).

Phyllis Beck Kritek, Negotiating at an Uneven Table: A Practical Approach to Working with Difference and Diversity (1994).

George Lakoff & Mark Johnson, Metaphors We Live By (1980).

John Allen Lemmon, Family Mediation Practice (1985).

Julie MacFarlane, The New Lawyer (2007).

Bernard Mayer, Beyond Neutrality: Confronting the Crisis in Conflict Resolution (2004).

Bernard Mayer, The Dynamics of Conflict Resolution: A Practitioner's Guide (2000).

Carrie Menkel-Meadow & Michael Wheeler, What's Fair: Ethics for Negotiators (2004).

Robert H. Mnookin, Scott R. Peppet & Andrew S. Tulumello, Beyond Winning: How Lawyers Help Clients Create Value in Negotiation (1999).

Christopher W. Moore, The Mediation Process: Practical Strategies for Resolving Conflict (2d. ed. 1996).

Forrest S. Mosten, The Complete Guide to Mediation (1997).

Kerry Patterson, Joseph Grenny, Ron McMillan & Al Switzler, Crucial Conversations: Tools for Talking When the Stakes Are High (2002).

Richard W. Shields, Judith P. Ryan & Victoria L. Smith, Collaborative Family Law: Another Way to Resolve Family Disputes (2003).

MARJORIE SILVER, ED., THE AFFECTIVE ASSISTANCE OF COUNSEL: PRACTICING LAW AS A HEALING PROFESSION (2007).

DENNIS P. STOLLE, DAVID B. WEXLER & BRUCE J. WINICK, PRACTICING THERAPEUTIC JURISPRUDENCE: LAW AS A HELPING PROFESSION (2000).

DOUGLAS STONE, BRUCE PATTON & SHEILA HEEN, DIFFICULT CONVERSATIONS: HOW TO DISCUSS WHAT MATTERS MOST (1999).

DEBORAH TANNEN, THE ARGUMENT CULTURE—MOVING FROM DEBATE TO DIALOGUE (1998).

PAULINE TESLER, J.D. & PEGGY THOMPSON, PH.D., COLLABORATIVE DIVORCE: THE REVOLUTIONARY NEW WAY TO RESTRUCTURE YOUR FAMILY, RESOLVE LEGAL ISSUES, AND MOVE ON WITH YOUR LIFE (2006).

PAULINE H. TESLER, COLLABORATIVE LAW: ACHIEVING EFFECTIVE RESOLUTION IN DIVORCE WITHOUT LITIGATION (American Bar Association, 2001).

WILLIAM URY, JEANNE M. BRETT & STEPHEN B. GOLDBERG, GETTING DISPUTES RESOLVED: DESIGNING SYSTEMS TO CUT THE COSTS OF CONFLICT (1988).

WILLIAM URY, GETTING PAST NO: NEGOTIATING YOUR WAY FROM CONFRONTATION TO COOPERATION (1991).

DIANE VAUGHAN, UNCOUPLING (1986).

JUDITH S. WALLERSTEIN & SANDRA BLAKESLEE, WHAT ABOUT THE KIDS? RAISING YOUR CHILDREN BEFORE, DURING AND AFTER DIVORCE (2003).

JUDITH S. WALLERSTEIN & JOAN BERLIN KELLY, SURVIVING THE BREAKUP: HOW CHILDREN AND PARENTS COPE WITH DIVORCE (1980).

STUART G. WEBB & RONALD D. OUSKY, THE COLLABORATIVE WAY TO DIVORCE: THE REVOLUTIONARY METHOD THAT RESULTS IN LESS STRESS, LOWER COSTS, AND HAPPIER KIDS—WITHOUT GOING TO COURT (2006).

DUDLEY WEEKS, THE EIGHT ESSENTIAL STEPS TO CONFLICT RESOLUTION: PRESERVING RELATIONSHIPS AT WORK, AT HOME, AND IN THE COMMUNITY (1992).

JOHN WINSLADE & GERALD MONK, NARRATIVE MEDIATION: A NEW APPROACH TO CONFLICT RESOLUTION (2001).

Websites and Web Pages

http://collaborativedivorcenewsblog.com: Pauline Tesler's collaborative divorce blog, including news items, articles, web links, and information about her schedule.

www.teslercollaboration.com: website for Tesler, Sandmann & Fishman law firm, including links, informational materials, and audio and video clips about collaborative law and collaborative divorce.

www.collaborativepracticesfbay.com: San Francisco Bay Area Collaborative Law Group website.

www.collaborativepractice.com: International Academy of Collaborative Professionals website for clients and members.

www.collaborativedivorcebook.com: excerpts from *Collaborative Divorce* by Tesler & Thompson, and video interview with authors.

Client Handout

Collaborative Divorce Handbook

Your Choices for Professional Legal Help with Ending a Marriage or Domestic Partnership

By Pauline H. Tesler

©2001, 2008, American Bar Association

1. What are my choices for professional help in my divorce or domestic partnership dissolution?

All separations and divorces involve a multitude of decisions and choices. Which professionals you select to assist you, and how you make use of their help, will surely affect how smooth a transition you and your spouse or partner are able to make from couple to single.

Some couples who communicate well and have no challenging financial or parenting issues can resolve all matters without any professional assistance at all, and then can go on to process their own divorce papers themselves through the courts. On the other end of the spectrum, some couples engage in drawn-out courtroom battles that cost dearly in emotional and financial resources and can take a very long time to complete. Most people's separations and divorces fall between these extremes.

Below are the choices for obtaining professional legal help during a separation or divorce. These options are available in most localities today. The list moves from choices involving the least degree of professional intervention and the most privacy and personal control, to choices involving far greater professional intervention and the least privacy and control. [The rest of this handbook will use the term "divorce," but the information about dispute resolution choices applies as well to the dissolution of nonmarital intimate partnerships and to certain other matters such as probate disputes, negotiating prenuptial agreements, and independent adoptions.]

> *a. Unbundled Legal Assistance:* People who choose this model act as their own "general contractor" and take primary responsibility for their own divorce, consulting with lawyers on an "as-needed" basis to get help in resolving specific issues, drafting papers, and so forth. The lawyer doesn't take over responsibility for managing the entire divorce. If you choose an "unbundled" divorce, your lawyer's role will be limited to providing the specific advice and help you ask for. You could also consult with more than one lawyer, or a mediator, in an "unbundled" approach. You could get help from your accountant—or you could do it all yourself.
>
> Just because you prefer an "unbundled" divorce does not necessarily mean your spouse will make the same choice. Consequently, in an unbundled

divorce you could be representing yourself with only occasional guidance from a lawyer, while a lawyer handled everything for your spouse in a conventional "take full charge" manner. This would put you at a disadvantage in negotiating solutions to disagreements.

b. Mediation: A single neutral person, who may be a lawyer, a mental health professional, a financial consultant, or simply someone with an interest in mediation, acts as the mediator for and with the couple. The mediator helps the couple reach agreement, but does not give individual legal advice, and may or may not prepare the divorce agreement. Very few mediators will process the divorce itself through the court system; you'd have to do that yourself or hire a lawyer to do it. Retaining your own lawyer to give you independent legal advice throughout a mediation is wise, and most good mediators recommend this. Waiting to secure independent legal advice until late in a mediation often causes difficulties. It is generally better for both spouses to have that legal advice available from the start. In some locales the two lawyers (yours and your spouse's) sit in on the mediation process, and in other locales they remain outside the mediation process, meeting privately with their own client to give legal advice. Either way, in a mediation, you and your partner should expect to negotiate face-to-face, directly, with the mediator's assistance. The two lawyers ordinarily do not take an active role in a mediation.

Mediators do not have to have to be licensed professionals in most jurisdictions, and in many jurisdictions mediation is not regulated by law. There are many approaches to mediation, all the way from something resembling a court-annexed settlement conference, to "anything goes–whatever works." In other words, each mediator has his or her own way of conducting mediation and there is no generally agreed upon set of rules, standards, or authorities that inform potential clients in advance exactly what kind of mediation is going to be provided by a particular mediator.

While mediation can work very well for motivated couples with emotional maturity and a shared desire to reach agreement, it can be challenging for many people to negotiate in this way face-to-face with a partner during the turmoil of ending an intimate relationship—especially where emotions run high, communications are difficult, or the playing field is uneven for other reasons.

c. Collaborative Law (also called "Collaborative Divorce" or "Collaborative Practice"): Each person retains his or her own trained collaborative lawyer to advise and assist in negotiating an agreement on all issues. All negotiations take place in "four-way" settlement meetings that both spouses and both lawyers attend; the lawyers never negotiate terms of settlement except with both clients present and participating. The lawyers cannot go to court or even threaten to go to court. Settlement is the only agenda. If either spouse chooses to go to court, both collaborative lawyers must withdraw, and both partners must retain new lawyers for the litigation process. Each spouse has built-in legal advice and advocacy at all times during negotiations, and each lawyer's job includes guiding his or her own client toward constructive behavior aimed at reasonable resolutions. Ordinarily the process proceeds in predictable structured stages that move through information gathering and goal setting to brainstorming and resolution. The legal advice is an integral part of the process, and your lawyer is always at your side helping and advising you, but all the decisions are made by you and your partner. The lawyers prepare and process all papers required for the divorce. Most people who choose collaborative divorce reach a full settlement agreement resolving all issues. Collaborative lawyers are fully licensed like other divorce lawyers, and are bound by all ethical and other rules for the practice of law. In addition, some states have statutes defining collaborative law, and there are international standards for the practice of collaborative law.

d. Interdisciplinary Collaborative Divorce: In many communities, there is the additional option of working with a collaborative divorce team, which includes not only two collaborative lawyers, but also a neutral financial consultant and two specially trained divorce coaches who teach communications skills, how to manage strong emotions, and how to build a parenting plan that meets the needs of the children, if any. The children's voice is brought into the coaching process by a child specialist who can explain how the divorce is affecting the children and what their concerns and needs may be, in ways parents can hear. This team approach allows the right professional with the right training and skills to step forward and assist with problems as they arise in the divorce and settlement negotiations. Surprisingly enough, this approach is very cost effective, because it does not ask lawyers to do work they are untrained for and that they therefore will do less efficiently and at a higher fee. There are international standards for the collaborative mental health and financial professionals who work on a collaborative divorce team. People who choose the collaborative divorce team approach have the best configuration of coordinated professional help during their divorce process that is currently available.

e. Conventional Representation: Each person hires any lawyer they choose, without any agreements in place between the spouses about how the legal divorce process will be handled or how they would like negotiations to be conducted. One or both lawyers may be good at settling cases, in which case the lawyers will at some point explore the possibilities for settlement—usually with their clients not present. In most instances the two lawyers also will be preparing your case for trial, right from the start. If the lawyers are not particularly good at, or interested in, settling the case, the lawyers' efforts will be aimed exclusively at preparing for trial, and settlement discussions may not begin until the trial date is close.

When you choose conventional representation, the pacing and objectives of your divorce process will tend to be dictated by what happens in court. There will be court timelines to meet, court paperwork rules to satisfy, and court appearances to make; and lawyers working in this manner generally limit their efforts both in court and in settlement negotiations to those matters about which local judges are permitted to make orders. Regardless of how the lawyers conduct themselves, it is a fact that most divorce matters (most lawyers estimate over 90 percent) do eventually end in a settlement, but these settlements too often occur at or near the time of trial, after considerable expense and ill will (and collateral damage to children) have been generated. Cases handled in a conventional manner often involve higher legal fees, and take longer to complete, than collaborative cases or mediated cases. The risk of a high-conflict divorce is higher than with mediation or collaborative divorce, as is the risk that "quick fix" settlements brokered close to the time of trial will be unsatisfactory and will lead to further conflict after the divorce judgment has been entered.

f. Arbitration, Private Judging, and Case Management: In some jurisdictions it is possible for divorcing couples and their lawyers to choose private judges or arbitrators who will be given the power to make some or all decisions for the couple, as an alternative to taking unresolved disputes into the public courts. While this approach permits the lawyers and their clients greater control over *who* will make the decisions and over *some* procedural rules, the decision-making process itself is not really very different from what a judge would do in court. Nor is the behavior of the lawyers: each spouse's lawyer tries to persuade the arbitrator or private judge that his or her client should win on all disputed issues; the kind of evidence that can be presented is highly restricted; and the judge decides the outcome.

Case management is an option that is sometimes available from private and some public judges. With case management, the judge is given greater power than judges ordinarily may have to streamline the procedural stages of pretrial preparation as well as settlement conferences.

These options can reduce the financial cost and delays associated with litigation in the public courts. The financial and emotional costs may still remain high, however, because positions still are likely to be polarized by the lawyers' trial-focused advocacy methods. When these methods are used, neither the lawyers nor the clients make a commitment to settlement as the goal, and the lawyers continue to represent the client whether the case settles or goes to trial. There are no built-in incentives or agreements in this approach that would encourage the lawyers to help you and your spouse reach an early settlement that both of you find acceptable.

g. "War": If one or both spouses are motivated primarily by strong emotion (fear, anger, guilt, grief, etc.) it can be very difficult to keep a realistic perspective on the divorce process, and it can be perilously easy to fall into extreme black-and-white thinking and look to the courts for revenge or validation. In this situation, reasonable accommodations become impossible. The lawyers for people who have declared war on one another often function as "alter egos" for these clients, acting as gladiators or hired guns instead of serving as wise counselors who help their clients arrive at sensible solutions. Such cases can drag on for many years. Few clients report satisfaction with the outcome of cases handled this way, regardless of who "won," and appeals and motions aimed at persuading the judge to change the orders that were issued after trial are commonplace, sometimes continuing for years after the divorce judgment is entered. This is the costliest form of conflict resolution, emotionally and financially. It is always destructive for the children involved—and often for the adults as well.

2. Can you say more about Collaborative Law?

Collaborative law is the newest divorce conflict-resolution model. It has been available in North America since 1990 and as of 2008 is being offered in 18 countries. In collaborative law, both spouses retain separate, specially trained lawyers whose only job is to help them arrive at an agreement that satisfactorily resolves the concerns most important to each of them—whether or not a judge has the power to issue orders about those concerns. If the lawyers do not succeed in helping the clients reach resolution, the lawyers are out of a job and can never act on behalf of either client in court proceedings against the other. All participants agree to work together respectfully, honestly, and in good faith to try to find acceptable solutions to the legitimate needs and concerns of both spouses and any children. Four creative minds work together to devise individualized settlement scenarios. Whatever matters to you and to your spouse, in terms of goals, priorities, and facts, will be brought to the table in a constructive way. The lawyers are responsible for keeping the process respectful and efficient, and for guiding the negotiations in a systematic, step-by-step manner that incorporates legal advice without giving the law more power over final solutions than it deserves. The couple themselves are in charge of all decisions. No one may go to court, or even threaten to do so, while the collaborative process is moving forward, and if either spouse decides to take matters to court, the collaborative process terminates and both lawyers are barred from any further involvement in the case. Lawyers hired for a collaborative representation can never under any circumstances go to court for the clients who retained them. Their job is to work 100 percent of the time toward a goal that everyone participating has identified as their sole purpose: a complete, satisfactory resolution of all issues, entirely outside the court system.

3. So, Collaborative Law is a kind of mediation?

No. Collaborative law is a cousin to mediation but it differs from mediation in ways that can be very important to a divorcing couple. In mediation, one neutral professional helps the parties try to resolve their issues face to face. While divorce mediation works very well for couples who cooperate well and whose goal is to reach a quick settlement agreement with a minimum of conflict and expense, and while many mediators are gifted and dedicated conflict-resolution professionals, mediation lacks the structural elements that make Collaborative Law so effective.

For instance, mediation can be difficult where the parties are not on a level playing field with one another, because a neutral mediator cannot give either party legal advice and cannot help either side advocate its position. If one spouse or the other becomes unreasonable or stubborn, or lacks negotiating skill, or is emotionally distraught or passive-aggressive, the mediation will become unbalanced or stalled, and if the mediator tries to deal with the problem, the mediator may be seen by one partner or the other as biased, whether or not that is so. If the mediator does not find a way to deal with these problems, the mediation can break down, or the agreement that results can be unfair. If there are lawyers for the parties, they are not necessarily present at the negotiations and their advice may come too late to be helpful. The lawyers are not required to sign agreements that they will not take matters to court, and so their role is not necessarily supportive of working harder to find a negotiated solution when difficulties arise in a mediation.

Collaborative Law was designed to deal with these problems, while maintaining the same absolute commitment to settlement as the sole agenda. Each side has legal advice and advocacy built in at all times during the collaborative process. Even if one party or the other lacks negotiating skill or financial understanding, or is emotionally upset or angry, the playing field can be leveled by the direct participation of the skilled legal advocates. In addition, collaborative lawyers can work in teams with the other collaborative divorce professionals (coaches, child specialists, financial consultants) to provide even greater support for reaching effective resolution. It is the job of the collaborative lawyers to work with their own clients if either or both are being unreasonable, to make sure that the process stays positive and productive. This is not part of the job description for lawyers in any other conflict-resolution mode, including mediation.

4. Is Collaborative Law only for divorces?

Collaborative lawyers can do everything that a conventional family lawyer does except go to court. They can negotiate nonmarital custody, parenting, and access agreements, premarital and postnuptial agreements, and agreements terminating gay and lesbian relationships. Collaborative Law can also be used in probate conflicts, business partnership dissolutions, employment and commercial conflicts, and much more. In fact, it is appropriate in any situation in which the parties who have issues to resolve all want a contained, creative, civilized process that builds in legal advice and counsel, aims solely at settlement, and distributes the risk of failure to the lawyers as well as the clients. But it is important that both collaborative lawyers be well-trained and know how to work effectively together in managing the collaborative negotiations. This is a special skill that needs to be learned.

5. How is Collaborative Law different from the traditional adversarial divorce process?

- In Collaborative Law, all participate in an open, honest exchange of information. There is no "hide the ball."
- In Collaborative Law, neither party takes advantage of the miscalculations or mistakes of the others, but instead identifies and corrects them.
- In Collaborative Law, both parties insulate their children from their conflicts. If coming up with the right shared parenting plan is challenging, they avoid the professional custody evaluation process, instead making use of specially trained coaches and a child-development specialist to arrive at solutions that both parents can accept, solutions that reflect the children's needs and concerns.
- Both parties in Collaborative Law use joint accountants, appraisers, and other advisors, instead of adversarial experts.
- In Collaborative Law, a respectful, creative effort to meet the legitimate needs and concerns of both spouses replaces tactical bargaining backed by threats of litigation. The focus is on constructive planning for the future rather than redress for past grievances.
- In Collaborative Law, agreements can address any matters of importance to the parties, regardless of whether a judge has the power to issue orders on the subject.
- In Collaborative Law, the lawyers must guide the process to settlement or withdraw from further participation, unlike adversarial lawyers and traditional consulting lawyers in a mediation, who remain involved whether the couple settles all issues or goes to trial.
- In Collaborative Law, there is parity of payment to each lawyer so that neither spouse's access to legal advice and counsel is disadvantaged compared to the other by lack of funds, a frequent problem in adversarial litigation.

DIVORCE: COLLABORATIVE VS. LITIGATION

	Collaborative	Litigation
Who Controls the Process	You and your spouse control the process and make final decisions	Judge controls process and makes final decisions
Degree of Opposition	You and your spouse pledge mutual respect and openness	Court process is based on an adversarial system
Cost	Costs are manageable, usually less expensive than litigation; team model is financially efficient in use of experts	Costs are unpredictable, can escalate rapidly, and can continue after trial in post-judgment litigation
Timetable	You and your spouse create the timetable	Judge sets the timetable, often with delays resulting from crowded court calendars
Use of Outside Experts	Jointly retained specialists provide information and guidance, helping you and your spouse develop informed, mutually beneficial solutions	Separate experts are hired to support the litigants' positions, often at great expense to both parties
Involvement of Lawyers	Your lawyers work toward a mutually created settlement	Lawyers fight to win, but someone loses
Privacy	The process and discussion or negotiation details are kept private	In many jurisdictions, dispute becomes a matter of public record and sometimes media attention
Facilitation of Communication	Team of collaborative practice specialists educate and assist you and your spouse to communicate more effectively with each other	No process designed to facilitate communication
Voluntary vs. Mandatory	Voluntary	Mandatory if no agreement
Lines of Communication	You and your spouse communicate directly with the assistance of members of your team	You and your spouse negotiate through your lawyers
Court Involvement	Outside court	Court-based

Source: International Academy of Collaborative Professionals.

6. What kind of information and documents are available in the Collaborative Law negotiations?

Both spouses and their lawyers commit in writing to disclose all documents and information that a fully informed decision maker would want to know about before reaching agreement. The information is exchanged early and voluntarily and is updated regularly. "Hide the ball" and stonewalling are not permitted. Both lawyers stake their professional integrity on helping their clients make full, early, voluntary disclosure of necessary information. Collaborative lawyers will not continue to represent a party who refuses to make necessary disclosures. The information-gathering phase of a collaborative divorce continues until all questions have been answered. Unlike "quick fix" settlement approaches, in Collaborative Law we defer considering options for settlement until the information-gathering and goal-setting phases are complete. For this reason, decisions in the collaborative process typically are based on more and better information than in other conflict-resolution processes, resulting in settlements that are more thorough and durable.

7. What happens if one side or the other does play "hide the ball" or is dishonest in some way, or misuses the Collaborative Law process to take advantage of the other party?

That can happen. There are no guarantees that one's rights will be protected if a participant in the collaborative process acts in bad faith. There also are no guarantees about that in mediation or conventional legal representation. What is different about collaborative law is that the collaborative agreement requires a lawyer to withdraw or even terminate the process upon becoming aware that his or her client is behaving in less than good faith.

For instance, if documents are altered or withheld, or if a spouse is deliberately delaying matters for economic or other gain, the collaborative lawyers have promised in advance that they will not continue to represent the client. The same is true if a spouse fails to keep agreements made during the course of negotiations— for instance, an agreement to consult a vocational counselor, or an agreement to engage in joint parenting counseling. In such a situation, a collaborative lawyer will counsel his or her client to honor the good-faith commitments made at the start, and will not continue to assist a person who declines to do what he or she promised to do. Many collaborative lawyers include in agreements with their own clients that they will terminate the collaborative process if this kind of bad faith should occur. International standards require those who do not terminate the process to withdraw from representing a client who is in bad faith.

8. How do I know whether it is safe for me to work in the Collaborative Law process?

The collaborative process does not guarantee you that every asset or debt or every dollar of income will be disclosed, any more than mediation or the conventional litigation process can guarantee you that. In the end, a dishonest person who works hard to conceal money can sometimes succeed, because the time and expense involved in investigating possible concealed assets is high, and the results are always uncertain at the start. Where there is a well-founded suspicion of concealed assets, Collaborative Law is generally not a good choice, because the methods for tracking concealed assets and income that are employed in conventional litigation might not be available in collaborative law, which relies upon voluntary disclosure. If unanswered questions about assets arise during the information-gathering phase of a collaborative case, the lawyers will keep asking until all the questions are answered. If there

SOME GROUND RULES DURING THE
COLLABORATIVE LAW PROCESS

While you and I cannot control how the other participants conduct themselves in negotiations, we can conduct ourselves in ways that have been proven to increase the chances of reaching agreement. Behaving in this way encourages similar behaviors from your spouse and his or her lawyer.

1. We will take turns speaking and not interrupt each other.
2. We will speak directly to one another rather than about one another, calling each other by our names, not "he" or "she."
3. We will not blame, attack, or engage in put-downs and will ask questions for the purposes of gaining clarity and understanding only, not to score points or win arguments.
4. We will avoid taking hard positions and instead will express ourselves in terms of personal needs and interests and the goals and outcomes we would like to achieve.
5. We will listen carefully and respectfully in order to understand better the other person's needs and interests and will not substitute planning our reply for real listening.
6. We recognize that even if we do not agree, each of us is entitled to respect for his or her own perspective.
7. We will not dwell on things that did not work in the past, but instead will focus on the future we would like to create.
8. We will make a sincere effort to avoid unproductive arguing, venting, and narratives, and we agree to work at all times during negotiations toward the most constructive and mutually acceptable agreement possible.
9. We will speak up if something is not working well in negotiations.
10. We will request a break when we need one, and will not remain at the negotiating table in a state of mind that is inconsistent with constructive problem-solving efforts.
11. While in negotiations, we will refrain from preemptive maneuvers, threats, ultimatums, and unilateral power plays.
12. We will take good physical and emotional care of ourselves so that each of us can participate fully and effectively in resolving our issues.

(Adapted from ground rules in wide use in the San Francisco Bay Area originally drafted by the Collaborative Council of the Redwood Empire.)

remain unanswered questions, either a neutral expert must be empowered to investigate and find satisfactory answers, or the process should terminate so that both parties can be represented by traditional lawyers.

You are generally the best judge of your spouse or partner's basic honesty. If you have confidence in your partner's basic honesty, then the process can be a good choice for you. If she would lie on an income tax return, she is probably not a good candidate for a Collaborative Law divorce, because the necessary honesty would be lacking. (Of course, she will be just as dishonest no matter what conflict-resolution option you choose. Surprisingly, some people who know they married a thoroughly dishonest spouse still prefer the cost-containment, direct negotiations, conflict management advantages, and wide open scope for settlement options that are characteristic in collaborative law.) The choice ultimately is yours. Discuss it with your lawyer.

9. How often do Collaborative Law cases fail to reach agreement?

We do not yet have large-scale studies about the percentage of collaborative cases that reach full settlement agreements, but collaborative lawyers who have been doing this work since the mid 1990's report that only about 5 percent of their collaborative cases terminate without a full settlement agreement. Some less experienced collaborative lawyers estimate as many as 10 to 15 percent of their collaborative cases end without reaching a full agreement. In other words, our best estimate is that overall roughly 9 out of 10 couples who choose Collaborative Law succeed in their goal of reaching a full settlement agreement in the collaborative process. There is of course no guarantee that any specific couple will be able to reach a full agreement in the collaborative process. But if both of you have a serious commitment to reaching a reasonable and civilized resolution, and understand the need to work constructively toward solutions, and if both of you choose capable collaborative lawyers who know how to work effectively together, there is every reason to expect success.

10. Is Collaborative Law the best choice for me?

It isn't for every person (or every lawyer), but it is worth considering if some or all of these are true for you:

- You are willing to work toward a civilized, respectful, lasting resolution of the issues rather than leaping toward a "quick fix."
- You care about the other person's needs and concerns sufficiently to seek solutions that might work for both of you, rather than always reaching for the biggest piece of the pie for yourself alone, on every issue.
- You would like to keep open the possibility of friendship with your partner down the road.
- You and your partner will be co-parenting children together and you want the best co-parenting relationship possible.
- You want to protect your children from the harm associated with litigated conflict resolution between parents.
- You and your partner have adult children together and recognize that they and any grandchildren will benefit when parents work toward a "good divorce."
- You and your partner have a circle of friends or extended family in common that you both want to remain connected to
- You have ethical or spiritual beliefs that place high value on taking personal responsibility for handling conflicts with integrity.
- You value privacy in your personal affairs and do not want details of your problems to be available in the public court record.
- You value control and autonomous decision making and do not want to hand over decisions about restructuring your financial and/or parenting future to a stranger (i.e., a judge).

- You recognize the restricted range of outcomes and rough, "cookie-cutter" justice generally available in the court system, and want a more creative and individualized range of choices available to you and your spouse or partner for resolving your issues.
- You prefer aiming for your best hopes rather than your worst fears in resolving divorce-related problems.
- You and your spouse are willing to devote your intelligence and energy toward creative problem solving rather than toward recriminations or revenge—fixing the problem rather than fixing blame.

Remember that you and your spouse or partner can have different reasons for choosing Collaborative Law. Talk with a collaborative lawyer, and suggest that your spouse do the same, for advice about whether it is worth considering in your situation. Visit www.collaborativepractice.com, www.teslercollaboration.com, and www.collaborativedivorcebook.com for more in-depth information about Collaborative Law and interdisciplinary team collaborative divorce.

11. My lawyer says she settles most of her cases. How is Collaborative Law different from what she does when she settles cases in a conventional family law practice?
Any experienced collaborative lawyer will tell you that there is a big difference between a settlement that is negotiated during the pressure and stress of a conventional litigation process, and a settlement that takes place in the context of a collaborative agreement that there will be no unilateral court proceedings or even the threat of court. Most conventional family law cases do eventually settle—but they reach settlement figuratively, if not literally, "on the courthouse steps." By that time, a great deal of money has been spent, and a great deal of emotional damage has often been caused. The settlements are reached under conditions of tension and anxiety, and both "buyer's remorse" and "seller's remorse" are common. Moreover, the settlements are reached in the shadow of trial, and for that reason they are generally constrained by what the lawyers believe the judge in the case is likely to do. The lawyers broker the terms of agreement, with the parties rarely if ever discussing solutions directly. The lawyers have a great deal of influence over what is treated as important, what is regarded as dispensable, and what solutions should and should not be recommended to their clients.

What happens in a typical Collaborative Law settlement could hardly be more different. The process is geared from the first to encourage creative, respectful collective problem solving. In a collaborative divorce, the people who will have to live with the solutions discuss them directly with one another, and they say "yes" only when the results look fully workable and satisfactory in light of all the facts and all the priorities and concerns. They are taught how to communicate clearly and listen respectfully. The lawyers discourage hasty resolution, instead urging their clients to wait until all information has been shared and all options have been considered, so that the final decisions about settlement reflect real resolution, not a quick fix.

Conventional "courthouse steps" settlements often fail to resolve the underlying concerns of either party, with both spouses leaving the settlement process frustrated and dissatisfied. In contrast, collaborative settlement agreements usually have lasting power because of that careful attention given every step of the way to reaching real resolution.

12. Why is Collaborative Law such an effective settlement process?

Because the collaborative lawyers have a completely different state of mind about their job than traditional lawyers generally bring to their work. We call it a "paradigm shift." Instead of being dedicated to getting the largest possible piece of the pie for their own client, no matter what the collateral human damage or financial cost, collaborative lawyers aim to help their clients achieve their best intentions for themselves and their children in their restructured families after the divorce.

Collaborative lawyers do not act as hired guns, nor do they take advantage of mistakes inadvertently made by the other side, nor do they threaten, or insult, or focus on the negative either in their own clients or on the other side. They expect and encourage the highest good-faith problem-solving behavior from their own clients and themselves, and they stake their own professional integrity on delivering that, in any collaborative representation they participate in.

Collaborative lawyers trust one another. They spend a great deal of their own time and money learning how to build effective working relationships with other collaborative lawyers, how to manage conflict, and how to guide negotiations effectively in collaborative cases. Like all lawyers, they still owe a primary allegiance and duty to their own clients, within all mandates of professional responsibility, but they know that the only way they can serve the interests of their clients who have selected Collaborative Law is to behave with, and demand, the highest integrity from themselves, their clients, and the other participants in the collaborative process.

Collaborative Law by its very structure offers a potential for creative problem solving that does not exist in the structure for either mediation or litigation, in that only Collaborative Law puts two lawyers in the same room pulling in the same direction with both clients to solve the same set of problems, without threats or ultimatums, using an agreed and highly structured good-faith process. Lawyers excel at solving problems, but in conventional litigation the adversarial nature of court-based conflict resolution encourages even the best family lawyers to pull in opposite directions for maximum economic and other advantage to one side without regard for the impact on the other spouse or the children. In Collaborative Law, the very structure of the process means that neither collaborative lawyer can succeed in the job they were both hired to do unless both of the lawyers can work together effectively to help their clients find solutions that both clients consider satisfactory. This is the special characteristic of collaborative law that is found in no other conflict-resolution process.

13. What if my spouse and I can reach agreement on almost everything, but there is one point on which we are stuck? Would we have to lose our collaborative lawyers and go to court?

In that situation it is possible under some circumstances, if everyone agrees (both lawyers and both clients), to submit just that one issue for decision by an arbitrator or private judge. We do this infrequently, and only with important limitations and safeguards built in, so that the integrity of the Collaborative Law process is not undermined. Everyone must agree that the good-faith atmosphere of the Collaborative Law process would not be damaged by submitting the issue for third-party decision, and everyone must agree on the issue and on who will be the decision maker.

Over the years, collaborative lawyers have found that if a couple can agree on all those procedural safeguards, then with a little more effort they almost always can also find a way to reach agreement themselves on the issue that is dividing them. For that reason, it has become rare to make use of arbitrators or private judges. Instead, most collaborative lawyers prefer to invite either the larger interdisciplinary collaborative divorce team, or a "super-mediator," into the collaborative four-way process to give the couple the best possible chance for solving their own problems, before resorting to a decision by a third party. After all, even the best judge will have less information about the facts of your own situation than you and your spouse have available in a collaborative divorce, and even the best judge lacks the time and the personal stake in outcome that you and your spouse can bring to the collaborative negotiating table. Judges have no magic, and they are the first to admit that their decisions are rarely if ever better than the ones couples arrive at themselves.

14. What if my spouse or partner chooses a lawyer who doesn't know about Collaborative Law?
Most collaborative lawyers—for very good reasons—will refuse to sign a Collaborative Law agreement if the other lawyer has no training in how to practice Collaborative Law. The success of the process depends on not just your lawyer, but your partner's lawyer as well. Most collaborative lawyers agree that working with an untrained lawyer involves an unacceptably high risk that the process will terminate without an agreement. This is because untrained lawyers lack essential skills and understandings, and have not yet built the necessary trust-based working relationships with other collaborative lawyers. They just don't know how to do the job.

Trust between the lawyers is essential for the Collaborative Law process to work at its best. Unless the lawyers can rely on one another's representations about full disclosure, for example, there can be too little protection against dishonesty by a party. If your lawyer lacks confidence that the other lawyer will withdraw from representing a dishonest client, it would be risky for you to sign on to a formal Collaborative Law process because you might agree to settlement terms based on false or incomplete information, or you might lose your lawyer if the Collaborative Law process fails because of lack of disclosure.

Similarly, Collaborative Law demands special skills from the lawyers—skills in guiding negotiations, and in managing conflict. They must have shared understandings about how the collaborative divorce will be handled: what will happen, and when, and how difficulties will be managed. These understandings and skills are quite different from what lawyers learn in law school and in the courts, and they can be developed only through training and experience. Without them, a lawyer would have a hard time working effectively in a Collaborative Law negotiation.

This doesn't mean your lawyer could not work cordially or cooperatively outside the collaborative process with an untrained lawyer, but caution is advised in signing the formal agreements that are the heart of Collaborative Law with an untrained lawyer representing your spouse. You and your spouse will get the best results by hiring two lawyers who both can show that they have committed to learning how to practice Collaborative Law at a high standard by obtaining training as well as experience in this new way of helping clients through divorce. You would not hire a dentist to perform open-heart surgery, and you would not want a litigator undertaking collaborative law.

15. Why is it so important to sign on formally to the official Collaborative Law Agreement? Why can't you work collaboratively with the other lawyer but still go to court if the process doesn't work?
There are two important reasons why the signed agreement that the lawyers can never go to court is the essential core element of a Collaborative Law representation.

One has to do with how clients behave, and the other has to do with how lawyers behave.

Effective collaborative negotiations and problem solving happen when both spouses and both lawyers recognize that although they are not on the same side, they are working toward one and the same goal. When that happens, the four people at the collaborative table become a problem-solving team, and remarkable solutions can be reached. But it's not easy for divorcing spouses to relax in the presence of one another, and when each has their own lawyer, suspicion and fear about hidden agendas can be a negative force that works against finding the best solutions. If you worry that your spouse's lawyer may have a secret intention to go to trial, or to use your words against you later, you are not likely to feel very comfortable about sharing information about what really matters to you in the divorce. This is the situation that exists in conventional settlement negotiations, either actually or potentially. But, when each spouse knows that the other lawyer cannot ever go to court as an adversary (which is the starting point in a Collaborative Law case), the climate at the negotiating table generally turns positive in a way that simply does not occur in conventional negotiations, where the lawyer across the table could at any time become your adversary in the courtroom. Settlements can and do happen all the time, even when lawyers can take matters to court, but the quality of both process and outcome in those cases just doesn't reach the high level that routinely exists in Collaborative Law.

Traditional lawyers have adversarial habits that they've applied in and out of courtrooms for so long that it is difficult for them even to see that those habits exist. Changing those habits of thought and behavior is not easy. When the lawyers can still take a problem to court as a fallback option when negotiations stall, their creative problem-solving capacity is actually crippled. This is because lawyers are impatient by nature, placing a premium on efficiency, and they are entirely comfortable in the conflict-ridden atmosphere of courts and trials. It is common for negotiations to hit rough spots, even in a collaborative divorce. When there is an apparent impasse in negotiations, lawyers who can go to court will probably do so, while collaborative lawyers simply roll up their sleeves and work harder. In other words, lawyers who can go to court tend to end negotiations much sooner than good collaborative lawyers do. When the lawyers cannot go to court, an apparent impasse liberates the creative problem solver within, motivating collaborative lawyers to help their clients find their own way through impasse. And finding their own solutions is what clients who choose Collaborative Law want.

When everyone at the negotiating table knows that it is up to the four of them and only the four of them to think their way through impasse to a solution or else the process fails and these lawyers are out of the picture, the special hypercreativity of Collaborative Law can be triggered. The moment when each person realizes that finding solutions for both parties' concerns is the responsibility of all four participants at the table is the moment when the magic can happen. When a divorcing couple finds their own solutions together, they almost always are more satisfied than when a solution—even the very same solution—is imposed on them by someone else.

Collaborative Law is not just two lawyers who like each other, or who agree to behave nicely, trying to settle cases. It is a special technique that demands special talents and procedures in order to work as promised. Any effort by parties and their lawyers to resolve conflicts cooperatively outside court is to be encouraged, but only Collaborative Law is Collaborative Law.

16. Why would a Collaborative Law case end in termination rather than in agreement?

While we lack formal research that could answer this question definitively, experienced collaborative lawyers report that when their cases terminate without an agreement, it is generally for one of these reasons:

- An inexperienced or ineffective collaborative lawyer is representing one party.
- One or both parties has a significant mental or emotional disability that interferes with constructive problem solving and follow-through.
- One or both parties has anger management or substance abuse problems.
- One or both parties lacked a full and authentic commitment to reaching an acceptable good-faith settlement outside the court system as a high priority.

Few experienced collaborative lawyers identify impasse in negotiations as a reason why Collaborative Law cases terminate.

17. How do I enlist my spouse in the process?

Talk with your spouse, and see whether there is a shared commitment to collaborative conflict resolution. Share materials with your spouse such as websites, this handbook, and books and articles that discuss Collaborative Law and collaborative divorce. If you do not feel comfortable doing this yourself, get help from a mutual friend or trusted counselor, or ask your lawyer to send an information packet. Encourage your spouse to select a lawyer who has experience and training in Collaborative Law and who works effectively with your own lawyer. Lawyers who trust one another are an excellent predictor of success in collaborative conflict resolution.

18. Is Collaborative Law possible if my spouse does not want to hire a lawyer?

No. The Collaborative Law model requires that each of you have a separate, trained collaborative lawyer who signs the agreement not to go to court if the process ends short of a full agreement. If your spouse has no lawyer, there is no one who can advise him or her, ensure that he or she participates constructively in negotiations, and guides the process from your spouse's side of the table. You could still hire a lawyer who might negotiate a settlement directly with your spouse, but it is not Collaborative Law without two collaborative lawyers.

19. How long will my divorce take if I use Collaborative Law?

The Collaborative Law process is flexible and can expand or contract to meet your specific needs. Most people require from four to seven of the four-way negotiating meetings to resolve all issues, though some divorces take less and some take more. You and your lawyer will prepare privately for these four-way meetings and will debrief after them. These meetings can be spaced with long intervals between, or close together, depending on the particular needs of the couple. Once the issues are resolved, the lawyers will complete the paperwork for the divorce. Time limits and requirements for divorce vary from state to state; ask your lawyer.

20. How expensive is Collaborative Law?

Collaborative lawyers generally charge by the hour as do conventional family lawyers. Rates vary from locale to locale and according to the experience of the lawyer.

No one can predict exactly what you will pay for this kind of representation because every case is different. Your issues may be simple or complex; you and your partner may have already reached agreement on most, some, or none, of your issues. You or your spouse may be very precise or very casual in your approach to resolving problems. You and your partner may be at very different emotional stages in coming to terms with separating from one another. You may communicate well with one another, or poorly. You may share many values and priorities for one another and the children after the divorce, or few. What can be said with confidence is that no other kind of professional conflict-resolution assistance can help as broad a range of divorcing couples to move through the divorce process respectfully and to reach high-quality, lasting solutions. While the cost of your own fees cannot be predicted accurately, a rough rule of thumb is that Collaborative Law representation will cost from from one-third to one-fifth as much as being represented conventionally by a lawyer who takes issues in your case to court for resolution.

Although Collaborative Law is efficient and cost-effective as compared to other approaches, it is still costly to retain lawyers and other professional helpers in a divorce, whatever dispute resolution mode you choose. The best reason to choose Collaborative Law isn't to save money, but rather to reach the best possible agreement you and your spouse are capable of devising.

21. Isn't mediation cheaper because only one neutral, instead of two lawyers, has to be paid?

No, mediation is not necessarily cheaper. No professional in a mediation has the job of helping each party separately to participate with maximum effectiveness in the process. Consequently, there can be more risk of a mediation becoming stalled than in Collaborative Law, where each lawyer takes responsibility for bringing his and her client to the four-way table ready to engage in constructive problem solving. The mediator must remain neutral and cannot work privately with the more troubled or uncooperative spouse to get past impasses. When a mediator must deal with difficult personalities, strong emotions, differences in negotiating skill, and other differences that cause a nonlevel playing field, the process can become inefficient and costly.

Also, most mediators strongly advise that independent lawyers for each party review and approve the mediated agreement. If the lawyers have not been a part of the negotiations, the lawyers may be unhappy with the results and a new phase of negotiations or even litigation may result. If the lawyers do participate, then three professionals are being paid in the mediation. The lawyers who serve as independent counsel in a mediation can be any lawyer that either party chooses. Such lawyers do not ordinarily commit to keep matters out of court, may have much or little skill in supporting client-centered resolution, and may sometimes even work at cross purposes to the mediator. Each of these situations involves fees and costs beyond those of the neutral mediator.

It is a false economy to select a conflict-resolution process that turns out to match poorly with your needs. It is not easy to predict in advance which couples will and which will not succeed in reaching full agreement in a mediation. Many people genuinely believe that they will have a very quick and simple divorce negotiation, but life can be surprising. Strong feelings arise unexpectedly; issues become more complicated than anyone anticipated. With Collaborative Law, couples have a process in place from the start that is well-equipped to deal with unexpected problems. Most lawyers with hands-on experience in mediation, traditional representation, and Collaborative Law believe that in most cases Collaborative Law can deal with these happenings more effectively than other conflict-resolution models—particularly since collaborative lawyers often can bring collaborative divorce coaches and financial consultants on as part of the professional team. Their services are brief, targeted, economical, and highly specialized. As a famous psychologist has said, "If the only tool you have is a hammer, all problems will tend to resemble nails." In Collaborative Law you have the best-stocked toolbox that we know of on call for professional help in conflict resolution. In the end, reaching a lasting, high-quality agreement will be more cost effective, when all is considered, than a settlement that doesn't satisfactorily meet the needs of every member of the family.

22. How does the cost of Collaborative Law compare with the cost of litigation?
Litigation is, quite simply, the most expensive way of resolving a conflict. By way of illustration, it is common for litigated divorces to begin with a motion for tempo-rary support. The result is exactly that—a temporary order, like a band-aid, rather than a final resolution of any issues. It is not uncommon for the bills for a single temporary support motion to equal or exceed the lawyers' fees and costs for an entire Collaborative Law representation.

23. How do I find a good collaborative lawyer?
You can do a Google search. You can go to the interactive "find a practitioner" section of the International Academy of Collaborative Professionals' website, www .collaborativepractice.com, which lists trained collaborative lawyers and other col-laborative professionals from 18 nations.

Seek out the best collaborative practitioner that you can locate; interview sev-eral, and ask for resumes. Ask how many collaborative cases the lawyer has han-dled and how many of them terminated without agreements. Ask what training the lawyer has in Collaborative Law, alternate dispute resolution, and conflict man-agement. Ask if the lawyer is a member in good standing of a local collaborative practice group. Above all, make sure that you feel comfortable with the person you select, because he or she will be your advisor and guide through a uniquely stressful and challenging time of life.

24. What can I expect during the collaborative law process?
Generally speaking, you can expect three stages to the collaborative law process. Stage 1 is about making and sustaining your commitments to the collaborative pro-cess. In stage 2, you will share and evaluate information. Finally, in stage 3 you will develop and evaluate options and reach solutions.

These three stages will occur through a series of four-way meetings—you, your lawyer, your spouse, and your spouse's lawyer. Typically, you can expect the fol-lowing during the four-way meetings:

Initial Four-way Meeting:
- Parties and lawyers become acquainted.
- Lawyers explain personal and ethical commitments to collaborative practice.
- Clients explain why they have chosen collaborative divorce and what their highest expectations are for the process.
- Legal divorce process in the jurisdiction is explained.
- Interest-based negotiations and self-determined decision making are dis-cussed and distinguished from conventional negotiations.
- The unique role of collaborative lawyers (guide to negotiations, facilitator of deep resolution, conflict manager, peacemaker) is discussed.
- The role of the law is explained (not a template for decisions; merely a default setting; something to be discussed later rather than sooner).
- Involvement of an interdisciplinary collaborative team is discussed.

What hopes do I and my partner have for ourselves and our children during and after the divorce?

What values and principles will I and my partner be guided by as we each work toward resolving our issues and achieving our goals?

Will I bring my full energy and good faith to the collaborative process? What promises can I make about how I will behave, both when things are going well and when they are not?

STAGE ONE

Making and sustaining your commitment to the collaborative processs (the focus of the first four-way)

To what extent am I determined to understand my partner's goals and priorities as fully as I understand my own?

What do I aim to achieve here? What are my highest and best intentions for myself, my divorcing partner, and my children, if any?

Why am I here? What has brought me to choose collaborative conflict resolution in my divorce?

- What constitutes effective good-faith participation in the process is reviewed:
    - We expect good preparation and follow-through from everyone
    - We plan agendas carefully and stick to them
    - We take homework assignments seriously
    - We honor interim agreements and understandings
    - We do not act unilaterally outside the meetings
    - We confine divorce-related efforts to the collaborative process and don't try to address issues outside meetings
    - We expect constructive, respectful efforts from all participants to devise mutually acceptable solutions
    - We don't hide facts or information and we do not conceal goals and concerns
- Collaborative participation documents are reviewed, discussed, and signed.
- Urgent matters are identified and a process for attending to them is agreed upon.

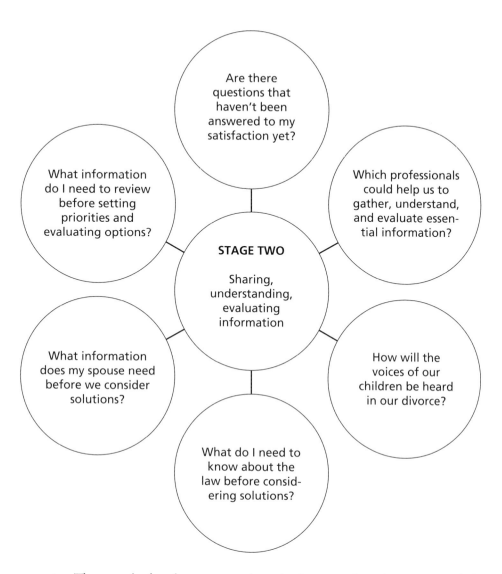

- The agenda for the next meeting, the homework assignments, and the schedule of forthcoming meetings are agreed upon.
- One of the lawyers later prepares and distributes the minutes of the meeting.

Subsequent Four-way Meetings:

- The meeting begins with review of the agenda and minutes of the previous meeting.
- Homework assignments are discussed.
- At the second (and perhaps third and fourth meetings if necessary) documents and financial information are exchanged and discussed.
- Initial divorce petition is filed at an agreed time.
- Goals, priorities, and values are identified and discussed.
- When all financial and other information has been gathered to everyone's satisfaction, we agree on the order in which we will address issues.
- We brainstorm possibilities for creative resolution of each issue.

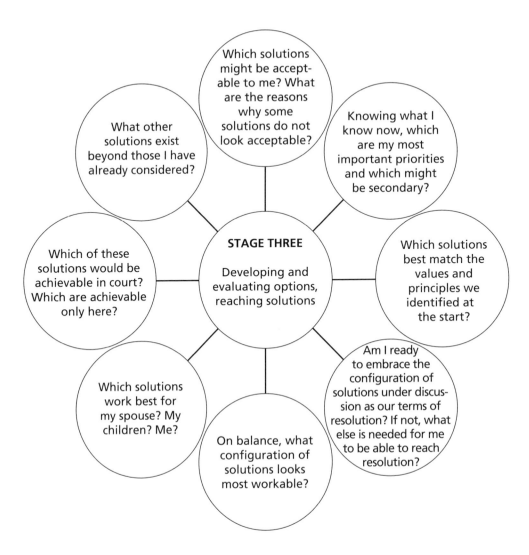

Which solutions might be acceptable to me? What are the reasons why some solutions do not look acceptable?

What other solutions exist beyond those I have already considered?

Knowing what I know now, which are my most important priorities and which might be secondary?

Which of these solutions would be achievable in court? Which are achievable only here?

STAGE THREE

Developing and evaluating options, reaching solutions

Which solutions best match the values and principles we identified at the start?

Which solutions work best for my spouse? My children? Me?

On balance, what configuration of solutions looks most workable?

Am I ready to embrace the configuration of solutions under discussion as our terms of resolution? If not, what else is needed for me to be able to reach resolution?

- We discuss the approaches to resolution that are available to judges as contrasted with the broader range of choices available to the parties in a collaborative process.
- We measure settlement options against the goals and priorities and values of each party.
- We arrive at a framework for resolution of all issues

The Final Four-way Meeting:

- We review, discuss, and sign the settlement agreement and related legal divorce papers.
- We focus on the accomplishments during the process .
- We help both parties anticipate future challenges and plan for collaborative resolution of them.
- We take time to acknowledge a job well done.

25. What can I do to ensure a successful collaborative law process?
You can ensure success by following the 10 collaborative commandments—plus one—throughout the collaborative process.

1. **See conflict as your ally, not your enemy.** Approach it with a constructive and curious attitude and it can help you reach more lasting solutions with your spouse than if it had not arisen. Ignoring differences or trying to force resolutions that fail to address them won't lead to a lasting resolution. Through conflict you can understand the roots of differences, and then look for acceptable ways to address them.

2. **Take personal responsibility–for your feelings, for your behavior, for your attitude.** No one can *make* you feel or do anything. You always have the choice of how you will respond. The lawyers have the responsibility of ensuring a respectful, civilized process but no one is perfect and bad moments can happen. Take a break, and decide how *you* wish to respond given your own personal goals and values. Blaming rarely if ever produces useful results.

3. **Speak up for your own needs, goals, and priorities.** Civility and respect are not the same as rolling over and playing dead. Saying "yes" to keep the peace will not lead to a lasting resolution. Ask for what you need, and not more than you need, and be prepared to explain why you need it. Your lawyer will help you express your needs and goals in clear, firm, constructive ways. In the rare event that no agreement can be devised that is good enough, you always have the option of terminating the collaborative process at any time if you think court is a better option for you.

4. **Pay serious attention to your partner or spouse's needs, goals, priorities, and interests.** Listen carefully. Ask questions to clarify so that you really understand. A full understanding is not the same as agreeing. But it is the doorway to out-of-the-box thinking about creative solutions that could possibly satisfy both you and your partner. You and your lawyer can't do that kind of thinking unless you work hard to understand what might work for your partner.

5. **Make sure every aspect of your own communications with your spouse or partner is constructive, not destructive.** This means not only the obvious aspects—no name calling, no shouting, no sarcasm or blaming. It also means paying attention to the very real but subtle ways that spouses express anger and blame – gestures, raised eyebrows, eye-rolling. And it means not talking about your spouse in the third person when he or she is right there at the table. Speak directly and civilly to him or her. Don't attribute beliefs or motives ("You just want . . ." or "He just thinks that I . . ." or "You always try to . . ."). Instead, express what you yourself think, feel, and want. Statements about yourself ("I don't understand that description of the condition of the roof") are not subject to dispute, while statements about your spouse ("She just wants to drive down the value of the house") generally lead to pointless argument. Please remember that a sentence that begins "I feel that you . . ." is not a statement about yourself.

6. **Bear in mind that you and your partner or spouse may be at very different stages in the emotional journey associated with separation and divorce.** It's both compassionate and smart to understand and respect those differences because they affect not only how you each feel, but also your energy, resil-

ience, and even capacity to think clearly. The person who initiated the divorce will often be further along in grieving and recovering from the loss of the marriage than the partner who didn't expect or want a separation. No one has control over how quickly they move through this grief and recovery process. Counseling helps but the bottom line is that a person who is pushed to go faster in negotiations than they can handle emotionally may need to terminate the collaborative process. It's wise to "make haste slowly" by accepting these timing differences as normal and inevitable and working with them constructively.

7. **Give at least as much—and maybe even more—attention to your own values and principles as you give to your legal rights and entitlements.** For solutions to look as good 10 years from now as they look today they must be congruent with your own personal values and principles. You are not bound by the limits on creative problem solving that the law imposes on judges.

8. **Be careful who you listen to and whose advice you take.** Friends and family who genuinely want to support you during a time of stress can actually behave in ways that undermine your commitment to a constructive, civilized divorce. Sometimes, friends and relatives mistakenly believe that attacking your spouse is the way to show their love for you. Few of them will have first-hand experience of collaborative divorce, while many will hold old beliefs that divorce always means war. It's important not to let their ideas influence you negatively. Tell these people that you appreciate their intentions but you prefer that they not discuss the actual divorce with you. Instead, they can invite you to dinner or give you tickets to the ball game.

9. **Stay focused on the present and future, not the past.** Focus on the past leads to feeling like a victim and looking for a perpetrator to blame. Whatever happened in the past, here you are today. You have complete freedom to decide how you wish to move forward. What you do today shapes the future for yourself and your children, if you have them. Keep your efforts focused on constructive ideas that could achieve your highest and best goals for the future.

10. **Avoid attachment to any one specific solution to an issue.** The best way to resolve an issue that involves differing interests and concerns is to examine a very broad spectrum of options. Be skeptical of any solution that you are already attached to before the collaborative process begins. Put it on a shelf and try to forget about it while you move through the proven steps that lead to wise, lasting solutions: begin with the facts, and with broad values and priorities. Then move to exploring specific interests and goals. Then, brainstorm to expand the range of possible options for resolution—including the one you put on the shelf, as well as many more. Only then is it time to evaluate options to see which of them can best meet the needs and interests you and your spouse have identified. Many people are amazed to discover options that can meet their needs far better than the one they originally put on the shelf.

11. **Be optimistic, stay positive.** Even the most challenging problems can be resolved where both parties share full intention to reach agreement. If you find yourself becoming discouraged or negative, take a break and work on understanding what is at the root of those feelings. Then work with your collaborative lawyer to find a constructive way to address what needs to be attended to.

26. Where can I go for more information?

The literature on the collaborative law process is growing. Below are selected materials for further reading:

Books

Ahrons, Constance, The Good Divorce: Keeping Your Family Together When Your Marriage Comes Apart, 1995.

Fisher, Roger, and Ertel, Danny, Getting Ready to Negotiate: The Getting to Yes Workbook, 1995.

Fisher, Roger, and Ury, William L., Getting to Yes: Negotiating Agreement Without Giving In, 1992.

Gold, Lois, Between Love & Hate: A Guide to Civilized Divorce, 1992.

Ricci, Isolina, Mom's House, Dad's House: Making Shared Custody Work, 1997.

Tesler, Pauline H., and Thompson, Peggy, Collaborative Divorce: The Revolutionary New Way to Restructure Your Family, Resolve Legal Issues, and Move On with Your Life, 2006.

Vaughan, Diane, Uncoupling: Turning Points in Intimate Relationships, 1990.

Wallerstein, Judith S. and Blakeslee, Sandra, What About the Kids? Raising Your Children Before, During, and After Divorce, 2003.

Webb, Stuart, and Ousky, Ron, The Collaborative Way to Divorce: The Revolutionary Method That Results in Less Stress, Lower Costs, and Happier Kids—Without Going to Court, 2006.

E-Book

Sedacca, Rosalind, How Do I Tell the Kids About the Divorce? A Create-a-Storybook™

Guide to Preparing Your Children with Love!, 2007. Downloadable e-book available at www.howdoitellthekids.com.

Web Resources

www.collaborativedivorcebook.com: book website offering excerpts from Tesler and Thompson's book, Collaborative Divorce, including video interview with authors and other resources for people thinking about divorce.

www.collaborativedivorcenews.com: Pauline Tesler's blog, offering news about collaborative divorce and collaborative law worldwide.

www.collaborativepractice.com: the website of the International Academy of Collaborative Professionals, an organization co-founded by Pauline Tesler.

www.collaborativepracticesfbay.com: Pauline Tesler's collaborative practice group, with links to collaborative documents, readings, and other resources for people considering divorce.

www.teslercollaboration.com: the author's website, with information about collaborative law and collaborative divorce, including links to video and audio material.

Index

ABA Committee on Ethics Opinion, 325–327
ABA Model Code, 145
ABA Model Rules, 133
Abney, Sherrie, 200
advice, legal, 69
agenda-setting, 59–60, 63–64, 65–66, 86–87
agreements. *See also* documents
  disqualification. *See* disqualification stipulations
  interim, 68
  participation. *See* participation agreements
  principles and guidelines. *See* principles and guidelines
  retainer, 157–158, 165
  settlement, 136, 139
airline travel metaphor, 312
alternative dispute resolution. *See also* arbitration; mediation
  dispute-resolution, 55, 56, 84, 108
  future disputes, 70, 130
  options under, 103–104
American Bar Association, 132–133
American Institute of Collaborative Professionals. *See* International Academy of Collaborative Professionals
Andrews, Bill, 200
appreciation, 73, 124
attorneys/lawyers
  as advocates, 11

bad faith and, 209
checklist for, 301–303
communicating with, 57, 110–111, 129–131
control by, 44, 46
detaching, 70–71
disqualification of. *See* disqualification stipulations
enthusiasm of, 35
fees. *See* fees
finding, 142
as gladiators, 2, 27–28, 29, 36, 38, 40, 47, 83, 309, 342
legal advice from, 69
mediation for, 100–102
professional responsibility. *See* professional responsibility
qualifications of, 4–5, 14
referring, 108, 176
relationships with, 39
responsibility of, 84. *See also* professional responsibility.
retooling, 27–48
selecting, 14
termination by. *See* termination.
withdrawal of. *See* withdrawal of counsel

bad faith. *See also* good faith
  generally, 12, 14
  secretive, 194, 209
  termination for, 130
bargaining. *See* negotiation
battle metaphors. *See* gladiators

beginner's mind
  environment, 88
  generally, 27, 80
  methods and, 34
  paradigm shift and, 36–37
  retooling and, 37
birthing metaphor, 312
Boyd, Don, 191
Branom, Debra, 200–201, 202
breathing, 46–47, 89, 115
brochures, 176
Burger, Warren, 139
Burke, Edmund, 97

California Family Code, 139
caucuses, 115, 123
ceremony, 72, 124
challenges, 24
children. *See also* custody; support
  development of, 34, 43, 47, 219
  litigation and, 1, 5, 25
  needs of, 32
Churchill, Winston, 171
civil rights litigation, 195
clients
  communication with, 53–63,
    97–107, 129–131, 140–141
  control by, 66
  difficult, 12, 25
  evaluation, 168, 184
  ideal, 98
  initial contact, 53–54, 55, 97–107,
    145
  responsibility of, 31, 39, 40, 56, 64,
    70, 106, 147
  retooling with, 28–30, 38, 39–40
  screening, 98, 99–100, 157
  self-selection, 83–84, 100, 106
  termination by. *See* termination
  types of, 13
collaborative case documents
  abuse of process, 253
  client duties, 251–252
  disqualification by court, 253
  divorce team and, 251
  election for termination, 254
  good faith negotiation, 251–252

  handbook, 339–361
  intervention, 249–250
  lawyer duties, 251–252
  limitations, 250
  new lawyer fees, 255–256
  new lawyer selection, 255–256
  participation, 250–251
  professional fees, 254–255
  retainer agreements, 157–158,
    226–232
  withdrawal of lawyer, 254
commercial practice, 191
communication. *See also* language
  basic skills, 107
  with clients, 53–63, 97–107,
    129–131, 140–141
  in letters, 121
  listening, 36, 39, 107, 121
  meta-messages, 34, 39
  with other attorneys, 57, 110–111,
    117–118
  with other professionals, 111–114
  retooling, 41–43, 45
  six-way, 12, 80, 81, 91
  between spouses, 44
  with spouses, 57
confidentiality, 136–137
conflict-resolution, 55–58
conflicts, 65–68, 102, 131, 147
consent, 20, 84
container, 59–60, 80
continuing education, 183. *See also*
  training
control
  attorney, 44, 46
  client, 66
  generally, 11, 18
  loss of, 25
  retooling, 41, 45
cooperation, 113. *See also* good faith
costs
  of collaborative law, 18, 181
  of experts, 18
  of litigation, 32, 33, 83–84
  of mediation, 139–141
counseling, 17, 99
Cox, Gay, 200

creativity
    encouraging, 16–17
    four-way meetings, 12
    generally, 5, 101
    impasses and, 45, 89–90
    retooling, 43
    six-way communications, 12
custody, 106

Daicoff, Susan, 8, 150
data-gathering forms
    IACP survey form, 169, 293–294
    internal data-gathering and
        evaluation form, 168, 279–284
    practice group data-gathering
        and evaluation form, 168–169,
        285–291
debriefing, 61, 63
deep, dark woods journey metaphor,
    310–311
demand, 27
detaching, 70–71
discovery
    explaining, 164
    generally, 10
dispute-resolution, 55, 56, 84
disqualification stipulations. *See
    also* termination; withdrawal
    of counsel
    experts and, 9, 10, 112–113
    explaining, 91, 161–163
    filing, 161
    generally, 17, 80
    impasses and, 17, 91
    necessity of, 14, 17, 109, 161–163
    obligations under, 14
    power of, 14–15, 17
    samples of, 257–262
documents. *See also* agreements
    for collaborative cases, 249–269
    evaluations, 168–169, 184
    for future dispute resolution, 70
    generally, 155–156
    information packets, 98, 108, 158,
        173, 175, 184–185
    sample letters, 158–159
    screening forms, 157

for termination, 164, 167
    for withdrawal of counsel, 164, 167
dominant paradigm, 28, 29, 30–31,
    81. *See also* litigation
durable power of attorney metaphor,
    312–313

EDS. *See* Electronic Data Systems
education, 162, 184–185. *See also*
    training
effectiveness of collaborative
    law, 4–6
Einstein, Albert, 1, 155
Electronic Data Systems (EDS),
    200–201
emotions. *See also* shadow state
    flooding, 62, 84–85
    four-way meetings, 62–63, 115
    in litigation, 213
    retooling, 27, 29–30, 39
    settlement and, 60–61, 68
employment disputes, 195
enthusiasm, 35
environment, 45
ethics. *See* professional responsibility
evaluations, 168–169, 184
experts
    costs of, 18
    disqualification of, 9, 10, 112
    five-way meetings, 113, 123
    initial contact with, 113
    marketing and, 176–177, 185
    neutrality of, 10
    reports, 114
    retooling with, 38, 43–45, 87
explanation, 124

Fairman, Christopher, 3
family relationships, 19, 32, 192. *See
    also* relational estate
Fasler, Karen, 200
fees. 138, 149. *See also* costs
fiduciary duties, 10
financial analysis, 219
financial disclosure form, 159,
    243–248
Fisher, Roger, 48

five-way meetings, 113, 123, 214

flooding, 62, 84–85

forgiveness, 38, 70

formal discovery, 210

four-way meetings. *See also*
    negotiation
    agenda-setting, 59–60, 64–65,
        65–66, 86–87
    benefits of, 12
    ceremony, 72, 124
    checklist for, 305–307
    creativity at, 12
    debriefing, 61, 63
    emotions during, 62–63, 115
    final, 70–72, 124
    first, 59–63, 115–116
    generally, 10
    language of, 108
    memorializing, 60
    metaphors at, 117, 123
    number of, 18, 65
    pacing, 66–67
    post-meeting conferences, 63,
        117–118
    pre-meeting conferences, 59–60,
        117–118
    retooling, 37
    transparency, 80, 81

frequently asked questions, 207–220

future dispute resolution, 164

Gandhi, M. K., 79

gladiators, 2, 27–28, 29, 36, 38, 40,
    47, 83, 211, 309, 342

goals
    highest, 60, 115
    identifying, 83–84, 102–106, 114
    of litigation, 15, 30–33, 47
    recalibrating, 67, 73
    retooling, 38, 39, 40, 42
    settlement as, 10, 12, 15
    transparency, 80

good faith. *See also* bad faith
    explaining, 104
    generally, 13, 209
    in retainer agreements, 158, 162

retooling, 45

transparency, 80, 81, 91

guidelines and principles. *See*
    principles and guidelines

Hague Convention, 141

hallmarks of collaborative law, 10

hardball tactics, 12

healing, 19

Hippocratic Oath, 20

Hoffman, David, 200

homework, 60, 63, 116, 117, 123

honesty, 157. *See also* trust

Hunter, Brad, 200

IACP ethical standards, 134, 315–319

IACP survey form, 169, 293–294

imbalances, 10, 12, 101, 111

immigration litigation, 195

impasses
    as magic moment, 91
    retooling, 45
    third-party resolution of, 17

income, 210, 215

information packets, 98, 108, 158,
    173, 175, 184–185

informed consent, 20, 84, 140–141

initial telephone screening form,
    157, 223

in propria persona, 108, 130, 158, 163

institutional changes, 195

intellectual property, 195

internal data-gathering and evaluation
    form, 168, 279–284

International Academy of
    Collaborative Professionals, 169,
    172, 176, 185, 216

intra-office forms
    collaborative retainer agreement,
        157–158, 226–232
    financial disclosure form, 243–248
    initial telephone screening form,
        157, 223
    new client basic information form,
        157, 224–225
    sample letters, 233–242

Johnston, Janet, 2
judges, 69, 179

Kass, Anne, 2–3
King, Donald M., 3, 25

Langenbahn, Stacey, 200
language, 56, 86, 108. *See also*
    communication
law, 69
lawyers. *See* attorneys/lawyers
letters, 121–122
Lincoln, Abraham, 23
listening, 36, 39, 107, 121. *See also*
    communication
litigation. *See also* dominant paradigm
    collaborative law compared, 15, 16
    costs of, 24, 32, 83–84
    Electronic Data systems in, 200–202
    as emergency room, 20, 69
    goals of, 15, 30–33, 47
    negotiations during, 45
    probate, 191–192, 195
    threats of, 10, 12, 14
Lucade, Max, 207

MacFarlane, Julie, 3
"magic moment," 91
malpractice, 23, 83, 142–145,
    210. *See also* professional
    responsibility
malpractice insurance carriers, 142–145
management, 47–48, 65–66
marathon metaphor, 313–314
marketing
    evaluation forms and, 168
    generally, 26, 176
    information packets, 129–131, 176
    practice groups, 26, 35, 129, 176
Maslow, Abraham, 214
Maxwell, Larry, 200
mediation
    collaborative law compared, 9–13,
        101
    costs of, 139–141
    neutrality of, 11

medical metaphor, 20
medicine, 20
meetings. *See* five-way meetings; four-
    way meetings
mental-health coaching, 219
mentors, 217
meta-mediator, 214
meta-messages, 34, 39
metaphors
    airline travel, 312
    birthing, 312
    deep, dark woods journey,
        310–311
    durable power of attorney,
        312–313
    four-way meetings, 117, 123
    generally, 27–28, 85, 309–314
    gladiator, 2, 29, 36, 38, 40, 47, 83,
        211, 309, 342
    marathon, 313–314
    medical, 20
    mountain climbing, 310
    peeling the onion, 85–86, 104, 114
    sack race, 314
    training horses, 314
    trip from here to there, 311–312
    whitewater rafting, 309–310
methods, 38, 39–40
modeling, 87
mountain climbing metaphor, 310

National Conference of
    Commissioners on Uniform
    State Laws (NCCUSL), 132
NCCUSL. *See* National Conference of
    Commissioners on Uniform State
    Laws
needs, 138, 146, 147. *See* goals
negotiation. *See also* four-way
    meetings
    interest-based, 71, 85–86, 104, 105,
        114, 120–121
    in litigation, 45
    positional, 114, 121, 123
    recalibrating, 67
    retooling, 43–45

neutrality
  of experts, 113
  of mediators, 11, 101
  negotiations, 41
new client basic information form,
    157, 224–225

O'Connor, Sandra Day, 129
opening
  with attorneys, 57, 111–114, 130
  with clients, 55, 97–107, 140–141
  options, 84
  with other spouses, 108–110
  with professionals, 111–114
overview of collaborative law, 3–6,
    9–20

paradigm, 28, 29, 30–31, 81. *See also*
    litigation
paradigm shift. *See also* retooling
  described, 26–27, 79–80, 146
  effecting, 36–37
participation agreements
  amending, 165
  commitments in, 14–17
  disqualification of counsel. *See*
    disqualification stipulations
  generally, 9, 60, 80, 155
  sample, 257–262
  termination, 142
  third party resolution under, 17,
    161–163
peeling the onion metaphor, 85–86,
    104, 114
persuasion, 98, 100, 104, 211, 219
physical space, 41, 48, 88–89,
    117, 123
post-meeting conferences, 63,
    117–118
practice group data-gathering and
    evaluation form, 168–169,
    285–291
practice groups, 26, 35, 134–136,
    148–150, 171–180, 212,
    217–220
practice protocols, 134–139
preconceptions, 34

preliminary informational session, 219
pre-meeting conferences, 59–60,
    117–118
preventive law, 19
principles and guidelines
  explaining, 104
  generally, 67, 160–161
privacy, 10, 18, 24
privileges, 136
probate litigation, 191–192, 195
professional responsibility
  documentation and, 130
  generally, 12, 23
  joint meetings, 108
  malpractice, 23, 84
  retainer agreements, 157–158
  zealous representation, 30, 48
professionals. *See* attorneys; experts
proposals, 123–124
prudence, 24–25

recalibration, 67, 73
reconciliation, 13
referrals, 108, 168, 176–177
relational estate, 36, 80–82. *See also*
    family relationships
relaxation, 46–47, 89–90, 115
remorse, 92. *See also* satisfaction
respect
  contractual, 9, 146
  self, 32, 82
responsibility. *See also* professional
    responsibility
  attorney, 84
  client, 31, 39, 40, 56, 64, 70
  missteps, 66
  transparency, 9, 11
retainer agreements, 157–158, 212
retooling
  attorneys, 23–52
  clients, 28–30
  communication, 41–43, 45
  control, 41, 45
  creativity, 43
  emotions, 27, 29–30, 39
  four-way meetings, 37
  goals, 38, 39, 40, 42

good faith, 45
methods, 38, 39–40, 41–42
negotiations, 43–45
tasks, 32–34
rewards. *See* satisfaction
Rose, Chip, 53, 92
Roseby, Vivienne, 2

sack race metaphor, 314
sample letter retaining neutral experts,
    163, 263–264
sample letter to client, 158–159,
    233–238
sample letter to nonclient partner or
    spouse, 239–241
sample letter to other collaborative
    lawyer, 158–159, 242
sample provision, 164
sample recitations, 163–164
samples. *See* agreements; documents
satisfaction. *See also* remorse
    attorney, 4–5, 19
    client, 5
screening, 97–98, 99–100, 106, 157
self-selection, 83–84, 100
settlement
    agreements, 160, 163–164
    conventional, 12
    emotions during, 60–61, 68
    encouraging, 14–16
    as primary goal, 10, 12
shadow state
    four-way meetings, 117–118
    generally, 29–30, 83, 85
    recalibrating, 73
six-way communications, 12, 80, 81
space, 39, 48, 88–89, 117, 123
speed. *See* pacing
spiritual practices, 5
spouses, 44, 108–110, 158–159, 208
staff, 98
stages, 53–74, 107
stipulations. *See* agreements;
    disqualification stipulations
stress, 5, 28, 65, 115. *See also*
    relaxation

Tannen, Deborah, 86
tasks, 32–34
tax fraud, 211
termination. *See also* disqualification
    stipulations; withdrawal of
    counsel
    for bad faith, 130, 167
    of collaborative representation, 167
    documents for, 167
therapeutic jurisprudence, 22
tools and resources for lawyers,
    221–336
training, 26. *See also* continuing
    education
training horses metaphor, 314
transference, 37, 47
transparency, 80, 81, 91
trip from here to there metaphor,
    311–312
trust, 54, 102, 116, 117, 211. *See also*
    honesty

uncertainty, 35
upgrades, 123
Ury, William, 48

visualization, 5
voluntary discovery, 209, 210

Webb, Stuart, 171, 214
websites, 172–173
whitewater rafting metaphor, 309–310
Winick, Bruce, 22, 150
withdrawal of counsel. *See also*
    disqualification stipulations;
    termination
    documents for, 136–137, 164–167
workshops. *See also* education;
    training

zealous representation, 30, 48, 136